The Collected Plays of

Edward Albee

The Collected Plays o:

Edward Albee

volume **1**

1958-65

The Zoo Story
The Death of Bessie Smith
The Sandbox
The American Dream
Who's Afraid of Virginia Woolf?
The Ballad of the Sad Cafe
Tiny Alice
Malcolm

OVERLOOK DUCKWORTH
Woodstock • New York • London

First published in the United States in 2004 by
Overlook Duckworth

NEW YORK:
The Overlook Press
141 Wooster Street
New York, NY 10012

WOODSTOCK:
The Overlook Press
One Overlook Drive
Woodstock, NY 12498
www.overlookpress.com
[for individual orders, bulk and special sales, contact our Woodstock office]

LONDON:
Gerald Duckworth & Co. Ltd.
Greenhill House
90-93 Cowcross Street
London EC1M 6BF

Cataloging-in-Publication Data is available from the Library of Congress

Book design and type formatting by Bernard Schleifer
Manufactured in the United States of America
3 5 7 9 8 6 4 2
ISBN-10   1-58567-529-6   ISBN-13   978-1-58567-529-6
ISBN-10   0-7156-3580-8 (UK)   ISBN-13   978-0-7156-3580-3 (UK)

Contents

NOTE: The plays contained within this anthology include some changes the author has made over the years. Although he may revisit these texts again one day, he considers them to be, at this point, the definitive versions for both reading and performance.

Introduction

HOW ODD IT FEELS TO BE WRITING ABOUT THINGS SO FAR IN THE PAST—so far in my past!

The eight plays collected here (Volume 1 of a set of three) were all composed at least forty years ago, were my first plays, except for a few truncated and derivative attempts at self done before I accomplished a sense of self, a sense that freed me, at twenty-eight, to write the work assembled here.

Still, I am looking back a long time, to my relative youth, to my beginnings. I wonder: what can I remember?, and how much of what I remember will have anything to do with fact—will not be either revisionist or plain guesswork?

As a character in one of my plays (which one I can't remember!) said, "The past is determined by what we choose to remember, and what we need to forget." . . . or some such thing!

The first four of these plays were written in a period of under two years (1957–59) on a big old manual typewriter which I had liberated from the Western Union Company, where I had worked as a messenger. How I lifted the damn thing (oh! a pun!) escapes me now.

In the *real* old days (my teens and earlier) I wrote by hand—even the two endless and unintentionally incoherent novels I excreted late in the nights I was supposed to be studying at home.

Later—"mid-period" plays on—I returned to manuscript, being sure, however, to transcribe them before too long, before my combination shorthand and scribble rendered my texts more guesswork than fact and far more experimental than intended.

Back to these eight. They vary in length from twelve minutes (*The Sandbox*) to three hours (*Who's Afraid of Virginia Woolf?*). They are—all of mine, even the shortest—"full-length" in that they are full to their lengths. The one-act play form is often scorned as being minor, or superficial, or some such nonsense, by people who forget that *Oedipus Rex* is a one-act play, as are many of Beckett's masterpieces. To my mind, many so-called "full length" plays are overly long and empty of persuasive content.

Carson McCullers' *The Ballad of the Sad Cafe* and James Purdy's *Malcolm* are adaptations of prose works which I felt would not lose and perhaps even gain by transformation to the stage. *The Ballad of the Sad Cafe* received greatly enthusiastic (or better) press, while *Malcolm* was excoriated by the New York reviewers.

Both Carson McCullers and James Purdy were very happy with my adaptations, and I remain convinced that *Malcolm* would have fared better had it been done off-Broadway, where works of its temperament are more welcome.

The Zoo Story had its world premiere in West Berlin, Germany, in the fall of 1959, *The American Dream* there also a year later—both in German translation. They both opened in New York City (in English, of course) a bit after. The other two one-act plays (*The Sandbox* and *The Death of Bessie Smith*) had their premieres in New York City. The press on all four was generally friendly, and I was accepted as—what?—a "rising talent"? Yes, I guess so.

Who's Afraid of Virginia Woolf? changed all that. It opened in New York *on* Broadway to mixed reviews in the dailies, and became a huge commercial success, mostly through word of mouth plus perceptive magazine appreciations. And I became the Great White Hope of the American theatre, or some such excess.

It is dangerous to have a huge commercial theatre success early on for, more often than not, your next plays will be judged not by how you're proceeding in your growth as a playwright, but by how similar your new work is to the blockbuster. My next play was *Tiny Alice*, a perfectly straightforward metaphysical melodrama having to do with the relationship of faith to sexual hysteria and the nonexistence of a god created by man in his own image.

Not quite your expected follow-up to *Who's Afraid of Virginia Woolf?*! And it suffered, of course. "Obstructionist," "pretentious," "opaque." Goodness! I should have stayed in the livingroom with a lot of drinks and yelling! But, I do not plan out my plays to fit in with either critical bias or commercial safety; nor do I worry that my themes may be difficult or dangerous and my techniques unconventional. I go with what my mind tells me it wants to do, and I take my chances. I think this is better than second- guessing the tastemakers; it gives me freedom for my wisdoms and my follies.

I never talk or write about what my plays are "about," their "meanings." I find them all quite clear (as I do Beckett, for example, one of the most naturalistic of playwrights) to anyone who approaches them as unique experiences and participates in them unfettered by notions of what a play should "be," what it should "say," or how it should go about its business.

Besides, I put them out of my mind soon after I've written them—by which I mean that the creation of them rids me of the need to mull the creation of them.

My career has had its ups and downs—in the sense of popularity, respect, comprehension, and tolerance. There was a period of time in the 70s and 80s when no one wanted to produce my work in New York. (Other cities, other countries did, of course, but to many minds, lack of New York exposure renders one invisible.) All that changed with some plays composed in the 90s and the new century—*Three Tall Women, The Play About the Baby,* and *The Goat or, Who is Sylvia?* I have become visible again. How long *this* will last I have no idea.

There are twenty-five or so plays in my quiver now, and I disown none of them. Indeed, *The Man Who Had Three Arms*, the most excoriated of all (by critics, not by audiences), remains one of my favorites.

The next two volumes of this collection will take you through the corpus and bring you up to date. I hope you will have as much enjoyment as I have had.

—EDWARD ALBEE
New York City
September 11, 2003

The Zoo Story

A PLAY IN ONE SCENE

For William Flanagan

FIRST PERFORMANCE

September 28, 1959, Berlin, Germany.
Schiller Theater Werkstatt.

The first American performance of *The Zoo Story* was presented by Richard Barr, H. B. Lutz, and Harry Joe Brown, Jr., under the auspices of Theatre 1960, at the Provincetown Playhouse in New York City on January 14, 1960. The production was directed by Milton Kattselas. The setting and lighting were by William Ritman. The cast was as follows:

JERRY	George Maharis
PETER	William Daniels

THE PLAYERS:

PETER

A man in his early forties, neither fat nor gaunt, neither hand-some nor homely. He wears tweeds, smokes a pipe, carries horn-rimmed glasses. Although he is moving into middle age, his dress and his manner would suggest a man younger.

JERRY

A man in his late thirties, not poorly dressed, but carelessly. What was once a trim and lightly muscled body has begun to go to fat; and while he is no longer handsome, it is evident that he once was. His fall from physical grace should not suggest debauchery; he has, to come closest to it, a great weariness.

THE SCENE

It is Central Park; a Sunday afternoon in summer; the present. There are two park benches, one toward either side of the stage; they both face the audience. Behind them: foliage, trees, sky. At the beginning, Peter is seated on one of the benches.

(As the curtain rises, PETER *is seated on the bench stage-right. He is reading a book. He stops reading, cleans his glasses, goes back to reading.* JERRY *enters.)*

JERRY

I've been to the zoo. (PETER *doesn't notice*) I said, I've been to the zoo. MISTER, I'VE BEEN TO THE ZOO!

PETER

Hm? . . . What? . . . I'm sorry, were you talking to me?

JERRY

I went to the zoo, and then I walked until I came here. Have I been walking north?

PETER *(Puzzled)*

North? Why . . . I . . . I think so. Let me see.

JERRY

(Pointing past the audience) Is that Fifth Avenue?

PETER

Why yes; yes, it is.

JERRY

And what is that cross street there; that one, to the right?

PETER

That? Oh, that's Seventy-fourth Street.

JERRY

And the zoo is around Sixty-fifth Street; so, I've been walking north.

PETER

(Anxious to get back to his reading) Yes; it would seem so.

JERRY

Good old north.

PETER

(Lightly, by reflex) Ha, ha.

JERRY

(After a slight pause) But not due north.

PETER

I . . . well, no, not due north; but, we . . . call it north. It's northerly.

JERRY

(Watches as PETER, *anxious to dismiss him, prepares his pipe)* Well, boy; *you're* not going to get lung cancer, are you?

PETER

(Looks up, a little annoyed, then smiles) No, sir. Not from this.

JERRY

No, sir. What you'll probably get is cancer of the mouth, and then you'll have to wear one of those things Freud wore after they took one whole side of his jaw away. What do they call those things?

PETER *(Uncomfortable)*

A prosthesis?

JERRY

The very thing! A prosthesis. You're an educated man, aren't you? Are you a doctor?

PETER

Oh, no; no. I read about it somewhere; *Time* magazine, I think. *(He turns to his book)*

JERRY

Well, *Time* magazine isn't for blockheads.

PETER

No, I suppose not.

JERRY

(After a pause) Boy, I'm glad that's Fifth Avenue there.

PETER *(Vaguely)*

Yes.

JERRY

I don't like the west side of the park much.

PETER

Oh? *(Then, slightly wary, but interested)* Why?

JERRY *(Offhand)*

I don't know.

PETER

Oh. *(He returns to his book)*

JERRY

(He stands for a few seconds, looking at PETER, *who finally looks up again, puzzled)* Do you mind if we talk?

PETER

(Obviously minding) Why . . . no, no.

JERRY

Yes you do; you do.

PETER

(Puts his book down, his pipe out and away, smiling) No, really; I don't mind.

JERRY

Yes you do.

PETER

(Finally decided) No; I don't mind at all, really.

JERRY

It's . . . it's a nice day.

PETER

(Stares unnecessarily at the sky) Yes. Yes, it is; lovely.

JERRY

I've been to the zoo.

PETER

Yes, I think you said so . . . didn't you?

JERRY

I bet you've got TV, huh?

PETER

Why yes, we have two; one for the children.

JERRY

You're married!

PETER

(With pleased emphasis) Why, certainly.

JERRY

It isn't a law, for God's sake.

PETER

No . . . no, of course not.

JERRY

And you have a wife.

PETER

(Bewildered by the seeming lack of communication) Yes!

JERRY

And you have children.

PETER

Yes; two.

JERRY

Boys?

PETER

No, girls . . . both girls.

JERRY

But you wanted boys.

PETER

Well . . . naturally, every man wants a son, but . . .

JERRY

(Lightly mocking) But that's the way the cookie crumbles?

PETER (Annoyed)

I wasn't going to say that.

JERRY

And you're not going to have any more kids, are you?

PETER

(A bit distantly) No. No more. (Then back, and irksome) Why did you say that? How would you know about that?

JERRY

The way you cross your legs, perhaps; something in the voice. Or maybe I'm just guessing. Is it your wife?

PETER (Furious)

That's none of your business! (A silence) Do you understand? (JERRY nods. PETER is quiet now) Well, you're right. We'll have no more children.

JERRY (Softly)

That is the way the cookie crumbles.

PETER (Forgiving)

Yes . . . I guess so.

JERRY

Do you mind if I ask you questions?

PETER

Oh, not really.

JERRY

I'll tell you why I do it; I don't talk to many people—except to say like: give me a beer, or where's the john, or what time does the feature go on, or keep your hands to yourself, buddy. You know—things like that.

PETER

I must say I don't . . .

JERRY

But every once in a while I like to talk to somebody, really *talk;* like to get to know somebody, know all about him.

PETER

(*Lightly laughing, still a little uncomfortable*) And am I the guinea pig for today?

JERRY

On a sun-drenched Sunday afternoon like this? Who better than a nice married man with two daughters and. . . uh . . . a dog? (PETER *shakes his head*) No? Two dogs. (PETER *shakes his head again*) Hm. No dogs? (PETER *shakes his head, sadly*) Oh, that's a shame. But you look like an animal man. CATS? (PETER *nods his head, ruefully*) Cats! But, that can't be your idea. No, sir. Your wife and daughters? (PETER *nods his head*) Is there anything else I should know?

PETER

(*He has to clear his throat*) There are . . . there are two parakeets. One . . . uh . . . one for each of my daughters.

JERRY

Birds.

PETER

My daughters keep them in a cage in their bedroom.

JERRY

Do they carry disease? The birds.

PETER

I don't believe so.

JERRY

That's too bad. If they did you could set them loose in the house and the cats could eat them and die, maybe. (PETER *looks blank for a moment, then laughs*) And what else? What do you do to support your enormous household?

PETER

I . . . uh . . . I have an executive position with a . . . a small publishing house. We . . . uh . . . we publish textbooks.

JERRY

That sounds nice; very nice. What do you make?

PETER *(Still cheerful)*

Now look here!

JERRY

Oh, come on.

PETER

Well, I make around two hundred thousand a year, but I don't carry more than forty dollars at any one time . . . in case you're a . . . a holdup man . . . ha, ha, ha.

JERRY

(Ignoring the above) Where do you live? (PETER *is reluctant*) Oh, look; I'm not going to rob you, and I'm not going to kidnap your parakeets, your cats, or your daughters.

PETER *(Too loud)*

I live between Lexington and Third Avenue, on Seventy-fourth Street.

JERRY

That wasn't so hard, was it?

PETER

I didn't mean to seem . . . ah . . . it's that you don't really carry on a conversation; you just ask questions. And I'm . . . I'm normally . . . uh . . . reticent. Why do you just stand there?

JERRY

Say, what's the dividing line between upper-middle-middle-class and lower-upper-middle-class?

PETER

My dear fellow, I . . .

JERRY

Don't my dear fellow me.

PETER *(Unhappily)*

Was I patronizing? I believe I was; I'm sorry. But, you see your question about the classes bewildered me.

JERRY

And when you're bewildered you become patronizing?

PETER

I . . . I don't express myself too well, sometimes. *(He attempts a joke on himself)* I'm in publishing, not writing.

JERRY

(Amused, but not at the humor) So be it. The truth *is: I* was being patronizing.

PETER

Oh, now; you needn't say that.

(*It is at this point that* JERRY *may begin to move about the stage with slowly increasing determination and authority, but pacing himself, so that the long speech about the dog comes at the high point of the arc*)

JERRY

All right. Who are your favorite writers? Baudelaire and Stephen King?

PETER *(Wary)*

Well, I like a great many writers; I have a considerable catholicity of taste, if I may say so. Those two men are fine, each in his way. *(Warming up)* Baudelaire, of course . . . uh . . . is by far the finer of the two, but Stephen King has a place . . . in our... uh . . . national . . .

JERRY

Skip it.

PETER

I . . . sorry.

JERRY

Do you know what I did before I went to the zoo today? I walked all the way up Fifth Avenue from Washington Square; all the way.

PETER

Oh; you live in Greenwich Village! *(This seems to enlighten* PETER)

JERRY

No, I don't. I took the subway down to the Village so I could walk all the way up Fifth Avenue to the zoo. It's one of those things a person has to do; sometimes a person has to go a very long distance out of his way to come back a short distance correctly.

PETER *(Almost pouting)*

Oh, I thought you lived in Greenwich Village.

JERRY

What were you trying to do? Make sense out of things? Bring order? The old pigeonhole bit? Well, that's easy; I'll tell you. I live in a four-story brownstone roominghouse on the Upper West Side between Columbus Avenue and Central Park West. I live on the top floor; rear; west. It's a laughably small room, and one of my walls is made of beaverboard; this beaverboard separates my room from another laughably small room, so I assume that the two rooms were once one room, a small room, but not necessarily laughable. The room beyond my beaverboard wall is occupied by a colored queen who always keeps his door open; well, not always but *always* when he's plucking his eyebrows, which he does with Buddhist concentration. This colored queen has rotten teeth, which is rare, and he has a Japanese kimono, which is also pretty rare; and he wears this kimono to and from the john in the hall, which is pretty frequent. I mean, he goes to the john a lot. He never bothers me, and he never brings anyone up to his room. All he does is pluck his eyebrows, wear his kimono and go to the john. Now, the two front rooms on my floor are a little larger, I guess; but they're pretty small, too. There's a Puerto Rican family in one of them, a husband, a wife, and some kids; I don't know how many. These people entertain a lot. And in the other front room, there's somebody living there, but I don't know who it is. I've never seen who it is. Never. Never ever.

PETER *(Embarrassed)*
Why . . . why do you live there?

JERRY
(From a distance again) I don't know.

PETER
It doesn't sound like a very nice place . . . where you live.

JERRY
Well, no; it isn't an apartment in the East Seventies. But, then again, I don't have one wife, two daughters, two cats and two parakeets. What I do have, I have toilet articles, a few clothes, a hot plate that I'm not supposed to have, a can opener, one that works with a key, you know; a knife, two forks, and two spoons, one small, one large; three plates, a cup, a saucer, a drinking glass, two picture frames, both empty, eight or nine books, a pack of pornographic playing cards, regular deck, an old Western Union type-writer that prints nothing but capital letters, and a small strongbox without a lock which has in it . . . what? Rocks! Some rocks . . . sea-rounded rocks I picked up on the beach when I was a kid. Under which . . . weighed down . . . are some letters . . . please letters . . . please why don't you do this, and please when will you do that letters. And when letters, too. When will you write? When will you come? When? These letters are from more recent years.

PETER
(Stares glumly at his shoes, then) About those two empty picture frames . . . ?

JERRY
I don't see why they need any explanation at all. Isn't it clear? I don't have pictures of anyone to put in them.

PETER
Your parents . . . perhaps . . . a girl friend . . .

JERRY
You're a very sweet man, and you're possessed of a truly enviable inno-cence. But good old Mom and good old Pop are dead . . . you know? . . .

I'm broken up about it, too . . . I mean really. BUT. That particular vaude-
ville act is playing the cloud circuit now, so I don't see how I can look at
them, all neat and framed. Besides, or, rather, to be pointed about it, good
old Mom walked out on good old Pop when I was ten and a half years old;
she embarked on an adulterous turn of our southern states . . . a journey
of a year's duration . . . and her most constant companion . . . among
others, among many others . . . was a Mr. Barleycorn. At least, that's what
good old Pop told me after he went down . . . came back . . . brought her
body north. We'd received the news between Christmas and New Year's,
you see, that good old Mom had parted with the ghost in some dump in
Alabama. And, without the ghost . . . she was less welcome. I mean, what
was she? A stiff . . . a northern stiff. At any rate, good old Pop celebrated
the New Year for an even two weeks and then slapped into the front of a
somewhat moving city omnibus, which sort of cleaned things out family-
wise. Well no; then there was Mom's sister, who was given neither to sin
nor the consolations of the bottle. I moved in on her, and my memory
of her is slight excepting I remember still that she did all things dourly:
sleeping, eating, working, praying. She dropped dead on the stairs to her
apartment, my apartment then, too, on the afternoon of my high school
graduation. A terribly middle-European joke, if you ask me.

PETER

Oh, my; oh, my.

JERRY

Oh, your what? But that was a long time ago, and I have no feeling about
any of it that I care to admit to myself. Perhaps you can see, though, why
good old Mom and good old Pop are frameless. What's your name? Your
first name?

PETER

I'm Peter.

JERRY

I'd forgotten to ask you. I'm Jerry.

PETER

(With a slight, nervous laugh) Hello, Jerry.

JERRY

(Nods his hello) And let's see now; what's the point of having a girl's picture, especially in two frames? I have two picture frames, you remember.
I never see the pretty little ladies more than once, and most of them
wouldn't be caught in the same room with a camera. It's odd, and I wonder if it's sad.

PETER

The girls?

JERRY

No. I wonder if it's sad that I never see the little ladies more than once. I've never been able to have sex with, or, how is it put?. . . make love to anybody more than once. Once; that's it. . . . Oh, wait; for a week and a half, when I was fifteen and I hang my head in shame that puberty was late . . . I was a h-o-m-o-s-e-x-u-a-l. I mean, I was queer . . . (*Very fast*) . . . queer, queer, queer . . . with bells ringing, banners snapping in the wind. And for those eleven days, I met at least twice a day with the park superintendent's son . . . a Greek boy, whose birthday was the same as mine, except he was a year older. I think I was very much in love . . . maybe just with sex. But that was the jazz of a very special hotel, wasn't it? And now; oh, do I love the little ladies; really, I love them. For about an hour.

PETER

Well, it seems perfectly simple to me . . .

JERRY (*Angry*)

Look! Are you going to tell me to get married and have parakeets?

PETER (*Angry himself*)

Forget the parakeets! And stay single if you want to. It's no business of mine. I didn't start this conversation in the . . .

JERRY

All right, all right. I'm sorry. All right? You're not angry?

PETER (*Laughing*)

No, I'm not angry.

JERRY (*Relieved*)

Good. (*Now back to his previous tone*) Interesting that you asked me about the picture frames. I would have thought that you would have asked me about the pornographic playing cards.

PETER

(*With a knowing smile*) Oh, I've seen those cards.

JERRY

That's not the point. (*Laughs*) I suppose when you were a kid you and your pals passed them around, or you had a pack of your own.

PETER

Well, I guess a lot of us did.

JERRY

And you threw them away just before you got married.

PETER

Oh, now; look here. I didn't *need* anything like that when I got older.

JERRY

No?

PETER (*Embarrassed*)

I'd rather not talk about these things.

JERRY

So? Don't. Besides, I wasn't trying to plumb your post-adolescent sexual life and hard times; what I wanted to get at is the value difference between pornographic playing cards when you're a kid, and pornographic playing cards when you're older. It's that when you're a kid you use the cards as a substitute for a real experience, and when you're older you use real experience as a substitute for the fantasy. But I imagine you'd rather hear about what happened at the zoo.

PETER (*Enthusiastic*)

Oh, yes; the zoo. (*Then, awkward*) That is . . . if you . . .

JERRY

Let me tell you about why I went. . . well, let me tell you some things. I've told you about the fourth floor of the roominghouse where I live. I think the rooms are better as you go down, floor by floor. I guess they are; I don't know. I don't know any of the people on the third and second floors. Oh, wait! I do know that there's a lady living on the third floor, in the front. I know because she cries all the time. Whenever I go out or come back in, whenever I pass her door, I always hear her crying, muffled, but . . . very determined. Very determined indeed. But the one I'm getting to, and all about the dog, is the landlady. I don't like to use words that are too harsh in describing people. I don't like to. But the landlady is a fat, ugly, mean, stupid, unwashed, misanthropic, cheap, drunken bag of garbage. And you may have noticed that I very seldom use profanity, so I can't describe her as well as I might.

PETER

You describe her . . . vividly.

JERRY

Well, thanks. Anyway, she has a dog, and I will tell you about the dog, and she and her dog are the gatekeepers of my dwelling. The woman is bad enough; she leans around in the entrance hall, spying to see that I don't bring in things or people, and when she's had her mid-afternoon pint of lemon-flavored gin she always stops me in the hall, and grabs ahold of my coat or my arm, and she presses her disgusting body up against me to keep me in a corner so she can talk to me. The smell of her body and her breath . . . you can't imagine it . . . and somewhere, somewhere in the back of that pea-sized brain of hers, an organ developed just enough to let her eat, drink, and emit, she has some foul parody of sexual desire. And I, Peter, I am the object of her sweaty lust.

PETER

That's disgusting. That's . . . horrible.

JERRY

But I have found a way to keep her off. When she talks to me, when she presses herself to my body and mumbles about her room and how I should come there, I merely say: but, Love; wasn't yesterday enough for you, and the day before? Then she puzzles, she makes slits of her tiny eyes, she sways a little, and then, Peter . . . and it is at this moment that I think I might be doing some good in that tormented house . . . a simple-minded smile begins to form on her unthinkable face, and she giggles and groans as she thinks about yesterday and the day before; as she believes and relives what never happened. Then, she motions to that black monster of a dog she has, and she goes back to her room. And I am safe until our next meeting.

PETER

It's so . . . unthinkable. I find it hard to believe that people such as that really *are*.

JERRY

(*Lightly mocking*) It's for reading about, isn't it?

PETER (*Seriously*)

Yes.

JERRY

And fact is better left to fiction. You're right, Peter. Well, what I have been meaning to tell you about is the dog; I shall, now.

PETER (*Nervously*)

Oh, yes; the dog.

JERRY

Don't go. You're not thinking of going, are you?

PETER

Well . . . no, I don't think so.

JERRY

(*As if to a child*) Because after I tell you about the dog, do you know what then? Then . . . then I'll tell you about what happened at the zoo.

PETER (*Laughing faintly*)

You're . . . you're full of stories, aren't you?

JERRY

You don't *have* to listen. Nobody is holding you here; remember that. Keep that in your mind.

PETER (*Irritably*)

PETER (*Irritably*)

I know that.

JERRY

You do? Good.

(The following long speech, it seems to me, should be done with a great deal of action, to achieve a hypnotic effect on PETER, *and on the audience, too. Some specific actions have been suggested, but the director and the actor playing Jerry might best work it out for themselves)*

ALL RIGHT. *(As if reading from a huge billboard)* THE STORY OF JERRY AND THE DOG! *(Natural again)* What I am going to tell you has something to do with how sometimes it's necessary to go a long distance out of the way in order to come back a short distance correctly; or, maybe I only think that it has something to do with that. But, it's why I went to the zoo today, and why I walked north . . . northerly, rather . . . until I came here. All right. The dog, I think I told you, is a black monster of a beast: an oversized head, tiny, tiny ears, and eyes . . . bloodshot, infected, maybe; and a body you can see the ribs through the skin. The dog is black, all black; all black except for the bloodshot eyes, and . . . yes . . . and an open sore on its . . . *right* forepaw; that is red, too. And, oh yes; the poor monster, and I do believe it's an old dog . . . it's certainly a misused one . . . almost always has an erection . . . of sorts. That's red, too. And . . . what else? . . . oh, yes; there's a gray-yellow-white color, too, when he bares his fangs. Like this: Grrrrrrr! Which is what he did when he saw me for the first time . . . the day I moved in. I worried about that animal the very first minute I met him. Now, animals don't take to me like Saint Francis had birds hanging off him all the time. What I mean is: Animals are indifferent to me . . . like people *(He smiles slightly)* . . . most of the time. But this dog wasn't indifferent. From the very beginning he'd snarl and then go for me, to get one of my legs. Not like he was rabid, you know; he was sort of a stumbly dog, but he wasn't half-assed, either. It was a good, stumbly run; but I always got away. He got a piece of my trouser leg, look, you can see right here, where it's mended; he got that the second day I lived there; but, I kicked free and got upstairs fast, so that was that. *(Puzzles)* I still don't know to this day how the other roomers manage it, but you know what I *think:* I think it had to do only with me. Cozy. So. Anyway, this went on for over a week, whenever I came in; but never when I went out. That's funny. Or, it *was* funny. I could pack up and live in the street for all the dog cared. Well, I thought about it up in my room one day, one of the times after I'd bolted upstairs, and I made up my mind. I decided: First, I'll kill the dog with kindness, and if that doesn't work . . . I'll just kill him. (PETER *winces*) Don't react, Peter; just listen. So, the next day I went out and bought a bag of hamburgers, medium rare, no catsup, no onion; and on the way home I threw away all the rolls and kept just the meat.

(Action for the following, perhaps)

When I got back to the roominghouse the dog was waiting for me. I half opened the door that led into the entrance hall, and there he was; waiting for me. It figured. I went in, very cautiously, and I had the hamburgers, you remember; I opened the bag, and I set the meat down about twelve feet from where the dog was snarling at me. Like so! He snarled; stopped snarling; sniffed; moved slowly; then faster; then faster toward the meat. Well, when he got to it he stopped, and he looked at me. I smiled; but ten-tatively, you understand. He turned his face back to the hamburgers, smelled, sniffed some more, and then . . . RRRAAAAGGGGGHHHH, like that . . . he tore into them. It was as if he had never eaten anything in his life before, except like garbage. Which might very well have been the truth. I don't think the landlady ever eats anything but garbage. But. He ate all the hamburgers, almost all at once, making sounds in his throat like a woman. *Then,* when he'd finished the meat, the hamburger, and tried to eat the paper, too, he sat down and smiled. I think he smiled; I know cats do. It was a very gratifying few moments. Then, BAM, he snarled and made for me again. He didn't get me this time, either. So, I got upstairs, and I lay down on my bed and started to think about the dog again. To be truthful, I was offended, and I was damn mad, too. It was six perfectly good hamburgers with not enough pork in them to make it disgusting. I was offended. But, after a while, I decided to try it for a few more days. If you think about it, this dog had what amounted to an antipathy toward me; really. And, I wondered if I mightn't overcome this antipathy. So, I tried it for five more days, but it was always the same: snarl, sniff, move; faster; stare; gobble; RAAGGGHHH; smile; snarl; BAM. Well, now; by this time Columbus Avenue was strewn with hamburger rolls and I was less offend-ed than disgusted. So, I decided to kill the dog.

*(*PETER *raises a hand in protest)*

Oh, don't be so alarmed, Peter; I didn't succeed. The day I tried to kill the dog I bought only one hamburger and what I thought was a murderous portion of rat poison. When I bought the hamburger I asked the man not to bother with the roll, all I wanted was the meat. I expected some reac-tion from him, like: we don't sell no hamburgers without rolls; or, wha' d'ya wanna do, eat it out'a ya han's? But no; he smiled benignly, wrapped up the hamburger in waxed paper, and said: A bite for ya pussy-cat? I wanted to say: No, not really; it's part of a plan to poison a dog I know. But, you can't say "a dog I know" without sounding funny; so I said, a little too loud, I'm afraid, and too formally: YES, A BITE FOR MY PUSSY-CAT. People looked up. It always happens when I try to simplify things; people look up. But that's neither hither nor thither. So. On my way back to the rooming-house, I kneaded the hamburger and the rat poison together between my hands, at that point feeling as much sadness as disgust. I opened the door to the entrance hall, and there the monster was, waiting to take the offer-ing and then jump me. Poor bastard; he never learned that the moment he took to smile before he went for me gave me time enough to get out of range. BUT, there he was; malevolence with an erection, waiting. I put the poison patty down, moved toward the stairs and watched. The poor animal gobbled the food down as usual, smiled, which made me almost sick, and then, BAM. But, I sprinted up the stairs, as usual, and the dog didn't get me, as usual. AND IT CAME TO PASS THAT THE BEAST WAS DEATHLY ILL. I knew this because he no longer attended me, and because the landlady sobered up. She stopped me in the hall the same evening of the attempted murder and confided the information that God had struck her puppy-dog a surely fatal blow. She had forgotten her be-wildered lust, and her eyes were wide open for the first time. They looked like the dog's eyes. She sniveled and implored me to pray for the animal. I wanted to say to her: Madam, I have myself to pray for, the colored queen, the Puerto Rican family, the person in the front room whom I've never seen, the woman who cries deliberately behind her closed door, and the rest of the people in all roominghouses, everywhere; besides, Madam, I don't understand how to pray. But . . . to simplify things . . . I told her I would pray. She looked up. She said that I was a liar, and that I probably wanted the dog to die. I told her, and there was so much truth here, that I didn't want the dog to die. I didn't, and not just because I'd poisoned him. I'm afraid that I must tell you I wanted the dog to live so that I could see what our new relationship might come to.

(PETER *indicates his increasing displeasure and slowly growing antagonism*)

Please understand, Peter; that sort of thing is important. You must believe me; it *is* important. We have to know the effect of our actions. (*Another deep sigh*) Well, anyway; the dog recovered. I have no idea why, unless he was a descendant of the puppy that guarded the gates of hell or some such resort. I'm not up on my mythology. (*He pronounces the word myth-*o-logy) Are you?

(PETER *sets to thinking, but* JERRY *goes on*)

At any rate, and you've missed the eight-thousand-dollar question, Peter; at any rate, the dog recovered his health and the landlady recovered her thirst, in no way altered by the bow-wow's deliverance. When I came home from a movie that was playing on Forty-second Street, a movie I'd seen, or one that was very much like one or several I'd seen, after the landlady told me puppykins was better, I was so hoping for the dog to be waiting for me. I was . . . well, how would you put it . . . enticed? . . . fascinated? . . . no, I don't think so . . . heart-shatteringly anxious, that's it; I was heart-shatteringly anxious to confront my friend again.

(PETER *reacts scoffingly*)

Yes, Peter; friend. That's the only word for it. I was heart-shatteringly et cetera to confront my doggy friend again. I came in the door and advanced, unafraid, to the center of the entrance hall. The beast was there . . . looking at me. And, you know, he looked better for his scrape with the nevermind. I stopped; I looked at him; he looked at me. I think . . . I think we stayed a long time that way . . . still, stone-statue . . . just looking at one another. I looked more into his face than he looked into mine. I mean, I can concentrate longer at looking into a dog's face than a dog can concentrate at looking into mine, or into anybody else's face, for that matter. But during that twenty seconds or two hours that we looked into each other's face, we made contact. Now, here is what I had wanted to happen: I loved the dog now, and I wanted him to love me. I had tried to love, and I had tried to kill, and both had been unsuccessful by themselves. I hoped . . . and I don't really know why I expected the dog to understand anything, much less my motivations . . . I hoped that the dog would understand.

(PETER *seems to be hypnotized*)

It's just . . . it's just that . . . (JERRY *is abnormally tense, now*) . . . it's just that if you can't deal with people, you have to make a start somewhere. WITH ANIMALS! *(Much faster now, and like a conspirator)* Don't you see? A person has to have some way of dealing with SOMETHING. If not with people . . . if not with people . . . SOMETHING. With a bed, with a cockroach, with a mirror . . . no, that's too hard, that's one of the last steps. With a cockroach, with a . . . with a . . . with a carpet, a roll of toilet paper . . . no, not that, either . . . that's a mirror, too; always check bleeding. You see how hard it is to find things? With a street corner, and too many lights, all colors reflecting on the oily-wet streets . . . with a wisp of smoke, a wisp . . . of smoke . . . with . . . with pornographic playing cards, with a strongbox . . . WITHOUT A LOCK . . . with love, with vomiting, with crying, with fury because the pretty little ladies aren't pretty little ladies, with making money with your body which is an act of love and I could prove it, with howling because you're alive; with God. How about that? WITH GOD WHO IS A COLORED QUEEN WHO WEARS A KIMONO AND PLUCKS HIS EYEBROWS, WHO IS A WOMAN WHO CRIES WITH DETERMINATION BEHIND HER CLOSED DOOR . . . with God who, I'm told, turned his back on the whole thing some time ago . . . with . . . someday, with people. (JERRY *sighs the next word heavily*) People. With an idea; a concept. And where better, where ever better in this humiliating excuse for a jail, where better to communicate one single, simpleminded idea than in an entrance hall? Where? It would be A START! Where better to make a beginning . . . to understand and just possibly be understood . . . a beginning of an understanding, than with . . .

(Here JERRY *seems to fall into almost grotesque fatigue*)

than with A DOG. Just that; a dog.

(Here there is a silence that might be prolonged for a moment or so; then JERRY *wearily finishes his story*)

A dog. It seemed like a perfectly sensible idea. Man is a dog's best friend, remember. So: the dog and I looked at each other. I longer than the dog.

And what I saw then has been the same ever since. Whenever the dog and I see each other we both stop where we are. We regard each other with a mixture of sadness and suspicion, and then we feign indifference. We walk past each other safely; we have an understanding. It's very sad, but you'll have to admit that it is an understanding. We had made many attempts at contact, and we had failed. The dog has returned to garbage, and I to solitary but free passage. I have not returned. I mean to say, I have *gained* solitary free passage, if that much further loss can be said to be gain. I have learned that neither kindness nor cruelty by themselves, independent of each other, creates any effect beyond themselves; and I have learned that the two combined, together, at the same time, are the teaching emotion. And what is gained is loss. And what has been the result: the dog and I have attained a compromise; more of a bargain, really. We neither love nor hurt because we do not try to reach each other. And, *was* trying to feed the dog an act of love? And, perhaps, was the dog's attempt to bite me *not* an act of love? If we can so misunderstand, well then, why have we invented the word love in the first place?

　　(There is silence. JERRY *moves to* PETER's *bench and sits down beside him. This is the first time that* JERRY *has sat down during the play.)*

The Story of Jerry and the Dog: the end.

　　(PETER *is silent)*

Well, Peter? (JERRY *is suddenly cheerful)* Well, Peter? Do you think I could sell that story to the *Reader's Digest* and make a couple of hundred bucks for *The Most Unforgettable Character I've Ever Met?* Huh?

　　(JERRY *is animated, but* PETER *is disturbed)*

Oh, come on now, Peter; tell me what you think.

PETER (Numb)

I . . . I don't understand what . . . I don't think I . . . *(Now, almost tearfully)* Why did you tell me all of this?

JERRY

Why not?

PETER

I DONT UNDERSTAND!

JERRY

(Furious, but whispering) That's a lie.

PETER

No. No, it's not.

JERRY (Quietly)

I tried to explain it to you as I went along. I went slowly; it all has to do with . . .

PETER

I DONT WANT TO HEAR ANY MORE. I don't understand you, or your landlady, or her dog . . .

JERRY

Her dog! I thought it was my . . . No. No, you're right. It *is* her dog. (*Looks at* PETER *intently, shaking his head*) I don't know what I was thinking about; of course you don't understand. (*In a monotone, wearily*) I don't live in your block I'm not married to two parakeets, or whatever your setup is. I am a *permanent transient,* and my home is the sickening roominghouses on the West Side of New York City, which is the greatest city in the world. Amen.

PETER

I'm . . . I'm sorry; I didn't mean to . . .

JERRY

Forget it. I suppose you don't quite know what to make of me, eh?

PETER (*A joke*)

We get all kinds in publishing. (*Chuckles*)

JERRY

You're a funny man. (*He forces a laugh*) You know that? You're a very . . . a richly comic person.

PETER

(*Modestly, but amused*) Oh, now, not really. (*Still chuckling*)

JERRY

Peter, do I annoy you, or confuse you?

PETER (*Lightly*)

Well, I must confess that this wasn't the kind of afternoon I'd anticipated.

JERRY

You mean, I'm not the gentleman you were expecting.

PETER

I wasn't expecting anybody.

JERRY

No, I don't imagine you were. But I'm here, and I'm not leaving.

PETER

(*Consulting his watch*) Well, you may not be, but I must be getting home now.

JERRY

Oh, come on; stay a while longer.

PETER

I really should get home; you see . . .

JERRY

(*Tickles* PETER's *ribs with his fingers*) Oh, come on.

PETER

(*He is very ticklish; as* JERRY *continues to tickle him his voice becomes falsetto*)
No, I . . . OHHHHH! Don't do that. Stop, Stop. Ohhh, no, no.

JERRY

Oh, come on.

PETER

(*As* JERRY *tickles*) Oh, hee, hee, hee. I must go. I . . . hee, hee, hee. After all, stop, stop, hee, hee, hee, after all, the parakeets will be getting dinner ready soon. Hee, hee. And the cats are setting the table. Stop, stop, and, and . . . (PETER *is beside himself now*) and we're having . . . hee, hee . . . uh . . . ho, ho, ho.

(JERRY *stops tickling* PETER, *but the combination of the tickling and his own mad whimsy has* PETER *laughing almost hysterically. As his laughter continues, then subsides,* JERRY *watches him, with a curious fixed smile*).

JERRY

Peter?

PETER

Oh, ha, ha, ha, ha, ha. What? What?

JERRY

Listen, now.

PETER

Oh, ho, ho. What . . . what is it, Jerry? Oh, my.

JERRY (*Mysteriously*)
Peter, do you want to know what happened at the zoo?

PETER

Ah, ha, ha. The what? Oh, yes; the zoo. Oh, ho, ho. Well, I had my own zoo there for a moment with . . . hee, hee, the parakeets getting dinner ready, and the . . . ha, ha, whatever it was, the . . .

JERRY (*Calmly*)
Yes, that was very funny, Peter. I wouldn't have expected it. But do you want to hear about what happened at the zoo, or not?

PETER

Yes. Yes, by all means; tell me what happened at the zoo. Oh, my. I don't know what happened to me.

JERRY

Now I'll let you in on what happened at the zoo; but first, I should tell you why I went to the zoo. I went to the zoo to find out more about the way people exist with animals, and the way animals exist with each other, and with people too. It probably wasn't a fair test, what with everyone separated by bars from everyone else, the animals for the most part from each other, and always the people from the animals. But, if it's a zoo, that's the way it is. *(He pokes* PETER *on the arm)* Move over.

PETER *(Friendly)*

I'm sorry, haven't you enough room? *(He shifts a little)*

JERRY *(Smiling slightly)*

Well, all the animals are there, and all the people are there, and it's Sunday and all the children are there. *(He pokes* PETER *again)* Move over.

PETER

(Patiently, still friendly) All right.

    (He moves some more, and JERRY *has all the room he might need)*

JERRY

And it's a hot day, so all the stench is there, too, and all the balloon sellers, and all the ice cream sellers, and all the seals are barking, and all the birds are screaming. *(Pokes* PETER *harder)* Move over!

PETER

(Beginning to be annoyed) Look here, you have more than enough room! *(But he moves more, and is now fairly cramped at one end of the bench)*

JERRY

And I am there, and it's feeding time at the lions' house, and the lion keeper comes into the lion cage, one of the lion cages, to feed one of the lions. *(Punches* PETER *on the arm, hard)* MOVE OVER!

PETER

(Very annoyed) I can't move over any more, and stop hitting me. What's the matter with you?

JERRY

Do you want to hear the story? *(Punches* PETER's *arm again)*

PETER *(Flabbergasted)*

I'm not so sure! I certainly don't want to be punched in the arm.

JERRY

(Punches PETER's *arm again)* Like that?

PETER

Stop it! What's the matter with you?

JERRY

I'm crazy, you bastard.

PETER

That isn't funny.

JERRY

Listen to me, Peter. I want this bench. You go sit on the bench over there, and if you're good I'll tell you the rest of the story.

PETER (*Flustered*)

But . . . whatever for? What *is* the matter with you? Besides, I see no reason why I should give up this bench. I sit on this bench almost every Sunday afternoon, in good weather. It's secluded here; there's never anyone sitting here, so I have it all to myself.

JERRY (*Softly*)

Get off this bench, Peter; I want it.

PETER

(*Almost whining*) No.

JERRY

I said I want this bench, and I'm going to have it. Now get over there.

PETER

People can't have everything they want. You should know that; it's a rule; people can have some of the things they want, but they can't have everything.

JERRY (*Laughs*)

Imbecile! You're slow-witted!

PETER

Stop that!

JERRY

You're a vegetable! Go lie down on the ground.

PETER (*Intense*)

Now *you* listen to me. I've put up with you all afternoon.

JERRY

Not really.

PETER

LONG ENOUGH. I've put up with you long enough. I've listened to you because you seemed . . . well, because I thought you wanted to talk to somebody.

JERRY

You put things well; economically, and, yet . . . oh, what is the word I want to put justice to your . . . JESUS, you make me sick . . . get off here and give me my bench.

PETER

MY BENCH!

JERRY

(Pushes PETER almost, but not quite, off the bench) Get out of my sight.

PETER

(Regaining his position) God da . . . mn you. That's enough! I've had enough of you. I will not give up this bench; you can't have it, and that's that. Now, go away.

(JERRY snorts but does not move)

Go away, I said.

(JERRY does not move)

Get away from here. If you don't move on . . . you're a bum . . . that's what y   o   u are. . . . If you don't move on, I'll get a policeman here and make you go.

(JERRY laughs, stays)

I warn you, I'll call a policeman.

JERRY (Softly)

You won't find a policeman around here; they're all over on the west side of the park chasing fairies down from trees or out of the bushes. That's all they do. That's their function. So scream your head off; it won't do you any good.

PETER

POLICE! I warn you, I'll have you arrested. POLICE! (Pause) I said POLICE! (Pause) I feel ridiculous.

JERRY

You look ridiculous: a grown man screaming for the police on a bright Sunday afternoon in the park with nobody harming you. If a policeman did fill his quota and come sludging over this way he'd probably take you in as a nut.

PETER

(With disgust and impotence) Great God, I just came here to read, and now you want me to give up the bench. You're mad.

JERRY

Hey, I got news for you, as they say. I'm on your precious bench, and you're never going to have it for yourself again.

PETER (Furious)

Look, you; get off my bench. I don't care if it makes any sense or not. I want this bench to myself; I want you OFF IT!

JERRY (Mocking)

Aw . . . look who's mad.

PETER

GET OUT!

JERRY

No.

PETER

I WARN YOU!

JERRY

Do you know how ridiculous you look *now?*

PETER

(His fury and self-consciousness have possessed him) It doesn't matter. *(He is almost crying)* GET AWAY FROM MY BENCH!

JERRY

Why? You have everything in the world you want; you've told me about your home, and your family, and *your own* little zoo. You have everything, and now you want this bench. Are these the things men fight for? Tell me, Peter, is this bench, this iron and this wood, is this your honor? Is this the thing in the world you'd fight for? Can you think of anything more absurd?

PETER

Absurd? Look, I'm not going to talk to you about honor, or even try to explain it to you. Besides, it isn't a question of honor; but even if it were, you wouldn't understand.

JERRY *(Contemptuously)*

You don't even know what you're saying, do you? This is probably the first time in your life you've had anything more trying to face than changing your cats' toilet box. Stupid! Don't you have any idea, not even the slightest, what other people *need?*

PETER

Oh, boy, listen to you; well, you don't need this bench. That's for sure.

JERRY

Yes; yes, I do.

PETER *(Quivering)*

I've come here for years; I have hours of great pleasure, great satisfaction, right here. And that's important to a man. I'm a responsible person, and I'm a GROWNUP. This is my bench, and you have no right to take it away from me.

JERRY

Fight for it, then. Defend yourself; defend your bench.

PETER

You've *pushed* me to it. Get up and fight.

JERRY

Like a man?

PETER (*Still angry*)

Yes, like a man, if you insist on mocking me even further.

JERRY

I'll have to give you credit for one thing: you *are* a vegetable, and a slightly nearsighted one, I think . . .

PETER

THAT'S ENOUGH. . . .

JERRY

. . . but, you know, as they say on TV all the time—you know—and I mean this, Peter, you have a certain dignity; it surprises me . . .

PETER

STOP!

JERRY

(*Rises lazily*) Very well, Peter, we'll battle for the bench, but we're not evenly matched.

(*He takes out and clicks open an ugly-looking knife*)

PETER

(*Suddenly awakening to the reality of the situation*)

You *are* mad! You're stark raving mad! YOU'RE GOING TO KILL ME!

(*But before* PETER *has time to think what to do,* JERRY *tosses the knife at* PETER's *feet*)

JERRY

There you go. Pick it up. You have the knife and we'll be more evenly matched.

PETER (*Horrified*)

No!

JERRY

(*Rushes over to* PETER, *grabs him by the collar;* PETER *rises; their faces almost touch*)

Now you pick up that knife and you fight with me. You fight for your self-respect; you fight for that goddamned bench.

PETER (*Struggling*)

No! Let . . . let go of me! He . . . Help!

JERRY

(*Slaps* PETER *on each "fight"*) You fight, you miserable bastard; fight for that bench; fight for your manhood, you pathetic little vegetable. (*Spits in* PETER's *face*) You couldn't even get your wife with a male child.

PETER

(Breaks away, enraged) It's a matter of genetics, not manhood, you . . . you monster.

> *(He darts down, picks up the knife and backs off a little; he is breathing heavily)*

I'll give you one last chance; get out of here and leave me alone!

> *(He holds the knife with a firm arm, but far in front of him, not to attack, but to defend)*

JERRY *(Sighs heavily)*

So be it!

> *(With a rush he charges* PETER *and impales himself on the knife. Tableau: For just a moment, complete silence,* JERRY *impaled on the knife at the end of* PETER's *still firm arm. Then* PETER *screams, pulls away, leaving the knife in* JERRY. JERRY *is motionless, on point. Then he, too, screams, and it must be the sound of an infuriated and fatally wounded animal. With the knife in him, he stumbles back to the bench that* PETER *had vacated. He crumbles there, sitting, facing* PETER, *his eyes wide in agony, his mouth open)*

PETER *(Whispering)*

Oh my God, oh my God, oh my God. . . .

> *(He repeats these words many times, very rapidly)*

JERRY

> *(*JERRY *is dying; but now his expression seems to change. His features relax, and while his voice varies, sometimes wrenched with pain, for the most part he seems removed from his dying. He smiles)*

Peter, thank you, Peter. I mean that now; thank you very much.

> *(*PETER's *mouth drops open. He cannot move; he is transfixed.)*

I came unto you *(He laughs, so faintly)* and you have comforted me. Dear Peter.

PETER

(Almost fainting) Oh my God!

JERRY

You'd better go now. Somebody might come by, and you don't want to be here when anyone comes.

PETER

> *(Does not move, but begins to weep)*

Oh my God, oh my God.

JERRY

And Peter, I'll tell you something now; you're not really a vegetable; it's all right, you're an animal. You're an animal, too. But you'd better hurry now, Peter. Hurry, you'd better go . . . see?

(JERRY *takes a handkerchief and with great effort and pain wipes the knife handle clean of fingerprints*)

Hurry away, Peter.

(PETER *begins to stagger away*)

Wait. . . wait, Peter. Take your book . . . book. Right here . . . beside me . . . on your bench . . . my bench, rather. Come . . . take your book.

(PETER *starts for the book, but retreats*)

Hurry . . . Peter.

(PETER *rushes to the bench, grabs the book, retreats*)

Very good, Peter . . . very good. Now . . . hurry away.

(PETER *hesitates for a moment, then flees, stage-left*)

Hurry away. . . . *(His eyes are closed now)* Hurry away, your parakeets are making the dinner . . . the cats . . . are setting the table . . .

PETER *(Offstage)*

(A pitiful howl)

OH MY GOD!

JERRY

(His eyes still closed, he shakes his head and speaks; a combination of scornful mimicry and supplication)

Oh . . . my . . . God.

(He is dead)

CURTAIN

The Death of Bessie Smith

A PLAY IN EIGHT SCENES

For Ned Rorem

FIRST PERFORMANCE

April 21, 1960, Berlin, Germany.
Schlosspark Theater

The first American performance of *The Death of Bessie Smith* was presented at the York Playhouse in New York City on January 24, 1961.

THE PLAYERS:

BERNIE

A Negro, about forty, thin.

JACK

A dark-skinned Negro, forty-five, bulky, with a deep voice and a mustache.

THE FATHER

A thin, balding white man, about fifty-five.

THE NURSE

A Southern white girl, full blown, dark or red-haired, pretty, with a wild laugh. Twenty-six.

THE ORDERLY

A light-skinned Negro, twenty-eight, clean-shaven, trim, prim.

SECOND NURSE

A Southern white girl, blond, not too pretty, about thirty.

THE INTERN

A Southern white man, blond, well put-together, with an amiable face; thirty.

THE SCENE

Afternoon and early evening, September 26, 1937. In and around the city of Memphis, Tennessee.

THE SET

The set for this play will vary, naturally, as stages vary—from theatre to theatre. So, the suggestions put down below, while they might serve as a useful guide, are but a general idea—what the author "sees."

What the author "sees" is this: The central and front area of the stage reserved for the admissions room of a hospital, for this is where the major portion of the action of the play takes place. The admissions desk and chair stage-center, facing the audience. A door, leading outside, stage-right; a door, leading to further areas of the hospital, stage-left. Very little more: a bench, perhaps; a chair or two. Running along the rear of the stage, and perhaps a bit on the sides, there should be a raised platform, on which, at various locations, against just the most minimal suggestions of sets, the other scenes of the play are performed. All of this very open, for the whole back wall of the stage is full of the sky, which will vary from scene to scene: a hot blue; a sunset; a great, red-orange-yellow sunset. Sometimes full, sometimes but a hint.

At the curtain, let the entire stage be dark against the sky, which is a hot blue. MUSIC against this, for a moment or so, fading to under as the lights come up on:

SCENE ONE

The corner of a barroom. BERNIE *seated at a table, a beer before him, with glass.* JACK *enters, tentatively, a beer bottle in his hand; he does not see* BERNIE.

BERNIE

(Recognizing JACK; *with pleased surprise)* Hey!

JACK

Hm?

BERNIE

Hey; Jack!

JACK

Hm? . . . What? . . . *(Recognizes him)* Bernie!

BERNIE

What you doin' here, boy? C'mon, sit down.

JACK

Well, I'll be damned . . .

BERNIE

C'mon, sit down, Jack.

JACK

Yeah . . . sure . . . well, I'll be damned. *(Moves over to the table; sits)* Bernie. My God, it's hot. How you been, boy?

BERNIE

Fine; fine. What you *doin'* here?

JACK

Oh, travelin'; travelin'.

BERNIE

On the move, hunh? Boy, you are the last person I expected t'walk in that door; small world, hunh?

JACK

Yeah; yeah.

BERNIE
On the move, hunh? Where you goin'?

JACK
(*Almost, but not quite, mysterious*) North.

BERNIE (*Laughs*)
North! North? That's a big place, friend: north.

JACK
Yeah . . . yeah, it is that: a big place.

BERNIE
(*After a pause; laughs again*) Well, *where*, boy? North *where?*

JACK
(*Coyly; proudly*) New York.

BERNIE
New York!

JACK
Unh-hunh; unh-hunh.

BERNIE
New York, hunh? Well. What you got goin' up there?

JACK
(*Coy again*) Oh . . . well . . . I got somethin' goin' up there. What *you* been up to, boy?

BERNIE
New York, hunh?

JACK
(*Obviously dying to tell about it*) Unh-hunh.

BERNIE
(*Knowing it*) Well, now, isn't that somethin'. Hey! You want a beer? You want another beer?

JACK
No, I gotta get . . . well, I don't know, I . . .

BERNIE
(*Rising from the table*) Sure you do. Hot like this? You need a beer or two, cool you off.

JACK
(*Settling back*) Yeah; why not? Sure, Bernie.

BERNIE
(*A dollar bill in his hand; moving off*) I'll get us a pair. New York, hunh? What's it all about, Jack? Hunh?

JACK (*Chuckles*)
Ah, you'd be surprised, boy; you'd be surprised.
(*Lights fade on this scene, come up on another, which is*)

SCENE TWO

Part of a screened-in porch; some wicker furniture, a little the worse for wear.

The NURSE's FATHER *is seated on the porch, a cane by his chair. Music, loud, from a phonograph, inside.*

FATHER
(*The music is too loud; he grips the arms of his chair; finally*) Stop it! Stop it! Stop it! Stop it!

NURSE (*From inside*)
What? What did you say?

FATHER
STOP IT!

NURSE
(*Appearing, dressed for duty*) I can't hear you; what do you want?

FATHER
Turn it off! Turn that goddamn music off!

NURSE
Honestly, Father . . .

FATHER
Turn it off!
    (*The* NURSE *turns wearily, goes back inside. Music stops*)
Goddamn Nigger records. (*To* NURSE, *inside*) I got a headache.

NURSE (*Re-entering*)
What?

FATHER
I said, I got a headache; you play those goddamn records all the time; blast my head off; you play those goddamn Nigger records full blast . . . me with a headache . . .

NURSE (*Wearily*)
You take your pill?

FATHER
No!

NURSE *(Turning)*

I'll get you your pills. . . .

FATHER

I don't want 'em!

NURSE *(Overpatiently)*

All right; then I won't get you your pills.

FATHER

(After a pause; quietly, petulantly) You play those goddamn records all the time. . . .

NURSE *(Impatiently)*

I'm sorry, Father; I didn't know you had your headache.

FATHER

Don't you use that tone with me!

NURSE

(With that tone) I wasn't using any tone . . .

FATHER

Don't argue!

NURSE

I am not arguing; I don't *want* to argue; it's too *hot* to argue. *(Pause; then quietly)* I don't see why a person can't play a couple of records around here without . . .

FATHER

Damn noise! That's all it is; damn noise.

NURSE

(After a pause) I don't suppose you'll drive me to work. I don't suppose, with your headache, you feel up to driving me to the hospital.

FATHER

No.

NURSE

I didn't think you would. And I suppose *you're* going to need the car, too.

FATHER

Yes.

NURSE

Yes; I figured you would. What are you going to do, Father? Are you going to sit here all afternoon on the porch, with your headache, and *watch* the car? Are you going to sit here and watch it all afternoon? You going to sit here with a shotgun and make sure the birds don't crap on it . . . or something?

FATHER

I'm going to need it.

NURSE

Yeah; sure.

FATHER

I said, I'm going to need it.

NURSE

Yeah . . . I heard you. You're going to need it.

FATHER

I am!

NURSE

Yeah; no doubt. You going to drive down to the Democratic Club, and sit around with that bunch of loafers? You going to play big politician today? Hunh?

FATHER

That's enough, now.

NURSE

You going to go down there with that bunch of bums . . . light up one of those expensive cigars, which you have no business smoking, which you can't afford, which *I* cannot afford, to put it more accurately . . . the same brand His Honor the mayor smokes . . . you going to sit down there and talk big, about how you and the mayor are like *this* . . . you going to pretend you're something more than you really are, which is nothing but . . .

FATHER

You be quiet, you!

NURSE

. . . a hanger-on . . . a flunky . . .

FATHER

YOU BE QUIET!

NURSE (*Faster*)

Is that what you need the car for, Father, and I am going to have to take that hot, stinking bus to the hospital?

FATHER

I said, quiet! (*Pause*) I'm sick and tired of hearing you disparage my friendship with the mayor.

NURSE (*Contemptuous*)

Friendship!

FATHER

That's right: friendship.

NURSE

I'll tell you what I'll do: Now that we have His Honor, the mayor, as a patient . . . when I get down to the hospital . . . if I ever get there on that damn bus . . . I'll pay him a call, and I'll just *ask* him about your "friendship" with him; I'll just . . .

FATHER

Don't you go disturbing him; you hear me?

NURSE

Why, I should think the mayor would be *delighted* if the daughter of one of his closest friends was to . . .

FATHER

You're going to make trouble!

NURSE *(Heavily sarcastic)*

Oh, how could I make trouble, Father?

FATHER

You be careful.

NURSE

Oh, that must be quite a friendship. Hey, I got a good idea: you could drive me down to the hospital and you could pay a visit to your good friend the mayor at the same time. Now, *that* is a good idea.

FATHER

Leave off! Just leave off!

NURSE

(Under her breath) You make me sick.

FATHER

What! What was that?

NURSE *(Very quietly)*

I said, you make me sick, Father.

FATHER

Yeah? Yeah?

(He takes his cane, raps it against the floor several times. This gesture, beginning in anger, alters, as it becomes weaker, to a helpless and pathetic flailing; eventually it subsides; the NURSE *watches it all quietly)*

NURSE *(Tenderly)*

Are you done?

FATHER

Go away; go to work.

NURSE

I'll get you your pills before I go.

FATHER *(Tonelessly)*

I said, I don't want them.

NURSE

I don't care whether you *want* them, or not. . . .

FATHER

I'm not one of your patients!

NURSE

Oh, and aren't I glad you're not.

FATHER

You give them better attention than you give me!

NURSE *(Wearily)*

I don't have patients, Father; I am not a floor nurse; will you get that into your head? I am on admissions; I am on the admissions desk. You *know* that; why do you pretend otherwise?

FATHER

If you were a . . . what-do-you-call-it . . . if you were a floor nurse . . . if you *were,* you'd give your patients better attention than you give me.

NURSE

'What *are* you, Father? What are you? Are you sick, or not? Are you a . . . a . . . a poor cripple, or are you planning to get yourself up out of that chair, after I go to work, and drive yourself down to the Democratic Club and sit around with that bunch of loafers? Make up your mind, Father; you can't have it every which way.

FATHER

Never mind.

NURSE

You can't; you just can't.

FATHER

Never mind, now!

NURSE

(After a pause) Well, I gotta get to work.

FATHER *(Sneering)*

Why don't you get your boyfriend to drive you to work?

NURSE

All right; leave off.

FATHER

Why don't you get him to come by and pick you up, hunh?

NURSE

I said, leave off!

FATHER

Or is he only interested in driving you back here at night . . . when it's nice and dark; when it's plenty dark for messing around in his car? Is that it? Why don't you bring him here and let *me* have a look at him; why don't you let me get a look at him some time?

NURSE *(Angry)*

Well, Father . . . *(A very brief gesture at the surroundings)* maybe it's because I don't want him to get a . . .

FATHER

I hear you; I hear you at night; I hear you gigglin' and carrying on out there in his car; I hear you!

NURSE

(Loud; to cover the sound of his voice) I'm going, Father.

FATHER

All right; get along, then; get on!

NURSE

You're damned right!

FATHER

Go on! Go!

(The NURSE *regards him for a moment; turns, exits)*

And don't stay out there all night in his car, when you get back. You hear me? *(Pause)* You hear me?

(Lights fade on this scene; come up on)

SCENE THREE

A bare area. JACK *enters, addresses his remarks off stage and to an invisible mirror on an invisible dresser. Music under this scene, as though coming from a distance.*

JACK

Hey . . . Bessie! C'mon, now. Hey . . . honey? Get your butt out of bed . . . wake up. C'mon; the goddamn afternoon's half gone; we gotta get movin'. Hey . . . I called that son-of-a-bitch in New York . . . *I* told him, all right. I told him what you said. Wake up, baby, we gotta get out of this dump; I

gotta get you to Memphis 'fore seven o'clock . . . and then . . . POW! . . .
we are headin' straight north. Here we come; NEW YORK. I told that bastard . . . I said: Look, you don't have no exclusive rights on Bessie . . .
nobody's got 'em . . . Bessie is doin' you a favor . . . she's doin' you a goddamn favor. She don't *have* to sing for you. I said: Bessie's tired . . . she
don't wanna travel now. An' he said: You don't *wanna* back out of this . . .
Bessie told me *herself* . . . and I said: Look . . . don't worry yourself . . .
Bessie said she'd cut more sides for you . . . she will . . . she'll make all the
goddamn new records you want. . . . What I mean to say *is,* just don't you
get any ideas about havin' exclusive rights . . . because nobody's got 'em.
(Giggles) I told him you was free as a bird, honey. Free as a goddamn bird.
(Looks in at her, shakes his head) Some bird! I been downstairs to check
us out. I go downstairs to check us out, and I run into a friend of mine . .
. and we sit in the bar and have a few, and he says: What're *you* doin' now;
what're you doin' in this crummy hotel? And I say: I am cartin' a bird
around with me. I'm cartin' her north; I got a fat lady upstairs; she is
sleepin' off last night. An' he says: You always got *some* fat lady upstairs,
somewhere; boy, I never seen it fail. An' I say: This ain't just no plain fat
lady I got upstairs . . . this is a celebrity, boy . . . this is a rich old fat singin'
lady . . . an' he laughed an' he said: Boy, who you got up there? I say: You
guess. An' he says: C'mon . . . I can't *guess.* An' I told him . . . I am travelin' with Miss Bessie Smith. An' he looked at me, an' he said, real quiet:
Jesus, boy, are you travelin' with Bessie? An' I said . . . an' real proud:
You're damn right I'm travelin' with Bessie. An' he wants to meet you; so
you get your big self out of bed; we're goin' to go downstairs, 'cause I
wanna show you off. C'mon, now; I mean I *gotta* show you off. 'Cause then
he said: Whatever *happened* to Bessie? An' I said: What do you mean,
whatever happened to Bessie? She's right upstairs. An' he said: I mean,
what's she been doin' the past four-five years? There was a time there, boy,
Chicago an' all, New York, she was the hottest goddamn thing goin'. Is she
still singin'? YOU HEAR THAT? That's what he said: Is she still singin'?
An' I said . . . I said, you been tired . . . you been restin'. You ain't been forgotten, honey, but they are askin' questions. SO YOU GET UP! We're dri-
vin' north tonight, an' when you get in New York . . . *you* show 'em where
you been. Honey, you're gonna go back on top again . . . I mean it . . . you
are. I'm gonna get you up to New York. 'Cause you gotta make that date.
I mean, sure, baby, you're free as a goddamn bird, an' I did tell that son-
of-a-bitch he don't have exclusive rights on you . . . but, honey . . . he *is*
interested . . . an' you gotta hustle for it now. You do; 'cause if you don't do
somethin', people are gonna stop askin' where you been the past four-five
years . . . they're gonna stop askin' anything at all! You hear? An' if I say
downstairs you're rich . . . that don't make it so, Bessie. No more, honey.
You gotta make this goddamn trip . . . you gotta get goin' again. *(Pleading)*
Baby? Honey? You know I'm not lyin' to you. C'mon now; get up. We go
downstairs to the bar an' have a few . . . see my friend . . . an' then we'll

get in that car . . . and *go*. 'Cause it's gettin' late, honey . . . it's gettin' awful late. *(Brighter)* Hey! You awake? *(Moving to the wings)* Well, c'mon, then, Bessie . . . let's get up. We're goin' north again!

(The lights fade on this scene.

Music.

The sunset is predominant)

JACK'S VOICE

Ha, ha; thanks; thanks a lot. *(Car door slams. Car motor starts)* O.K.; here we go; we're on our way. *(Sound of car motor gunning, car moving off, fading)*

(The sunset dims again.

Music, fading, as the lights come up on)

SCENE FOUR

The admissions room of the hospital. The NURSE *is at her desk; the* ORDERLY *stands to one side.*

ORDERLY

The mayor of Memphis! I went into his room and there he was; the mayor of Memphis. Lying right there, flat on his belly . . . a cigar in his mouth . . . an unlit cigar stuck in his mouth, chewing on it, chewing on a big, unlit cigar . . . shuffling a lot of papers in his hands, a pillow shoved up under his chest to give him some freedom for all those papers . . . and I came in, and I said: Good afternoon, Your Honor . . . and he swung his face 'round and he looked at me and he shouted: My ass hurts, you get the hell out of here!

NURSE *(Laughs freely)*

His Honor has got his ass in a sling, and that's for sure.

ORDERLY

And I got out; I left very quickly; I closed the door fast.

NURSE

The mayor and his hemorrhoids . . . the mayor's late hemorrhoids . . . are a matter of deep concern to this institution, for the mayor built this hospital; the mayor is here with his ass in a sling, and the seat of government is now in Room 206 . . . so you be nice and respectful. *(Laughs)* There is a man two rooms down who walked in here last night after you went off . . . that man walked in here with his hands over his gut to keep his insides from spilling right out on this desk . . .

ORDERLY

I heard. . . .

NURSE

. . . and that man may live, or he may not live, and the wagers are heavy that he will not live . . . but we are not one bit more concerned for that man than we are for His Honor . . . no sir.

ORDERLY *(Chuckling)*

I like your contempt.

NURSE

You what? You like my *contempt,* do you? Well now, don't misunderstand me. Just what do you think I meant? What have you got it in your mind that I was saying?

ORDERLY

Why, it's a matter of proportion. Surely you don't *condone* the fact that the mayor and his piles, and that poor man lying up there . . . ?

NURSE

Condone! Will you listen to that: condone! My! Aren't you the educated one? What . . . what does that word mean, boy? That word condone? Hunh? You do talk some, don't you? You have a great deal to learn. Now it's true that the poor man lying up there with his guts coming out could be a Nigger for all the attention he'd get if His Honor should start shouting for something . . . he could be on the operating table . . . and they'd drop his insides right on the floor and come running if the mayor should want his cigar lit. . . . But that is the way things *are.* Those are facts. You had better acquaint yourself with some realities.

ORDERLY

I know . . . I know the mayor is an important man. He is impressive . . . even lying on his belly like he is. . . . I'd like to get to talk to him.

NURSE

Don't you know it! TALK to him! Talk to the mayor? What for?

ORDERLY

I've told you. I've told you I don't intend to stay here carrying crap pans and washing out the operating theatre until I have a . . . a long gray beard . . . I'm . . . I'm going beyond that.

NURSE *(Patronizing)*

Sure.

ORDERLY

I've told you . . . I'm going beyond that. This . . .

NURSE

(*Shakes her head in amused disbelief*) Oh, my. Listen . . . you should count yourself lucky, boy. Just what do you think is going to happen to you? Is His Honor, the mayor, going to rise up out of his sickbed and take a personal interest in you? Write a letter to the President, maybe? And is Mr. Roosevelt going to send his wife, Lady Eleanor, down here after you? Or is it in your plans that you are going to be handed a big fat scholarship somewhere to the north of Johns Hopkins? Boy, you just don't know! I'll tell you something . . . you are lucky as you are. Whatever do you expect?

ORDERLY

What's been promised. . . . Nothing more. Just that.

NURSE

Promised! Promised? Oh, boy, I'll tell you about promises. Don't you know yet that everything is promises . . . and that is all there is to it? Promises . . . nothing more! I am personally sick of promises. Would you like to hear a little poem? Would you like me to recite some verse for you? Here is a little poem: "You kiss the Niggers and I'll kiss the Jews and we'll stay in the White House as long as we choose." And that . . . according to what I am told . . . that is what Mr. and Mrs. Roosevelt sit at the breakfast table and sing to each other over their orange juice, right in the White House. Promises, boy! Promises . . . and that is what they are going to stay.

ORDERLY

There are *some* people who believe in more than promises. . . .

NURSE

Hunh?

ORDERLY (*Cautious now*)

I say, there are some people who believe in more than promises; there are some people who believe in action.

NURSE

What's that? What did you say?

ORDERLY

Action . . . ac— . . . Never mind.

NURSE (*Her eyes narrow*)

No . . . no, go on now . . . action? What kind of action do you mean?

ORDERLY

I don't *mean* anything . . . all I said was . . .

NURSE

I heard you. You know . . . I know what you been doing. You been listening to the great white doctor again . . . that big, good-looking blond intern you *admire* so much because he is so liberal-thinking, eh? My suitor? *(Laughs)* My suitor . . . my very own white knight, who is wasting his time patching up decent folk right here when there is dying going on in Spain. *(Exaggerated)* Oh, there is dying in Spain. And he is held here! That's who you have been listening to.

ORDERLY

I don't mean that. . . . I don't pay any attention . . . *(Weakly)* to that kind of talk. I do my job here . . . I try to keep . . .

NURSE *(Contemptuous)*

You try to keep yourself on the good side of everybody, don't you, boy? You stand there and you nod your kinky little head and say yes'm, yes'm, at everything I say, and then when he's here you go off in a corner and you get him and you sympathize with him . . . you get him to tell you about . . . promises! . . . and . . . and . . . action! . . . I'll tell you right now, he's going to get himself into trouble . . . and you're helping him right along.

ORDERLY

No, now. I don't . . .

NURSE *(With some disgust)*

All that talk of his! Action! I know all what he talks about . . . like about that bunch of radicals came through here last spring . . . causing the rioting . . . that arson! Stuff like that. Didn't . . . didn't you have someone get banged up in that?

ORDERLY *(Contained)*

My uncle got run down by a lorry full of state police . . .

NURSE

. . . which the Governor called out because of the rioting . . . and that arson! Action! That was a fine bunch of action. Is that what you mean? Is that what you get him off in a corner and get him to talk about . . . and pretend you're interested? Listen, boy . . . if you're going to get yourself in with those folks, you'd better . . .

ORDERLY *(Quickly)*

I'm not mixed up with any folks . . . honestly . . . I'm not. I just want to . .
.

NURSE

I'll tell you what you just want. . . . I'll tell you what you just want if you have any mind to keep this good job you've got. . . . You just shut your ears . . . and you keep that mouth closed tight, too. All this talk about what you are going to go beyond! You keep walking a real tight line here, and . . . and at night . . . *(She begins to giggle)* . . . and at night, if you want to, on your own time . . . at night you keep right on putting that bleach on your hands and your neck and your face . . .

ORDERLY

I do no such thing!

NURSE *(In full laughter)*

. . . and you keep right on bleaching away . . . b-l-e-a-c-h-i-n-g a-w-a-y . . . but you do that on your own time . . . you can do all that on your own time.

ORDERLY *(Pleading)*

I do no such thing!

NURSE

The hell you don't! You are such a . . .

ORDERLY

That kind of talk is very . . .

NURSE

. . . you are so mixed up! You are going to be one funny sight. You, over there in a corner playing up to him . . . well, boy, you are going to be one funny sight come the millennium. . . . The great black mob marching down the street, banners in the air . . . that great black mob . . . and you right there in the middle, your bleached-out, snowy-white face in the middle of the pack like that . . . *(She breaks down in laughter)* . . . oh . . . oh, my . . . oh. I tell you, that will be quite a sight.

ORDERLY *(Plaintive)*

I wish you'd stop that.

NURSE

Quite a sight.

ORDERLY

I wish you wouldn't make fun of me . . . I don't give you any cause.

NURSE

Oh, my . . . oh, I *am* sorry . . . I am *so* sorry.

ORDERLY

I don't think I give you any cause. . . .

NURSE

You don't, eh?

ORDERLY

No.

NURSE

Well . . . you *are* a true little gentleman, that's for sure . . . you *are* polite . . . and deferential . . . and you are a genuine little ass-licker, if I ever saw one. Tell me, boy . . .

ORDERLY

(Stiffening a little) There is no need . . .

NURSE

(Maliciously solicitous) Tell me, boy . . . is it true that you have Uncle Tom'd yourself right out of the bosom of your family . . . right out of your circle of acquaintances? Is it true, young man, that you are now an inhabitant of no-man's-land, on the one side shunned and disowned by your brethren, and on the other an object of contempt and derision to your betters? Is that your problem, son?

ORDERLY

You . . . you shouldn't do that. I . . . work hard . . . I try to advance myself . . . I give nobody trouble.

NURSE

I'll tell you what you do. . . . You go north, boy . . . you go up to New York City, where nobody's any better than anybody else . . . get up north, boy. *(Abrupt change of tone)* But before you do anything like that, you run on downstairs and get me a pack of cigarettes.

ORDERLY

(Pauses. Is about to speak; thinks better of it; moves off to door, rear) Yes'm. *(Exits)*

NURSE

(Watches him leave. After he is gone, shakes her head, laughs, parodies him)
Yes'm . . . yes'm . . . ha, ha, ha! You white Niggers kill me.
(She picks up her desk phone, dials a number, as the lights come up on)

SCENE FIVE

Which is both the hospital set of the preceding scene and, as well, on the raised platform, another admissions desk of another hospital. The desk is empty. The phone rings, twice. The SECOND NURSE comes in, slowly, filing her nails, maybe.

SECOND NURSE

(Lazily answering the phone) Mercy Hospital.

NURSE

Mercy Hospital! Mercy, indeed, you away from your desk all the time. *Some* hospitals are run better than *others; some* nurses stay at their posts.

SECOND NURSE *(Bored)*

Oh, hi. What do you want?

NURSE

I don't *want* anything. . . .

SECOND NURSE

(Pause) Oh. Well, what did you call for?

NURSE

I didn't call *for* anything. I *(Shrugs)* just called.

SECOND NURSE

Oh.

(The lights dim a little on the two nurses.

Music.

Car sounds up)

JACK'S VOICE

(Laughs) I tell you, honey, he didn't like that. No, sir, he didn't. You comfortable, honey. Hunh? You just lean back and enjoy the ride, baby; we're makin' good time. Yes, we are makin' . . . WATCH OUT! WATCH . . .

(Sound of crash. . . . Silence)

Honey . . . baby . . . we have crashed . . . you all right? . . . BESSIE! BESSIE!

(Music up again, fading as the lights come up full again on the two nurses)

NURSE

. . . and, what else? Oh, yeah; *we* have got the mayor here.

SECOND NURSE

That's nice. What's he doin'?

NURSE

He isn't *doin'* anything; he is a patient here.

SECOND NURSE

Oh. Well, *we* had the mayor's wife *here* . . . last April.

NURSE

Unh-hunh. Well, *we* got the mayor *here*, now.

SECOND NURSE *(Very bored)*

Unh-hunh. Well, that's nice.

NURSE

(Turns, sees the INTERN *entering)* Oh, lover-boy just walked in; I'll call you later, hunh?

SECOND NURSE

Unh-hunh.

(They both hang up. The lights fade on the SECOND NURSE*)*

SCENE SIX

NURSE

Well, how is the Great White Doctor this evening?

INTERN *(Irritable)*

Oh . . . drop it.

NURSE

Oh, my . . . where is your cheerful demeanor this evening, Doctor?

INTERN

(Smiling in spite of himself) How do you do it? How do you manage to just dismiss things from your mind? How can you say a . . . cheerful hello to someone . . . dismissing from your mind . . . excusing yourself for the vile things you have said the evening before?

NURSE *(Lightly)*

I said nothing vile. I put you in your place . . . that's all. I . . . I merely put you in your place . . . as I have done before . . . and as I shall do again.

INTERN

(Is about to say something; thinks better of it; sighs) Never mind . . . forget about it . . . Did you *see* the sunset?

NURSE *(Mimicking)*

No, I didn't *see* the sunset. *What* is it doing?

INTERN

(Amused. Puts it on heavily) The west is burning . . . fire has enveloped fully half of the continent . . . the . . . the fingers of the flame stretch upward to the stars . . . and . . . and there is a monstrous burning circumference hanging on the edge of the world.

NURSE *(Laughs)*

Oh, my . . . oh, my.

INTERN *(Serious)*

It's a truly beautiful sight. Go out and have a look.

NURSE *(Coquettish)*

Oh, Doctor, I am chained to my desk of pain, so I must rely on you. . . . Talk the sunset to me, you . . . you monstrous burning intern hanging on the edge of my circumference . . . ha, ha, *ha.*

INTERN

(*Leans toward her*) When?

NURSE

When?

INTERN (*Lightly*)

When . . . when are you going to let me nearer, woman?

NURSE

Oh, my!

INTERN

Here am I . . . here am I tangential, while all the while I would serve more nobly as a radiant, not outward from, but reversed, plunging straight to your lovely vortex.

NURSE (*Laughs*)

Oh, la! You must keep your mind off my lovely vortex . . . you just remain . . . uh . . . tangential.

INTERN (*Mock despair*)

How is a man to fulfill himself? Here I offer you love . . . consider the word . . . love. . . . Here I offer you my love, my self . . . my bored bed . . .

NURSE

I note your offer . . . your offer is noted. (*Holds out a clipboard*) Here . . . do you want your reports?

INTERN

No . . . I don't want my reports. Give them here. (*Takes the clipboard*)

NURSE

And while you're here with your hot breath on me, hand me a cigarette. I sent the Nigger down for a pack. I ran out. (*He gives her a cigarette*) Match?

INTERN

Go light it on the sunset. (*Tosses match to her*) He says you owe him for three packs.

NURSE

(*Lights her cigarette*) Your bored bed . . . indeed.

INTERN

Ma'am . . . the heart yearns, the body burns . . .

NURSE

And *I* haven't time for *in*terns.

INTERN

. . . the heart yearns, the body burns . . . and I haven't time . . . Oh, I don't know . . . the things you women can do to art.

(More intimate, but still light)

Have you told your father, yet? Have you told your father that I am hopelessly in love with you? Have you told him that at night the sheets of my bed are like a tent, poled center-upward in my love for you?

NURSE *(Wry)*

I'll tell him . . . I'll tell my father just that . . . just what you said . . . and he'll be down here after you for talking to a young lady like that! Really!

INTERN

My God! I forgot myself! A cloistered maiden in whose house trousers are never mentioned . . . in which flies, I am sure, are referred to only as winged bugs. Here I thought I was talking to someone, to a certain young nurse, whose collection of anatomical jokes for all occasions . . .

NURSE *(Giggles)*

Oh, you be still, now. *(Lofty)* Besides, just because I play coarse and flip around here. . . to keep my place with the rest of you . . . don't you think for a minute that I relish this turn to the particular from the general. . . . If you don't mind, we'll just cease this talk.

INTERN *(Half sung)*

I'm always in tumescence for you. You'd never guess the things I . . .

NURSE *(Blush-giggle)*

Now stop that! Really, I mean it!

INTERN

Then marry me, woman. If nothing else, marry me.

NURSE

Don't, now.

INTERN

(Joking and serious at the same time) Marry me.

NURSE

(Matter-of-fact, but not unkindly) I am sick of this talk. My poor father may have some funny ideas; he may be having a pretty hard time reconciling himself to things as they are. But not me! Forty-six dollars a month! Isn't that right? Isn't that what you make? Forty-six dollars a month! Boy, you can't afford even to think about marrying. You can't afford marriage. . . . Best you can afford is lust. That's the best you can afford.

INTERN *(Scathing)*

Oh . . . gentle woman . . . nineteenth-century lady out of place in this vulgar time . . . maiden versed in petit point and murmured talk of the weather . . .

NURSE

Now I mean it . . . you can cut that talk right out.

INTERN

. . . type my great-grandfather fought and died for . . . forty-six dollars a month and the best I can afford is lust! Jesus, woman!

NURSE

All right . . . you can quit making fun of me. You can quit it right this minute.

INTERN

I! Making fun of *you* . . . !

NURSE

I am tired of being toyed with; I am tired of your impractical propositions. Must you dwell on what is not going to happen? Must you ask me, constantly, over and over again, the same question to which you are already aware you will get the same answer? Do you get pleasure from it? What unreasonable form of contentment do you derive from persisting in this?

INTERN *(Lightly)*

Because I love you?

NURSE

Oh, that would help matters along; it really would . . . even if it were *true*. The economic realities would pick up their skirts, whoop, and depart before the lance-high, love-smit knight. My knight, whose real and true interest, if we come right down to it, as indicated in the order of your propositions, is, and always has been, a convenient and uncomplicated bedding down.

INTERN

(Smiling, and with great gallantry) I have offered to marry you.

NURSE

Yeah . . . sure . . . you have offered to marry me. The United States is chuck-full of girls who have heard that great promise—I will marry you . . . I will marry you . . . IF! If! The great promise with its great conditional attached to it. . . .

INTERN *(Amused)*

Who are you pretending to be?

NURSE *(Abrupt)*

What do you mean?

INTERN *(Laughing)*

Oh, *nothing.*

NURSE

(Regards him silently for a moment; then) Marry me! Do you know . . . do you know that Nigger I sent to fetch me a pack of butts . . . do you know

he is in a far better position . . . realistically, economically . . . to ask to marry me than you are? Hunh? Do you know that? That Nigger! Do you know that Nigger outearns you . . . and by a *lot?*

INTERN

(Bows to her) I know he does . . . and I know what value you, you and your famous family, put on such things. So, I have an idea for you . . . why don't you just *ask* that Nigger to marry you? 'Cause, boy, he'd never ask you! I'm sure if you told your father about it, it would give him some pause at first, because we know what type of man your father is . . . don't we? . . . But then he would think about it . . . and realize the advantages of the match . . . realistically . . . economically . . . and he would find some way to adjust his values, in consideration of your happiness, and security. . . .

NURSE

(Flicks her still-lit cigarette at him, hard; hits him with it) You are disgusting!

INTERN

Damn you, bitch!

NURSE

Disgusting!

INTERN

Realistic . . . practical . . . *(A little softer, now)* Your family is a famous *name,* but those thousand acres are *gone,* and the pillars of your house are blistered and flaking . . . *(Harder)* Not that your family ever *had,* within human memory, a thousand acres to *go* . . . *or* a house with pillars in the first place. . . .

NURSE *(Angry)*

I am fully aware of what is true and what is not true. *(Soberly)* Go about your work and leave me be.

INTERN *(Sweetly)*

Aw.

NURSE

I said . . . leave me be.

INTERN

(Brushing himself) It is a criminal offense to set fire to interns . . . orderlies you may burn at will, unless you have other plans for them . . . but interns . . .

NURSE

. . . are a dime a dozen. *(Giggles)* Did I burn you?

INTERN

No, you did not burn me.

NURSE

That's too bad . . . would have served you right if I had. *(Pauses; then smiles)* I'm sorry, honey.

INTERN *(Mock formal)*

I accept your apology . . . and I await your surrender.

NURSE *(Laughs)*

Well, you just await it. *(A pause)* Hey, what are you going to do about the mayor being here now?

INTERN

What am I supposed to do about it? I am on emergencies, and he is not an emergency case.

NURSE

I told you . . . I told you what you should do.

INTERN

I know . . . I should go upstairs to his room . . . I should pull up a chair, and I should sit down and I should say, How's tricks, Your Honor?

NURSE

Well, you make fun if you want to . . . but if you listen to me, you'll know you need some people *behind* you.

INTERN

Strangers!

NURSE

Strangers don't stay strangers . . . not if you don't let them. He could do something for you if he had a mind to.

INTERN

Yes he could . . . indeed, he *could* do something for me. . . . He could give me his car . . . he could make me a present of his Cord automobile. . . . That would be the finest thing any mayor ever did for a private citizen. Have you seen that car?

NURSE

Have I seen that car? Have I seen this . . . have I seen that? Cord automobiles and . . . and sunsets . . . those are . . . fine preoccupations. Is that what you think about? Huh? Driving a fine car into a fine sunset?

INTERN *(Quietly)*

Lord knows, I'd like to get away from here.

NURSE *(Nodding)*

I know . . . I know. Well, maybe you're going to *have* to get away from here. People are aware how dissatisfied you are . . . people have heard a lot about your . . . dissatisfaction. . . . My father has heard . . . people got wind of the way you feel about things. People here aren't good enough for your attentions. . . . Foreigners . . . a bunch of foreigners who are cutting each other up in their own business . . . that's where you'd like to be, isn't it?

INTERN *(Quietly; intensely)*
There are over half a million people killed in that war! Do you know that? By airplanes. . . . Civilians! You misunderstand me so! I am . . . all right . . . this way. . . . My dissatisfactions . . . you call them that . . . my dissatisfactions have nothing to do with loyalties. . . . I am not concerned with politics . . . but I have a sense of urgency . . . a dislike of waste . . . stagnation . . . I am *stranded* . . . *here.* . . . My talents are not large . . . but the emergencies of the emergency ward of this second-rate hospital in this second-rate state . . . No! . . . it isn't enough. Oh, you listen to me. If I could . . . if I could bandage the arm of one person . . . if I could be over there right this minute . . . you could take the city of Memphis . . . you could take the whole state . . . and don't you forget I was born here . . . you could take the whole goddamn state. . . .

NURSE *(Hard)*
Well, I have a very good idea of how we could arrange that. I have a dandy idea. . . . We could just tell the mayor about the way you feel, and he'd be delighted to help you on your way . . . out of this hospital at the very least, and maybe out of the state! And I don't think he'd be giving you any Cord automobile as a going-away present, either. He'd set you out, all right . . . he'd set you right out on your *butt!* That's what he'd do.

INTERN
(With a rueful half-smile) Yes . . . yes . . . I imagine he would. I feel lucky . . . I feel doubly fortunate, now . . . having you . . . feeling the way we do about each other.

NURSE
You are so sarcastic!

INTERN
Well, how the hell do you expect me to behave?

NURSE
Just . . . *(Laughs)* . . . oh, boy, this is good . . . just like I told the Nigger . . . you walk a straight line, and you do your job . . . *(Turns coy, here)* . . . and . . . and unless you are kept late by some emergency more pressing than your . . . *(Smiles wryly)* . . . "love" . . . for me . . . I may let you drive me home tonight . . . in your beat-up Chevy.

INTERN
Woman, as always I anticipate with enormous pleasure the prospect of driving you home . . . a stop along the way . . . fifteen minutes or so . . . of tantalizing preliminary love play ending in an infuriating and inconclusive

wrestling match, during which you hiss of the . . . the liberties I should not take, and I sound the horn once or twice accidentally with my elbow . . .

(*She giggles at this*)

. . . and finally, in my beat-up car, in front of your father's beat-up house . . . a kiss of searing intensity . . . a hand in the right place . . . briefly . . . and your hasty departure within. I am looking forward to this ritual. . . as I always do.

NURSE (*Pleased*)

Why, thank you.

INTERN

I look forward to this ritual because of how it sets me apart from other men . . .

NURSE

Aw . . .

INTERN

. . . because I am probably the only white man under sixty in two counties who has *not* had the pleasure of . . .

NURSE

LIAR! You no-account mother-grabbing son of a Nigger!

INTERN (*Laughs*)

Boy! Watch you go!

NURSE

FILTH! You are filth!

INTERN

I am honest . . . an honest man. Let me make you an honest woman.

NURSE

(*Steaming . . . her rage between her teeth*) You have done it, boy . . . you have played around with me and you have done it. I am going to get you. . . . I am going to fix you . . . I am going to see to it that you are *through* here . . . do you understand what I'm telling you?

INTERN

There is no ambiguity in your talk now, honey.

NURSE

You're damn right there isn't.

(*The* ORDERLY *re-enters from stage-rear. The* NURSE *sees him*)

Get out of here!

(*But he stands there*)

Do you hear me? You get the hell out of here! GO!

(*He retreats, exits, to silence*)

INTERN *(Chuckling)*

King of the castle. My, you *are* something.

NURSE

Did you get what I was telling you?

INTERN

Why, I heard every word . . . every sweet syllable. . . .

NURSE

You have overstepped yourself . . . and you are going to wish you hadn't. I'll get my father . . . I'll have you done with *myself*

INTERN *(Cautious)*

Aw, come on, now.

NURSE

I mean it.

INTERN *(Lying badly)*

Now look . . . you don't think I meant . . .

NURSE *(Mimicking)*

Now you don't think I meant . . . *(Laughs broadly)* Oh, my . . . you are the funny one.

    (Her threat, now, has no fury, but is filled with quiet conviction)

I said I'll fix you . . . and I will. You just go along with your work . . . you do your job . . . but what I said . . . you keep that burning in the back of your brain. We'll go right along, you and I, and we'll be civil . . . and it'll be as though nothing had happened . . . nothing at all. *(Laughs again)* Honey, your neck is in the *noose* . . . and I have a whip . . . and I'll set the horse from under you . . . when it pleases me.

INTERN *(Wryly)*

It's going to be nice around here.

NURSE

Oh, yes it is. I'm going to enjoy it . . . I really am.

INTERN

Well. . . I'll forget about driving you home tonight. . . .

NURSE

Oh, no . . . you will *not* forget about driving me home tonight. You will drive me home *tonight* . . . you will drive me home *tonight* . . . and *tomorrow* night . . . you will see me to my *door* . . . you will be my gallant. We will have things between us a little bit the way I am told things *used* to be. You will *court* me, boy, and you will do it *right!*

INTERN

(Stares at her for a moment) You impress me. No matter what else, I've got to admit that.

(The NURSE *laughs wildly at this.*

Music.

The lights on this hospital set fade, and come up on the SECOND NURSE, *at her desk, for)*

SCENE SEVEN

JACK

(Rushing in) Ma'am, I need help, quick!

SECOND NURSE

What d'you want here?

JACK

There has been an accident, ma'am . . . I got an injured woman outside in my car. . . .

SECOND NURSE

Yeah? Is that so? Well, you sit down and wait. . . . You go over there and sit down and wait a while.

JACK

This is an emergency! There has been an accident!

SECOND NURSE

YOU WAIT! You just sit down and wait!

JACK

This woman is badly . . .

SECOND NURSE

YOU COOL YOUR HEELS!

JACK

Ma'am . . . I got Bessie Smith out in that car there. . . .

SECOND NURSE

I DONT CARE WHO YOU GOT OUT THERE, NIGGER. YOU COOL YOUR HEELS!

(Music up.

The lights fade on this scene, come up again on the main hospital scene, on the NURSE *and the* INTERN, *for)*

SCENE EIGHT

(Music fades)

NURSE *(Loud)*

Hey, Nigger . . . Nigger!
(The ORDERLY *re-enters)*
Give me my cigarettes.

INTERN

I think I'll . . .

NURSE

You stay here!
(The ORDERLY *hands the nurse the cigarettes, cautious and attentive to see what is wrong)*
A person could die for a smoke, the time you take. What'd you do . . . sit downstairs in the can and rest your small, shapely feet . . . hunh?

ORDERLY

You told me to . . . go back outside . . .

NURSE

Before that! What'd you do . . . go to the cigarette *factory?* Did you take a quick run up to Winston-Salem for these?

ORDERLY

No . . . I . . .

NURSE

Skip it. *(To the* INTERN*)* Where? Where were you planning to go?

INTERN *(Too formal)*

I beg your pardon?

NURSE

I said . . . where did you want to go to? Were you off for coffee?

INTERN

Is that what you want? Now that you have your cigarettes, have you hit upon the idea of having coffee, too? Now that he is back from one errand, are you planning to send me on another?

NURSE *(Smiling wickedly)*

Yeah . . . I think I'd like that . . . keep both of you jumping. I *would* like coffee, and I *would* like you to get it for me. So why don't you just trot right across the hall and get me some? And I like it good and hot . . . and strong . . .

INTERN

. . . and black . . . ?

NURSE

Cream! . . . and sweet . . . and in a hurry!

INTERN

I guess your wish is my command . . . hunh?

NURSE

You bet it is!

INTERN

(Moves halfway to the door, stage-rear, then pauses)

I just had a lovely thought . . . that maybe sometime when you are sitting there at your desk opening mail with that stiletto you use for a letter opener, you might slip and tear open your arm . . . then you could come running into the emergency . . . and I could be there when you came running in, blood coming out of you like water out of a faucet . . . and I could take ahold of your arm . . . and just hold it . . . just hold it . . . and watch it flow . . . just hold on to you and watch your blood flow . . .

NURSE

(Grabs up the letter opener . . . holds it up)

This? More likely between your ribs!

INTERN *(Exiting)*

One coffee, lady.

NURSE

(After a moment of silence, throws the letter opener back down on her desk)

I'll take care of him. CRACK! I'll crack that whip. *(To the* ORDERLY*)* What are you standing there for . . . hunh? You like to watch what's going on?

ORDERLY

I'm no voyeur.

NURSE

You what? You like to listen in? You take pleasure in it?

ORDERLY

I said no.

NURSE *(Half to herself)*

I'll bet you don't. I'll take care of him . . . talking to me like that . . . I'll crack that whip. Let him just wait.

(To the ORDERLY, *now)*

My father says that Francisco Franco is going to be victorious in that war over there . . . that he's going to win . . . and that it's just wonderful.

ORDERLY

He does?

NURSE

Yes, he does. My father says that Francisco Franco has got them licked, and that they're a bunch of radicals, anyway, and it's all to the good . . . just wonderful.

ORDERLY

Is that so?

NURSE

I've told you my father is a . . . a historian, so he isn't just anybody. His opinion counts for something special. It *still* counts for something special. He says anybody wants to go over there and get mixed up in that thing has got it coming to him . . . whatever happens.

ORDERLY

I'm sure your father is an informed man, and . . .

NURSE

What?

ORDERLY

I said . . . I said . . . I'm sure your father is an informed man, and . . . his opinion is to be respected.

NURSE

That's right, boy . . . you just jump to it and say what you think people want to hear . . . you be both sides of the coin. Did you . . . did you hear him threaten me there? Did you?

ORDERLY

Oh, now . . . I don't think . . .

NURSE (*Steely*)

You heard him threaten me!

ORDERLY

I don't think . . .

NURSE

For such a smart boy . . . you are so dumb. I don't know what I am going to do with you.

(*She is thinking of the* INTERN *now, and her expression shows it*)

You refuse to comprehend things and that bodes badly . . . it does. Especially considering it is all but arranged . . .

ORDERLY

What is all but arranged?

NURSE

(A great laugh, but mirthless. She is barely under control)
Why, don't you know, boy? Didn't you know that you and I are practically engaged?

ORDERLY

I . . . I don't . . .

NURSE

Don't you know about the economic realities? Haven't you been appraised of the way things *are? (She giggles)* Our knights are gone forth into sunsets . . . behind the wheels of Cord cars . . . the acres have diminished and the paint is flaking . . . that there is a great . . . *abandonment?*

ORDERLY *(Cautious)*

I don't understand you . . .

NURSE

No kidding? (Her *voice shakes*) No kidding . . . you don't understand me? Why? What's the matter, boy, don't you get the idea?

ORDERLY *(Contained, but angry)*

I think you'd tire of riding me some day. I think you *would* . . .

NURSE

You go up to Room 206, right now . . . you go up and tell the mayor that when his butt's better we have a marrying job for him.

ORDERLY *(With some distaste)*

Really . . . you go much too far. . . .

NURSE

Oh, I do, do I? Well, let me tell you something . . . I am sick of it! I am *sick.* I am sick of everything in this hot, stupid, fly-ridden *world.* I am sick of the disparity between things as they are, and as they should be! I am sick of this desk . . . this uniform . . . it scratches. . . . I am sick of the sight of *you* . . . the *thought* of you makes me . . . *itch.* . . . I am sick of *him. (Soft now: a chant)* I am sick of talking to people on the phone in this damn stupid hospital. . . . I am sick of the smell of Lysol . . . I could die of it. . . . I am sick of going to bed and I am sick of waking up. . . . I am tired . . . I am tired of the truth . . . and I am tired of lying about the truth . . . I am tired of my skin. . . . I WANT OUT!

ORDERLY

(After a short pause) Why don't you go into emergency . . . and lie down?
    (He approaches her)

NURSE

Keep away from me.

(At this moment the outside door bursts open and JACK *plunges into the room. He is all these things: drunk, shocked, frightened. His face should be cut, but no longer bleeding. His clothes should be dirtied . . . and in some disarray. He pauses, a few steps into the room, breathing hard)*

NURSE

Whoa! Hold on there, you.

ORDERLY *(Not advancing)*

What do you want?

JACK

(After more hard breathing; confused) What . . . ?

NURSE

You come banging in through that door like that? What's the matter with you? *(To the* ORDERLY*)* Go see what's the matter with him.

ORDERLY *(Advancing slightly)*

What do you *want?*

JACK *(Very confused)*

What do I want . . . ?

ORDERLY *(Backing off)*

You can't come in here like this . . . banging your way in here . . . don't you know any better?

NURSE

You drunk?

JACK

(Taken aback by the irrelevance) I've been drinking . . . yes . . . all right . . . I'm drunk. *(Intense)* I got someone outside . . .

NURSE

You stop that yelling. This is a white hospital, you.

ORDERLY *(Nearer the* NURSE*)*

That's right. She's right. This is a private hospital . . . a semi-private hospital. If you go on . . . into the city . . .

JACK *(Shakes his head)*

No. . . .

NURSE

Now you listen to me, and you get this straight . . . *(Pauses just percepti-bly, then says the word, but with no special emphasis)* . . . Nigger . . . this is a semiprivate white hospital . . .

JACK *(Defiant)*

I don't care!

NURSE

Well, you *get* on. . . .

ORDERLY

(As the INTERN *re-enters with two containers of coffee)*
You go on now . . . you go . . .

INTERN

What's all this about?

ORDERLY

I told him to go on into Memphis . . .

INTERN

Be quiet. *(To* JACK*)* What is all this about?

JACK

Please . . . I got a woman . . .

NURSE

You been told to move on.

INTERN

You got a woman . . .

JACK

Outside . . . in the car. . . . There was an accident . . . there is blood. . . . Her arm
. . .

INTERN

(After thinking for a moment, looking at the NURSE, *moves toward the outside door)*
All right . . . we'll go see. *(To the* ORDERLY, *who hangs back)* Come on, you
. . . let's go.

ORDERLY

(Looks to the NURSE*)* We told him to go on into Memphis.

NURSE

(To the INTERN, *her eyes narrowing)* Don't you go out there!

INTERN

(Ignoring her; to the ORDERLY*)* You heard me . . . come on!

NURSE *(Strong)*
I told you . . . DON'T GO OUT THERE!

INTERN *(Softly, sadly)*
Honey . . . you going to fix me? You going to have the mayor throw me out
of here on my butt? Or are you going to arrange it in Washington to have
me *deported?* What *are* you going to do . . . hunh?

NURSE *(Between her teeth)*
Don't go out there . . .

INTERN
Well, honey, whatever it is you're going to do . . . it might as well be now
as any other time.
   (He and the ORDERLY *move to the outside door)*

NURSE
   (Half angry, half plaintive, as they exit)
Don't go!
   (After they exit)
I warn you! I *will* fix you. You go out that door . . . you're through here.
   *(*JACK *moves to a vacant area near the bench, stage-right. The*
   NURSE *lights a cigarette)*
I told you I'd fix you . . . I'll fix you. *(Now, to* JACK*)* I think I said this was
a white hospital.

JACK *(Wearily)*
I know, lady . . . you told me.

NURSE
(Her attention on the door) You don't have sense enough to do what you're
told . . . you make trouble for yourself . . . you make trouble for other people.

JACK *(Sighing)*
I don't care . . .

NURSE
You'll care!

JACK
(Softly, shaking his head) No . . . I won't care. *(Now, half to her, half to himself)* We were driving along . . . not very fast . . . I don't think we were driving fast . . . we were in a hurry, yes . . . and I had been drinking . . . *we* had
been drinking . . . but I *don't* think we were driving fast . . . not too fast . . .

NURSE
(Her speeches now are soft comments on his)
. . . driving drunk on the road . . . it not even dark yet . . .

JACK

. . . but then there was a car . . . I hadn't seen it . . . it couldn't have seen me . . . from a side road . . . hard, fast, sudden . . . *(Stiffens)* . . . *CRASH! (Loosens)* . . . and we weren't thrown . . . both of us . . . both cars stayed on the road . . . but we were stopped . . . my motor, running. . . . I turned it off . . . the door . . . the right door was all smashed in. . . . That's all it was . . . no more damage than that . . . but we had been riding along . . . laughing . . . it was cool driving, but it was warm out . . . and she had her arm out the window . . .

NURSE

. . . serves you right . . . drinking on the road . . .

JACK

. . . and I said . . . I said, Honey, we have crashed . . . you all right? *(His face contorts)* And I looked . . . and the door was all pushed in . . . she was caught there . . . where the door had pushed in . . . her right side, crushed into the torn door, the door crushed into her right side. . . . BESSIE! BESSIE! . . . *(More to the* NURSE, *now)* . . . but ma'am . . . her arm . . . her right arm . . . was torn off . . . almost torn off from her shoulder . . . and there was blood . . . SHE WAS BLEEDING SO . . . !

NURSE *(From a distance)*

Like water from a faucet . . . ? Oh, that is terrible . . . terrible . . .

JACK

I didn't wait for nothin' . . . the other people. . . the other car . . . I started up . . . I started . . .

NURSE *(More alert)*

You took *off?* . . . You took off from an accident?

JACK

Her arm, ma'am . . .

NURSE

You probably got police looking for you right now . . . you know that?

JACK

Yes, ma'am . . . I suppose so . . . and I drove . . . there was a hospital about a mile up . . .

NURSE

(Snapping to attention) THERE! You went somewhere *else?* You been somewhere else already? What are you doing *here* with that woman then, hunh?

JACK

At the hospital . . . I came in to the desk and I told them what had happened. . . and they said, you sit down and wait . . . you go over there and sit down and wait a while. WAIT! It was a white hospital, ma'am . . .

NURSE
This is a white hospital, too.

JACK
I said . . . this is an emergency . . . there has been an accident. . . . YOU
WAIT! You just sit down and wait. . . . I told them . . . I told them it was
an emergency. . . . I said . . . this woman is badly hurt. . . . YOU COOL
YOUR HEELS! . . . I said, Ma'am, I got Bessie Smith out in that car there
. . . I DONT CARE WHO YOU GOT OUT THERE, NIGGER . . . YOU
COOL YOUR HEELS! . . . I couldn't wait there . . . her in the car . . . so
I left there . . . I drove on . . . I stopped on the road and I was told where
to come . . . and I came here.

NURSE *(Numb, distant)*
I know who she is . . . I heard her sing. *(Abruptly)* You give me your name!
You can't take off from an accident like that . . . I'll phone the police; I'll
tell them where you are!
  (The INTERN *and the* ORDERLY *re-enter. Their uniforms are blood-
  ied. The* ORDERLY *moves stage-rear, avoiding* JACK. *The intern
  moves in, staring at* JACK*)*

NURSE
He drove away from an accident . . . he just took off . . . and he didn't come
right here, either . . . he's been to one hospital *already.* I *warned* you not
to get mixed up in this. . . .

INTERN *(Softly)*
Shut up!
  (Moves toward JACK, *stops in front of him)*
You tell me something . . .

NURSE
I warned you! You didn't listen to me . . .

JACK
You want my name, too . . . is that what you want?

INTERN
No, that's not what I want.
  (He is contained, but there is a violent emotion inside him)
You tell me something. When you brought her here . . .

JACK
I brought her here . . . They wouldn't help her . . .

INTERN
All right. When you brought her here . . . when you brought this woman
here . . .

NURSE

Oh, this is no plain woman . . . this is no ordinary Nigger . . . this is Bessie Smith!

INTERN

When you brought this woman *here* . . . when you drove up *here* . . . when you brought this woman *here* . . . DID YOU KNOW SHE WAS DEAD?

(Pause)

NURSE

Dead! . . . This Nigger brought a dead woman here?

INTERN

(Afraid of the answer) Well . . . ?

NURSE *(Distantly)*

Dead . . . dead.

JACK

(Wearily; turning, moving toward the outside door) Yes . . . I knew she was dead. She died on the way here.

NURSE

(Snapping to) Where you going? Where do you think you're going? I'm going to get the police here for you!

JACK

(At the door)

Just outside.

INTERN

(As JACK *exits)*

WHAT DID YOU EXPECT *ME* TO DO, EH? WHAT WAS *I* SUP-POSED TO DO?

*(*JACK *pauses for a moment, looks at him blankly, closes the door behind him)*

TELL ME! WHAT WAS I SUPPOSED TO DO?

NURSE *(Slyly)*

Maybe . . . maybe he thought you'd bring her back to life . . . great white doctor. *(Her laughter begins now, mounts to hysteria)* Great . . .white . . . doctor. . . . Where are you going to go now . . . great . . . white . . . doctor? You are finished. You have had your last patient here. . . . Off you go, boy! You have had your last patient . . . a Nigger . . . a dead Nigger lady . . . WHO SINGS. Well . . . I sing, too, boy . . . I sing real good. You want to hear me sing? Hunh? You want to hear the way I sing? HUNH?

(Here she begins to sing and laugh at the same time. The singing is tuneless, almost keening, and the laughter is almost crying)

INTERN

(Moves to her)

Stop that! Stop that!

(But she can't. Finally he slaps her hard across the face. Silence. She is frozen, with her hand to her face where he hit her. He backs toward the rear door)

ORDERLY

(His back to the wall)

I never heard of such a thing . . . bringing a dead woman here like that. . . . I don't know what people can be thinking of sometimes. . . .

(The INTERN *exits. The room fades into silhouette again. . . . The great sunset blazes; music up)*

CURTAIN

The Sandbox

A BRIEF PLAY, IN MEMORY OF MY

GRANDMOTHER (1876–1959)

The Sandbox was produced by Lion Associates at the Jazz Gallery in New York City on May 16, 1960. It was staged by Lawrence Arrick. Original music was composed by William Flanagan. The cast was as follows:

YOUNG MAN	Alan Helm
MOMMY	Jane Hoffman
DADDY	Richard Woods
GRANDMA	Sudie Bond
MUSICIAN	Hal McKusick

THE PLAYERS:

THE YOUNG MAN

Twenty-five. A good-looking, well-built boy in a bathing suit.

MOMMY

Fifty-five. A well-dressed, imposing woman.

DADDY

Sixty. A small man; gray, thin.

GRANDMA

Eighty-six. A tiny, wizened woman with bright eyes.

THE MUSICIAN

No particular age, but young would be nice.

Note:

When, in the course of the play, MOMMY and DADDY call each other by these names, there should be no suggestion of regionalism. These names are of empty affection and point up the pre-senility and vacuity of their characters.

THE SCENE

A bare stage, with only the following: Near the footlights, far stage-right, two simple chairs set side by side, facing the audience; near the footlights, far stage-left, a chair facing stage-right with a music stand before it; farther back, and stage-center, slightly elevated and raked, a large child's sandbox with a toy pail and shovel; the background is the sky, which alters from brightest day to deepest night.

At the beginning, it is brightest day; the YOUNG MAN *is alone on stage, to the rear of the sandbox, and to one side. He is doing calisthenics; he does calisthenics until quite at the very end of the play. These calisthenics, employing the arms only, should suggest the beating and fluttering of wings. The* YOUNG MAN *is, after all, the Angel of Death.*

MOMMY *and* DADDY *enter from stage-left,* MOMMY *first.*

MOMMY

(Motioning to DADDY*)* Well, here we are; this is the beach.

DADDY *(Whining)*

I'm cold.

MOMMY

(Dismissing him with a little laugh) Don't be silly; it's as warm as toast. Look at that nice young man over there: *he* doesn't think it's cold. *(Waves to the* YOUNG MAN*)* Hello.

YOUNG MAN

(With an endearing smile) Hi!

MOMMY *(Looking about)*

This will do perfectly . . . don't you think so, Daddy? There's sand there . . . and the water beyond. What do you think, Daddy?

DADDY *(Vaguely)*

Whatever you say, Mommy.

MOMMY

(With the same little laugh) Well, of course . . . whatever I say. Then, it's settled, is it?

DADDY *(Shrugs)*

She's *your* mother, not mine.

MOMMY

I know she's my mother. What do you take me for? *(A pause)* All right, now; let's get on with it. *(She shouts into the wings, stage-left)* You! Out there! You can come in now.

(The MUSICIAN *enters, seats himself in the chair, stage-left, places music on the music stand, is ready to play.* MOMMY *nods approvingly)*

MOMMY

Very nice; very nice. Are you ready, Daddy? Let's go get Grandma.

DADDY

Whatever you say, Mommy.

MOMMY

(Leading the way out, stage-left) Of course, whatever I say. *(To the* MUSI-CIAN*)* You can begin now.

> *(The* MUSICIAN *begins playing;* MOMMY *and* DADDY *exit; the* MUSI-CIAN, *all the while playing, nods to the* YOUNG MAN*)*

YOUNG MAN

(With the same endearing smile) Hi!

> *(After a moment,* MOMMY *and* DADDY *re-enter, carrying* GRANDMA. *She is borne in by their hands under her armpits; she is quite rigid; her legs are drawn up; her feet do not touch the ground; the expression on her ancient face is that of puzzlement and fear)*

DADDY

Where do we put her?

MOMMY

(The same little laugh) Wherever I say, of course. Let me see . . . well . . . all right, over there . . . in the sandbox. *(Pause)* Well, what are you waiting for, Daddy? . . . The sandbox!

> *(Together they carry* GRANDMA *over to the sandbox and more or less dump her in)*

GRANDMA

(Righting herself to a sitting position; her voice a cross between a baby's laugh and cry) Ahhhhhh! Graaaaa!

DADDY *(Dusting himself)*

What do we do now?

MOMMY

(To the MUSICIAN*)* You can stop now.

> *(The* MUSICIAN *stops)*

(Back to DADDY*)* What do you mean, what do we do now? We go over there and sit down, of course. *(To the* YOUNG MAN*)* Hello there.

YOUNG MAN

(Again smiling) Hi!

> *(MOMMY *and* DADDY *move to the chairs, stage-right, and sit down. A pause)*

GRANDMA

(Same as before) Ahhhhhh! Ah-haaaaaa! Graaaaaa!

DADDY

Do you think . . . do you think she's . . . comfortable?

MOMMY *(Impatiently)*

How would I know?

DADDY

(Pause) What do we do now?

MOMMY

(As if remembering) We . . . wait. We . . . sit here . . . and we wait . . . that's what we do.

DADDY

(After a pause) Shall we talk to each other?

MOMMY

(With that little laugh; picking something off her dress) Well, *you* can talk, if you want to . . . if you can think of anything to *say* . . . if you can think of anything *new*.

DADDY *(Thinks)*

No . . . I suppose not.

MOMMY

(With a triumphant laugh) Of course not!

GRANDMA

(Banging the toy shovel against the pail) Haaaaaa! Ahhaaaaaa!

MOMMY

(Out over the audience) Be quiet, Grandma . . . just be quiet, and wait.

　　(GRANDMA *throws a shovelful of sand at* MOMMY)

MOMMY

(Still out over the audience) She's throwing sand at me! You stop that, Grandma; you stop throwing sand at Mommy! *(To* DADDY) She's throwing sand at me.

　　(DADDY *looks around at* GRANDMA, *who screams at him)*

GRANDMA

GRAAAAA!

MOMMY

Don't look at her. Just . . . sit here . . . be very still . . . and wait. *(To the* MUSICIAN) You . . . uh . . . you go ahead and do whatever it is you do.

　　(The MUSICIAN *plays)*

　　(MOMMY *and* DADDY *are fixed, staring out beyond the audience.* GRANDMA *looks at them, looks at the* MUSICIAN, *looks at the sandbox, throws down the shovel)*

GRANDMA

Ah-haaaaaa! Graaaaaa! *(Looks for reaction; gets none. Now . . . directly to the audience)* Honestly! What a way to treat an old woman! Drag her out of the house. . . stick her in a car . . . bring her out here from the city . . . dump her in a pile of sand . . . and leave her here to set. I'm eighty-six years old! I was married when I was seventeen. To a farmer. He died when I was thirty. *(To the* MUSICIAN*)* Will you stop that, please?

(The MUSICIAN *stops playing)*

I'm a feeble old woman . . . how do you expect anybody to hear me over that peep! peep! peep! *(To herself)* There's no respect around here. *(To the* YOUNG MAN*)* There's no respect around here!

YOUNG MAN

(Same smile) Hi!

GRANDMA

(After a pause, a mild double-take, continues, to the audience) My husband died when I was thirty *(indicates* MOMMY*)*, and I had to raise that big cow over there all by my lonesome. You can imagine what *that* was like. Lordy! *(To the* YOUNG MAN*)* Where'd they get *you?*

YOUNG MAN

Oh . . . I've been around for a while.

GRANDMA

I'll bet you have! Heh, heh, heh. Will you look at you!

YOUNG MAN

(Flexing his muscles) Isn't that something? *(Continues his calisthenics)*

GRANDMA

Boy, oh boy; I'll say. Pretty good.

YOUNG MAN *(Sweetly)*

I'll say.

GRANDMA

Where ya from?

YOUNG MAN

Southern California.

GRANDMA *(Nodding)*

Figgers, figgers. What's your name, honey?

YOUNG MAN

I don't know. . . .

GRANDMA

(To the audience) Bright, too!

YOUNG MAN

I mean . . . I mean, they haven't given me one yet . . . the studio . . .

GRANDMA

(Giving him the once-over) You don't say . . . you don't say. Well . . . uh, I've got to talk some more . . . don't you go 'way.

YOUNG MAN

Oh, no.

GRANDMA

(Turning her attention back to the audience) Fine; fine. *(Then, once more, back to the* YOUNG MAN*)* You're . . . you're an actor, hunh?

YOUNG MAN *(Beaming)*

Yes. I am.

GRANDMA

(To the audience again; shrugs) I'm smart that way. *Anyhow,* I had to raise . . . *that* over there all by my lonesome; and what's next to her there . . . that's what she married. Rich? I tell you . . . money, money, money. They took me off the *farm* . . . which was real decent of them . . . and they moved me into the big town house with *them* . . . fixed a nice place for me under the stove . . . gave me an army blanket . . . and my own dish . . . my very own dish! So, what have I got to complain about? Nothing, of course. I'm not complaining. *(She looks up at the sky, shouts to someone offstage)* Shouldn't it be getting dark now, dear?

> *(The lights dim; night comes on. The* MUSICIAN *begins to play; it becomes deepest night. There are spots on all the players, including the* YOUNG MAN, *who is, of course, continuing his calisthenics)*

DADDY *(Stirring)*

It's nighttime.

MOMMY

Shhhh. Be still . . . wait.

DADDY *(Whining)*

It's so hot.

MOMMY

Shhhhhh. Be still . . . wait.

GRANDMA

(To herself) That's better. Night. *(To the* MUSICIAN*)* Honey, do you play all through this part?

> *(The* MUSICIAN *nods)*

Well, keep it nice and soft; that's a good boy.

(The MUSICIAN *nods again; plays softly)*

That's nice.

(There is an off-stage rumble)

DADDY *(Starting)*

What was that?

MOMMY

(Beginning to weep) It was nothing.

DADDY

It was . . . it was . . . thunder . . . or a wave breaking . . . or something.

MOMMY

(Whispering, through her tears) It was an off-stage rumble. and you know what *that* means. . . .

DADDY

I forget. . . .

MOMMY

(Barely able to talk) It means the time has come for poor Grandma . . . and I can't bear it!

DADDY *(Vacantly)*

I . . . I suppose you've got to be brave.

GRANDMA *(Mocking)*

That's right, kid; be brave. You'll bear up; you'll get over it.

(Another off-stage rumble . . . louder)

MOMMY

Ohhhhhhhhhh . . . poor Grandma . . . poor Grandma. . . .

GRANDMA *(To* MOMMY*)*

I'm fine! I'm all right! It hasn't happened yet!

(A violent off-stage rumble. All the lights go out, save the spot on the YOUNG MAN; *the* MUSICIAN *stops playing)*

MOMMY

Ohhhhhhhhhh . . . Ohhhhhhhhhh. . . .

(Silence)

GRANDMA

Don't put the lights up yet . . . I'm not ready; I'm not quite ready. *(Silence)* All right, dear . . . I'm about done.

(The lights come up again, to brightest day; the MUSICIAN *begins to play.* GRANDMA *is discovered, still in the sandbox, lying on her side, propped up on an elbow, half covered, busily shoveling sand over herself)*

GRANDMA (*Muttering*)

I don't know how I'm supposed to do anything with this goddamn toy shovel. . . .

DADDY

Mommy! It's daylight!

MOMMY (*Brightly*)

So it is! Well! Our long night is over. We must put away our tears, take off our mourning . . . and face the future. It's our duty.

GRANDMA

(*Still shoveling; mimicking*) . . . take off our mourning . . . face the future. . . . Lordy!

>(MOMMY *and* DADDY *rise, stretch.* MOMMY *waves to the* YOUNG MAN)

YOUNG MAN

(*With that smile*) Hi!

>(GRANDMA *plays dead.* (!) MOMMY *and* DADDY *go over to look at her; she is a little more than half buried in the sand; the toy shovel is in her hands, which are crossed on her breast*)

MOMMY

(*Before the sandbox; shaking her head*) Lovely! It's . . . it's hard to be sad . . . she looks . . . so happy. (*With pride and conviction*) It pays to do things well. (*To the* MUSICIAN) All right, you can stop now, if you want to. I mean, stay around for a swim, or something; it's all right with us. (*She sighs heavily*) Well, Daddy . . . off we go.

DADDY

Brave Mommy!

MOMMY

Brave Daddy!

>(*They exit, stage-left*)

GRANDMA

(*After they leave; lying quite still*) It pays to do things well. . . . Boy, oh boy! (*She tries to sit up*) . . . well, kids . . . (*but she finds she can't*) . . . I . . . I can't get up. I . . . I can't move. . . .

>(*The* YOUNG MAN *stops his calisthenics, nods to the* MUSICIAN, *walks over to* GRANDMA, *kneels down by the sandbox*)

GRANDMA

I . . . can't move. . . .

YOUNG MAN

Shhhhh . . . be very still. . . .

GRANDMA

I . . . I can't move. . . .

YOUNG MAN

Uh . . . ma'am; I . . . I have a line here.

GRANDMA

Oh, I'm sorry, sweetie; you go right ahead.

YOUNG MAN

I am . . . uh . . . I am . . .

GRANDMA

Take your time, dear.

YOUNG MAN

(*Prepares; delivers the line like a real amateur*) I am the Angel of Death. I am . . . uh . . . I am come for you.

GRANDMA

What . . . wha . . . (*Then, with resignation*) . . . ohhhh . . . ohhhh . . . I see.
(*The* YOUNG MAN *bends over, kisses* GRANDMA *gently on the forehead*)

GRANDMA

(*Her eyes closed, her hands folded on her breast again, the shovel between her hands, a sweet smile on her face*)
Well . . . that was very nice, dear . . .

YOUNG MAN

(*Still kneeling*) Shhhhhh . . . be still. . . .

GRANDMA

What I meant was . . . you did that very well, dear. . . .

YOUNG MAN (*Blushing*)

. . . oh . . .

GRANDMA

No; I mean it. You've got that . . . you've got a quality.

YOUNG MAN

(*With his endearing smile*) Oh . . . thank you; thank you very much . . . ma'am.

GRANDMA

(*Slowly; softly—as the* YOUNG MAN *puts his hands on top of* GRANDMA's)
You're . . . you're welcome . . . dear.
(*Tableau. The* MUSICIAN *continues to play as the curtain slowly comes down*)

CURTAIN

The American Dream

A PLAY IN ONE SCENE

For David Diamond

The American Dream was first produced by Theatre 1961, Richard Barr and Clinton Wilder, at the York Playhouse, New York City, on January 24, 1961. It wasdirected by Alan Schneider. The sets and costumes were by William Ritman. The cast was as follows:

DADDY	John C. Becher
MOMMY	Jane Hoffman
GRANDMA	Sudie Bond
MRS. BARKER	Nancy Cushman
THE YOUNG MAN	Ben Piazza

THE PLAYERS

MOMMY

DADDY

GRANDMA

MRS. BARKER

YOUNG MAN

THE SCENE

A living room. Two armchairs, one toward either side of the stage, facing each other diagonally out toward the audience. Against the rear wall, a sofa. A door, leading out from the apartment, in the rear wall, far stage-right. An archway, leading to other rooms, in the side wall, stage-left.

At the beginning, MOMMY *and* DADDY *are seated in the armchairs,* DADDY *in the armchair stage-left,* MOMMY *in the other.*

Curtain up. A silence. Then:

MOMMY

I don't know what can be keeping them.

DADDY

They're late, naturally.

MOMMY

Of course, they're late; it never fails.

DADDY

That's the way things are today, and there's nothing you can do about it.

MOMMY

You're quite right.

DADDY

When we took this apartment, they were quick enough to have me sign the lease; they were quick enough to take my check for two months' rent in advance . . .

MOMMY

And one month's security . . .

DADDY

. . . and one month's security. They were quick enough to check my references; they were quick enough about all that. But now! But now, try to get the icebox fixed, try to get the doorbell fixed, try to get the leak in the johnny fixed! Just try it . . . they aren't so quick about *that.*

MOMMY

Of course not; it never fails. People think they can get away with anything these days . . . and, of course they can. I went to buy a new hat yesterday.
    (Pause)
I said, I went to buy a new hat yesterday.

DADDY

Oh! Yes . . . yes.

MOMMY

Pay attention.

DADDY

I *am* paying attention, Mommy.

MOMMY

Well, be sure you do.

DADDY

Oh, I am.

MOMMY

All right, Daddy; now listen.

DADDY

I'm listening, Mommy.

MOMMY

You're sure!

DADDY

Yes . . . yes, I'm sure. I'm all ears.

MOMMY

(*Giggles at the thought; then*)

All right, now. I went to buy a new hat yesterday and I said, "I'd like a new hat, please." And so, they showed me a few hats, green ones and blue ones, and I didn't like any of them, not one bit. What did I say? What did I just say?

DADDY

You didn't like any of them, not one bit.

MOMMY

That's right; you just keep paying attention. And then they showed me one that I did like. It was a lovely little hat, and I said, "Oh, this is a lovely little hat; I'll take this hat; oh my, it's lovely. What color is it?" And they said, "Why, this is beige; isn't it a lovely little beige hat?" And I said, "Oh, it's just lovely." And so, I bought it.

(*Stops, looks at* DADDY)

DADDY

(*To show he is paying attention*)

And so you bought it.

MOMMY

And so I bought it, and I walked out of the store with the hat right on my head, and I ran spang into the chairman of our woman's club, and she said, "Oh, my dear, isn't that a lovely little hat? Where did you get that lovely little hat? It's the loveliest little hat; I've always wanted a wheat-colored hat *myself*." And, I said, "Why, no, my dear; this hat is beige; beige." And she laughed and said, "Why no, my dear, that's a wheat-colored hat . . . wheat. I know beige from wheat." And I said, "Well, my dear, I know beige from wheat, too." What did I say? What did I just say?

DADDY

(Tonelessly)
Well, my dear, I know beige from wheat, too.

MOMMY

That's right. And she laughed, and she said, "Well, my dear, they certainly put one over on you. That's wheat if I ever saw wheat. But it's lovely, just the same." And then she walked off. She's a dreadful woman, you don't know her; she has dreadful taste, two dreadful children, a dreadful house, and an absolutely adorable husband who sits in a wheelchair all the time. You don't know him. You don't know anybody, do you? She's just a dreadful woman, but she *is* chairman of our woman's club, so naturally I'm terribly fond of her. So, I went right back into the hat shop, and I said, "Look here; what do you mean selling me a hat that you say is beige, when it's wheat all the time . . . wheat! I can tell beige from wheat any day in the week, but not in this artificial light of yours." They have artificial light, Daddy.

DADDY

Have they!

MOMMY

And I said, "The minute I got outside I could tell that it wasn't a beige hat at all; it was a wheat hat." And they said to me, "How could you tell that when you had the hat on the top of your head?" Well, that made me angry, and so I made a scene right there; I screamed as hard as I could; I took my hat off and I threw it down on the counter, and oh, I made a terrible scene. I said, I made a terrible scene.

DADDY

(Snapping to)
Yes . . . yes . . . good for you!

MOMMY

And I made an absolutely terrible scene; and they became frightened, and they said, "Oh, madam; oh, madam." But I kept right on, and finally they admitted that they might have made a mistake; so they took my hat into the back, and then they came out again with a hat that looked exactly like it. I took one look at it, and I said, "This hat is wheat-colored; wheat." Well, of course, they said, "Oh, no, madam, this hat is beige; you go outside and see." So, I went outside, and lo and behold, it *was* beige. So I bought it.

DADDY

(Clearing his throat)

I would imagine that it was the same hat they tried to sell you before.

MOMMY

(With a little laugh)

Well, of course it was!

DADDY

That's the way things are today; you just can't get satisfaction; you just try.

MOMMY

Well, I got satisfaction.

DADDY

That's right, Mommy. You did get satisfaction, didn't you?

MOMMY

Why are they so late? I don't know what can be keeping them.

DADDY

I've been trying for two weeks to have the leak in the johnny fixed.

MOMMY

You can't get satisfaction; just try. I can get satisfaction, but you can't.

DADDY

I've been trying for two weeks and it isn't so much for my sake; I can always go to the club.

MOMMY

It isn't so much for my sake, either; I can always go shopping.

DADDY

It's really for Grandma's sake.

MOMMY

Of course it's for Grandma's sake. Grandma cries every time she goes to the johnny as it is; but now that it doesn't work it's even worse, it makes Grandma think she's getting feeble-headed.

DADDY

Grandma is getting feeble-headed.

MOMMY

Of course Grandma is getting feeble-headed, but not about her johnny-do's.

DADDY

No; that's true. I must have it fixed.

MOMMY

WHY are they so late? I don't know what can be keeping them.

DADDY

When they came here the first time, they were ten minutes early; they were quick enough about it then.

(*Enter* GRANDMA *from the archway, stage-left. She is loaded down with boxes, large and small, neatly wrapped and tied.*)

MOMMY

Why Grandma, look at you! What *is* all that you're carrying?

GRANDMA

They're boxes. What do they look like?

MOMMY

Daddy! Look at Grandma; look at all the boxes she's carrying!

DADDY

My goodness, Grandma; look at all those boxes.

GRANDMA

Where'll I put them?

MOMMY

Heavens! I don't know. Whatever are they for?

GRANDMA

That's nobody's damn business.

MOMMY

Well, in that case, put them down next to Daddy; there.

GRANDMA

(*Dumping the boxes down, on and around* DADDY's *feet*)

I sure wish you'd get the john fixed.

DADDY

Oh, I do wish they'd come and fix it. We hear you . . . for hours . . . whimpering away. . . .

MOMMY

Daddy! What a terrible thing to say to Grandma!

GRANDMA

Yeah. For shame, talking to me that way.

DADDY

I'm sorry, Grandma.

MOMMY

Daddy's sorry, Grandma.

GRANDMA

Well, all right. In that case I'll go get the rest of the boxes. I suppose I deserve being talked to that way. I've gotten so old. Most people think that when you get so old, you either freeze to death, or you burn up. But you don't. When you get so old, all that happens is that people talk to you that way.

DADDY

(Contrite)

I said I'm sorry, Grandma.

MOMMY

Daddy said he was sorry.

GRANDMA

Well, that's all that counts. People being sorry. Makes you feel better; gives you a sense of dignity, and that's all that's important . . . a sense of dignity. And it doesn't matter if you don't care, or not, either. You got to have a sense of dignity, even if you don't care, 'cause, if you don't have that, civilization's doomed.

MOMMY

You've been reading my book club selections again!

DADDY

How dare you read Mommy's book club selections, Grandma!

GRANDMA

Because I'm old! When you're old you gotta do something. When you get old, you can't talk to people because people snap at you. When you get so old, people talk to you that way. That's why you become deaf, so you won't be able to hear people talking to you that way. And that's why you go and hide under the covers in the big soft bed, so you won't feel the house shaking from people talking to you that way. That's why old people die, eventually. People talk to them that way. I've got to go and get the rest of the boxes.

(GRANDMA exits)

DADDY

Poor Grandma, I didn't mean to hurt her.

MOMMY

Don't you worry about it; Grandma doesn't know what she means.

DADDY

She knows what she says, though.

MOMMY

Don't you worry about it; she won't know that soon. I love Grandma.

DADDY

I love her, too. Look how nicely she wrapped these boxes.

MOMMY

Grandma has always wrapped boxes nicely. When I was a little girl, I was very poor, and Grandma was very poor, too, because Grandpa was in heaven. And every day, when I went to school, Grandma used to wrap a box for me, and I used to take it with me to school; and when it was lunchtime, all the little boys and girls used to take out their boxes of lunch, and they weren't wrapped nicely at all, and they used to open them and eat their chicken legs and chocolate cakes; and I used to say, "Oh, look at my lovely lunch box; it's so nicely wrapped it would break my heart to open it." And so, I wouldn't open it.

DADDY

Because it was empty.

MOMMY

Oh no. Grandma always filled it up, because she never ate the dinner she cooked the evening before; she gave me all her food for my lunch box the next day. After school, I'd take the box back to Grandma, and she'd open it and eat the chicken legs and chocolate cake that was inside. Grandma used to say, "I love day-old cake." That's where the expression day-old cake came from. Grandma always ate everything a day late. I used to eat all the other little boys' and girls' food at school, because they thought my lunch box was empty. They thought my lunch box was empty, and that's why I wouldn't open it. They thought I suffered from the sin of pride, and since that made them better than me, they were very generous.

DADDY

You were a very deceitful little girl.

MOMMY

We were very poor! But then I married you, Daddy, and now we're very rich.

DADDY

Grandma isn't rich.

MOMMY

No, but you've been so good to Grandma she feels rich. She doesn't know you'd like to put her in a nursing home.

DADDY

I wouldn't!

MOMMY

Well, heaven knows, *I* would! I can't stand it, watching her do the cooking and the housework, polishing the silver, moving the furniture. . . .

DADDY

She likes to do that. She says it's the least she can do to earn her keep.

MOMMY

Well, she's right. You can't live off people. I can live off you, because I married you. And aren't you lucky all I brought with me was Grandma. A lot of women I know would have brought their whole families to live off you. All I brought was Grandma. Grandma is all the family I have.

DADDY

I feel very fortunate.

MOMMY

You should. I have a right to live off of you because I married you, and because I used to let you get on top of me and bump your uglies; and I have a right to all your money when you die. And when you do, Grandma and I can live by ourselves . . . if she's still here. Unless you have her put away in a nursing home.

DADDY

I have no intention of putting her in a nursing home.

MOMMY

Well, I wish somebody would do something with her!

DADDY

At any rate, you're very well provided for.

MOMMY

You're my sweet Daddy; that's very nice.

DADDY

I love my Mommy.

(*Enter* GRANDMA *again, laden with more boxes*)

GRANDMA

(*Dumping the boxes on and around* DADDY's *feet*)
There; that's the lot of them.

DADDY

They're wrapped so nicely.

GRANDMA

(*To* DADDY)
You won't get on my sweet side that way . . .

MOMMY

Grandma!

GRANDMA

. . . telling me how nicely I wrap boxes. Not after what you said: how I whimpered for hours. . . .

MOMMY

Grandma!

GRANDMA

(To MOMMY*)*

Shut up!

(To DADDY*)*

You don't have any feelings, that's what's wrong with you. Old people make all sorts of noises, half of them they can't help. Old people whimper, and cry, and belch, and make great hollow rumbling sounds at the table; old people wake up in the middle of the night screaming, and find out they haven't even been asleep; and when old people *are* asleep, they try to wake up, and they can't . . . not for the longest time.

MOMMY

Homilies, homilies!

GRANDMA

And there's more, too.

DADDY

I'm really very sorry, Grandma.

GRANDMA

I know you are, Daddy; it's Mommy over there makes all the trouble. If you'd listened to me, you wouldn't have married her in the first place. She was a tramp and a trollop and a trull to boot, and she's no better now.

MOMMY

Grandma!

GRANDMA

(To MOMMY*)*

Shut up!

(To DADDY*)*

When she was no more than eight years old she used to climb up on my lap and say, in a sickening little voice, "When I gwo up, I'm going to mahwy a wich old man; I'm going to set my wittle were end right down in a tub o' butter, that's what I'm going to do." And I warned you, Daddy; I told you to stay away from her type. I told you to. I did.

MOMMY

You stop that! You're my mother, not his!

GRANDMA

I am?

DADDY

That's right, Grandma. Mommy's right.

GRANDMA

Well, how would you expect somebody as old as I am to remember a thing like that? You don't make allowances for people. I want an allowance. I want an allowance!

DADDY

All right, Grandma; I'll see to it.

MOMMY

Grandma! I'm ashamed of you.

GRANDMA

Humf! It's a fine time to say that. You should have gotten rid of me a long time ago if that's the way you feel. You should have had Daddy set me up in business somewhere . . . I could have gone into the fur business, or I could have been a singer. But no; not you. You wanted me around so you could sleep in my room when Daddy got fresh. But now it isn't important, because Daddy doesn't want to get fresh with you any more, and I don't blame him. You'd rather sleep with me, wouldn't you, Daddy?

MOMMY

Daddy doesn't want to sleep with anyone. Daddy's been sick.

DADDY

I've been sick. I don't even want to sleep in the apartment.

MOMMY

You see? I told you.

DADDY

I just want to get everything over with.

MOMMY

That's right. Why are they so late? Why can't they get here on time?

GRANDMA

(An owl)

Who? Who? . . . Who? Who?

MOMMY

You know, Grandma.

GRANDMA

No, I don't.

MOMMY

Well, it doesn't really matter whether you do or not.

DADDY

Is that true?

MOMMY

Oh, more or less. Look how pretty Grandma wrapped these boxes.

GRANDMA

I didn't really like wrapping them; it hurt my fingers, and it frightened me.
But it had to be done.

MOMMY

Why, Grandma?

GRANDMA

None of your damn business.

MOMMY

Go to bed.

GRANDMA

I don't want to go to bed. I just got up. I want to stay here and watch.
Besides . . .

MOMMY

Go to bed.

DADDY

Let her stay up, Mommy; it isn't noon yet.

GRANDMA

I want to watch; besides . . .

DADDY

Let her watch, Mommy.

MOMMY

Well all right, you can watch; but don't you dare say a word.

GRANDMA

Old people are very good at listening; old people don't like to talk; old
people have colitis and lavender perfume. Now I'm going to be quiet.

DADDY

She never mentioned she wanted to be a singer.

MOMMY

Oh, I forgot to tell you, but it was ages ago.
    (*The doorbell rings*)
Oh, goodness! Here they are!

GRANDMA

Who? Who?

MOMMY

Oh, just some people.

GRANDMA

The van people? Is it the van people? Have you finally done it? Have you called the van people to come and take me away?

DADDY

Of course not, Grandma!

GRANDMA

Oh, don't be too sure. She'd have you carted off too, if she thought she could get away with it.

MOMMY

Pay no attention to her, Daddy.
  (*An aside to* GRANDMA)
My God, you're ungrateful!
  (*The doorbell rings again*)

DADDY

  (*Wringing his hands*)
Oh dear; oh dear.

MOMMY

  (*Still to* GRANDMA)
Just you wait; I'll fix your wagon.
  (*Now, to* DADDY)
Well, go let them in, Daddy. What are you waiting for?

DADDY

I think we should talk about it some more. Maybe we've been hasty . . . a little hasty, perhaps.
  (*Doorbell rings again*)
I'd like to talk about it some more.

MOMMY

There's no need. You made up your mind; you were firm; you were masculine and decisive.

DADDY

We might consider the pros and the . . .

MOMMY

I won't argue with you; it has to be done; you were right. Open the door.

DADDY

But I'm not sure that . . .

MOMMY

Open the door.

DADDY

Was I firm about it?

MOMMY

Oh, so firm; so firm.

DADDY

And was I decisive?

MOMMY

SO decisive! Oh, I shivered.

DADDY

And masculine? Was I really masculine?

MOMMY

Oh, Daddy, you were so masculine; I shivered and fainted.

GRANDMA

Shivered and fainted, did she? Humf!

MOMMY

You be quiet.

GRANDMA

Old people have a right to talk to themselves; it doesn't hurt the gums, and it's comforting.

(Doorbell rings again)

DADDY

(Backing off from the door)
Maybe we can send them away.

MOMMY

Oh, look at you! You're turning into jelly; you're indecisive; you're a woman.

DADDY

All right. Watch me now; I'm going to open the door. Watch. Watch!

MOMMY

We're watching; we're watching.

GRANDMA

I'm not.

DADDY

Watch now; it's opening.
(He opens the door)
It's open!
(MRS. BARKER steps into the room)
Here they are!

MOMMY

Here they are!

GRANDMA

Where?

DADDY

Come in. You're late. But, of course, we expected you to be late; we were saying that we expected you to be late.

MOMMY

Daddy, don't be rude! We were saying that you just can't get satisfaction these days, and we were talking about you, of course. Won't you come in?

MRS. BARKER

Thank you. I don't mind if I do.

MOMMY

We're very glad that you're here, late as you are. You do remember us, don't you? You were here once before. I'm Mommy, and this is Daddy, and that's Grandma, doddering there in the corner.

MRS. BARKER

Hello, Mommy; hello, Daddy; and hello there, Grandma.

DADDY

Now that you're here, I don't suppose you could go away and maybe come back some other time.

MRS. BARKER

Oh no; we're much too efficient for that. I said, hello there, Grandma.

MOMMY

Speak to them, Grandma.

GRANDMA

I don't see them.

DADDY

For shame, Grandma; they're here.

MRS. BARKER

Yes, we're here, Grandma. I'm Mrs. Barker. I remember you; don't you remember me?

GRANDMA

I don't recall. Maybe you were younger, or something.

MOMMY

Grandma! What a terrible thing to say!

MRS. BARKER

Oh now, don't scold her, Mommy; for all she knows she may be right.

DADDY

Uh . . . Mrs. Barker, is it? Won't you sit down?

MRS. BARKER

I don't mind if I do.

MOMMY

Would you like a cigarette, and a drink, and would you like to cross your legs?

MRS. BARKER

You forget yourself, Mommy; I'm a professional woman. But I will cross my legs.

DADDY

Yes, make yourself comfortable.

MRS. BARKER

I don't mind if I do.

GRANDMA

Are they still here?

MOMMY

Be quiet, Grandma.

MRS. BARKER

Oh, we're still here. My, what an unattractive apartment you have!

MOMMY

Yes, but you don't know what a trouble it is. Let me tell you . . .

DADDY

I was saying to Mommy . . .

MRS. BARKER

Yes, I know. I was listening outside.

DADDY

About the icebox, and . . . the doorbell . . . and the . . .

MRS. BARKER

. . . and the johnny. Yes, we're very efficient; we have to know everything in our work.

DADDY

Exactly what do you do?

MOMMY

Yes, what is your work?

MRS. BARKER

Well, my dear, for one thing, I'm chairman of your woman's club.

MOMMY

Don't be ridiculous. I was talking to the chairman of my woman's club just yester— Why, so you are. You remember, Daddy, the lady I was telling you about? The lady with the husband who sits in the *swing?* Don't you remember?

DADDY

No . . . no . . .

MOMMY

Of course you do. I'm so sorry, Mrs. Barker. I would have known you anywhere, except in this artificial light. And look! You have a hat just like the one I bought yesterday.

MRS. BARKER

(With a little laugh)

No, not really; this hat is cream.

MOMMY

Well, my dear, that may look like a cream hat to you, but I can . . .

MRS. BARKER

Now, now; you seem to forget who I am.

MOMMY

Yes, I do, don't I? Are you sure you're comfortable? Won't you take off your dress?

MRS. BARKER

I don't mind if I do.

(She removes her dress)

MOMMY

There. You must feel a great deal more comfortable.

MRS. BARKER

Well, I certainly *look* a great deal more comfortable.

DADDY

I'm going to blush and giggle.

MOMMY

Daddy's going to blush and giggle.

MRS. BARKER

(Pulling the hem of her slip above her knees)

You're lucky to have such a man for a husband.

MOMMY

Oh, don't I know it!

DADDY

I just blushed and giggled and went sticky wet.

MOMMY

Isn't Daddy a caution, Mrs. Barker?

MRS. BARKER

Maybe if I smoked . . . ?

MOMMY

Oh, that isn't necessary.

MRS. BARKER

I don't mind if I do.

MOMMY

No; no, don't. Really.

MRS. BARKER

I don't mind . . .

MOMMY

I won't have you smoking in my house, and that's that! You're a professional woman.

DADDY

Grandma drinks AND smokes; don't you, Grandma?

GRANDMA

No.

MOMMY

Well, now, Mrs. Barker; suppose you tell us why you're here.

GRANDMA

(As MOMMY *walks through the boxes)*
The boxes . . . the boxes . . .

MOMMY

Be quiet, Grandma.

DADDY

What did you say, Grandma!

GRANDMA

(As MOMMY *steps on several of the boxes)*
The boxes, damn it!

MRS. BARKER

Boxes; she said boxes. She mentioned the boxes.

DADDY

What about the boxes, Grandma? Maybe Mrs. Barker is here because of the boxes. Is that what you meant, Grandma?

GRANDMA

I don't know if that's what I meant or not. It's certainly not what I *thought* I meant.

DADDY

Grandma is of the opinion that . . .

MRS. BARKER

Can we assume that the boxes are for us? I mean, can we assume that you had us come here for the boxes?

MOMMY

Are you in the habit of receiving boxes?

DADDY

A very good question.

MRS. BARKER

Well, that would depend on the reason we're here. I've got my fingers in so many little pies, you know. Now, I can think of one of my little activities in which we are in the habit of receiving *baskets;* but more in a literary sense than really. We *might* receive boxes, though, under very special circumstances. I'm afraid that's the best answer I can give you.

DADDY

It's a very interesting answer.

MRS. BARKER

I thought so. But, does it help?

MOMMY

No; I'm afraid not.

DADDY

I wonder if it might help us any if I said I feel misgivings, that I have definite qualms.

MOMMY

Where, Daddy?

DADDY

Well, mostly right here, right around where the stitches were.

MOMMY

Daddy had an operation, you know.

MRS. BARKER

Oh, you poor Daddy! I didn't know; but then, how could I?

GRANDMA

You might have asked; it wouldn't have hurt you.

MOMMY

Dry up, Grandma.

GRANDMA

There you go. Letting your true feelings come out. Old people aren't dry enough, I suppose. My sacks are empty, the fluid in my eyeballs is all caked on the inside edges, my spine is made of sugar candy, I breathe ice; but you don't hear me complain. Nobody hears old people complain because people think that's all old people do. And *that's* because old people are gnarled and sagged and twisted into the shape of a complaint.

(*Signs off*)

That's all.

MRS. BARKER

What was wrong, Daddy?

DADDY

Well, you know how it is: the doctors took out something that was there and put in something that wasn't there. An operation.

MRS. BARKER

You're very fortunate, I should say.

MOMMY

Oh, he is; he is. All his life, Daddy has wanted to be a United States Senator; but now . . . why now he's changed his mind, and for the rest of his life he's going to want to be Governor . . . it would be nearer the apartment, you know.

MRS. BARKER

You *are* fortunate, Daddy.

DADDY

Yes, indeed; except that I get these qualms now and then, definite ones.

MRS. BARKER

Well, it's just a matter of things settling; you're like an old house.

MOMMY

Why Daddy, thank Mrs. Barker.

DADDY

Thank you.

MRS. BARKER

Ambition! That's the ticket. I have a brother who's very much like you, Daddy . . . ambitious. Of course, he's a great deal younger than you; he's even younger than I am . . . if such a thing is possible. He runs a little newspaper. Just a little newspaper . . . but he runs it. He's chief cook and bottle washer of that little newspaper, which he calls *The Village Idiot*. He has such a sense of humor; he's so self-deprecating, so modest. And he'd never admit it himself, but he *is* the Village Idiot.

MOMMY

Oh, I think that's just grand. Don't you think so, Daddy?

DADDY

Yes, just grand.

MRS. BARKER

My brother's a dear man, and he has a dear little wife, whom he loves, dearly. He loves her so much he just can't get a sentence out without mentioning her. He wants everybody to know he's married. He's really a stickler on that point; he can't be introduced to anybody and say hello without adding, "Of course, I'm married." As far as I'm concerned, he's the chief exponent of Woman Love in this whole country; he's even been written up in psychiatric journals because of it.

DADDY

Indeed!

MOMMY

Isn't that lovely.

MRS. BARKER

Oh, I think so. There's too much woman hatred in this country, and that's a fact.

GRANDMA

Oh, I don't know.

MOMMY

Oh, I think that's just grand. Don't you think so, Daddy?

DADDY

Yes, just grand.

GRANDMA

In case anybody's interested . . .

MOMMY

Be quiet, Grandma.

GRANDMA

Nuts!

MOMMY

Oh, Mrs. Barker, you *must* forgive Grandma. She's rural.

MRS. BARKER

I don't mind if I do.

DADDY

Maybe Grandma has something to say.

MOMMY

Nonsense. Old people have nothing to say; and if old people *did* have something to say, nobody would listen to them.

(*To* GRANDMA)

You see? I can pull that stuff just as easy as you can.

GRANDMA

Well, you got the rhythm, but you don't really have the quality. Besides, you're middle-aged.

MOMMY

I'm proud of it!

GRANDMA

Look. I'll show you how it's really done. Middle-aged people think they can do anything, but the truth is that middle-aged people can't do most things as well as they used to. Middle-aged people think they're special because they're like everybody else. We live in the age of deformity. You see? Rhythm *and* content. You'll learn.

DADDY

I do wish I weren't surrounded by women; I'd like some men around here.

MRS. BARKER

You can say that again!

GRANDMA

I don't hardly count as a woman, so can I say my piece?

MOMMY

Go on. Jabber away.

GRANDMA

It's very simple; the fact is, these boxes don't have anything to do with why this good lady is come to call. Now, if you're interested in knowing why these boxes *are* here . . .

MOMMY

Well, nobody *is* interested!

GRANDMA

You can be as snippety as you like for all the good it'll do you.

DADDY

You two will have to stop arguing.

MOMMY

I don't argue with her.

DADDY

It will just have to stop.

MOMMY

Well, why don't you call a van and have her taken away?

GRANDMA

Don't bother; there's no need.

DADDY

No, now, perhaps I can go away myself. . . .

MOMMY

Well, one or the other; the way things are now it's impossible. In the first place, it's too crowded in this apartment.

(*To* GRANDMA)

And it's you that takes up all the space, with your enema bottles, and your Pekinese, and God-only-knows-what-else . . . and now all these boxes. . . .

GRANDMA

These boxes are . . .

MRS. BARKER

I've never heard of enema *bottles* . . .

GRANDMA

She means enema bags, but she doesn't know the difference. Mommy comes from extremely bad stock. And besides, when Mommy was born . . . well, it was a difficult delivery, and she had a head shaped like a banana.

MOMMY

You ungrateful—Daddy? Daddy, you see how ungrateful she is after all these years, after all the things we've done for her?

(*To* GRANDMA)

One of these days you're going away in a van; that's what's going to happen to you!

GRANDMA

Do tell!

MRS. BARKER

Like a banana?

GRANDMA

Yup, just like a banana.

MRS. BARKER

My word!

MOMMY

You stop listening to her; she'll say anything. just the other night she called Daddy a hedgehog.

MRS. BARKER

She didn't!

GRANDMA

That's right, baby; you stick up for me.

MOMMY

I don't know where she gets the words; on the television, maybe.

MRS. BARKER

Did you really call him a hedgehog?

GRANDMA

Oh look; what difference does it make whether I did or not?

DADDY

Grandma's right. Leave Grandma alone.

MOMMY

(To DADDY)
How dare you!

GRANDMA

Oh, leave her alone, Daddy; the kid's all mixed up.

MOMMY

You see? I told you. It's all those television shows. Daddy, you go right into
Grandma's room and take her television and shake all the tubes loose.

DADDY

Don't mention tubes to me.

MOMMY

Oh! Mommy forgot!
(To MRS. BARKER)
Daddy has tubes now, where he used to have tracts.

MRS. BARKER

Is that a fact!

GRANDMA

I know why this dear lady is here.

MOMMY

You be still.

MRS. BARKER

Oh, I do wish you'd tell me.

MOMMY

No! No! That wouldn't be fair at all.

DADDY

Besides, she knows why she's here; she's here because we called them.

MRS. BARKER

La! But that still leaves me puzzled. I know I'm here because you called us, but I'm such a busy girl, with this committee and that committee, and the Responsible Citizens Activities I indulge in.

MOMMY

Oh my; busy, busy.

MRS. BARKER

Yes, indeed. So I'm afraid you'll have to give me some help.

MOMMY

Oh, no. No, you must be mistaken. I can't believe we asked you here to give you any help. With the way taxes are these days, and the way you can't get satisfaction in ANYTHING . . . no, I don't believe so.

DADDY

And if you need help . . . why, I should think you'd apply for a Fulbright Scholarship. . . .

MOMMY

And if not that . . . why, then a Guggenheim Fellowship. . . .

GRANDMA

Oh, come on; why not shoot the works and try for the Prix de Rome.

(Under her breath to MOMMY *and* DADDY*)*

Beasts!

MRS. BARKER

Oh, what a jolly family. But let me think. I'm knee-deep in work these days; there's the Ladies' Auxiliary Air Raid Committee, for one thing; how do you feel about air raids?

MOMMY

Oh, I'd say we're hostile.

DADDY

Yes, definitely; we're hostile.

MRS. BARKER

Then, you'll be no help there. There's too much hostility in the world these days as it is; but I'll not badger you! There's a surfeit of badgers as well.

GRANDMA

While we're at it, there's been a run on old people, too. The Department of Agriculture, or maybe it wasn't the Department of Agriculture—anyway, it was some department that's run by a girl—put out figures showing that ninety per cent of the adult population of the country is over eighty years old . . . or eighty per cent is over ninety years old . . .

MOMMY

You're such a liar! You just finished saying that everyone is middle-aged.

GRANDMA

I'm just telling you what the government says . . . that doesn't have anything to do with what . . .

MOMMY

It's that television! Daddy, go break her television.

GRANDMA

You won't find it.

DADDY

(Wearily getting up)
If I must . . . I must.

MOMMY

And don't step on the Pekinese; it's blind.

DADDY

It may be blind, but Daddy isn't.
(He exits, through the archway, stage-left)

GRANDMA

You won't find *it,* either.

MOMMY

Oh, I'm so fortunate to have such a husband. Just think: I could have
a husband who was poor, or argumentative, or a husband who sat in a
wheelchair all day . . . OOOOHHHH! *What* have I said? What *have*
I said?

GRANDMA

You said you could have a husband who sat in a wheel . . .

MOMMY

I'm mortified! I could die! I could cut my tongue out! I could . . .

MRS. BARKER

(Forcing a smile)
Oh, now . . . now . . . don't think about it . . .

MOMMY

I could . . . why, I could . . .

MRS. BARKER

. . . don't think about it . . . really . . .

MOMMY

You're quite right. I won't think about it, and that way I'll forget that I ever said it, and that way it will be all right.

    (Pause)

There . . . I've forgotten. Well, now, now that Daddy is out of the room we can have some girl talk.

MRS. BARKER

I'm not sure that I . . .

MOMMY

You *do* want to have some girl talk, don't you?

MRS. BARKER

I was going to say I'm not sure that I wouldn't care for a glass of water. I feel a little faint.

MOMMY

Grandma, go get Mrs. Barker a glass of water.

GRANDMA

Go get it yourself. I quit.

MOMMY

Grandma loves to do little things around the house; it gives her a false sense of security.

GRANDMA

I quit! I'm through!

MOMMY

Now, you be a good Grandma, or you know what will happen to you. You'll be taken away in a van.

GRANDMA

You don't frighten me. I'm too old to be frightened. Besides . . .

MOMMY

WELL! I'll tend to you later. I'll hide your teeth . . . I'll . . .

GRANDMA

Everything's hidden.

MRS. BARKER

I *am* going to faint. I *am*.

MOMMY

Good heavens! I'll go myself.

    (As she exits, through the archway, stage-left)

I'll fix you, Grandma. I'll take care of you later.

    (She exits)

GRANDMA

Oh, go soak your head.

(To MRS. BARKER)

Well, dearie, how do you feel?

MRS. BARKER

A little better, I think. Yes, much better, thank you, Grandma.

GRANDMA

That's good.

MRS. BARKER

But . . . I feel so lost . . . not knowing why I'm here . . . and, on top of it, they say I was here before.

GRANDMA

Well, you were. You weren't *here*, exactly, because we've moved around a lot, from one apartment to another, up and down the social ladder like mice, if you like similes.

MRS. BARKER

I don't . . . particularly.

GRANDMA

Well, then, I'm sorry.

MRS. BARKER

(Suddenly)

Grandma, I feel I can trust you.

GRANDMA

Don't be too sure; it's every man for himself around this place. . . .

MRS. BARKER

Oh . . . is it? Nonetheless, I really do feel that I can trust you. *Please* tell me why they called and asked us to come.

GRANDMA

Well, I'll give you a hint. That's the best I can do, because I'm a muddlehead-ed old woman. Now listen, because it's important. Once upon a time, not too very long ago, but a long enough time ago . . . oh, about twenty years ago . . . there was a man very much like Daddy, and a woman very much like Mommy, who were married to each other, very much like Mommy and Daddy are mar-ried to each other; and they lived in an apartment very much like one that's very much like this one, and they lived there with an old woman who was very much like yours truly, only younger, because it was some time ago; in fact, they were all somewhat younger.

MRS. BARKER

How fascinating!

GRANDMA

Now, at the same time, there was a dear lady very much like you, only younger then, who did all sorts of Good Works. . . . And one of the Good Works this dear lady did was in something very much like a volunteer capacity for an organization very much like the Bye-Bye Adoption Service, which is nearby and which was run by a terribly deaf old lady very much like the Miss Bye-Bye who runs the Bye-Bye Adoption Service nearby.

MRS. BARKER

How enthralling!

GRANDMA

Well, be that as it may. Nonetheless, one afternoon this man, who was very much like Daddy, and this woman who was very much like Mommy came to see this dear lady who did all the Good Works, who was very much like you, dear, and they were very sad and very hopeful, and they cried and smiled and bit their fingers, and they said all the most intimate things.

MRS. BARKER

How spellbinding! What did they say?

GRANDMA

Well, it was very sweet. The woman, who was very much like Mommy, said that she and the man who was very much like Daddy had never been blessed with anything very much like a bumble of joy.

MRS. BARKER

A what?

GRANDMA

A bumble; a bumble of joy.

MRS. BARKER

Oh, like bundle.

GRANDMA

Well, yes; very much like it. Bundle, bumble; who cares? At any rate, the woman, who was very much like Mommy, said that they wanted a bumble of their own, but that the man, who was very much like Daddy, couldn't have a bumble; and the man, who was very much like Daddy, said that yes, they had wanted a bumble of their own, but that the woman, who was very much like Mommy, couldn't have one, and that now they wanted to buy something very much like a bumble.

MRS. BARKER

How engrossing!

GRANDMA

Yes. And the dear lady, who was very much like you, said something that was very much like, "Oh, what a shame; but take heart . . . I think we have just the bumble *for* you." And, well, the lady, who was very much like Mommy, and the man, who was very much like Daddy, cried and smiled and bit their fingers, and said some more intimate things, which were totally irrelevant but which were pretty hot stuff, and so the dear lady, who was very much like you, and who had something very much like a penchant for pornography, listened with something very much like enthusiasm. "Whee," she said. "Whoooopeeeeee!" But that's beside the point.

MRS. BARKER

I suppose *so*. But how gripping!

GRANDMA

Anyway . . . they *bought* something very much like a bumble, and they took it away with them. But . . . things didn't work out very well.

MRS. BARKER

You mean there was trouble?

GRANDMA

You got it.
(*With a glance through the archway*)
But, I'm going to have to speed up now because I think I'm leaving soon.

MRS. BARKER

Oh. Are you really?

GRANDMA

Yup.

MRS. BARKER

But old people don't go anywhere; they're either taken places, or put places.

GRANDMA

Well, this old person is different. Anyway . . . things started going badly.

MRS. BARKER

Oh yes. Yes.

GRANDMA

Weeeeellll . . . in the first place, it turned out the bumble didn't look like either one of its parents. That was enough of a blow, but things got worse. One night, it cried its heart out, if you can imagine such a thing.

MRS. BARKER

Cried its heart out! Well!

GRANDMA

But that was only the beginning. Then it turned out it only had eyes for its Daddy.

MRS. BARKER

For its Daddy! Why, any self-respecting woman would have gouged those eyes right out of its head.

GRANDMA

Well, she did. That's exactly what she did. But then, it kept its nose up in the air.

MRS. BARKER

Ufggh! How disgusting!

GRANDMA

That's what they thought. But *then,* it began to develop an interest in its you-know-what.

MRS. BARKER

In its you-know-what! Well! I hope they cut its hands off at the wrists!

GRANDMA

Well, yes, they did that eventually. But first, they cut off its you-know-what.

MRS. BARKER

A much better idea!

GRANDMA

That's what they thought. But after they cut off its you-know-what, it *still* put its hands under the covers, *looking* for its you-know-what. So, finally, they *had* to cut off its hands at the wrists.

MRS. BARKER

Naturally!

GRANDMA

And it was such a resentful bumble. Why, one day it called its Mommy a dirty name.

MRS. BARKER

Well, I hope they cut its tongue out!

GRANDMA

Of course. And then, as it got bigger, they found out all sorts of terrible things about it, like: it didn't have a head on its shoulders, it had no guts, it was spineless, its feet were made of clay . . . just dreadful things.

MRS. BARKER

Dreadful!

GRANDMA

So you can understand how they became discouraged.

MRS. BARKER

I certainly can! And what did they do?

GRANDMA

What did they do? Well, for the last straw, it finally up and died; and you can imagine how *that* made them feel, their having paid for it, and all. So, they called up the lady who sold them the bumble in the first place and told her to come right over to their apartment. They wanted satisfaction; they wanted their money back. That's what they wanted.

MRS. BARKER

My, my, my.

GRANDMA

How do you like *them* apples?

MRS. BARKER

My, my, my.

DADDY

(Off stage)

Mommy! I can't find Grandma's television, and I can't find the Pekinese, either.

MOMMY

(Off stage)

Isn't that funny! And I can't find the water.

GRANDMA

Heh, heh, heh. I told them everything was hidden.

MRS. BARKER

Did you hide the water, too?

GRANDMA

(Puzzled)

No. No, I didn't do *that*.

DADDY

(Off stage)

The truth of the matter is, I can't even find Grandma's room.

GRANDMA

Heh, heh, heh.

MRS. BARKER

My! You certainly did hide things, didn't you?

GRANDMA

Sure, kid, sure.

MOMMY

(Sticking her head in the room)

Did you ever hear of such a thing, Grandma? Daddy can't find your television, and he can't find the Pekinese, and the truth of the matter is he can't even find your room.

GRANDMA

I told you. I hid everything.

MOMMY

Nonsense, Grandma! Just wait until I get my hands on you. You're a troublemaker . . . that's what you are.

GRANDMA

Well, I'll be out of here pretty soon, baby.

MOMMY

Oh, you don't know how right you are! Daddy's been wanting to send you away for a long time now, but I've been restraining him. I'll tell you one thing, though . . . I'm getting sick and tired of this fighting, and I might just let him have his way. Then you'll see what'll happen. Away you'll go; in a van, too. I'll let Daddy call the van man.

GRANDMA

I'm way ahead of you.

MOMMY

How can you be so old and so smug at the same time? You have no sense of proportion.

GRANDMA

You just answered your own question.

MOMMY

Mrs. Barker, I'd much rather you came into the kitchen for that glass of water, what with Grandma out here, and all.

MRS. BARKER

I don't see what Grandma has to do with it; and besides, I don't think you're very polite.

MOMMY

You seem to forget that you're a guest in this house . . .

GRANDMA

Apartment!

MOMMY

Apartment! And that you're a professional woman. So, if you'll be so good as to come into the kitchen, I'll be more than happy to show you where the

water is, and where the glass is, and then you can put two and two together, if you're clever enough.

(She vanishes)

MRS. BARKER

(After a moment's consideration)
I suppose she's right.

GRANDMA

Well, that's how it is when people call you up and ask you over to do something for them.

MRS. BARKER

I suppose you're right, too. Well, Grandma, it's been very nice talking to
you.

GRANDMA

And I've enjoyed listening. Say, don't tell Mommy or Daddy that I gave
you that hint, will you?

MRS. BARKER

Oh, dear me, the hint! I'd forgotten about it, if you can imagine such a
thing. No, I won't breathe a word of it to them.

GRANDMA

I don't know if it helped you any . . .

MRS. BARKER

I can't tell, yet. I'll have to. . . what *is* the word I want? . . . I'll have to relate
i   t
. . . that's it . . . I'll have to relate it to certain things that I *know*, and . . .
draw . . . conclusions. . . . What I'll really have to do is to see if it applies
to anything. I mean, after all, I *do* do volunteer work for an adoption service, but it isn't very much *like* the Bye-Bye Adoption Service . . . it *is* the
Bye-Bye Adoption Service . . . and while I can remember Mommy and
Daddy coming to see me, oh about twenty years ago, about buying a bumble, I can't quite remember anyone very much *like* Mommy and Daddy
coming to see me about buying a bumble. Don't you see? It really presents
quite a problem. . . . I'll have to think about it . . . mull it . . . but at any
rate, it was truly first-class of you to try to help me. Oh, will you still be
here after I've had my drink of water?

GRANDMA

Probably . . . I'm not as spry as I used to be.

MRS. BARKER

Oh. Well, I won't say good-by then.

GRANDMA

No. Don't.

(MRS. BARKER *exits through the archway*)

People don't say good-by to old people because they think they'll frighten them. Lordy! If they only knew how awful "hello" and "my, you're looking chipper" sounded, they wouldn't say those things either. The truth is, there isn't much you *can* say to old people that doesn't sound just terrible.

(*The doorbell rings*)

Come on in!

(*The* YOUNG MAN *enters.* GRANDMA *looks him over*)

Well, now, aren't you a breath of fresh air!

YOUNG MAN

Hello there.

GRANDMA

My, my, my. Are you the van man?

YOUNG MAN

The what?

GRANDMA

The van man. The van man. Are you come to take me away?

YOUNG MAN

I don't know what you're talking about.

GRANDMA

Oh.

(*Pause*)

Well.

(*Pause*)

My, my, aren't you something!

YOUNG MAN

Hm?

GRANDMA

I said, my, my, aren't you something.

YOUNG MAN

Oh. Thank you.

GRANDMA

You don't sound very enthusiastic.

YOUNG MAN

Oh, I'm . . . I'm used to it.

GRANDMA

Yup . . . yup. You know, if I were about a hundred and fifty years younger I could go for you.

YOUNG MAN

Yes, I imagine so.

GRANDMA

Unh-hunh . . . will you look at those muscles!

YOUNG MAN

(*Flexing his muscles*)

Yes, they're quite good, aren't they?

GRANDMA

Boy, they sure are. They natural?

YOUNG MAN

Well the basic structure was there, but I've done some work, too . . . you know, in a gym.

GRANDMA

I'll bet you have. You ought to be in the movies, boy.

YOUNG MAN

I know.

GRANDMA

Yup! Right up there on the old silver screen. But I suppose you've heard that before.

YOUNG MAN

Yes, I have.

GRANDMA

You ought to try out for them . . . the movies.

YOUNG MAN

Well, actually, I may have a career there yet. I've lived out on the West Coast almost all my life . . . and I've met a few people who . . . might be able to help me. I'm not in too much of a hurry, though. I'm almost as young as I look.

GRANDMA

Oh, that's nice. And will you look at that face!

YOUNG MAN

Yes, it's quite good, isn't it? Clean-cut, Midwest farm boy type, almost insultingly good-looking in a typically American way. Good profile, straight nose, honest eyes, wonderful smile . . .

GRANDMA

Yup. Boy, you know what you are, don't you? You're the American Dream, that's what you are. All those other people, they don't know what they're talking about. You . . . *you* are the American Dream.

YOUNG MAN

Thanks.

MOMMY

(Off stage)
Who rang the doorbell?

GRANDMA

(Shouting off stage)
The American Dream!

MOMMY

(Off stage)
What? What was that, Grandma?

GRANDMA

(Shouting)
The American Dream! The American Dream! Damn it!

DADDY

(Off stage)
How's that, Mommy?

MOMMY

(Off stage)
Oh, some gibberish; pay no attention. Did you find Grandma's room?

DADDY

(Off stage)
No. I can't even find Mrs. Barker.

YOUNG MAN

What was all that?

GRANDMA

Oh, that was just the folks, but let's not talk about them, honey; let's talk about you.

YOUNG MAN

All right.

GRANDMA

Well, let's see. If you're not the van man, what are you doing here?

YOUNG MAN

I'm looking for work.

GRANDMA

Are you! Well, what kind of work?

YOUNG MAN

Oh, almost anything . . . almost anything that pays. I'll do almost anything for money.

GRANDMA

Will you . . . will you? Hmmmm. I wonder if there's anything you could do around here?

YOUNG MAN

There might be. It looked to be a likely building.

GRANDMA

It's always looked to be a rather unlikely building to me, but I suppose you'd know better than I.

YOUNG MAN

I can sense these things.

GRANDMA

There *might* be something you could do around here. Stay there! Don't come any closer.

YOUNG MAN

Sorry.

GRANDMA

I don't mean I'd *mind*. I don't know whether I'd mind, or not. . . . But it wouldn't look well; it would look just *awful*.

YOUNG MAN

Yes; I suppose so.

GRANDMA

Now, stay there, let me concentrate. What could you do? The folks have been in something of a quandary around here today, sort of a dilemma, and I wonder if you mightn't be some help.

YOUNG MAN

I hope so . . . if there's money in it. Do you have any money?

GRANDMA

Money! Oh, there's more money around here than you'd know what to do with.

YOUNG MAN

I'm not so sure.

GRANDMA

Well, maybe not. Besides, I've got money of my own.

YOUNG MAN

You have?

GRANDMA

Sure. Old people quite often have lots of money; more often than most people expect. Come here, so I can whisper to you . . . not too close. I might faint.

YOUNG MAN

Oh, I'm sorry.

GRANDMA

It's all right, dear. Anyway . . . have you ever heard of that big baking contest they run? The one where all the ladies get together in a big barn and bake away?

YOUNG MAN

I'm . . . not . . . sure. . . .

GRANDMA

Not so close. Well, it doesn't matter whether you've heard of it or not. The important thing is—and I don't want anybody to hear this . . . the folks think I haven't been out of the house in eight years—the important thing is that I won first prize in that baking contest this year. Oh, it was in all the papers; not under my own name, though. I used a *nom de boulangère;* I called myself Uncle Henry.

YOUNG MAN

Did you?

GRANDMA

Why not? I didn't see any reason not to. I look just as much like an old man as I do like an old woman. And you know what I called it . . . what I won for?

YOUNG MAN

No. What did you call it?

GRANDMA

I called it Uncle Henry's Day-Old Cake.

YOUNG MAN

That's a very nice name.

GRANDMA

And it wasn't any trouble, either. All I did was go out and get a store-bought cake, and keep it around for a while, and then slip it in, unbeknownst to anybody. Simple.

YOUNG MAN

You're a very resourceful person.

GRANDMA

Pioneer stock.

YOUNG MAN

Is all this true? Do you want me to believe all this?

GRANDMA

Well, you can believe it or not . . . it doesn't make any difference to me.
All *I* know is, Uncle Henry's Day-Old Cake won me twenty-five thousand
smackerolas.

YOUNG MAN

Twenty-five thou—

GRANDMA

Right on the old loggerhead. Now . . . how do you like them apples?

YOUNG MAN

Love 'em.

GRANDMA

I thought you'd be impressed.

YOUNG MAN

Money talks.

GRANDMA

Hey! You look familiar.

YOUNG MAN

Hm? Pardon?

GRANDMA

I said, you look familiar.

YOUNG MAN

Well, I've done some modeling.

GRANDMA

No . . . no. I don't mean that. You look familiar.

YOUNG MAN

Well, I'm a type.

GRANDMA

Yup; you sure are. Why do you say you'd do almost anything for money . .
. if you don't mind my being nosy?

YOUNG MAN

No, no. It's part of the interview. I'll be happy to tell you. It's that I
have no talents at all, except what you see . . . my person; my body, my
face. In every other way I am incomplete, and I must therefore . . .
compensate.

GRANDMA

What do you mean, incomplete? You look pretty complete to me.

YOUNG MAN

I think I can explain it to you, partially because you're very old, and very old people have perceptions they keep to themselves, because if they expose them to other people . . . well, you know what ridicule and neglect are.

GRANDMA

I do, child, I do.

YOUNG MAN

Then listen. My mother died the night that I was born, and I never knew my father; I doubt my mother did. But, I wasn't alone, because lying with me . . . in the placenta . . . there was someone else . . . my brother . . . my twin.

GRANDMA

Oh, my child.

YOUNG MAN

We were identical twins . . . he and I . . . not fraternal . . . identical; we were derived from the same ovum; and in *this,* in that we were twins not from separate ova but from the same one, we had a kinship such as you cannot imagine. We . . . we felt each other breathe . . . his heartbeats thundered in my temples . . . mine in his . . . our stomachs ached and we cried for feeding at the same time . . . are you old enough to understand?

GRANDMA

I think so, child; I think I'm nearly old enough.

YOUNG MAN

I hope so. But we were separated when we were still very young, my brother, my twin and I . . . inasmuch as you can separate one being. We were torn apart . . . thrown to opposite ends of the continent. I don't know what became of my brother . . . to the rest of myself . . . except that, from time to time, in the years that have passed, I have suffered losses . . . that I can't explain. A fall from grace . . . a departure of innocence . . . loss. . . loss. How can I put it to you? All right; like this: Once . . . it was as if all at once my heart . . . became numb . . . almost as though I . . . almost as though . . . just like that . . . it had been wrenched from my body . . . and from that time I have been unable to love. Once . . . I was asleep at the time . . . I awoke, and my eyes were burning. And since that time I have been unable to see anything, *anything,* with pity, with affection . . . with anything but . . . cool disinterest. And my groin . . . even there . . . since one time . . . one specific agony . . . since then

I have not been able to *love* anyone with my body. And even my hands . . . I cannot touch another person and feel love. And there is more . . . there are more losses, but it all comes down to this: I no longer have the capacity to feel anything. I have no emotions. I have been drained, torn asunder . . . disemboweled. I have, now, only my person . . . my body, my face. I use what I have . . . I let people love me . . . I accept the syntax around me, for while I know I cannot relate . . . I know I must be related *to*. I let people love me . . . I let people touch me . . . I let them draw pleasure from my groin . . . from my presence . . . from the fact of me . . . but, that is all it comes to. As I told you, I am incomplete . . . I can feel nothing. I can feel nothing. And so . . . here I am . . . as you see me. I am . . . but this . . . what you see. And it will always be thus.

GRANDMA

Oh, my child; my child.

(Long pause; then)

I was mistaken . . . before. I don't know you from somewhere, but I knew . . . once . . . someone very much like you . . . or, very much as perhaps you were.

YOUNG MAN

Be careful; be very careful. What I have told you may not be true. In my profession . . .

GRANDMA

Shhhhhh.

(The YOUNG MAN *bows his head, in acquiescence)*

Someone . . . to be more precise . . . who might have turned out to be very much like you might have turned out to be. And . . . unless I'm terribly mistaken . . . you've found yourself a job.

YOUNG MAN

What are my duties?

MRS. BARKER

(Off stage)

Yoo-hoo! Yoo-hoo!

GRANDMA

Oh-oh. You'll . . . you'll have to play it by ear, my dear . . . unless I get a chance to talk to you again. I've got to go into my act, now.

YOUNG MAN

But, I . . .

GRANDMA

Yoo-hoo!

MRS. BARKER

(Coming through archway)

Yoo-hoo . . . oh, there you are, Grandma. I'm glad to see somebody. I can't find Mommy or Daddy.

(Double takes)

Well . . . who's this?

GRANDMA

This? Well . . . uh . . . oh, this is the . . . uh . . . the van man. That's who it is . . . the van man.

MRS. BARKER

So! It's true! They *did* call the van man. They *are* having you carted away.

GRANDMA

(Shrugging)

Well, you know. It figures.

MRS. BARKER

(To YOUNG MAN*)*

How dare you cart this poor old woman away!

YOUNG MAN

(After a quick look at GRANDMA, *who nods)*

I do what I'm paid to do. I don't ask any questions.

MRS. BARKER

(After a brief pause)

Oh.

(Pause)

Well, you're quite right, of course, and I shouldn't meddle.

GRANDMA

(To YOUNG MAN*)*

Dear, will you take my things out to the van?

(She points to the boxes)

YOUNG MAN

(After only the briefest hesitation)

Why certainly.

GRANDMA

(As the YOUNG MAN *takes up half the boxes, exits by the front door)*

Isn't that a nice young van man?

MRS. BARKER

(Shaking her head in disbelief, watching the YOUNG MAN *exit)*

Unh-hunh . . . some things have changed for the better. I remember
when I had *my* mother carted off . . . the van man who came for her
wasn't anything near as nice as this one.

GRANDMA

Oh, did you have your mother carted off, too?

MRS. BARKER *(Cheerfully)*

Why certainly! Didn't you?

GRANDMA *(Puzzling)*

No . . . no, I didn't. At least, I can't remember. Listen dear; I got to talk to
you for a second.

MRS. BARKER

Why certainly, Grandma.

GRANDMA

Now, listen.

MRS. BARKER

Yes, Grandma. Yes.

GRANDMA

Now listen carefully. You got this dilemma here with Mommy and
Daddy . . .

MRS. BARKER

Yes! I wonder where they've gone to.

GRANDMA

They'll be back in. Now, LISTEN!

MRS. BARKER

Oh, I'm sorry.

GRANDMA

Now, you got this dilemma here with Mommy and Daddy, and I think I got
the way out for you.

(The YOUNG MAN *re-enters through the front door)*

Will you take the rest of my things out now, dear?

(To MRS. BARKER, *while the* YOUNG MAN *takes the rest of the boxes,
exits again by the front door)*

Fine. Now listen, dear.

(She begins to whisper in MRS. BARKER's *ear)*

MRS. BARKER

Oh! Oh! Oh! I don't think I could . . . do you really think I could? Well, why not? What a wonderful idea . . . what an absolutely wonderful idea!

GRANDMA

Well, yes, I thought it was.

MRS. BARKER

And you so old!

GRANDMA

Heh, heh, heh.

MRS. BARKER

Well, I think it's absolutely marvelous, anyway. I'm going to find Mommy and Daddy right now.

GRANDMA

Good. You do that.

MRS. BARKER

Well, now. I think I will say good-by. I can't thank you enough.
    (*She starts to exit through the archway*)

GRANDMA

You're welcome. Say it!

MRS. BARKER

Huh? What?

GRANDMA

Say good-by.

MRS. BARKER

Oh. Good-by.
    (*She exits*)
Mommy! I say, Mommy! Daddy!

GRANDMA

Good-by.
    (*By herself now, she looks about*)
Ah me.
    (*Shakes her head*)
Ah me.
    (*Takes in the room*)
Good-by.
    (*The* YOUNG MAN *re-enters*)
Oh, hello, there.

YOUNG MAN

All the boxes are outside.

GRANDMA

(A little sadly)

I don't know why I bother to take them with me. They don't have much in them . . . some old letters, a couple of regrets . . . Pekinese . . . blind at that . . . the television . . . my Sunday teeth . . . eighty-six years of living . . . some sounds . . . a few images, a little garbled by now . . . . and, well . . .

(She shrugs)

. . . you know . . . the things one accumulates.

YOUNG MAN

Can I get you . . . a cab, or something?

GRANDMA

Oh no, dear . . . thank you just the same. I'll take it from here.

YOUNG MAN

And what shall I do now?

GRANDMA

Oh, you stay here, dear. It will all become clear to you. It will be explained. You'll understand.

YOUNG MAN

Very well.

GRANDMA

(After one more look about)

Well . . .

YOUNG MAN

Let me see you to the elevator.

GRANDMA

Oh . . . that *would* be nice, dear.

(They both exit by the front door, slowly)

(Enter MRS. BARKER, *followed by* MOMMY *and* DADDY)

MRS. BARKER

. . . and I'm happy to tell you that the whole thing's settled. Just like that.

MOMMY

Oh, we're so glad. We were afraid there might be a problem, what with delays, and all.

DADDY

Yes, we re very relieved.

MRS. BARKER

Well, now; that's what professional women are for.

MOMMY

Why . . . where's Grandma? Grandma's not here! Where's Grandma? And look! The boxes are gone, too. Grandma's gone, and so are the boxes. She's taken off and she's stolen something! Daddy!

MRS. BARKER

Why, Mommy, the van man was here.

MOMMY

(Startled)

The what?

MRS. BARKER

The van man. The van man was here.

(The lights might dim a little, suddenly)

MOMMY

(Shakes her head)

No, that's impossible.

MRS. BARKER

Why, I saw him with my own two eyes.

MOMMY

(Near tears)

No, no, that's impossible. No. There's no such thing as the van man. There is no van man. We . . . we made him up. Grandma? Grandma?

DADDY

(Moving to MOMMY*)*

There, there, now.

MOMMY

Oh Daddy . . . where's Grandma?

DADDY

There, there, now.

(While DADDY *is comforting* MOMMY, GRANDMA *comes out, stage right, near the footlights)*

GRANDMA

(To the audience)

Shhhhhh! I want to watch this.

(She motions to MRS. BARKER, *who, with a secret smile, tiptoes to the front door and opens it. The* YOUNG MAN *is framed therein. Lights up full again as he steps into the room)*

MRS. BARKER

Surprise! Surprise! Here we are!

MOMMY

What? What?

DADDY

Hm? What?

MOMMY

(Her tears merely sniffles now)

What surprise?

MRS. BARKER

Why, I told you. The surprise I told you about.

DADDY

You . . . you know, Mommy.

MOMMY

Sur . . . prise?

DADDY

(Urging her to cheerfulness)

You remember, Mommy; why we asked . . . uh . . . what's-her-name to come here?

MRS. BARKER

Mrs. Barker, if you don't mind.

DADDY

Yes. Mommy? You remember now? About the bumble . . . about wanting satisfaction?

MOMMY

(Her sorrow turning into delight)

Yes. Why yes! Of course! Yes! Oh, how wonderful!

MRS. BARKER

(To the YOUNG MAN*)*

This is Mommy.

YOUNG MAN

How . . . how do you do?

MRS. BARKER

(Stage whisper)

Her name's Mommy.

YOUNG MAN

How . . . how do you do, Mommy?

MOMMY

Well! Hello there!

MRS. BARKER

(To the YOUNG MAN)
And that is Daddy.

YOUNG MAN

How do you do, sir?

DADDY

How do you do?

MOMMY

(Herself again, circling the young man, feeling his arm, poking him)
Yes, sir! Yes, sirree! Now this is more like it. Now this is a great deal more like it! Daddy! Come see. Come see if this isn't a great deal more like it.

DADDY

I . . . I can see from here, Mommy. It does look a great deal more like it.

MOMMY

Yes, sir. Yes sirree! Mrs. Barker, I don't know *how* to thank you.

MRS. BARKER

Oh, don't worry about that. I'll send you a bill in the mail.

MOMMY

What this really calls for is a celebration. It calls for a drink.

MRS. BARKER

Oh, what a nice idea.

MOMMY

There's some sauterne in the kitchen.

YOUNG MAN

I'll go.

MOMMY

Will you? Oh, how nice. The kitchen's through the archway there.
(As the YOUNG MAN *exits: to* MRS. BARKER)
He's very nice. Really top notch; much better than the other one.

MRS. BARKER

I'm glad you're pleased. And I'm glad everything's all straightened out.

MOMMY

Well, at least we know why we sent for you. We're glad that's cleared up. By the way, what's his name?

MRS. BARKER

Ha! Call him whatever you like. He's yours. Call him what you called the other one.

MOMMY

Daddy? What did we call the other one?

DADDY

(Puzzles)

Why . . .

YOUNG MAN

(Re-entering with a tray on which are a bottle of sauterne and five glasses)

Here we are!

MOMMY

Hooray! Hooray!

MRS. BARKER

Oh, good!

MOMMY

(Moving to the tray)

So, let's— Five glasses? Why five? There are only four of us. Why five?

YOUNG MAN

(Catches GRANDMA's *eye;* GRANDMA *indicates she is not there)*

Oh, I'm sorry.

MOMMY

You must learn to count. We're a wealthy family, and you must learn to count.

YOUNG MAN

I will.

MOMMY

Well, everybody take a glass.

(They do)

And we'll drink to celebrate. To satisfaction! Who says you can't get satisfaction these days!

MRS. BARKER

What dreadful sauterne!

MOMMY

Yes, isn't it?

(To YOUNG MAN, *her voice already a little fuzzy from the wine)*

You don't know how happy I am to see you! Yes sirree. Listen, that time we had with . . . with the other one. I'll tell you about it some time.

(*Indicates* MRS. BARKER)

I'll tell you all about it.

(*Sidles up to him a little*)

Maybe . . . maybe later tonight.

YOUNG MAN

(*Not moving away*)

Why yes. That would be very nice.

MOMMY

(*Puzzles*)

Something familiar about you . . . you know that? I can't quite place it. . . .

GRANDMA

(*Interrupting . . . to audience*)

Well, I guess that just about wraps it up. I mean, for better or worse, this is a comedy, and I don't think we'd better go any further. No, definitely not. So, let's leave things as they are right now . . . while everybody's happy . . . while everybody's got what he wants . . . or everybody's got what he thinks he wants. Good night, dears.

CURTAIN

Who's Afraid of Virginia Woolf?

For Richard Barr
and Clinton Wilder

The world premier of *Who's Afraid of Virginia Woolf?* was presented by Theater 1963 (Richard Barr and Clinton Wilder), A.B.W. Productions, Inc., and Pisces Productions, Inc. at the Billy Rose Theatre in New York City on October 13, 1962. The production was directed by Alan Schneider. The production design was by William Ritman. The cast was as follows:

MARTHA	Uta Hagen
GEORGE	Arthur Hill
NICK	George Grizzard
HONEY	Melinda Dillon

THE PLAYERS

MARTHA

A large, boisterous woman, fifty-two, looking somewhat younger. Ample, but not fleshy.

GEORGE

Her husband, forty-six. Thin; hair going gray.

HONEY

Twenty-six, a petite blond girl, rather plain.

NICK

Late twenties, her husband. Blond, well put-together, good-looking.

THE SCENE

The living room of a house on the campus of a small New England college.

ACT ONE

FUN AND GAMES

(Set in darkness. Crash against front door. MARTHA's *laughter heard. Front door opens, lights are switched on.* MARTHA *enters, followed by* GEORGE)

MARTHA

Jesus . . .

GEORGE

. . . Shhhhhhh . . .

MARTHA

. . . H. Christ . . .

GEORGE

For God's sake, Martha, it's two o'clock in the . . .

MARTHA

Oh, George!

GEORGE

Well, I'm *sorry*, but . . .

MARTHA

What a cluck! What a cluck you are.

GEORGE

It's late, you know? Late.

MARTHA
(Looks about the room. Imitates Bette Davis)
What a dump. Hey, what's that from? "What a dump!"

GEORGE

How would I know what . . .

MARTHA

Aw, come on! What's it from? *You* know . . .

GEORGE

. . . Martha . . .

MARTHA

WHAT'S IT FROM, FOR CHRIST'S SAKE?

GEORGE *(Wearily)*

What's what from?

MARTHA

I just told you; I just did it. "What a dump!" Hunh? What's that from?

GEORGE

I haven't the faintest idea what . . .

MARTHA

Dumbbell! It's from some goddamn Bette Davis picture . . . some goddamn Warner Brothers epic . . .

GEORGE

I can't remember all the pictures that . . .

MARTHA

Nobody's asking you to remember every single goddamn Warner Brothers epic . . . just one! One single little epic! Bette Davis gets peritonitis in the end . . . she's got this big black fright wig she wears all through the picture and she gets peritonitis, and she's married to Joseph Cotten or something . . .

GEORGE

. . . Some*body* . . .

MARTHA

. . . some*body* . . . and she wants to go to Chicago all the time, 'cause she's in love with that actor with the scar. . . . But she gets sick, and she sits down in front of her dressing table . . .

GEORGE

What actor? What scar?

MARTHA

I can't remember his name, for God's sake. What's the name of the *picture?* I want to know what the name of the *picture* is. She sits down in front of her dressing table . . . and she's got this peritonitis . . . and she tries to put her lipstick on, but she can't . . . and she gets it all over her face . . . but she decides to go to Chicago anyway, and . . .

GEORGE

Chicago! It's called *Chicago.*

MARTHA

Hunh? What . . . what is?

GEORGE

The picture . . . it's called *Chicago* . . .

MARTHA

Good grief! Don't you know *anything?* *Chicago* was a 'thirties musical, starring little Miss Alice *Faye.* Don't you know *anything?*

GEORGE

Well, that was probably before my *time,* but . . .

MARTHA

Can it! Just cut that out! This picture . . . Bette Davis comes home from a hard day at the grocery store . . .

GEORGE

She works in a grocery store?

MARTHA

She's a housewife; she buys things . . . and she comes home with the groceries, and she walks into the modest living room of the modest cottage modest Joseph Cotten has set her up in . . .

GEORGE

Are they married?

MARTHA *(Impatiently)*

Yes. They're married. To each other. Cluck! And she comes in, and she looks around, and she puts her groceries down, and she says, "What a dump!"

GEORGE

(Pause) Oh.

MARTHA

(Pause) She's discontent.

GEORGE

(Pause) Oh.

MARTHA

(Pause) Well, what's the name of the picture?

GEORGE

I really don't know, Martha . . .

MARTHA

Well, think!

GEORGE

I'm tired, dear . . . it's late . . . and besides . . .

MARTHA

I don't know what you're so tired about . . . you haven't *done* anything all day; you didn't have any classes, or anything . . .

GEORGE

Well, I'm tired. . . . If your father didn't set up these goddamn Saturday night orgies all the time . . .

MARTHA

Well, that's too bad about you, George . . .

GEORGE (*Grumbling*)

Well, that's how it is, anyway.

MARTHA

You didn't *do* anything; you never *do* anything; you never *mix*. You just sit around and *talk*.

GEORGE

What do you want me to do? Do you want me to act like you? Do you want me to go around all night *braying* at everybody, the way you do?

MARTHA (*Braying*)

I DON'T BRAY!

GEORGE (*Softly*)

All right . . . you don't bray.

MARTHA (*Hurt*)

I do not *bray*.

GEORGE

All right. I said you didn't bray.

MARTHA (*Pouting*)

Make me a drink.

GEORGE

What?

MARTHA (*Still softly*)

I said, make me a drink.

GEORGE

(*Moving to the portable bar*)

Well, I don't suppose a nightcap'd kill either one of us . . .

MARTHA

A nightcap! Are you kidding? We've got guests.

GEORGE (*Disbelieving*)

We've got what?

MARTHA

Guests. GUESTS.

GEORGE

GUESTS!

MARTHA

Yes . . . guests . . . people. . . . We've got guests coming over.

GEORGE

When?

MARTHA

NOW!

GEORGE

Good Lord, Martha . . . do you know what time it . . . *Who's* coming over?

MARTHA

What's-their-name.

GEORGE

Who?

MARTHA

WHAT'S-THEIR-NAME!

GEORGE

Who what's-their-name?

MARTHA

I don't know what their name is, George. . . . You met them tonight . . . they're new . . . he's in the math department, or something. . . .

GEORGE

Who . . . who are these people?

MARTHA

You met them tonight, George.

GEORGE

I don't remember meeting anyone tonight . . .

MARTHA

Well you did . . . Will you give me my drink, please. . . . He's in the math department . . . about thirty, blond, and . . .

GEORGE

. . . and good-looking . . .

MARTHA

Yes . . . and good-looking. . . .

GEORGE

It figures.

MARTHA

. . . and his wife's a mousey little type, without any hips, or anything.

GEORGE *(Vaguely)*

Oh.

MARTHA

You remember them now?

GEORGE

Yes, I guess so, Martha. . . . But why in God's name are they coming over here now?

MARTHA

(In a so-there voice)
Because Daddy said we should be nice to them, that's why.

GEORGE *(Defeated)*

Oh, Lord.

MARTHA

May I have my drink, please? Daddy said we should be nice to them. Thank you.

GEORGE

But why now? It's after two o'clock in the morning, and . . .

MARTHA

Because Daddy said we should be nice to them!

GEORGE

Yes. But I'm sure your father didn't mean we were supposed to stay up all *night* with these people. I mean, we could have them over some Sunday or something. . . .

MARTHA

Well, never mind. . . . Besides, it *is* Sunday. Very early Sunday.

GEORGE

I mean . . . it's ridiculous. . . .

MARTHA

Well, it's *done!*

GEORGE

(Resigned and exasperated)
All right. Well . . . where are they? If we've got guests, where are they?

MARTHA

They'll be here soon.

GEORGE

What did they do . . . go home and get some sleep first, or something?

MARTHA

They'll *be* here!

GEORGE

I wish you'd *tell* me about something sometime. . . . I wish you'd stop *springing* things on me all the time.

MARTHA

I don't *spring* things on you all the time.

GEORGE

Yes, you do . . . you really do . . . you're always *springing* things on me.

MARTHA *(Friendly-patronizing)*

Oh, George!

GEORGE

Always.

MARTHA

Poor Georgie-Porgie, put-upon pie! *(As he sulks)* Awwwwww . . . what are you doing? Are you sulking? Hunh? Let me see . . . are you sulking? Is that what you're doing?

GEORGE *(Very quietly)*

Never mind, Martha. . . .

MARTHA

AWWWWWWWWWW!

GEORGE

Just don't bother yourself. . . .

MARTHA

AWWWWWWWWWW! *(No reaction)* Hey! *(No reaction)* HEY!

(GEORGE looks at her, put-upon)

Hey. *(She sings)* Who's afraid of Virginia Woolf,

Virginia Woolf,

Virginia Woolf . . .

Ha, ha, ha, HA! *(No reaction)* What's the matter . . . didn't you think that was funny? Hunh? *(Defiantly)* I thought it was a scream . . . a real scream. You didn't like it, hunh?

GEORGE

It was all right, Martha. . . .

MARTHA

You laughed your head off when you heard it at the party.

GEORGE

I smiled. I didn't laugh my head off . . . I smiled, you know? . . . it was all right.

MARTHA (*Gazing into her drink*)

You laughed your goddamn head off.

GEORGE

It was all right. . . .

MARTHA (*Ugly*)

It was a scream!

GEORGE (*Patiently*)

It was very funny; yes.

MARTHA

(*After a moment's consideration*)

You make me puke!

GEORGE

What?

MARTHA

Uh . . . you make me puke?

GEORGE

(*Thinks about it . . . then . . .*)

That wasn't a very nice thing to say, Martha.

MARTHA

That wasn't *what*?

GEORGE

. . . a very nice thing to say.

MARTHA

I like your anger. I think that's what I like about you most . . . your anger. You're such a . . . such a simp! You don't even have the . . . the what? . . .

GEORGE

. . . guts? . . .

MARTHA

PHRASEMAKER! (*Pause . . . then they both laugh*) Hey, put some more ice in my drink, will you? You never put any ice in my drink. Why is that, hunh?

GEORGE *(Takes her drink)*

I always put ice in your drink. You eat it, that's all. It's that habit you have . . .
chewing your ice cubes . . . like a cocker spaniel. You'll crack your big teeth.

MARTHA

THEY'RE MY BIG TEETH!

GEORGE

Some of them . . . some of them.

MARTHA

I've got more teeth than you've got.

GEORGE

Two more.

MARTHA

Well, two more's a lot more.

GEORGE

I suppose it is. I suppose it's pretty remarkable . . . considering how old
you are.

MARTHA

YOU CUT THAT OUT! *(Pause)* You're not so young yourself.

GEORGE

(With boyish pleasure . . . a chant)

I'm six years younger than you are. . . . I always have been and I always
will be.

MARTHA *(Glumly)*

Well . . . you're going bald.

GEORGE

So are you. *(Pause . . . they both laugh)* Hello, honey.

MARTHA

Hello. C'mon over here and give your Mommy a big sloppy kiss.

GEORGE

. . . oh, now . . .

MARTHA

I WANT A BIG SLOPPY KISS!

GEORGE *(Preoccupied)*

I don't *want* to kiss you, Martha. Where *are* these people? Where are
these *people* you invited over?

MARTHA

They stayed on to talk to Daddy. . . . They'll be here. . . . *Why* don't you
want to kiss me?

GEORGE

(Too matter-of-fact)

Well, dear, if I kissed you I'd get all excited . . . I'd get beside myself, and I'd take you, by force, right here on the living room rug, and then our little guests would walk in, and . . . well, just think what your father would say about *that*.

MARTHA

You pig!

GEORGE *(Haughtily)*

Oink! Oink!

MARTHA

Ha, ha, ha, HA! Make me another drink . . . lover.

GEORGE *(Taking her glass)*

My God, you can swill it down, can't you?

MARTHA

(Imitating a tiny child)

I'm firsty.

GEORGE

Jesus!

MARTHA *(Swinging around)*

Look, sweetheart, I can drink you under any goddamn table you want . . . so don't worry about me!

GEORGE

Martha, I gave you the prize years ago. . . . There isn't an abomination award going that you . . .

MARTHA

I swear . . . if you existed I'd divorce you. . . .

GEORGE

Well, just stay on your feet, that's all. . . . These people are your guests, you know, and . . .

MARTHA

I can't even see you . . . I haven't been able to see you for years. . . .

GEORGE

. . . if you pass out, or throw up, or something . . .

MARTHA

. . . I mean, you're a blank, a cipher. . . .

GEORGE

. . . and try to keep your clothes on, too. There aren't many more sickening sights than you with a couple of drinks in you and your skirt up over your head. . . .

MARTHA

. . . a zero. . . .

GEORGE

. . . your *heads,* I should say. . . .
    (The front doorbell chimes)

MARTHA

Party! Party!

GEORGE *(Murderously)*

I'm really looking forward to this, Martha. . . .

MARTHA *(Same)*

Go answer the door.

GEORGE *(Not moving)*

You answer it.

MARTHA

Get to that door, you.
    (He does not move)
I'll fix you, you . . .

GEORGE *(Fake-spits)*

. . . to you . . .
    (Door chime again)

MARTHA

(Shouting . . . to the door)
C'MON IN! *(To* GEORGE, *between her teeth)* I said, get over there!

GEORGE

(Moving toward the door)

All right, love . . . whatever love wants. Isn't it nice the way some people
have manners, though, even in this day and age? Isn't it nice that some
people won't just come breaking into other people's houses even if they *do*
hear some sub-human monster yowling at 'em from inside . . . ?

MARTHA

FUCK YOU!

(Simultaneously with MARTHA's *last remark,* GEORGE *flings open
the front door.* HONEY *and* NICK *are framed in the entrance. There
is a brief silence, then . . .)*

GEORGE

(Ostensibly a pleased recognition of HONEY *and* NICK, *but really
satisfaction at having* MARTHA's *explosion overheard)*

Ahhhhhhhhh!

MARTHA

(A little too loud . . . to cover)

HI! Hi, there . . . c'mon in!

HONEY *and* NICK *(ad lib)*

Hello, here we are . . . hi . . . *etc.*

GEORGE

(Very matter-of-factly)

You must be our little guests.

MARTHA

Ha, ha, ha, HA! Just ignore old sour-puss over there. C'mon in, kids . . . give your coats and stuff to sour-puss.

NICK *(Without expression)*

Well, now, perhaps we shouldn't have come . . .

HONEY

Yes . . . it *is* late, and . . .

MARTHA

Late! Are you kidding? Throw your stuff down anywhere and c'mon in.

GEORGE

(Vaguely . . . walking away)

Anywhere . . . furniture, floor . . . doesn't make any difference around this place.

NICK *(To* HONEY*)*

I told you we shouldn't have come.

MARTHA *(Stentorian)*

I said c'mon in! Now c'mon!

HONEY

(Giggling a little as she and NICK *advance)*

Oh, dear.

GEORGE

(Imitating HONEY's *giggle)*

Hee, hee, hee, hee.

MARTHA *(Swinging on* GEORGE*)*

Look, muckmouth . . . you cut that out!

GEORGE

(Innocence and hurt)

Martha! *(To* HONEY *and* NICK*)* Martha's a devil with language; she really is.

MARTHA

Hey, *kids* . . . sit down.

HONEY *(As she sits)*

Oh, isn't this lovely!

NICK *(Perfunctorily)*

Yes indeed . . . very handsome.

MARTHA

Well, thanks.

NICK

(Indicating the abstract painting)
Who . . . who did the . . . ?

MARTHA

That? Oh, that's by . . .

GEORGE

. . . some Greek with a mustache Martha attacked one night in . . .

HONEY

(To save the situation)
Oh, ho, ho, ho, HO.

NICK

It's got a . . . a . . .

GEORGE

A quiet intensity?

NICK

Well, no . . . a . . .

GEORGE

Oh. *(Pause)* Well, then, a certain noisy relaxed quality, maybe?

NICK

(Knows what GEORGE is doing, but stays grimly, coolly polite)
No. What I meant was . . .

GEORGE

How about . . . uh . . . a quietly noisy relaxed intensity.

HONEY

Dear! You're being joshed.

NICK *(Cold)*

I'm aware of that.
(A brief, awkward silence)

GEORGE *(Truly)*

I *am* sorry.

(NICK *nods condescending forgiveness*)

GEORGE

What it is, actually, is it's a pictorial representation of the order of Martha's mind.

MARTHA

Ha, ha, ha, HA! Make the kids a drink, George. What do you want, kids? What do you want to drink, hunh?

NICK

Honey? What would you like?

HONEY

I don't know, dear . . . A little brandy, maybe. "Never mix—never worry." *(She giggles)*

GEORGE

Brandy? Just brandy? Simple; simple. *(Moves to the portable bar)* What about you . . . uh . . .

NICK

Bourbon on the rocks, if you don't mind.

GEORGE *(As he makes drinks)*

Mind? No, I don't mind. I don't think I mind. Martha? Rubbing alcohol for you?

MARTHA

Sure. "Never mix—never worry."

GEORGE

Martha's tastes in liquor have come down . . . simplified over the years . . . crystallized. Back when I was courting Martha—well, I don't know if that's exactly the right word for it—but back when I was courting Martha . . .

MARTHA *(Cheerfully)*

Screw, sweetie!

GEORGE

(Returning with HONEY *and* NICK's *drinks)*

At any rate, back when I was courting Martha, she'd order the damnedest things! You wouldn't believe it! We'd go into a bar . . . you know, a *bar* . . . a whiskey, beer, and bourbon *bar* . . . and what she'd do would be, she'd screw up her face, think real hard, and come up with . . . brandy Alexanders, creme de cacao frappes, gimlets, flaming punch bowls . . . seven-layer liqueur things.

MARTHA

They were good . . . I liked them.

GEORGE

Real lady-like little drinkies.

MARTHA

Hey, where's my rubbing alcohol?

GEORGE

(Returning to the portable bar)

But the years have brought to Martha a sense of essentials . . . the knowledge that cream is for coffee, lime juice for pies . . . and alcohol *(Brings* MARTHA *her drink)* pure and simple . . . here you are, angel . . . for the pure and simple. *(Raises his glass)* For the mind's blind eye, the heart's ease, and the liver's craw. Down the hatch, all.

MARTHA *(To them all)*

Cheers, dears. *(They all drink)* You have a poetic nature, George . . . a Dylan Thomas-y quality that gets me right where I live.

GEORGE

Vulgar girl! With guests here!

MARTHA

Ha, ha ha, HA! *(To* HONEY *and* NICK) Hey; hey!

(Sings, conducts with her drink in her hand.
HONEY *joins in toward the end)*

Who's afraid of Virginia Woolf,
             Virginia Woolf,
             Virginia Woolf,
Who's afraid of Virginia Woolf . . .

*(*MARTHA *and* HONEY *laugh;* NICK *smiles)*

HONEY

Oh, wasn't that funny? That was so funny . . .

NICK *(Snapping to)*

Yes . . . yes, it was.

MARTHA

I thought I'd bust a gut; I really did. . . . I really thought I'd bust a gut laughing. George didn't like it . . . George didn't think it was funny at all.

GEORGE

Lord, Martha, do we have to go through this again?

MARTHA

I'm trying to shame you into a sense of humor, angel, that's all.

GEORGE

(Overpatiently, to HONEY *and* NICK*)*

Martha didn't think I laughed loud enough. Martha thinks that unless . . . as she demurely puts it . . . that unless you "bust a gut" you aren't amused. You know? Unless you carry on like a hyena you aren't having any fun.

HONEY

Well, I certainly had fun . . . it was a *wonderful* party.

NICK

(Attempting enthusiasm)

Yes . . . it certainly was.

HONEY *(To* MARTHA*)*

And your father! Oh! He is so marvelous!

NICK *(As above)*

Yes . . . yes, he is.

HONEY

Oh, I tell you.

MARTHA *(Genuinely proud)*

He's quite a guy, isn't he? Quite a guy.

GEORGE *(at* NICK*)*

And you'd better believe it!

HONEY *(Admonishing* GEORGE*)*

Ohhhhhhhhh! He's a wonderful man.

GEORGE

I'm not trying to tear him down. He's a god, we all know that.

MARTHA

You lay off my father!

GEORGE

Yes, love. (To NICK) All I mean is . . . when you've had as many of these faculty parties as I have . . .

NICK

(Killing the attempted rapport)

I rather appreciated it. I mean, aside from enjoying it, I appreciated it. You know, when you're new at a place.

*(*GEORGE *eyes him suspiciously)*

Meeting everyone, getting introduced around . . . getting to know some of the men. . . . When I was teaching in Kansas . . .

HONEY

You won't believe it, but we had to make our way all by *ourselves* . . . isn't that right, dear?

NICK

Yes, it is. . . . We . . .

HONEY

. . . We had to make our own way. . . . I had to go up to wives . . . in the library, or at the supermarket . . . and say, "Hello, I'm new here . . . you must be Mrs. So-and-so, Doctor So-and-so's wife." It really wasn't very nice at all.

MARTHA

Well, *Daddy* knows how to run things.

NICK

(Not enough enthusiasm)
He's a remarkable man.

MARTHA

You bet your sweet life.

GEORGE

(To NICK . . . *a confidence, but not whispered)*
Let me tell you a secret, baby. There are easier things in the world, if you happen to be teaching at a university, there are easier things than being married to the daughter of the president of that university. There are easier things in this world.

MARTHA

(Loud . . . to no one in particular)
It *should* be an extraordinary opportunity . . . for *some* men it would be the chance of a lifetime!

GEORGE

(To NICK . . . *a solemn wink)*
There are, believe me, easier things in this world.

NICK

Well, I can understand how it might make for some . . . awkwardness, perhaps . . . conceivably, but . . .

MARTHA

Some men would give their right arm for the chance!

GEORGE *(Quietly)*
Alas, Martha, in reality it works out that the sacrifice is usually of a somewhat more private portion of the anatomy.

MARTHA

(A snarl of dismissal and contempt)
NYYYYAAAAHHHHH!

HONEY *(Rising quickly)*
I wonder if you could show me where the . . . *(Her voice trails off)*

GEORGE

(To MARTHA, *indicating* HONEY*)*
Martha . . .

NICK *(To* HONEY*)*
Are you all right?

HONEY

Of course, dear. I want to . . . put some powder on my nose.

GEORGE

(As MARTHA *is not getting up)*
Martha, won't you show her where we keep the . . . euphemism?

MARTHA

Hm? What? Oh! Sure! *(Rises)* I'm sorry, c'mon. I want to show you the
house.

HONEY

I think I'd like to . . .

MARTHA

. . . wash up? Sure . . . c'mon with me. *(Takes* HONEY *by the arm. To the
men)* You two do some men talk for a while.

HONEY *(To* NICK*)*
We'll be back, dear.

MARTHA *(To* GEORGE*)*
Honestly, George, you burn me up!

GEORGE *(Happily)*
All right.

MARTHA

You really do, George.

GEORGE

O.K. Martha . . . O.K. Just . . . trot along.

MARTHA

You really do.

GEORGE

O.K. O.K. Vanish.

MARTHA

(Practically dragging HONEY *out with her)* C'mon . . .

GEORGE

Vanish. *(The women have gone)* So? What'll it be?

NICK

Oh, I don't know . . . I'll stick to bourbon, I guess.

GEORGE

(Takes NICK's *glass, goes to portable bar)*
That what you were drinking over at Parnassus?

NICK

Over at . . .?

GEORGE

Parnassus.

NICK

I don't understand . . .

GEORGE

Skip it. *(Hands him his drink)* One bourbon.

NICK

Thanks.

GEORGE

It's just a private joke between li'l ol' Martha and me. *(They sit)* So?
(Pause) So . . . you're in the math department, eh?

NICK

No . . . uh, no.

GEORGE

Martha said you were. I think that's what she said. *(Not too friendly)* What
made you decide to be a teacher?

NICK

Oh . . . well, the same things that . . . uh . . . motivated you, I imagine.

GEORGE

What were they?

NICK *(Formal)*

Pardon?

GEORGE

I said, what were they? What were the things that motivated me?

NICK *(Laughing uneasily)*

Well . . . I'm sure I don't know.

GEORGE

You just finished saying that the things that motivated you were the same things that motivated me.

NICK *(With a little pique)*

I said I *imagined* they were.

GEORGE

Oh. *(Off-hand)* Did you? *(Pause)* Well. . . . *(Pause)* You like it here?

NICK *(Looking about the room)*

Yes . . . it's . . . it's fine.

GEORGE

I mean the University.

NICK

Oh. . . . I thought you meant . . .

GEORGE

Yes . . . I can see you did. *(Pause)* I meant the University.

NICK

Well, I . . . I like it . . . fine. *(As* GEORGE *just stares at him)* Just fine. *(Same)* You . . . you've been here quite a long time, haven't you?

GEORGE

(Absently, as if he had not heard) What? Oh . . . yes. Ever since I married . . . uh, what's-her-name . . . uh, Martha. Even before that. *(Pause)* Forever. *(To* himself*)* Dashed hopes, and good intentions, Good, better, best, bested. *(Back to* NICK*)* How do you like that for a declension, young man? Eh?

NICK

Sir, I'm sorry if we . . .

GEORGE

(With an edge in his voice)

You didn't answer my question.

NICK

Sir?

GEORGE

Don't you condescend to me! *(Toying with him)* I asked you how you liked that for a declension: Good; better; best, bested. Hm? Well?

NICK *(With some distaste)*

I really don't know what to say.

GEORGE

(Feigned incredulousness)
You really don't know what to *say?*

NICK *(Snapping it out)*
All right . . . what do you want me to say? Do you want me to say it's funny, so you can contradict me and say it's sad? Or do you want me to say it's sad so you can turn around and say no, it's funny. You can play that damn little game any way you want to, you know!

GEORGE *(Feigned awe)*
Very good! Very good!

NICK

(Even angrier than before)
And when my wife comes back, I think we'll just . . .

GEORGE *(Sincere)*
Now, now . . . calm down, my boy. Just . . . calm down. *(Pause)* All right? *(Pause)* You want another drink? Here, give me your glass.

NICK
I still have one. I do think that when my wife comes downstairs . . .

GEORGE
Here . . . I'll freshen it. Give me your glass. *(Takes it)*

NICK
What I mean is . . . you two . . . you and your wife . . . seem to be having *some* sort of a . . .

GEORGE
Martha and I are having . . . nothing. Martha and I are merely . . . exercising . . . that's all . . . we're merely walking what's left of our wits. Don't pay any attention to it.

NICK *(Undecided)*
Still . . .

GEORGE

(An abrupt change of pace)
Well, now . . . let's sit down and talk, hunh?

NICK *(Cool again)*
It's just that I don't like to . . . become involved . . . *(An afterthought)* uh . . . in other people's affairs.

GEORGE *(Comforting a child)*
Well, you'll get over that . . . small college and all. Musical beds is the faculty sport around here.

NICK

Sir?

GEORGE

I said, musical beds is the faculty . . . Never mind. I wish you wouldn't go "Sir" like that . . . not with the question mark at the end of it. You know? Sir? I know it's meant to be a sign of respect for your *(Winces)* elders . . . but . . . uh . . . the way you do it . . . uh . . . Sir? . . . Madam?

NICK

(With a small, noncommittal smile)
No disrespect intended.

GEORGE

How old *are* you?

NICK

Twenty-eight.

GEORGE

I'm forty something. *(Waits for reaction . . . gets none)* Aren't you surprised? I mean . . . don't I look older? Doesn't this . . . *gray* quality suggest the fifties? Don't I sort of fade into backgrounds . . . get lost in the cigarette smoke? Hunh?

NICK

(Looking around for an ash tray)
I think you look . . . fine.

GEORGE

I've always been lean . . . I haven't put on five pounds since I was your age. I don't have a paunch, either. . . . What I've got . . . I've got this little distension just below the belt . . . but it's hard . . . It's not soft flesh. I use the handball courts. How much do *you* weigh?

NICK

I . . .

GEORGE

Hundred and fifty-five, sixty . . . something like that? Do you play handball?

NICK

Well, yes . . . no . . . I mean, not very well.

GEORGE

Well, then . . . we shall play some time. Martha is a hundred and eight . . . years *old*. She weighs somewhat more than that. How old is *your* wife?

NICK

(A little bewildered)
She's twenty-six.

GEORGE

Martha is a remarkable woman. I would imagine she weighs around a hundred and ten.

NICK

Your . . . wife . . . weighs . . . ?

GEORGE

No, no, my boy. Yours! *Your* wife. My wife is Martha.

NICK

Yes . . . I know.

GEORGE

If you were married to Martha you would know what it means. *(Pause)* But then, if I were married to your wife I would know what that means, too . . . wouldn't I?

NICK *(After a pause)*
Yes.

GEORGE

Martha says you're in the Math Department, or something.

NICK

(As if for the hundredth time)
No . . . I'm not.

GEORGE

Martha is seldom mistaken . . . maybe you *should* be in the Math Department, or something.

NICK

I'm a biologist. I'm in the Biology Department.

GEORGE

(After a pause)
Oh. *(Then, as if remembering something)* OH!

NICK

Sir?

GEORGE

You're the one! You're the one's going to make all that trouble . . . making everyone the same, rearranging the chromozones, or whatever it is. Isn't that right?

NICK *(With that small smile)*

Not exactly: chromo*somes*.

GEORGE

I'm very mistrustful. Do you believe . . . *(Shifting in his chair)* . . . do you believe that people learn nothing from history? Not that there is nothing to learn, mind you, but that people learn nothing? I am in the History Department.

NICK

Well . . .

GEORGE

I am a Doctor. A.B. . . . M.A. . . . PH.D. . . . ABMAPHID! Abmaphid has been variously described as a wasting disease of the frontal lobes, and as a wonder drug. It is actually both. I'm really very mistrustful. Biology, hunh?

(NICK *does not answer . . . nods . . . looks*)

I read somewhere that science fiction is really not fiction at all . . . that you people are rearranging my genes, so that everyone will be like everyone else. Now, I won't have that! It would be a . . . shame. I mean . . . look at me! Is it really such a good idea . . . if everyone was forty something and looked fifty-five? You didn't answer my question about history.

NICK

This genetic business you're talking about . . .

GEORGE

Oh, that. *(Dismisses it with a wave of his hand)* That's very upsetting . . . very . . . disappointing. But history is a great deal more . . . disappointing. I am in the History Department.

NICK

Yes . . . you told me.

GEORGE

I know I told you. . . . I shall probably tell you several more times. Martha tells me often, that I am *in* the History Department . . . as opposed to *being* the History Department . . . in the sense of *running* the History Department. I do not run the History Department.

NICK

Well, I don't run the Biology Department.

GEORGE

You're twenty-one!

NICK

Twenty-eight.

GEORGE

Twenty-eight! Perhaps when you're forty something and look fifty-five, you will run the History Department . . .

NICK

. . . Biology . . .

GEORGE

. . . the Biology Department. I *did* run the History Department, for four years, during the war, but that was because everybody was away. Then . . . everybody came back . . . because nobody got killed. That's New England for you. Isn't that amazing? Not one single man in this whole place got his head shot off. That's pretty irrational. *(Broods)* Your wife *doesn't* have any hips . . . has she . . . does she?

NICK

What?

GEORGE

I don't mean to suggest that I'm hip-happy. . . . I'm not one of those thirty-six, twenty-two, seventy-eight men. Nosiree . . . not me. Everything in proportion. I was implying that your wife is . . . slim-hipped.

NICK

Yes . . . she is.

GEORGE

(Looking at the ceiling)
What are they *doing* up there? I assume that's where they are.

NICK *(False heartiness)*

You know women.

GEORGE

(Gives NICK *a long stare, of feigned incredulity . . . then his attention moves)*
Not one son-of-a-bitch got killed. Of course, nobody bombed Washington. No . . . that's not fair. You have any kids?

NICK

Uh . . . no . . . not yet. *(Pause)* You?

GEORGE

(A kind of challenge)
That's for me to know and you to find out.

NICK

Indeed?

GEORGE

No kids, hunh?

NICK

Not yet.

GEORGE

People do . . . uh . . . have kids. That's what I meant about history. You people are going to make them in test tubes, aren't you? You biologists.
Babies. Then the rest of us . . . them as wants to . . . can screw to their
heart's content.

(NICK, *who can think of nothing better to do, laughs mildly*)

But you *are* going to have kids . . . anyway. In spite of history.

NICK *(Hedging)*

Yes . . . certainly. We . . . want to wait . . . a little until we're settled.

GEORGE

And this . . . *(With a handsweep taking in not only the room, the house, but
the whole countryside)* . . . this is your heart's content—Illyria . . . Penguin
Island . . . Gomorrah. . . . You think you're going to be happy here in New
Carthage, eh?

NICK *(A little defensively)*

I hope we'll stay here.

GEORGE

And every definition has its boundaries, eh? Well, it isn't a bad college, I
guess. I mean . . . it'll do. It isn't M.I.T. . . . it isn't U.C.L.A. . . . it isn't the
Sorbonne . . . or Moscow U. either, for that matter.

NICK

I don't mean . . . forever.

GEORGE

Well, don't you let that get bandied about. The old man wouldn't like it.
Martha's father expects loyalty and devotion out of his . . . staff. I was
going to use another word. Martha's father expects his . . . staff . . . to
cling to the walls of this place, like the ivy . . . to come here and grow
old . . . to fall in the line of service. One man, a professor of Latin and
Elocution, actually fell in the cafeteria line, one lunch. He was buried,
as many of us have been, and as many more of us will be, under the
shrubbery around the chapel. It is said . . . and I have no reason to doubt
it . . . that we make excellent fertilizer. But the old man is not going to
be buried under the shrubbery . . . the old man is not going to die.
Martha's father has the staying power of one of those Micronesian tor-
toises. There are rumors . . . which you must not breathe in front of
Martha, for she foams at the mouth . . . that the old man, her father, is
over two hundred years old. There is probably an irony involved in this,

but I am not drunk enough to figure out what it is. How many kids you going to have?

NICK

I . . . I don't know. . . . My wife is . . .

GEORGE

Slim-hipped. *(Rises)* Have a drink.

NICK

Yes.

GEORGE

MARTHA! *(No answer)* DAMN IT! *(To* NICK*)* You asked me if I knew women. . . . Well, one of the things I do *not* know about them is what they talk about while the men are talking. *(Vaguely)* I must find out some time.

MARTHA'S VOICE

WHADD'YA WANT?

GEORGE *(To* NICK*)*

Isn't that a wonderful sound? What I mean is . . . what do you think they really *talk* about . . . or don't you care?

NICK

Themselves, I would imagine.

MARTHA'S VOICE

GEORGE?

GEORGE *(To* NICK*)*

Do you find women . . . puzzling?

NICK

Well . . . yes and no.

GEORGE

(With a knowing nod)
Unh-hunh. *(Moves toward the hall, almost bumps into* HONEY, *re-entering)* Oh! Well, here's one of you, at least.

    *(*HONEY *moves toward* NICK. GEORGE *goes to the hall)*

HONEY *(To* GEORGE*)*

She'll be right down. *(To* NICK*)* You must see this house, dear . . . this is such a wonderful old house.

NICK

Yes, I . . .

GEORGE

MARTHA!

MARTHA'S VOICE
FOR CHRIST'S SAKE, HANG ON A MINUTE, WILL YOU?

HONEY (*To* GEORGE)
She'll be right down . . . she's changing.

GEORGE (*Incredulous*)
She's *what?* She's changing?

HONEY
Yes.

GEORGE
Her clothes?

HONEY
Her dress.

GEORGE (*Suspicious*)
Why?

HONEY
(*With a nervous little laugh*)
Why, I imagine she wants to be . . . comfortable.

GEORGE
(*With a threatening look toward the hall*) Oh she does, does she?

HONEY
Well, heavens, I should think . . .

GEORGE
YOU DON'T KNOW!

NICK
(*As* HONEY *starts*)
You feel all right?

HONEY
(*Reassuring, but with the echo of a whine. A long-practiced tone*)
Oh, yes, dear . . . perfectly fine.

GEORGE
(*Fuming . . . to himself*)
So she wants to be comfortable, does she? Well, we'll see about that.

HONEY (*To* GEORGE, *brightly*)
I didn't know until just a minute ago that you had a *son.*

GEORGE

(Wheeling, as if struck from behind)
WHAT?

HONEY

A son! I hadn't known.

NICK

You to know and me to find out. Well, he must be quite a big . . .

HONEY

Twenty-one . . . twenty-one tomorrow . . . tomorrow's his birthday.

NICK *(A victorious smile)*

Well!

GEORGE *(To* HONEY*)*

She told you about him?

HONEY *(Flustered)*

Well, *yes*. Well, I mean . . .

GEORGE *(Nailing it down)*

She told you about him.

HONEY *(A nervous giggle)*

Yes.

GEORGE *(Strangely)*

You say she's changing?

HONEY

Yes . . .

GEORGE

And she mentioned . . . ?

HONEY

(Cheerful, but a little puzzled)
. . . your son's birthday . . . yes.

GEORGE

(More or less to himself)
O.K., Martha . . . O.K.

NICK

You look pale, Honey. Do you want a . . . ?

HONEY

Yes, dear . . . a little more brandy, maybe. Just a drop.

GEORGE

O.K., Martha.

NICK

May I use the . . . uh . . . bar?

GEORGE

Hm? Oh, yes . . . yes . . . by all means. Drink away . . . you'll need it as the years go on. *(For* MARTHA, *as if she were in the room)* You goddamn destructive . . .

HONEY *(To cover)*

What time is it, dear?

NICK

Two-thirty.

HONEY

Oh, it's so late . . . we *should* be getting home.

GEORGE

(Nastily, but he is so preoccupied he hardly notices his own tone)
For what? You keeping the babysitter up, or something?

NICK

(Almost a warning)
I told you we didn't have children.

GEORGE

Hm? *(Realizing)* Oh, I'm sorry. I wasn't even listening . . . or thinking . . . *(With a flick of his hand)* . . . whichever one applies.

NICK *(Softly, to* HONEY*)*

We'll go in a little while.

GEORGE *(Driving)*

Oh no, now . . . you mustn't. Martha is changing . . . and Martha is not changing for *me*. Martha hasn't changed for *me* in years. If Martha is changing, it means we'll be here for . . . days. You are being accorded an honor, and you must not forget that Martha is the daughter of our beloved boss. She is his . . . right ball, you might say.

NICK

You might not understand this . . . but I wish you wouldn't talk that way in front of my wife.

HONEY

Oh, now . . .

GEORGE *(Incredulous)*

Really? Well, you're quite right. . . . We'll leave that sort of talk to Martha.

MARTHA *(Entering)*

What sort of talk?

(MARTHA *has changed her clothes, and she looks, now, more com-*
fortable and . . . and this is most important . . . most voluptuous)

GEORGE

There you are, my pet.

NICK *(Impressed; rising)*

Well, now . . .

GEORGE

Why, Martha . . . your Sunday chapel dress!

HONEY *(Slightly disapproving)*

Oh, that's most attractive.

MARTHA *(Showing off)*

You like it? Good! *(To* GEORGE) What the hell do you mean screaming up
the stairs at me like that?

GEORGE

We got lonely, darling . . . we got lonely for the soft purr of your little voice.

MARTHA

(Deciding not to rise to it)

Oh. Well, then, you just trot over to the barie-poo . . .

GEORGE

(Taking the tone from her)

. . . and make your little mommy a gweat big dwink.

MARTHA *(Giggles)*

That's right. *(To* NICK) Well, did you two have a nice little talk? You men
solve the problems of the world, as usual?

NICK

Well, no, we . . .

GEORGE *(Quickly)*

What we did, actually, if you really want to know, what we did actually is
try to figure out what you two were talking about.

(HONEY *giggles;* MARTHA *laughs)*

MARTHA *(To* HONEY)

Aren't they something? Aren't these . . . *(Cheerfully disdainful)* . . .
men the absolute end? *(To* GEORGE) Why didn't you sneak upstairs and
listen in?

GEORGE

Oh, I wouldn't have *listened*, Martha. . . . I would have *peeked*.

(HONEY *giggles;* MARTHA *laughs*)

NICK

(*To* GEORGE, *with false heartiness*)

It's a conspiracy.

GEORGE

And now we'll never know. Shucks!

MARTHA

(*To* NICK, *as* HONEY *beams*)

Hey, you must be quite a boy, getting your Masters when you were . . . what? . . . twelve? You hear that, George?

NICK

Twelve-and-a-half, actually. No, nineteen really. (*To* HONEY) Honey, you needn't have mentioned that. It . . .

HONEY

Ohhhh . . . I'm *proud* of you. . . .

GEORGE (*Seriously, if sadly*)

That's very . . . impressive.

MARTHA (*Aggressively*)

You're damned right!

GEORGE (*Between his teeth*)

I said I was impressed, Martha. I'm beside myself with jealousy. What do you want me to do, throw up? (*To* NICK) That really is very impressive. (*To* HONEY) You should be right proud.

HONEY (*Coy*)

Oh, he's a pretty nice fella.

GEORGE (*To* NICK)

I wouldn't be surprised if you *did* take over the History Department one of these days.

NICK

The Biology Department.

GEORGE

The *Biology* Department . . . of course. I seem preoccupied with history. Oh! What a remark. (*He strikes a pose, his hand over his heart, his head raised, his voice stentorian*) "I am preoccupied with history."

MARTHA

(As HONEY *and* NICK *chuckle)*

Ha, ha, ha, HA!

GEORGE *(With some disgust)*

I think I'll make *myself* a drink.

MARTHA

George is not preoccupied with *history*. . . . George is preoccupied with the *History Department*. George is preoccupied with the History Department because . . .

GEORGE

. . . because he is *not* the History Department, but is only *in* the History Department. We know, Martha . . . we went all through it while you were upstairs . . . getting up. There's no need to go through it again.

MARTHA

That's right, baby . . . keep it clean. *(To the others)* George is bogged down in the History Department. He's an old bog in the History Department, that's what George is. A bog. . . . A fen. . . . A.G.D. swamp. Ha, ha, ha HA! A swamp! Hey, swamp! Hey SWAMPY!

GEORGE

(With a great effort controls himself . . . then, as if she had said nothing more than "George, dear" . . .)

Yes, Martha? Can I get you something?

MARTHA *(Amused at his game)*

Well . . . uh . . . sure, you can light my cigarette, if you're of a mind to.

GEORGE

(Considers, then moves off)

No . . . there are limits. I mean, man can put up with only so much without he descends a rung or two on the old evolutionary ladder . . . *(Now a quick aside to* NICK*)* . . . which is up your line . . . *(Then back to* MARTHA*)* . . . sinks, Martha, and it's a funny ladder . . . you can't reverse yourself . . . start back up once you're descending.

*(*MARTHA *blows him an arrogant kiss)*

Now . . . I'll hold your hand when it's dark and you're afraid of the bogey man, and I'll tote your gin bottles out after midnight, so no one'll see . . . but I will not light your cigarette. And that, as they say, is that.

(Brief silence)

MARTHA *(Under her breath)*

Jesus! *(Then, immediately, to* NICK*)* Hey, you played football, hunh?

HONEY

(As NICK *seems sunk in thought)*

Dear . . .

NICK

Oh! Oh, yes . . . I was a . . . quarterback . . . but I was much more . . . adept . . . at boxing, really.

MARTHA *(With great enthusiasm)*

BOXING! You hear that, George?

GEORGE *(Resignedly)*

Yes, Martha.

MARTHA

(To NICK, *with peculiar intensity and enthusiasm)*

You musta been pretty good at it . . . I mean, you don't look like you got hit in the face at all.

HONEY *(Proudly)*

He was intercollegiate state middleweight champion.

NICK *(Embarrassed)*

Honey . . .

HONEY

Well, you were.

MARTHA

You look like you still got a pretty good body *now*, too . . . is that right? Have you?

GEORGE *(Intensely)*

Martha . . . decency forbids . . .

MARTHA

(To GEORGE . . . *still staring at* NICK, *though)*

SHUT UP! *(Now, back to* NICK) Well, have you? Have you kept your body?

NICK

(Unself-conscious . . . almost encouraging her)

It's still pretty good. I work out.

MARTHA *(With a half-smile)*

Do you!

NICK

Yeah.

HONEY

Oh, yes . . . he has a very . . . firm body.

MARTHA

(Still with that smile . . . a private communication with NICK*)*
Have you! Oh, I think that's very nice.

NICK

(Narcissistic, but not directly for MARTHA*)*
Well, you never know . . . *(shrugs)* . . . you know . . . once you have it . . .

MARTHA

. . . you never know when it's going to come in handy.

NICK

I was going to say . . . why give it up until you have to.

MARTHA

I couldn't agree with you more.
   *(They both smile, and there is a rapport of some unformed sort
   established)*
I couldn't agree with you more.

GEORGE

Martha, your obscenity is more than . . .

MARTHA

George, here, doesn't cotton much to body talk . . . do you sweetheart?
(No reply) George isn't too happy when we get to muscle. You know . . .
flat bellies, pectorals . . .

GEORGE *(To* HONEY*)*
Would you like to take a walk around the garden?

HONEY *(Chiding)*
Oh, now . . .

GEORGE *(Incredulous)*
You're amused? *(Shrugs)* All right.

MARTHA

Paunchy over there isn't too happy when the conversation moves to muscle. How much do you weigh?

NICK

A hundred and sixty-five, a hundred and . . .

MARTHA

Still at the old middleweight limit, eh? That's pretty good.
   (Swings around)
Hey George, tell 'em about the boxing match *we* had.

GEORGE

(Slamming his drink down, moving toward the hall)

Christ!

MARTHA

George! Tell 'em about it!

GEORGE

(With a sick look on his face)

You tell them, Martha. You're good at it.

(Exits)

HONEY

Is he . . . all right?

MARTHA *(Laughs)*

Him? Oh, sure. George and I had this boxing match . . . Oh, Lord, twenty years ago . . . a couple of years after we were married.

NICK

A boxing match? The two of you?

HONEY

Really?

MARTHA

Yup . . . the two of us . . . really.

HONEY

(With a little shivery giggle of anticipation)

I can't imagine it.

MARTHA

Well, like I say, it was twenty years ago, and it wasn't in a ring, or anything like that, you know what I mean. It was wartime, and Daddy was on this physical fitness kick . . . Daddy's always admired physical fitness . . . says a man is only part brain . . . he has a body, too, and it's his responsibility to keep both of them up . . . you know?

NICK

Unh-hunh.

MARTHA

Says the brain can't work unless the body's working, too.

NICK

Well, that's not exactly so . . .

MARTHA

Well, maybe that *isn't* what he says . . . something like it. *But* . . . it was wartime, and Daddy got the idea all the men should learn how to box . . .

self-defense. I suppose the idea was if the Germans landed on the coast, or something, the whole faculty'd go out and punch 'em to death. . . . I don't know.

NICK

It was probably more the principle of the thing.

MARTHA

No kidding. Anyway, so Daddy had a couple of us over one Sunday and we went out in the back, and Daddy put on the gloves himself. Daddy's a strong man. . . . Well, *you* know.

NICK

Yes . . . yes.

MARTHA

And he asked George to box with him. Aaaaannnnd . . . George didn't *want* to . . . probably something about not wanting to bloody-up his meal ticket . . .

NICK

Unh-hunh.

MARTHA

. . . Anyway, George said he didn't want to, and Daddy was saying, "Come on, young man . . . what sort of son-in-law *are* you?" . . . and stuff like that.

NICK

Yeah.

MARTHA

So, while this was going on . . . I don't know why I *did* it . . . I got into a pair of gloves myself . . . you know, I didn't lace 'em up, or anything . . . and I snuck up behind George, just kidding, and I yelled "Hey George!" and at the same time I let go sort of a roundhouse right . . . just kidding, you know?

NICK

Unh-hunh.

MARTHA

. . . and George wheeled around real quick, and he caught it right in the jaw . . . Pow! (NICK *laughs*) I hadn't meant it . . . honestly. Anyway . . . POW! Right in the jaw . . . and he was off balance . . . he must have been . . . and he stumbled back a few steps, and then, CRASH, he landed . . . flat . . . in a huckleberry bush!

(NICK *laughs.* HONEY *goes tsk, tsk, tsk, tsk, and shakes her head*)
It was awful, really. It was funny, but it was awful.

(*She thinks, gives a muffled laugh in rueful contemplation of the incident*)

I think it's colored our whole life. Really I do! It's an excuse, anyway.

(GEORGE *enters now, his hands behind his back. No one sees him*)

It's what he uses for being bogged down, anyway . . . why he hasn't *gone* anywhere.

(GEORGE *advances.* HONEY *sees him*)

MARTHA

And it was an *accident* . . . a real, goddamn accident!

(GEORGE *takes from behind his back a short-barreled shotgun, and calmly aims it at the back of* MARTHA's *head.* HONEY *screams . . . rises.* NICK *rises, and, simultaneously,* MARTHA *turns her head to face* GEORGE. GEORGE *pulls the trigger*)

GEORGE

POW!!!

(*Pop! From the barrel of the gun blossoms a large red and yellow Chinese parasol.* HONEY *screams again, this time less, and mostly from relief and confusion*)

You're dead! Pow! You're dead!

NICK (*Laughing*)

Good Lord.

(HONEY *is beside herself.* MARTHA *laughs too . . . almost breaks down, her great laugh booming.* GEORGE *joins in the general laughter and confusion. It dies, eventually*)

HONEY

Oh! My goodness!

MARTHA (*Joyously*)

Where'd you get that, you bastard?

NICK

(*His hand out for the gun*)

Let me see that, will you?

(GEORGE *hands him the gun*)

HONEY

I've never been so frightened in my life! Never!

GEORGE

(*A trifle abstracted*)

Oh, I've had it awhile. Did you like that?

MARTHA (*Giggling*)

You bastard.

HONEY *(Wanting attention)*

I've *never* been so frightened . . . never.

NICK

This is quite a gadget.

GEORGE *(Leaning over MARTHA)*

You liked that, did you?

MARTHA

Yeah . . . that was pretty good. *(Softer)* C'mon . . . give me a kiss.

GEORGE

(Indicating NICK and HONEY)

Later, sweetie.

(But MARTHA will not be dissuaded. They kiss, GEORGE standing, leaning over MARTHA's chair. She takes his hand, places it on her stage-side breast. He breaks away)

Oh-ho! That's what you're after, is it? What are we going to have . . . blue games for the guests? Hunh? Hunh?

MARTHA *(Angry-hurt)*

You . . . prick!

GEORGE

(A Pyrrhic victory)

Everything in its place, Martha . . . everything in its own good time.

MARTHA

(An unspoken epithet)

You . . .

GEORGE

(Over to NICK, who still has the gun)

Here, let me show you . . . it goes back in, like this.

(Closes the parasol, reinserts it in the gun)

NICK

That's damn clever.

GEORGE *(Puts the gun down)*

Drinks now! Drinks for all!

(Takes NICK's glass without question . . . goes to MARTHA)

MARTHA *(Still angry-hurt)*

I'm not finished.

HONEY

(As GEORGE *puts out his hand for her glass)*

Oh, I think I need *something.*

(He takes her glass, moves back to the portable bar)

NICK

Is that Japanese?

GEORGE

Probably.

HONEY *(To* MARTHA*)*

I was never so frightened in my life. Weren't you frightened? Just for a second?

MARTHA

(Smothering her rage at GEORGE*)*

I don't remember.

HONEY

Ohhhh, now . . . I bet you were.

GEORGE

Did you really think I was going to kill you, Martha?

MARTHA *(Dripping contempt)*

You? . . . Kill me? . . . That's a laugh.

GEORGE

Well, now, I might . . . some day.

MARTHA

Fat chance.

NICK

(As GEORGE *hands him his drink)*

Where's the john?

GEORGE

Through the hall there . . . and down to your left.

HONEY

Don't you come back with any guns, or anything, now.

NICK *(Laughs)*

Oh, no.

MARTHA

You don't need any props, do you, baby?

NICK

Unh-unh.

MARTHA *(Suggestive)*

I'll bet not. No fake Jap gun for you, eh?

NICK

(Smiles at MARTHA. *Then, to* GEORGE, *indicating a side table near the hall)*

May I leave my drink here?

GEORGE

(As NICK *exits without waiting for a reply)*

Yeah . . . sure . . . why not? We've got half-filled glasses everywhere in the house, wherever Martha forgets she's left them . . . in the freezer, on the edge of the bathtub. . . . I even found one in the linen closet once.

MARTHA

(Amused in spite of herself)

You did not!

GEORGE

Yes I did.

MARTHA *(Ibid)*

You did *not!*

GEORGE

(Giving HONEY *her brandy)*

Yes I *did.* *(To* HONEY) Brandy doesn't give you a hangover?

HONEY

I never mix. And then, I don't drink very much, either.

GEORGE

(Grimaces behind her back)

Oh . . . that's good. Your . . . your husband was telling me all about the . . . chromosomes.

MARTHA *(Ugly)*

The what?

GEORGE

The chromosomes, Martha . . . the genes, or whatever they are. *(To* HONEY) You've got quite a . . . terrifying husband.

HONEY

(As if she's being joshed)

Ohhhhhhhhh . . .

GEORGE

No, really. He's quite terrifying, with his chromosomes, and all.

MARTHA

He's in the Math Department.

GEORGE

No, Martha . . . he's a biologist.

MARTHA *(Her voice rising)*

He's in the *Math* Department!

HONEY *(Timidly)*

Uh . . . biology.

MARTHA *(Unconvinced)*

Are you *sure?*

HONEY *(With a little giggle)*

Well, I ought to. *(Then as an afterthought)* Be.

MARTHA *(Grumpy)*

I suppose *so.* I don't know who said he was in the Math Department.

GEORGE

You did, Martha.

MARTHA

(By way of irritable explanation)

Well, I can't be expected to remember *everything.* I meet fifteen new teachers and their goddamn wives . . . present company outlawed, of course . . . (HONEY *nods, smiles sillily*) . . . and I'm supposed to remember *everything. (Pause)* So? He's a biologist. Good for him. Biology's even better. It's less . . . abstruse.

GEORGE

Abstract.

MARTHA

ABSTRUSE! In the sense of recondite. *(Sticks her tongue out at* GEORGE*)* Don't you tell me words. Biology's even better. It's . . . right at the *meat* of things.

(NICK *reenters)*

You're right at the meat of things, baby.

NICK

(Taking his drink from the side table)

Oh?

HONEY *(With that giggle)*

They thought you were in the Math Department.

NICK

Well, maybe I ought to be.

MARTHA

You stay right where you are . . . you stay right at the . . . *meat* of things.

GEORGE

You're obsessed with that phrase, Martha. . . . It's ugly.

MARTHA

(*Ignoring* GEORGE . . . *to* NICK)

You stay right there. (*Laughs*) Hell, you can take over the History
Department just as easy from there as anywhere else. God knows, *somebody's* going to take over the History Department, *some* day, and it ain't
going to be Georgie-boy, there . . . that's for sure. Are ya, swampy . . . are
ya, hunh?

GEORGE

In my mind, Martha, you are buried in cement, right up to your neck.
(MARTHA *giggles*) No . . . right up to your nose . . . that's much quieter.

MARTHA (*To* NICK)

Georgie-boy, here, says you're terrifying. Why are you terrifying?

NICK (*With a small smile*)

I didn't know I was.

HONEY (*A little thickly*)

It's because of your chromosomes, dear.

NICK

Oh, the chromosome business. . . .

MARTHA (*To* NICK)

What's all this about chromosomes?

NICK

Well, chromosomes are . . .

MARTHA

I know what chromosomes are, sweetie, I love 'em.

NICK

Oh . . . Well, then.

GEORGE

Martha eats them . . . for breakfast . . . she sprinkles them on her cereal.
(*To* MARTHA, *now*) It's very simple, Martha, this young man is working on
a system whereby chromosomes can be altered . . . well not all by himself—he probably has one or two co-conspirators—the genetic makeup of
a sperm cell changed, reordered . . . *to* order, actually . . . for hair and eye
color, stature, potency . . . I imagine . . . hairiness, features, health . . . and
mind. Most important . . . Mind. All imbalances will be corrected, sifted

out . . . Propensity for various diseases will be gone, longevity assured. We will have a race of men . . . test-tube-bred . . . incubator-born . . . superb and sublime.

MARTHA *(Impressed)*

Hunh!

HONEY

How exciting!

GEORGE

But! Everyone will tend to be rather the same. . . . Alike. Everyone . . . and I'm sure I'm not wrong here . . . will tend to look like this young man *here*.

MARTHA

That's not a bad idea.

NICK *(Impatient)*

All right, now . . .

GEORGE

It will, on the surface of it, be all rather pretty . . . quite jolly. But of course there will be a dank side to it, too. A certain amount of regulation will be necessary . . . uh . . . for the experiment to succeed. A certain number of sperm tubes will have to be cut.

MARTHA

Hunh! . . .

GEORGE

Millions upon millions of them . . . millions of tiny little slicing operations that will leave just the smallest scar, on the underside of the scrotum (MARTHA *laughs*) but which will assure the sterility of the imperfect . . . the ugly, the stupid . . . the . . . unfit.

NICK *(Grimly)*

Now look . . . !

GEORGE

. . . with this, we will have, in time, a race of glorious men.

MARTHA

Hunh!

GEORGE

I suspect we will not have much music, much painting, but we will have a civilization of men, smooth, blond, and right at the middleweight limit.

MARTHA

Awww . . .

GEORGE

. . . a race of scientists and mathematicians, each dedicated to and working for the greater glory of the super-civilization.

MARTHA

Goody.

GEORGE

There will be a certain . . . loss of liberty, I imagine, as a result of this experiment . . . but diversity will no longer be the goal. Cultures and races will eventually vanish . . . the ants will take over the world.

NICK

Are you finished?

GEORGE (*Ignoring him*)

And I, naturally, am rather opposed to all this. History, which is my field . . . history, of which I am one of the most famous bogs . . .

MARTHA

Ha, ha, HA!

GEORGE

. . . will lose its glorious variety and unpredictability. I, and with me the . . . the surprise, the multiplexity, the sea-changing rhythm of . . . history, will be eliminated. There will be order and constancy . . . and I am unalterably opposed to it. I will not give up Berlin!

MARTHA

You'll give up Berlin, sweetheart. You going to defend it with your paunch?

HONEY

I don't see what Berlin has to *do* with anything.

GEORGE

There is a saloon in West Berlin where the barstools are five feet high. And the earth . . . the floor . . . is . . . so . . . far . . . below you. I will not give up things like that. No . . . I won't. I will fight you, young man . . . one hand on my scrotum, to be sure . . . but with my free hand I will battle you to the death.

MARTHA (*Mocking, laughing*)

Bravo!

NICK (*To* GEORGE)

That's right. And I am going to be the wave of the future.

MARTHA

You bet you are, baby.

HONEY (*Quite drunk—to* NICK)

I don't see why you want to do all those things, dear. You never told me.

NICK (*Angry*)

Oh for God's sake!

HONEY (*Shocked*)

OH!

GEORGE

The most profound indication of a social malignancy . . . no sense of humor.
None of the monoliths could take a joke. Read history. I know something
about history.

NICK

(*To* GEORGE, *trying to make light of it all*)

You . . . you don't know much about science, do you?

GEORGE

I know something about history. I know when I'm being threatened.

MARTHA

(*Salaciously—to* NICK)

So, everyone's going to look like you, eh?

NICK

Oh, sure. I'm going to be a personal fucking machine!

MARTHA

Isn't that nice.

HONEY

(*Her hands over her ears*)

Dear, you mustn't . . . you mustn't . . . you mustn't.

NICK (*Impatiently*)

I'm sorry, Honey.

HONEY

Such language. It's . . .

NICK

I'm *sorry*. All right?

HONEY (*Pouting*)

Well . . . all right. (*Suddenly she giggles insanely, subsides. To* GEORGE) . . .
When is your son? (*Giggles again*)

GEORGE

What?

NICK (*Distastefully*)

Something about your son.

GEORGE

SON!

HONEY

When is . . . where is your son . . . coming home? *(Giggles)*

GEORGE

Ohhhh. *(Too formal)* Martha? When is our son coming home?

MARTHA

Never mind.

GEORGE

No, no . . . I want to know . . . you brought it out into the open. When is he coming home, Martha?

MARTHA

I said never mind. I'm sorry I brought it up.

GEORGE

Him up . . . not it. You brought *him* up. Well, more or less. When's the little bugger going to appear, hunh? I mean isn't tomorrow meant to be his birthday, or something?

MARTHA

I don't want to talk about it!

GEORGE *(Falsely innocent)*

But Martha . . .

MARTHA

I DON'T WANT TO TALK ABOUT IT!

GEORGE

I'll bet you don't. *(To* HONEY *and* NICK*)* Martha does not want to talk about it . . . him. Martha is sorry she brought it up . . . him.

HONEY *(Idiotically)*

When's the little bugger coming home? *(Giggles)*

NICK

Honey, don't you think you . . . ?

GEORGE

Yes, Martha . . . since you had the bad taste to bring the matter up in the first place . . . when *is* the little bugger coming home?

MARTHA

George talks disparagingly about the little bugger because . . . well, because he has problems.

GEORGE

The little bugger has problems? What problems has the little bugger got?

MARTHA

Not the little bugger . . . stop calling him that! You! You've got problems.

GEORGE (*Feigned disdain*)
I've never heard of anything more ridiculous in my life.

HONEY
Neither have I!

NICK
Honey . . .

MARTHA
George's biggest problem about the little . . . ha, ha, ha, HA! . . . about our son, about our great big son, is that deep down in the private-most pit of his gut, he's not completely sure it's his own kid.

GEORGE (*Deeply serious*)
My God, you're a wicked woman.

MARTHA
And I've told you a million times, baby . . . I wouldn't conceive with any-one but you . . . you know that, baby.

GEORGE
A deeply wicked person.

HONEY
(*Deep in drunken grief*)
My, my, my, my. Oh, my.

NICK
I'm not sure that this is a subject for . . .

GEORGE
Martha's lying. I want you to know that, right now. Martha's lying. (MARTHA *laughs*) There are very few things in this world that I *am* sure of . . . national boundaries, the level of the ocean, political allegiances, practical morality . . . none of these would I stake my stick on any more . . . but the one thing in this whole sinking world that I am sure of is my partnership, my chromosomological partnership in the . . . creation of our . . . blond-eyed, blue-haired . . . son.

HONEY
Oh, I'm so glad!

MARTHA
That was a very pretty speech, George.

GEORGE
Thank you, Martha.

MARTHA
You rose to the occasion . . . good. Real good.

HONEY

Well . . . real well.

NICK

Honey . . .

GEORGE

Martha knows . . . she knows better.

MARTHA *(Proudly)*

I know better. I been to college like everybody else.

GEORGE

Martha been to college. Martha been to a convent when she were a little twig of a thing, too.

MARTHA

And I was an atheist. *(Uncertainly)* I still am.

GEORGE

Not an atheist, Martha . . . a pagan. *(To* HONEY *and* NICK) Martha is the only true pagan on the Eastern Seaboard.
   (MARTHA *laughs*)

HONEY

Oh, that's nice. Isn't that nice, dear?

NICK *(Humoring her)*

Yes . . . wonderful.

GEORGE

And Martha paints blue circles around her things.

NICK

You do?

MARTHA

   (Defensively, for the joke's sake)
Sometimes. *(Beckoning)* You wanna see?

GEORGE *(Admonishing)*

Tut, tut, tut.

MARTHA

Tut, tut yourself . . . you old floozie!

HONEY

He's not a floozie . . . he can't be a floozie . . . you're a floozie.
   (Giggles)

MARTHA

   (Shaking a finger at HONEY)
Now you watch yourself!

HONEY (*Cheerfully*)

All right. I'd like a nipper of brandy, please.

NICK

Honey, I think you've had enough, now. . . .

GEORGE

Nonsense! Everybody's ready, I think. (*Takes glasses, etc.*)

HONEY (*Echoing* GEORGE)

Nonsense.

NICK (*Shrugging*)

O.K.

MARTHA (*To* GEORGE)

Our son does *not* have blue hair . . . or blue eyes, for that matter. He has green eyes . . . like me.

GEORGE

He has blue eyes, Martha.

MARTHA (*Determined*)

Green.

GEORGE (*Patronizing*)

Blue, Martha.

MARTHA (*Ugly*)

GREEN! (*To* HONEY *and* NICK) He has the loveliest green eyes . . . they aren't all flaked with brown and gray, you know . . . hazel . . . they're real green . . . deep, pure green eyes . . . like mine.

NICK (*Peers*)

Your eyes are . . . brown, aren't they?

MARTHA

GREEN! (*A little too fast*) Well, in some lights they *look* brown, but they're green. Not green like his . . . more hazel. George has watery blue eyes . . . milky blue.

GEORGE

Make up your mind, Martha.

MARTHA

I was giving you the benefit of the doubt. (*Now back to the others*) Daddy has green eyes, too.

GEORGE

He does not! Your father has tiny red eyes . . . like a white mouse. In fact, he *is* a white mouse.

MARTHA

You wouldn't dare say a thing like that if he was here! You're a coward!

GEORGE (*To* HONEY *and* NICK)

You know . . . that great shock of white hair, and those little beady red eyes . . . a great big white mouse.

MARTHA

George hates Daddy . . . not for anything Daddy's done to him, but for his own . . .

GEORGE

(*Nodding . . . finishing it for her*)

. . . inadequacies.

MARTHA

That's right. You hit it . . . right on the snout. (*Seeing* GEORGE *exiting*) Where do you think *you're* going?

GEORGE

We need some more booze, angel.

MARTHA

Oh. (*Pause*) So, go.

GEORGE (*Exiting*)

Thank you.

MARTHA

(*Seeing that* GEORGE *has gone*)

He's a good bartender . . . a good bar nurse. The S.O.B., he hates my father. You know that?

NICK

(*Trying to make light of it*)

Oh, come on.

MARTHA (*Offended*)

You think I'm kidding? You think I'm joking? I never joke . . . I don't have a sense of humor. (*Almost pouting*) I have a fine sense of the ridiculous, but no sense of humor. (*Affirmatively*) I have no sense of humor!

HONEY (*Happily*)

I haven't, either.

NICK (*Half-heartedly*)

Yes, you have, Honey . . . a quiet one.

HONEY (*Proudly*)

Thank you.

MARTHA

You want to know *why* the S.O.B. hates my father? You want me to tell you? All right. . . . I will now tell you why the S.O.B. hates my father.

HONEY
(Swinging to some sort of attention)
Oh, good!

MARTHA *(Sternly, to* HONEY*)*
Some people feed on the calamities of others.

HONEY *(Offended)*
They do not!

NICK
Honey . . .

MARTHA
All right! Shut up! Both of you! *(Pause)* All right, now. Mommy died early,
see, and I sort of grew up with Daddy. *(Pause—thinks)* . . . I went away to
school, and stuff, but I more or less grew up with him. Jesus, I admired
that guy! I worshipped him . . . I absolutely worshipped him. I still do. And
he was pretty fond of me, too . . . you know? We had a real . . . rapport
going . . . a real rapport.

NICK
Yeah, yeah.

MARTHA
And Daddy built this college . . . I mean, he built it up from what it was
. . . it's his whole life. He *is* the college.

NICK
Unh-hunh.

MARTHA
The college is him. You know what the endowment was when he took over,
and what it is *now?* You look it up some time.

NICK
I know . . . I read about it. . . .

MARTHA
Shut up and listen . . . (As *an afterthought)* . . . cutie. So after I got done
with college and stuff, I came back here and sort of . . . sat around, for a
while. I wasn't married, or anything. Wellllll, I'd *been* married . . . sort of
I . . . for a week, my sophomore year at Miss Muff's Academy for Young
Ladies . . . college. A kind of junior Lady Chatterly arrangement, as it
turned out . . . the marriage. (NICK *laughs)* He mowed the lawn at Miss
Muff's, sitting up there, all naked, on a big power mower, mowing away.
But Daddy and Miss Muff got together and put an end to that . . . real
quick . . . annulled . . . which is a laugh . . . because theoretically you can't
get an annulment if there's entrance. Ha! Anyway, so I was revirginized,
finished at Miss Muff's . . . where they had one less gardener's boy, and a

real shame, that was . . . and I came back here and sort of sat around for a while. I was hostess for Daddy and I took care of him . . . and it was . . . nice. It was very nice.

NICK

Yes . . . yes.

MARTHA

What do you mean, yes, yes? How would you know?

(NICK *shrugs helplessly*)

Lover.

(NICK *smiles a little*)

And I got the idea, about then, that I'd marry into the college . . . which didn't seem to be quite as stupid as it turned out. I mean, Daddy had a sense of history . . . of . . . continuation . . . Why don't you come over here and sit by me?

NICK

(*Indicating* HONEY, *who is barely with it*)

I . . . don't think I . . . should . . . I . . . .

MARTHA

Suit yourself. A sense of continuation . . . history . . . and he'd always had it in the back of his mind to . . . *groom* someone to take over . . . some time, when he quit. A succession . . . you know what I mean?

NICK

Yes, I do.

MARTHA

Which is natural enough. When you've made something, you want to pass it on, to somebody. So, I was sort of on the lookout, for . . . prospects with the new men. An heir-apparent. (*Laughs*) It wasn't *Daddy's* idea that I had to necessarily marry the guy. I mean, I wasn't the albatross . . . you didn't have to take me to get the prize, or anything like that. It was something *I* had in the back of *my* mind. And a lot of the new men were married . . . naturally.

NICK

Sure.

MARTHA

(*With a strange smile*)

Like you, baby.

HONEY

(*A mindless echo*)

Like you, baby.

MARTHA *(Ironically)*

But then George came along . . . along come George.

GEORGE

(Reentering, with liquor)

And along came George, bearing hooch. What are you doing now, Martha?

MARTHA *(Unfazed)*

I'm telling a story. Sit down . . . you'll learn something.

GEORGE

(Stays standing. Puts the liquor on the portable bar)

All rightie.

HONEY

You've come back!

GEORGE

That's right.

HONEY

Dear! He's come back!

NICK

Yes, I see . . . I see.

MARTHA

Where was I?

HONEY

I'm *so* glad.

NICK

Shhhhh.

HONEY *(Imitating him)*

Shhhhh.

MARTHA

Oh yeah. And along came George. That's right. WHO was young . . . intelligent . . . and . . . bushy-tailed, . . . and sort of cute . . . if you can imagine it . . .

GEORGE

. . . and younger than you . . .

MARTHA

. . . and younger than me . . .

GEORGE

. . . by six years . . .

MARTHA

. . . by six years. . . . It doesn't bother me, George. . . . And along he came, bright-eyed, into the History Department. And you know what I did, dumb cluck that I am? You know what I did? I fell for him.

HONEY *(Dreamy)*

Oh, that's nice.

GEORGE

Yes, she did. You should have seen it. She'd sit outside of my room, on the lawn, at night, and she'd howl and claw at the turf . . . I couldn't work.

MARTHA *(Laughs, really amused)*

I actually fell for him . . . it . . . that, there.

GEORGE

Martha's a Romantic at heart.

MARTHA

That I am. So, I actually fell for him. And the match seemed . . . practical, too. You know, Daddy was looking for someone to . . .

GEORGE

Just a minute, Martha . . .

MARTHA

. . . take over, some time, when he was ready to . . .

GEORGE *(Stony)*

Just a minute, Martha.

MARTHA

. . . retire, and so I thought . . .

GEORGE

STOP IT, MARTHA!

MARTHA *(Irritated)*

Whadda you want?

GEORGE *(Too patiently)*

I'd thought you were telling the story of our courtship, Martha . . . I didn't know you were going to start in on the other business.

MARTHA *(So-thereish)*

Well, I am!

GEORGE

I wouldn't, if I were you.

MARTHA

Oh . . . you wouldn't? Well, you're not!

GEORGE

Now, you've already sprung a leak about you-know-what . . .

MARTHA *(A duck)*

What? What?

GEORGE

. . . about the apple of our eye . . . the sprout . . . the little bugger . . . *(spits it out)* . . . our *son* . . . and if *you start* in on this other business, I warn you, Martha, it's going to make me angry.

MARTHA *(Laughing at him)*

Oh, it is, is it?

GEORGE

I warn you.

MARTHA *(Incredulous)*

You *what?*

GEORGE *(Very quietly)*

I warn you.

NICK

Do you really think we have to go through . . . ?

MARTHA

I stand warned! *(Pause . . . then, to* HONEY *and* NICK*)* So, anyway, I married the S.O.B., and I had it all planned out. . . . He was the groom . . . he was going to be groomed. He'd take over some day . . . first, he'd take over the History Department, and then, when Daddy retired, he'd take over the college . . . you know? That's the way it was supposed to be.

(To GEORGE, *who is at the portable bar with his back to her)*

You getting angry, baby? Hunh? *(Now back)* That's the way it was *supposed* to be. Very simple. And Daddy seemed to think it was a pretty good idea, too. For a while. Until he watched for a couple of years! *(To* GEORGE *again)* You getting angrier? *(Now back)* Until he watched for a couple of years and started thinking maybe it wasn't such a good idea after all . . . that maybe Georgie-boy didn't have the *stuff* . . . that he didn't have it in him!

GEORGE

(Still with his back to them all)

Stop it, Martha.

MARTHA *(Viciously triumphant)*

The hell I will! You see, George didn't have much . . . push . . . he wasn't particularly . . . aggressive. In fact he was sort of a . . . *(Spits the word at* GEORGE's *back)* . . . a FLOP! A great . . . big . . . fat . . . FLOP!

(CRASH! Immediately after FLOP! GEORGE *breaks a bottle against the portable bar and stands there, still with his back to them all, holding the remains of the bottle by the neck. There is a silence, with everyone frozen. Then . . .)*

GEORGE *(Almost crying)*

I said stop, Martha.

MARTHA

(After considering what course to take)

I hope that was an empty bottle, George. You don't want to waste good liquor . . . not on your salary.

(GEORGE *drops the broken bottle on the floor, not moving)*

Not on an Associate Professor's salary. *(To* NICK *and* HONEY) I mean, he'd be . . . no good . . . at trustees' dinners, fund raising. He didn't have any . . . personality, you know what I mean? Which was disappointing to Daddy, as you can imagine. So, here I am, stuck with this flop . . .

GEORGE *(Turning around)*

. . . don't go on, Martha. . . .

MARTHA

. . . this BOG in the History Department . . .

GEORGE

. . . don't, Martha, don't . . .

MARTHA	GEORGE
(Her voice rising to match his)	*(Under her, then covering, to drown her)*

. . . who's married to the President's daughter, who's expected to *be* somebody, not just some nobody, some bookworm, somebody who's so damn . . . contemplative, he can't make anything out of himself, somebody without the *guts* to make anybody proud of him . . . ALL RIGHT, GEORGE!	I said, don't. All right . . . all right: *(Sings)* Who's afraid of Virginia Woolf,
	          Virginia Woolf,
	          Virginia Woolf,
	Who's afraid of Virginia Woolf,
	early in the morning.

GEORGE *and* HONEY

(Who joins him drunkenly)

Who's afraid of Virginia Woolf,
          Virginia Woolf,
          Virginia Woolf . . . *(etc.}*

MARTHA

STOP IT!

(A brief silence)

HONEY
(Rising, moving toward the hall)
I'm going to be sick . . . I'm going to be sick . . . I'm going to vomit.
(Exits)

NICK *(Going after her)*
Oh, for God's sake!
(Exits)

MARTHA
(Going after them, looks back at GEORGE, *contemptuously)*
Jesus! *(Exits.* GEORGE *is alone on stage)*

CURTAIN

ACT TWO

WALPURGISNACHT

GEORGE, *by himself:* NICK *reenters.*

NICK *(After a silence)*
I . . . guess . . . she's all right. *(No answer)* She . . . really shouldn't drink. *(No answer)* She's . . . frail. *(No answer)* Uh . . . slim-hipped, as you'd have it. (GEORGE *smiles vaguely)* I'm really very sorry.

GEORGE *(Quietly)*
Where's my little yum yum? Where's Martha?

NICK
She's making coffee . . . in the kitchen. She . . . gets sick quite easily.

GEORGE *(Preoccupied)*
Martha? Oh no, Martha hasn't been sick a day in her life, unless you count the time she spends in the rest home. . . .

NICK *(He, too, quietly)*
No, no; *my* wife . . . *my* wife gets sick quite easily. Your wife is Martha.

GEORGE *(With some rue)*
Oh, yes . . . I know.

NICK *(A statement of fact)*
She doesn't really spend any time in a rest home.

GEORGE
Your wife?

NICK
No. Yours.

GEORGE
Oh! Mine. *(Pause)* No, no, she doesn't . . . *I* would; I mean if I were . . . her . . . she . . . *I* would. But I'm not . . . and so I don't. *(Pause)* I'd like to, though. It gets pretty bouncy around here sometimes.

NICK *(Coolly)*

Yes . . . I'm sure.

GEORGE

Well, you saw an example of it.

NICK

I try not to . . .

GEORGE

Get involved. Um? Isn't that right?

NICK

Yes . . . that's right.

GEORGE

I'd imagine not.

NICK

I find it . . . embarrassing.

GEORGE *(Sarcastic)*

Oh, you do, hunh?

NICK

Yes. Really. Quite.

GEORGE *(Mimicking him)*

Yes. Really. Quite. *(Then aloud, but to himself)* IT'S DISGUSTING!

NICK

Now look! I didn't have anything . . .

GEORGE

DISGUSTING! *(Quietly, but with great intensity)* Do you think I like hav-
ing that . . . whatever-it-is . . . ridiculing me, tearing me down, in front of . . .
(Waves his hand in a gesture of contemptuous dismissal) YOU? Do you think
I *care* for it?

NICK *(Cold—unfriendly)*

Well, no . . . I don't imagine you care for it at all.

GEORGE

Oh, you don't imagine it, hunh?

NICK *(Antagonistic)*

No . . . I don't. I don't imagine you do!

GEORGE *(Withering)*

Your sympathy disarms me . . . your . . . your compassion makes me weep!
Large, salty, unscientific tears!

NICK *(With great disdain)*
I just don't see why you feel you have to subject *other* people to it.

GEORGE
I?

NICK
If you and your . . . wife . . . want to go at each other, like a couple of . . .

GEORGE
I! Why *I* want to!

NICK
. . . animals, I don't see why you don't do it when there aren't any . . .

GEORGE
(Laughing through his anger)
Why, you smug, self-righteous little . . .

NICK *(A genuine threat)*
CAN . . . IT . . . MISTER!

GEORGE
. . . scientist.

NICK
I've never hit an older man.

GEORGE *(Considers it)*
Oh. *(Pause)* You just hit younger men . . . and children . . . women . . .
birds. *(Sees that* NICK *is not amused)* Well, you're quite right, of course. It
isn't the prettiest spectacle . . . seeing a couple of middle-age types hack-
ing away at each other, all red in the face and winded, missing half the
time.

NICK
Oh, you two don't miss . . . you two are pretty good. Impressive.

GEORGE
And impressive things impress you, don't they? You're . . . easily impressed
. . . sort of a . . . pragmatic idealism.

NICK *(A tight smile)*
No, it's that sometimes I can admire things that I don't admire. Now, flag-
ellation isn't my idea of good times, but . . .

GEORGE
. . . but you can admire a good flagellator . . . a real pro.

NICK
Unh-hunh . . . yeah.

GEORGE

Your wife throws up a lot, eh?

NICK

I didn't say that. . . . I said she gets sick quite easily.

GEORGE

Oh. I thought by sick you meant . . .

NICK

Well, it's true. . . . She . . . she does throw up a lot. Once she starts . . . there's practically no stopping her. . . . I mean, she'll go right on . . . for hours. Not all the time, but . . . regularly.

GEORGE

You can tell time by her, hunh?

NICK

Just about.

GEORGE

Drink?

NICK

Sure. (*With no emotion, except the faintest distaste, as* GEORGE *takes his glass to the bar*) I married her because she was pregnant.

GEORGE

(*Pause*) Oh? (*Pause*) But you said you didn't have any children . . . When I asked you, you said. . . .

NICK

She wasn't . . . really. It was a hysterical pregnancy. She blew up, and then she went down.

GEORGE

And while she was up, you married her.

NICK

And then she went down.

(*They both laugh, and are a little surprised that they do*)

GEORGE

Uh . . . Bourbon *is* right.

NICK

Uh . . . yes, Bourbon.

GEORGE (*At the bar, still*)

When I was sixteen and going to prep school, during the Punic Wars, a bunch of us used to go into New York on the first day of vacations, before we fanned out to our homes, and in the evening this bunch of us used to go to this gin mill owned by the gangster-father of one of us—for this was during the Great Experiment, or Prohibition, as it is more frequently called, and it was a bad time for the liquor lobby, but a fine time for the crooks and the cops—and we would go to this gin mill, and we would drink with the grown-ups and listen to the jazz. And one time, in the bunch of us, there was this boy who was fifteen, and he had killed his mother with a shotgun some years before—accidentally, completely accidentally, without even an unconscious motivation, I have no doubt, no doubt at all—and this one evening this boy went with us, and we ordered our drinks, and when it came his turn he said, I'll have bergin . . . give me some bergin, please . . . bergin and water. Well, we all laughed . . . he was blond and he had the face of a cherub, and we all laughed, and his cheeks went red and the color rose in his neck, and the assistant crook who had taken our order told people at the next table what the boy had said, and then they laughed, and then more people were told and the laughter grew, and more people and more laughter, and no one was laughing more than us, and none of us more than the boy who had shot his mother. And soon, everyone in the gin mill knew what the laughter was about, and everyone started ordering bergin, and laughing when they ordered it. And soon, of course, the laughter became less general, but it did not subside, entirely, for a very long time, for always at this table or that someone would order bergin and a new area of laughter would rise. We drank free that night, and we were bought champagne by the management, by the gangster-father of one of us. And, of course, we suffered the next day, each of us, alone, on his train, away from New York, each of us with a grown-up's hangover . . . but it was the grandest day of my . . . youth.

(Hands NICK a drink on the word)

NICK (Very quietly)
Thank you. What . . . what happened to the boy . . . the boy who had shot his mother?

GEORGE
I won't tell you.

NICK
All right.

GEORGE
The following summer, on a country road, with his learner's permit in his pocket and his father on the front seat to his right, he swerved the car, to avoid a porcupine, and drove straight into a large tree.

NICK (Faintly pleading)
No.

GEORGE

He was not killed, of course. And in the hospital, when he was conscious and out of danger, and when they told him that his father *was* dead, he began to laugh, I have been told, and his laughter grew and he would not stop, and it was not until after they jammed a needle in his arm, not until after that, until his consciousness slipped away from him, that his laughter subsided . . . stopped. And when he was recovered from his injuries enough so that he could be moved without damage should he struggle, he was put in an asylum. That was thirty years ago.

NICK

Is he . . . still there?

GEORGE

Oh, yes. And I'm told that for these thirty years he has . . . not . . . uttered . . . one . . . sound.

(A rather long silence: five seconds, please)

MARTHA! *(Pause)* MARTHA!

NICK

I told you . . . she's making coffee.

GEORGE

For your hysterical wife, who goes up and down.

NICK

Went. Up and down.

GEORGE

Went. No more?

NICK

No more. Nothing.

GEORGE

(After a sympathetic pause)

The saddest thing about men . . . Well, no, one of the saddest things about men is the way they age . . . some of them. Do you know what it is with insane people? Do you? . . . the quiet ones?

NICK

No.

GEORGE

They don't change . . . they don't grow old.

NICK

They must.

GEORGE

Well, eventually, probably, yes. But they don't . . . in the usual sense. They maintain a . . . a firm-skinned serenity . . . the . . . the under-use of everything leaves them . . . quite whole.

NICK

Are you recommending it?

GEORGE

No. Some things are sad, though. *(Imitates a pep-talker)* But ya jest gotta buck up an' face 'em, 'at's all. Buck up! *(Pause)* Martha doesn't have hysterical pregnancies.

NICK

My wife had *one.*

GEORGE

Yes. Martha doesn't have pregnancies at all.

NICK

Well, no . . . I don't imagine so . . . now. Do you have any other kids? Do you have any daughters, or anything?

GEORGE

(As if it's a great joke)
Do we have any *what?*

NICK

Do you have any . . . I mean, do you have only one . . . kid . . . uh . . . your son?

GEORGE

(With a private knowledge)
Oh no . . . just one . . . one boy . . . our son.

NICK

Well . . . *(Shrugs)* . . . that's nice.

GEORGE

Oh ho, ho. Yes, well, he's a . . . comfort, a bean bag.

NICK

A what?

GEORGE

A bean bag. Bean bag. You wouldn't understand. *(Overdistinct)* Bean . . . bag.

NICK

I *heard* you . . . I didn't say I was deaf . . . I said I didn't understand.

GEORGE

You didn't say that at all.

NICK

I meant I was *implying* I didn't understand. *(Under his breath)* For Christ's sake!

GEORGE

You're getting testy.

NICK *(Testy)*

I'm sorry.

GEORGE

All I said was, our son . . . the apple of our three eyes, Martha being a Cyclops . . . our son is a bean bag, and you get testy.

NICK

I'm sorry! It's late, I'm tired, I've been drinking since nine o'clock, my wife is vomiting, there's been a lot of screaming going on around here. . . .

GEORGE

And so you're testy. Naturally. Don't . . . worry about it. Anybody who comes here ends up getting . . . testy. It's expected . . . don't be upset.

NICK *(Testy)*

I'm not upset!

GEORGE

You're testy.

NICK

Yes.

GEORGE

I'd like to set you straight about something . . . while the little ladies are out of the room . . . I'd like to set you straight about what Martha said.

NICK

I don't . . . make judgments, so there's no need, really, unless you . . .

GEORGE

Well, I want to. I know you don't like to become involved . . . I know you like to . . . preserve your scientific detachment in the face of—for lack of a better word—Life . . . and all . . . but still, I want to tell you.

NICK *(A tight, formal smile)*

I'm a . . . guest. You go right ahead.

GEORGE

(Mocking appreciation)

Oh . . . well, thanks. Now! That makes me feel all warm and runny inside.

NICK

Well, if you're going to . . .

MARTHA'S VOICE

HEY!

NICK

. . . if you're going to start that kind of stuff again . . .

GEORGE

Hark! Forest sounds.

NICK

Hm?

GEORGE

Animal noises.

MARTHA (*Sticking her head in*)

Hey!

NICK

Oh!

GEORGE

Well, here's nursie.

MARTHA (*To* NICK)

We're sitting up . . . we're having coffee, and we'll be back in.

NICK (*Not rising*)

Oh . . . is there anything I should do?

MARTHA

Nayh. You just stay here and listen to George's side of things. Bore your-self to death.

GEORGE

Monstre!

MARTHA

Cochon!

GEORGE

Bête!

MARTHA

Canaille!

GEORGE

Putain!

MARTHA

(*With a gesture of contemptuous dismissal*)

Yaaaahhhh! (As *she goes*) You clean up the mess you made, George?

GEORGE

(MARTHA *goes.* GEORGE *speaks to the empty hallway*)

No, Martha, I did not clean up the mess I made. I've been trying for years to clean up the mess I made.

NICK

Have you?

GEORGE

Hm?

NICK

Have you been trying for years?

GEORGE

(*After a long pause . . . looking at him*)

Accommodation, malleability, adjustment . . . those do seem to be in the order of things, don't they?

NICK

Don't try to put me in the same class with you!

GEORGE

(*Pause*) Oh. (*Pause*) No, of course not. Things are simpler with you . . . you marry a woman because she's all blown up . . . while I, in my clumsy, old-fashioned way . . .

NICK

There was more to it than that!

GEORGE

Sure! I'll bet she has money, too!

NICK

(*Looks hurt. Then, determined, after a pause*)

Yes.

GEORGE

Yes? (*Joyfully*) YES! You mean I was right? I hit it?

NICK

Well, you see . . .

GEORGE

My God, what archery! First try, too. How about that!

NICK

You see . . .

GEORGE

There were other things.

NICK

Yes.

GEORGE

To compensate.

NICK

Yes.

GEORGE

There always are. *(Sees that* NICK *is reacting badly)* No, I'm sure there are. I didn't mean to be . . . flip. There are *always* compensating factors . . . as in the case of Martha and myself. . . . Now, on the surface of it . . .

NICK

We sort of grew up together, you know . . .

GEORGE

. . . it looks to be a kind of knock-about, drag-out affair, on the *surface* of it . . .

NICK

We knew each other from, oh God, I don't know, when we were *six,* or something. . . .

GEORGE

. . . but somewhere back there, at the beginning of it, right when I first came to New Carthage, back then . . .

NICK *(With some irritation)*

I'm *sorry.*

GEORGE

Hm? Oh. No, no . . . *I'm* sorry.

NICK

No . . . it's . . . it's all right.

GEORGE

No . . . you go ahead.

NICK

No . . . please.

GEORGE

I insist. . . . You're a guest. You go first.

NICK

Well, it seems a little silly . . . now.

GEORGE

Nonsense! *(Pause)* But if you were six, she must have been four, or something.

NICK

Maybe I was eight . . . she was six. We . . . we used to play . . . doctor.

GEORGE

That's a good healthy heterosexual beginning.

NICK *(Laughing)*

Yup.

GEORGE

The scientist even then, eh?

NICK *(Laughs)*

Yeah. And it was . . . always taken for granted . . . you know . . . by our families, and by us, too, I guess. And . . . so, we did.

GEORGE

(Pause) Did what?

NICK

We got married.

GEORGE

When you were eight?

NICK

No. No, of course not. Much later.

GEORGE

I wondered.

NICK

I wouldn't say there was any . . . particular *passion* between us, even at the beginning . . . of our marriage, I mean.

GEORGE

Well, certainly no surprise, no earth-shaking discoveries, after Doctor, and all.

NICK *(Uncertainly)*

No . . .

GEORGE

Everything's all pretty much the same, anyway . . . in *spite* of what they say about Chinese women.

NICK

What is that?

GEORGE

Let me freshen you up. *(Takes* NICK's *glass)*

NICK

Oh, thanks. After a while you don't get any drunker, do you?

GEORGE

Well, you *do* . . . but it's different . . . everything slows down. . . . you get
sodden. . . . unless you can up-chuck . . . like your wife . . . then you can
sort of start all over again.

NICK

Everybody drinks a lot here in the East. *(Thinks about it)* Everybody
drinks a lot in the Middle-west, too.

GEORGE

We drink a great deal in this country, and I suspect we'll be drinking a
great deal more, too . . . if we survive. We should be Arabs or Italians . . .
the Arabs don't drink, and the Italians don't get drunk much, except on
religious holidays. We should live on Crete, or something.

NICK

(Sarcastically . . . as if killing a joke)

And that, of course, would make us cretins.

GEORGE *(Mild surprise)*

So it would. *(Hands* NICK *his drink)* Tell me about your wife's money.

NICK *(Suddenly suspicious)*

Why?

GEORGE

Well . . . don't, then.

NICK

What do you want to know about my wife's money for? *(Ugly)* Hunh?

GEORGE

Well, I thought it would be nice.

NICK

No you didn't.

GEORGE

(Still deceptively bland)

All right. . . . I want to know about your wife's money because . . .
well, because I'm fascinated by the methodology . . . by the pragmatic
accommodation by which you wave-of-the-future boys are going to take
over.

NICK

You're starting in again.

GEORGE

Am I? No I'm not. Look . . . Martha has money too. I mean, her father's been robbing this place blind for years, and . . .

NICK

No, he hasn't. He has not.

GEORGE

He hasn't?

NICK

No.

GEORGE *(Shrugs)*

Very well. . . . Martha's father has *not* been robbing this place blind for years, and Martha does not have any money. O.K.?

NICK

We were talking about *my* wife's money . . . not yours.

GEORGE

O.K. . . . talk.

NICK

No. *(Pause)* My father-in-law . . . was a man of the Lord, and he was very rich.

GEORGE

What faith?

NICK

He . . . my father-in-law . . . was called by God when he was six, or something, and he started preaching, and he baptized people, and he saved them, and he traveled around a lot, and he became pretty famous . . . not like some of them, but he became pretty famous . . . and when he died he had a lot of money.

GEORGE

God's money.

NICK

No . . . his own.

GEORGE

What happened to God's money?

NICK

He spent God's money . . . and he saved his own. He built hospitals, and he sent off Mercy ships, and he brought the outhouses indoors, and he brought the people outdoors, into the sun, and he built three churches, or whatever they were, and two of them burned down . . . and he ended up pretty rich.

GEORGE *(After considering it)*

Well, I think that's very nice.

NICK

Yes. *(Pause. Giggles a little)* And so, my wife's got some money.

GEORGE

But not God's money.

NICK

No. Her own.

GEORGE

Well, I think that's very nice.

(NICK *giggles a little*)

Martha's got money because Martha's father's second wife . . . not Martha's mother, but after Martha's mother died . . . was a very old lady with warts who was very rich.

NICK

She was a witch.

GEORGE

She was a *good* witch, and she married the white mouse . . .

(NICK *begins to giggle*)

. . . with the tiny red eyes . . . and he must have nibbled her warts, or something like that, because she went up in a puff of smoke almost immediately. POUF!

NICK

POUF!

GEORGE

POUF! And all that was left, aside from some wart medicine, was a big fat will. . . . A peach pie, with some for the township of New Carthage, some for the college, some for Martha's daddy, and just this much for Martha.

NICK *(Quite beside himself)*

Maybe . . . maybe my father-in-law and the witch with the warts should have gotten together, because he was a mouse, too.

GEORGE *(Urging NICK on)*

He was?

NICK *(Breaking down)*

Sure . . . he was a church mouse! *(They both laugh a great deal, but it is sad laughter . . . eventually they subside, fall silent)* Your wife never mentioned a stepmother.

GEORGE *(Considers it)*

Well . . . maybe it isn't true.

NICK *(Narrowing his eyes)*

And maybe it is.

GEORGE

Might be . . . might not. Well, I think your story's a lot nicer . . . about your pumped-up little wife, and your father-in-law who was a priest . . .

NICK

He was not a priest . . . he was a man of God.

GEORGE

Yes.

NICK

And my wife wasn't pumped up . . . she blew up.

GEORGE

Yes, yes.

NICK *(Giggling)*

Get things straight.

GEORGE

I'm sorry . . . I will. I'm sorry.

NICK

O.K.

GEORGE

You realize, of course, that I've been drawing you out on this stuff, not because I'm interested in your terrible lifehood, but only because you represent a direct and pertinent threat to my lifehood, and I want to get the goods on you.

NICK *(Still amused)*

Sure . . . sure.

GEORGE

I mean . . . I've warned you . . . you stand warned.

NICK

I stand warned *(Laughs)* It's you sneaky types worry me the most, you know. You ineffectual sons of bitches . . . you're the worst.

GEORGE

Yes . . . we are. Sneaky. An elbow in your steely-blue eye . . . a knee in your solid gold groin . . . we're the worst.

NICK

Yup.

GEORGE

Well, I'm glad you don't believe me. . . . I know you've got history on your side, and all . . .

NICK

Unh-unh. *You've* got history on *your* side. . . . I've got biology on mine.
History, biology.

GEORGE

I know the difference.

NICK

You don't act it.

GEORGE

No? I thought we'd decided that you'd take over the History Department first, before you took over the whole works. You know . . . a step at
a time.

NICK

(Stretching . . . luxuriating . . . playing the game)

Nyaah . . . what I thought I'd do is . . . I'd sort of insinuate myself generally, play around for a while, find all the weak spots, shore 'em up, but with
my own name plate on 'em . . . become sort of a fact, and then turn into a
. . . a what. . .?

GEORGE

An inevitability.

NICK

Exactly. . . . An inevitability. You know. . . . Take over a few courses from
the older men, start some special groups for myself . . . plow a few pertinent wives. . . .

GEORGE

Now that's it! You can take over all the courses you want to, and get as
much of the young elite together in the gymnasium as you like, but until
you start plowing pertinent wives, you really aren't working. The way to a
man's heart is through his wife's belly, and don't you forget it.

NICK *(Playing along)*

Yeah. . . . I know.

GEORGE

And the women around here are no better than puntas—you know,
South American ladies of the night. You know what they do in South
America . . . in Rio? The puntas? Do you know? They hiss . . . like geese.
. . . They stand around in the street and they hiss at you . . . like a bunch
of geese.

NICK

Gangle.

GEORGE

Hm?

NICK

Gangle . . . gangle of geese . . . not bunch . . . gangle.

GEORGE

Well, if you're going to get all cute about it, all ornithological, it's gaggle . . . not gangle, *gaggle.*

NICK

Gaggle? Not gangle?

GEORGE

Yes, gaggle.

NICK *(Crestfallen)*

Oh.

GEORGE

Oh. Yes. . . . Well they stand around on the street and they hiss at you, like a bunch of geese. All the faculty wives, downtown in New Carthage, in front of the A&P, hissing away like a bunch of geese. That's the way to power—plow 'em all!

NICK *(Still playing along)*

I'll bet you're right.

GEORGE

Well, I am.

NICK

And I'll bet your wife's the biggest goose in the gangle . . . *gaggle,* isn't she . . . ? Her father president, and all.

GEORGE

You bet your historical inevitability she is!

NICK

Yessirree. *(Rubs his hands together)* Well now, I'd just better get her off in a corner and mount her like a goddamn dog, eh?

GEORGE

Why, you'd certainly better.

NICK

(Looks at GEORGE *a minute, his expression a little sick)*

You know, I almost think you're serious.

GEORGE *(Toasting him)*

No, baby . . . *you* almost think you're serious, and it scares the hell out of you.

NICK *(Exploding in disbelief)*

ME!

GEORGE *(Quietly)*

Yes . . . you.

NICK

You're kidding!

GEORGE *(Like a father)*

I wish I were . . . I'll give you some good advice if you want me to. . . .

NICK

Good advice! From you? Oh boy! *(Starts to laugh)*

GEORGE

You haven't learned yet. . . . Take it wherever you can get it. . . . Listen to me, now.

NICK

Come off it!

GEORGE

I'm giving you good advice, now.

NICK

Good God . . . !

GEORGE

There's quicksand here, and you'll be dragged down, just as . . .

NICK

Oh boy . . . !

GEORGE

. . . before you know it . . . sucked down. . . .
    (NICK *laughs derisively*)
You disgust me on principle, and you're a smug son of a bitch personally, but I'm trying to give you a survival kit. DO YOU HEAR ME?

NICK *(Still laughing)*

I hear you. You come in loud.

GEORGE

ALL RIGHT!

NICK

Hey, Honey.

GEORGE *(Silence. Then quietly)*

All right . . . O.K. You want to play it by ear, right? Everything's going to work out anyway, because the time-table's history, right?

NICK

Right . . . right. You just tend to your knitting, grandma. . . . I'll be O.K.

GEORGE *(After a silence)*

I've tried to . . . tried to reach you . . . to . . .

NICK *(Contemptuously)*

. . . make contact?

GEORGE

Yes.

NICK *(Still)*

. . . communicate?

GEORGE

Yes. Exactly.

NICK

Aw . . . that *is* touching . . . that is . . . downright moving . . . that's what it is. *(With sudden vehemence)* UP YOURS!

GEORGE *(Brief pause)*

Hm?

NICK *(Threatening)*

You heard me!

GEORGE *(At* NICK, *not to him)*

You take the trouble to construct a civilization . . . to . . . to build a society, based on the principles of . . . of principle . . . you endeavor to make communicable sense out of natural order, morality out of the unnatural disorder of man's mind . . . you make government and art, and realize that they are, must be, both the same . . . you bring things to the saddest of all points . . . to the point where there *is* something to lose . . . then all at once, through all the music, through all the sensible sounds of men building, attempting, comes the *Dies Irae*. And what is it? What does the trumpet sound? Up yours. I suppose there's justice to it, after all the years. . . . Up yours.

NICK

(Brief pause . . . then applauding)

Ha, ha! Bravo! Ha, ha! *(Laughs on)*

(And MARTHA *reenters, leading* HONEY, *who is wan but smiling bravely)*

HONEY *(Grandly)*

Thank you . . . thank you.

MARTHA

Here we are, a little shaky, but on our feet.

GEORGE

Goodie.

NICK

What? Oh . . . OH! Hi, Honey . . . you better?

HONEY

A little bit, dear. . . . I' d better sit down, though.

NICK

Sure . . . c'mon . . . you sit by me.

HONEY

Thank you, dear.

GEORGE (*Beneath his breath*)

Touching . . . touching.

MARTHA (*To* GEORGE)

Well? Aren't you going to apologize?

GEORGE (*Squinting*)

For what, Martha?

MARTHA

For making the little lady throw up, what else?

GEORGE

I did not make her throw up.

MARTHA

You most certainly did!

GEORGE

I did not!

HONEY (*Papal gesture*)

No, now . . . no.

MARTHA (*To* GEORGE)

Well, who do you think did . . . Sexy over there? You think he made his *own* little wife sick?

GEORGE (*Helpfully*)

Well, you make *me* sick.

MARTHA

THAT'S DIFFERENT!

HONEY

No, now. I . . . I throw up . . . I mean, I get sick . . . occasionally, all by myself . . . without any reason.

GEORGE

Is that a fact?

NICK

You're . . . you're delicate, Honey.

HONEY *(Proudly)*

I've always done it.

GEORGE

Like Big Ben.

NICK *(A warning)*

Watch it!

HONEY

And the doctors say there's nothing wrong with me . . . organically. You know?

NICK

Of course there isn't.

HONEY

Why, just before we got married, I developed . . . appendicitis . . . or everybody *thought* it was appendicitis . . . but it turned out to be . . . it was a . . . *(laughs briefly)* . . . false alarm.

(GEORGE *and* NICK *exchange glances*)

MARTHA *(To* GEORGE*)*

Get me a drink.

(GEORGE *moves to the bar*)

George makes everybody sick. . . . When our son was just a little boy, he used to . . .

GEORGE

Don't, Martha . . .

MARTHA

. . . he used to throw up all the time, because of George . . .

GEORGE

I said, don't!

MARTHA

It got so bad that whenever George came into the room he'd start right in retching, and . . .

GEORGE

. . . the real reason *(Spits out the words)* our son . . . used to throw up all the time, wife and lover, was nothing more complicated than that he couldn't stand you fiddling at him all the time, breaking into his bedroom with your kimono flying, fiddling at him all the time, with your liquor breath on him, and your hands all over his . . .

MARTHA

YEAH? And I suppose that's why he ran away from home twice in one month, too. *(Now to the guests)* Twice in one month! Six times in one year!

GEORGE *(Also to the guests)*

Our son ran away from home all the time because Martha here used to corner him.

MARTHA *(Braying)*

I NEVER CORNERED THE SON OF A BITCH IN MY LIFE!

GEORGE

(Handing MARTHA *her drink)*

He used to run up to me when I'd get home, and he'd say, "Mama's always coming at me." That's what he'd say.

MARTHA

Liar!

GEORGE *(Shrugging)*

Well, that's the way it was . . . you were always coming at him. I thought it was very embarrassing.

NICK

If you thought it was so embarrassing, what are you talking about it for?

HONEY *(Admonishing)*

Dear . . . !

MARTHA

Yeah! *(To* NICK) Thanks, sweetheart.

CEORCE *(To them all)*

I didn't want to talk about him at all . . . I would have been perfectly happy not to discuss the whole subject. . . . I never want to talk about it.

MARTHA

Yes you do.

GEORGE

When we're alone, maybe.

MARTHA

We're alone!

GEORGE

Uh . . . no, Love . . . we've got guests.

MARTHA

(With a covetous look at NICK)

We sure have.

HONEY

Could I have a little brandy? I think I'd like a little brandy.

NICK

Do you think you should?

HONEY

Oh yes . . . yes, dear.

GEORGE

(Moving to the bar again)
Sure! Fill 'er up!

NICK

Honey, I don't think you . . .

HONEY *(Petulance creeping in)*
It will steady me, *dear.* I feel a little unsteady.

GEORGE

Hell, you can't walk steady on half a bottle . . . got to do it right.

HONEY

Yes. *(To* MARTHA*)* I love brandy . . . I really do.

MARTHA *(Somewhat abstracted)*
Good for you.

NICK *(Giving up)*
Well, if you think it's a good idea. . . .

HONEY *(Really testy)*
I know what's best for me, dear.

NICK *(Not even pleasant)*
Yes . . . I'm sure you do.

HONEY

*(*GEORGE *hands her a brandy)*
Oh, goodie! Thank you. *(To* NICK*)* Of course I do, dear.

GEORGE *(Pensively)*
I used to drink brandy.

MARTHA *(Privately)*
You used to drink bergin, too.

GEORGE *(Sharp)*
Shut up, Martha!

MARTHA

(Her hand over her mouth in a little girl gesture)
Oooooops.

NICK
(Something having clicked, vaguely)
Hm?

GEORGE *(Burying it)*
Nothing . . . nothing.

MARTHA *(She, too)*
You two men have it out while we were gone? George tell you his side of
things? He bring you to tears, hunh?

NICK
Well . . . no . . .

GEORGE
No, what we did, actually, was . . . we sort of danced around.

MARTHA
Oh, yeah? Cute!

HONEY
Oh, I love dancing.

NICK
He didn't mean that, Honey.

HONEY
Well, I didn't think he did! Two grown men dancing . . . heavens!

MARTHA
You mean he didn't start in on how he would have amounted to something
if it hadn't been for Daddy? How his high moral sense wouldn't even let
him *try* to better himself? No?

NICK *(Qualified)*
No . . .

MARTHA
And he didn't run on about how he tried to publish a goddamn book, and
Daddy wouldn't let him.

NICK
A book? No.

GEORGE
Please, Martha. . . .

NICK *(Egging her on)*
A book? What book?

GEORGE *(Pleading)*
Please. Just a book.

MARTHA (*Mock incredulity*)

Just a book!

GEORGE

Please, Martha!

MARTHA (*Almost disappointed*)

Well, I guess you didn't get the whole sad story. What's the matter with you, George? You given up?

GEORGE (*Calm . . . serious*)

No . . . no. It's just I've got to figure out some new way to fight you, Martha. Guerilla tactics, maybe . . . internal subversion . . . I don't know. Something.

MARTHA

Well, you figure it out, and you let me know when you do.

GEORGE (*Cheery*)

All right, Love.

HONEY

Why don't we dance? I'd love some dancing.

NICK

Honey . . .

HONEY

I would! I'd love some dancing.

NICK

Honey . . .

HONEY

I *want* some! I want some dancing!

GEORGE

All right . . . ! For heaven's sake . . . we'll have some dancing.

HONEY (*All sweetness again*)

(*To* MARTHA) Oh, I'm so glad . . . I just love dancing. Don't you?

MARTHA (*With a glance at* NICK)

Yeah . . . yeah, that's not a bad idea.

NICK (*Genuinely nervous*)

Gee.

GEORGE

Gee.

HONEY

I dance like the wind.

MARTHA *(Without comment)*

Yeah?

GEORGE *(Picking a record)*

Martha had her daguerreotype in the paper once . . . oh, 'bout twenty five years ago. . . . Seems she took second prize in one o' them seven-day dancin' contest things . . . biceps all bulging, holding up her partner.

MARTHA

Will you put a record on and shut up?

GEORGE

Certainly, Love. *(To all)* How are we going to work this? Mixed doubles?

MARTHA

Well, you certainly don't think I'm going to dance with *you*, do you?

GEORGE *(Considers it)*

Noooooo . . . not with him around . . . that's for sure. And not with twin-kle-toes here, either.

HONEY

I'll dance with anyone . . . I'll dance by myself.

NICK

Honey . . .

HONEY

I dance like the wind.

GEORGE

All right, kiddies . . . choose up and hit the sack.
(Music starts. . . . Second movement, Beethoven's 7th Symphony)

HONEY

(Up, dancing by herself)
De, de de *da* da, da-da de, da *da*-da de da . . . wonderful . . . !

NICK

Honey . . .

MARTHA

All right, George . . . cut that out!

HONEY

Dum, de de da da, da-da de, dum de *da* da da . . . Wheeeee . . . !

MARTHA

Cut it out, George!

GEORGE

(Pretending not to hear)
What, Martha? What?

NICK

Honey . . .

MARTHA

(As GEORGE *turns up the volume)*
CUT IT OUT, GEORGE!

GEORGE

WHAT?

MARTHA

(Gets up, moves quickly, threateningly, to GEORGE*)*
All right, you son of a bitch . . .

GEORGE

(Record off, at once. Quietly)
What did you say, Love?

MARTHA

You son of a . . .

HONEY

(In an arrested posture)
You stopped! Why did you stop?

NICK

Honey . . .

HONEY *(To* NICK, *snapping)*
Stop that!

GEORGE

I thought it was fitting, Martha.

MARTHA

Oh you did, hunh?

HONEY

You're always *at* me when I'm having a good time.

NICK *(Trying to remain civil)*
I'm sorry, Honey.

HONEY

Just . . . leave me alone!

GEORGE

Well, why don't *you* choose, Martha? *(Moves away from the phonograph
. . . leaves it* to MARTHA) Martha's going to run things . . . the little lady's
going to lead the band.

HONEY

I like to dance and you don't want me to.

NICK

I like you to dance.

HONEY

Just . . . leave me alone. *(She sits . . . takes a drink)*

GEORGE

Martha's going to put on some rhythm she understands . . . Sacre du
Printemps, maybe. *(Moves . . . sits by* HONEY) Hi, sexy.

HONEY

(A little giggle-scream)
Oooooohhhhh!

GEORGE *(Laughs mockingly)*
Ha, ha, ha, ha, ha. Choose it, Martha . . . do your stuff!

MARTHA

(Concentrating on the machine)
You're damn right!

GEORGE *(To* HONEY)
You want to dance with me, angel-tits?

NICK

What did you call my wife?

GEORGE *(Derisively)*
Oh boy!

HONEY *(Petulantly)*
No! If I can't do my interpretive dance, I don't want to dance with anyone.
I'll just sit here and. . . . *(Shrugs . . . drinks)*

MARTHA

(Record on . . . a jazzy slow pop tune)
O.K. stuff, let's go. *(Grabs* NICK)

NICK

Hm? Oh . . . hi.

MARTHA

Hi. *(They dance, close together, slowly)*

HONEY (*Pouting*)

We'll just sit here and watch.

GEORGE

That's *right!*

MARTHA (*To* NICK)

Hey, you *are* strong, aren't you?

NICK

Unh-hunh.

MARTHA

I like that.

NICK

Unh-hunh.

HONEY

They're dancing like they've danced before.

GEORGE

It's a familiar dance . . . they both know it. . . .

MARTHA

Don't be shy.

NICK

I'm . . . not. . . .

GEORGE (*To* HONEY)

It's a very old ritual, monkey-nipples . . . old as they come.

HONEY

I . . . I don't know what you mean.

(NICK *and* MARTHA *move apart now, and dance on either side of where* GEORGE *and* HONEY *are sitting; they face each other, and while their feet move but little, their bodies undulate congruently. . . . It is as if they were pressed together*)

MARTHA

I like the way you move.

NICK

I like the way you move, too.

GEORGE (*To* HONEY)

They like the way they move.

HONEY (*Not entirely with it*)

That's nice.

MARTHA (*To* NICK)

I'm surprised George didn't give you his side of things.

GEORGE (*To* HONEY)

Aren't they cute?

NICK

Well, he didn't.

MARTHA

That surprises me.

(*Perhaps* MARTHA'*s statements are more or less in time to the music*)

NICK

Does it?

MARTHA

Yeah . . . he usually does . . . when he gets the chance.

NICK

Well, what do you know.

MARTHA

It's really a very sad story.

GEORGE

You have ugly talents, Martha.

NICK

Is it?

MARTHA

It would make you weep.

GEORGE

Hideous gifts.

NICK

Is that so?

GEORGE

Don't encourage her.

MARTHA

Encourage me.

NICK

Go on.

(*They may undulate toward each other and then move back*)

GEORGE

I warn you . . . don't encourage her.

MARTHA

He warns you . . . don't encourage me.

NICK

I heard him . . . tell me more.

MARTHA

(Consciously making rhymed speech)
Well, Georgie-boy had lots of big ambitions
in spite of something funny in his past. . . .

GEORGE *(Quietly warning)*

Martha . . .

MARTHA

Which Georgie-boy here turned into a novel. . . .
His first attempt and also his last. . . .
Hey! I rhymed! I rhymed!

GEORGE

I warn you, Martha.

NICK

Yeah . . . you rhymed. Go on, go on.

MARTHA

But daddy took a look at Georgie's novel . . .

GEORGE

You're looking for a punch in the mouth. . . . You know that, Martha.

MARTHA

Do tell! . . . and he was very shocked by what he read.

NICK

He was?

MARTHA

Yes . . . he was. . . . A novel all about a naughty boy-child . . .

GEORGE *(Rising)*

I will not tolerate this!

NICK *(Offhand, to* GEORGE*)*

Oh, can it.

MARTHA

. . . ha, ha!
naughty boychild
who . . . uh . . . who killed his mother and his father dead.

GEORGE

STOP IT, MARTHA!

MARTHA

And Daddy said . . . Look here, I will not let you publish such a thing. . . .

GEORGE

(Rushes to phonograph . . . rips the record off)
That's it! The dancing's over. That's it. Go on now!

NICK

What do you think you're doing, hunh?

HONEY *(Happily)*

Violence! Violence!

MARTHA

(Loud: a pronouncement)
And Daddy said . . . Look here, kid, you don't think for a second I'm going to let you publish this crap, do you? Not on your life, baby . . . not while you're teaching here. . . . You publish that goddamn book and you're out . . . on your ass!

GEORGE

DESIST! DESIST!

MARTHA

Ha, ha, ha, HA!

NICK *(Laughing)*

De . . . sist!

HONEY

Oh, violence . . . violence!

MARTHA

Why, the idea! A teacher at a respected, conservative institution like this, in a town like New Carthage, publishing a book like that? If you respect your position here, young man, young . . . whippersnapper, you'll just withdraw that manuscript. . . .

GEORGE

I will not be made mock of!

NICK

He will not be made mock of, for Christ's sake. *(Laughs)*
(HONEY joins in the laughter, not knowing exactly why)

GEORGE

I will not!
(All three are laughing at him)
(Infuriated) THE GAME IS OVER!

MARTHA *(Pushing on)*

Imagine such a thing! A book about a boy who murders his mother and kills his father, and pretends it's all an accident!

HONEY

(Beside herself with glee)

An accident!

NICK

(Remembering something related)

Hey . . . wait a minute . . . .

MARTHA *(Her own voice now)*

And you want to know the clincher? You want to know what big brave Georgie said to Daddy?

GEORGE

NO! NO! NO! NO!

NICK

Wait a minute now . . .

MARTHA

Georgie said . . . but Daddy . . . I mean . . . ha, ha, ha, ha . . . but *Sir,* it isn't a *novel* at all. . . . *(Other voice)* Not a novel? *(Mimicking* GEORGE's *voice)* No, sir . . . it isn't a novel at all . . .

GEORGE *(Advancing on her)*

You will not say this!

NICK *(Sensing the danger)*

Hey.

MARTHA

The hell I won't. Keep away from me, you bastard!

(Backs off a little . . . uses GEORGE's *voice again)*

No, Sir, this isn't a novel at all . . . this is the truth . . . this really happened . . . TO ME!

GEORGE *(On her)*

I'LL KILL YOU!

(Grabs her by the throat. They struggle)

NICK

HEY! *(Comes between them)*

HONEY *(Wildly)*

VIOLENCE! VIOLENCE!

*(*GEORGE, MARTHA, *and* NICK *struggle . . . yells, etc.)*

MARTHA

IT HAPPENED! TO ME! TO ME!

GEORGE

YOU SATANIC BITCH!

NICK

STOP THAT! STOP THAT!

HONEY

VIOLENCE! VIOLENCE!

(The other three struggle. GEORGE's *hands are on* MARTHA's *throat.*
NICK *grabs him, tears him from* MARTHA, *throws him on the floor.*
GEORGE, *on the floor;* NICK *over him;* MARTHA *to one side, her hand
on her throat)*

NICK

That's enough now!

HONEY

(Disappointment in her voice)

Oh . . . oh . . . oh . . .

*(*GEORGE *drags himself into a chair. He is hurt, but it is more a
profound humiliation than a physical injury)*

GEORGE

(They watch him . . . a pause . . .)

All right . . . all right . . . very quiet now . . . we will all be . . . very quiet.

MARTHA

(Softly, with a slow shaking of her head)

Murderer. Mur . . . der . . . er.

NICK *(Softly to* MARTHA)

O.K. now . . . that's enough.

*(A brief silence. They all move around a little, self-consciously,
like wrestlers flexing after a fall)*

GEORGE

*(Composure seemingly recovered, but there is a great nervous
intensity)*

Well! That's one game. What shall we do now, hunh?

*(*MARTHA *and* NICK *laugh nervously)*

Oh come on . . . let's think of something else. We've played Humiliate the
Host . . . we've gone through that one . . . what shall we do now?

NICK

Aw. . . . look . . .

GEORGE

AW LOOK! *(Whines it)* Awww . . . looooook. *(Alert)* I mean, come on! We must know other games, college-type types like us . . . that can't be the . . . limit of our vocabulary, can it?

NICK

I think maybe . . .

GEORGE

Let's see now . . . what else can we do? There are other games. How about . . . how about . . . Hump the Hostess? HUNH?? How about that? How about Hump the Hostess? *(To* NICK*)* You wanna play that one? You wanna play Hump the Hostess? HUNH? HUNH?

NICK *(A little frightened)*

Calm down, now.

(MARTHA *giggles quietly)*

GEORGE

Or is that for later . . . mount her like a goddamn dog?

HONEY

(Wildly toasting everybody)

Hump the Hostess!

NICK *(To* HONEY *. . . sharply)*

Just shut up . . . will you?

(HONEY *does, her glass in mid-air)*

GEORGE

You don't wanna play that now, hunh? You wanna save that game till later? Well, what'll we play now? We gotta play a game.

MARTHA *(Quietly)*

Portrait of a man drowning.

GEORGE

(Affirmatively, but to none of them)

I am not drowning.

HONEY

(To NICK, *tearfully indignant)*

You told me to shut up!

NICK *(Impatiently)*

I'm sorry.

HONEY *(Between her teeth)*

No you're not.

NICK

(To HONEY, *even more impatiently)*

I'm sorry.

GEORGE

(Claps his hands together, once, loud)

I've got it! I'll tell you what game we'll play. We're done with Humiliate the
Host . . . this round, anyway . . . we re done with that . . . and we don't want
to play Hump the Hostess, yet . . . not yet . . . so I know what we'll play . . .
We'll play a round of Get the Guests. How about that? How about a little
game of Get the Guests?

MARTHA

(Turning away, a little disgusted)

Jesus, George.

GEORGE

Book dropper! Child mentioner!

HONEY

I don't like these games.

NICK

Yeah. . . . I think maybe we've had enough of games, now. . . .

GEORGE

Oh, no . . . oh, no . . . we haven't. We've had only one game. . . . Now we're
going to have another. You can't fly on one game.

NICK

I think maybe . . .

GEORGE *(With great authority)*

SILENCE! *(It is respected)* Now, how are we going to play Get the
Guests?

MARTHA

For God's sake, George . . .

GEORGE

You be quiet!

*(*MARTHA *shrugs)*

I wonder. . . . I wonder. *(Puzzles . . . then . . .)* O.K.! Well . . . Martha . . .
in her indiscreet way . . . well, not really indiscreet, because Martha is a
naive, at heart . . . anyway, Martha told you all about my first novel. True
or false? Hunh? I mean, true or false that there ever was such a thing. HA!
But, Martha told you about it . . . my first novel, my . . . memory book . . .
which I'd sort of preferred she hadn't, but hell, that's blood under the
bridge. BUT! what she didn't do . . . what Martha didn't tell you about is
she didn't tell us all about my *second* novel.

(MARTHA *looks at him with puzzled curiosity*)

No, you didn't know about that, did you, Martha? About my second novel, true or false. True or false?

MARTHA (*Sincerely*)

No.

GEORGE

No.

(*He starts quietly but as he goes on, his tone becomes harsher, his voice louder*)

Well, it's an allegory, really—probably—but it can be read as straight, cozy prose . . . and it's all about a nice young couple who come out of the Middle-west. It's a bucolic you see. AND, this nice young couple comes out of the Middle-west, and he's blond and about thirty, and he's a scientist, a teacher, a scientist . . . and his mouse is a wifey little type who gargles brandy all the time . . . and . . .

NICK

Just a minute here . . .

GEORGE

. . . and they got to know each other when they was only teensie little types, and they used to get under the vanity table and poke around, and . . .

NICK

I said JUST A MINUTE!

GEORGE

This is my game! You played yours . . . you people. This is my game!

HONEY (*Dreamy*)

I want to hear the story. I love stories.

MARTHA

George, for heaven's sake . . .

GEORGE

AND! And Mousie's father was a holy man, see, and he ran sort of a traveling clip joint, based on Christ and all those girls, and he took the faithful . . . that's all . . . just took 'em . . .

HONEY (*Puzzling*)

This is familiar . . .

NICK (*Voice shaking a little*)

No kidding!

GEORGE

. . . and he died eventually, Mousie's pa, and they pried him open, and all sorts of money fell out. . . . Jesus money, Mary money . . . LOOT!

HONEY *(Dreamy, puzzling)*

I've heard this story before.

NICK

(With quiet intensity . . . to waken her)

Honey . . .

GEORGE

But that's in the backwash, in the early part of the book. Anyway, Blondie and his frau out of the plain states came.

(Chuckles)

MARTHA

Very funny, George . . .

GEORGE

. . . thank you . . . and settled in a town just like nouveau Carthage here . . .

NICK *(Threatening)*

I don't think you'd better go on, mister . . .

GEORGE

Do you not!

NICK *(Less certainly)*

No. I . . . I don't think you'd better.

HONEY

I love familiar stories . . . they're the best.

GEORGE

How right you are. But Blondie was in disguise, really, all got up as a teacher, 'cause his baggage ticket had bigger things writ on it . . . H.I. HI! Historical inevitability.

NICK

There's no need for you to go any further, now . . .

HONEY

(Puzzling to make sense out of what she is hearing)

Let them go on.

GEORGE

We shall. And he had this baggage with him, and part of this baggage was in the form of his mouse . . .

NICK

We don't have to listen to this!

HONEY

Why not?

GEORGE

Your bride has a point. And one of the things nobody could understand about Blondie was his baggage . . . his mouse, I mean, here he was, pan-Kansas swimming champeen, or something, and he had this mouse, of whom he was solicitous to a point that faileth human understanding . . . given that she was sort of a simp, in the long run. . . .

NICK

This isn't fair of you. . . .

GEORGE

Perhaps not. Like, as I said, his mouse, she tooted brandy immodestly and spent half of her time in the upchuck. . . .

HONEY (*Focussing*)

I know these people. . . .

GEORGE

Do you! . . . But she was a money baggage amongst other things . . . Godly money ripped from the golden teeth of the unfaithful, a pragmatic extension of the big dream . . . and she was put up with . . .

HONEY (*Some terror*)

I don't like this story. . . .

NICK (*Surprisingly pleading*)

Please . . . please don't.

MARTHA

Maybe you better stop, George. . . .

GEORGE

. . . and she was put up with . . . STOP? Ha-ha.

NICK

Please . . . please don't.

GEORGE

Beg, baby.

MARTHA

George . . .

GEORGE

. . . and . . . oh, we get a flashback here, to How They Got Married.

NICK

NO!

GEORGE (*Triumphant*)

YES!

NICK (*Almost whining*)

Why?

GEORGE

How They Got Married. Well, how they got married is this. . . . The Mouse got all puffed up one day, and she went over to Blondie's house, and she stuck out her puff, and she said . . . look at me.

HONEY *(White . . . on her feet)*

I . . . don't . . . like this.

NICK *(To* GEORGE*)*

Stop it!

GEORGE

Look at me . . . I'm all puffed up. Oh my goodness, said Blondie . . .

HONEY *(As from a distance)*

. . . and so they were married . . .

GEORGE

. . . and so they were married . . .

HONEY

. . . and then . . .

GEORGE

. . . and then . . .

HONEY *(Hysteria)*

WHAT? . . . and then, WHAT?

NICK

NO! NO!

GEORGE *(As if to a baby)*

. . . and then the puff went *away* . . . like magic . . . pouf!

NICK *(Almost sick)*

Jesus God . . .

HONEY

. . . the puff went away . . .

GEORGE *(Softly)*

. . . pouf.

NICK

Honey . . . I didn't mean to . . . honestly, I didn't mean to . . .

HONEY

You . . . you told them. . . .

NICK

Honey . . . I didn't mean to. . . .

HONEY

(With outlandish horror)

You . . . told them! You told them! OOOOHHHH! Oh, no, no, no, no! You couldn't have told them . . . oh, noooo!

NICK

Honey, I didn't mean to. . . .

HONEY *(Grabbing at her belly)*

Ohhhhh . . . nooooo.

NICK

Honey . . . baby . . . I'm sorry . . . I didn't mean to. . . .

GEORGE

(Abruptly and with some disgust)

And that's how you play Get the Guests.

HONEY

I'm going to . . . I'm going to be sick. . . .

GEORGE

Naturally!

NICK

Honey . . .

GEORGE

HEY! How do you do it? Hunh? How do you make your secret little murders studboy doesn't know about, hunh? Pills? PILLS? You got a secret supply of pills? Or what? Apple jelly? WILL POWER?

HONEY *(Hysterical)*

Leave me alone . . . I'm going . . . to . . . . be . . . sick.

(She runs out of the room)

MARTHA

(Shaking her head, watching HONEY's *retreating form)*

God Almighty.

GEORGE *(Shrugging)*

The patterns of history.

NICK *(Quietly shaking)*

You shouldn't have done that . . . you shouldn't have done that at all.

GEORGE *(Calmly)*

I hate hypocrisy.

NICK

That was cruel . . . and vicious. . . .

GEORGE

. . . she'll get over it . . .

NICK

. . . and damaging . . . !

GEORGE

. . . she'll recover. . . .

NICK

DAMAGING!! TO ME!!

GEORGE *(With wonder)*

To you!

NICK

TO ME!!

GEORGE

To you!!

NICK

YES!!

GEORGE

Or, beautiful . . . beautiful. By God, you gotta have a swine to show you where the truffles are. *(So calmly)* Well, you just rearrange your alliances, boy. You just pick up the pieces where you can . . . you just look around and make the best of things . . . you scramble back up on your feet.

MARTHA *(Quietly, to* NICK*)*

Go look after your wife.

GEORGE

Yeah . . . go pick up the pieces and plan some new strategy.

NICK

(To GEORGE, *as he moves toward the hall)*

You're going to regret this.

GEORGE

Probably. I regret everything.

NICK

I mean, I'm going to make you regret this.

GEORGE *(Softly)*

No doubt. Acute embarrassment, eh?

NICK

I'll play the charades like you've got 'em set up . . . I'll play in your language . . . I'll be what you say I am.

GEORGE

You are already . . . you just don't know it.

NICK *(Shaking within)*

No . . . no. Not really. But I'll *be* it, mister . . . I'll show you something come to life you'll wish you hadn't set up.

GEORGE

Go clean up the mess.

NICK *(Quietly . . . intensely)*

You just wait, mister.

(*He exits. Pause.* GEORGE *smiles at* MARTHA)

MARTHA

Very good, George.

GEORGE

Thank you, Martha.

MARTHA

Really good.

GEORGE

I'm glad you liked it.

MARTHA

I mean . . . You did a good job . . . you really fixed it.

GEORGE

Unh-hunh.

MARTHA

It's the most . . . life you've shown in a long time.

GEORGE

You bring out the best in me, baby.

MARTHA

Yeah . . . pigmy hunting!

GEORGE

PIGMY!

MARTHA

You're really a bastard.

GEORGE

I? I?

MARTHA

Yeah . . . you.

GEORGE

Baby, if quarterback there is a pigmy, you've certainly changed your style. What are you after now . . . giants?

MARTHA

You make me sick.

GEORGE

It's perfectly all right for you. . . . I mean, you can make your own rules . . . you can go around like a hopped-up Arab, slashing away at everything in sight, scarring up half the world if you want to. But somebody else try it . . . no sir!

MARTHA

You miserable . . .

GEORGE (*Mocking*)

Why baby, I did it all for you. I thought you'd like it, sweetheart . . . it's sort of to your taste . . . blood, carnage and all. Why, I thought you'd get all excited . . . sort of heave and pant and come running at me, your melons bobbling.

MARTHA

You've really screwed up, George.

GEORGE (*Spitting it out*)

Oh, for God's sake, Martha!

MARTHA

I mean it . . . you really have.

GEORGE

(*Barely contained anger now*)

You can sit there in that chair of yours, you can sit there with the gin running out of your mouth, and you can humiliate me, you can tear me apart . . . ALL NIGHT . . . and that's perfectly all right . . . that's O.K. . . .

MARTHA

YOU CAN STAND IT!

GEORGE

I CANNOT STAND IT!

MARTHA

YOU CAN STAND IT!! YOU MARRIED ME FOR IT!!

(*A silence*)

GEORGE (*Quietly*)

That is a desperately sick lie.

MARTHA

DON'T YOU KNOW IT, EVEN YET?

GEORGE *(Shaking his head)*

Oh . . . Martha.

MARTHA

My arm has gotten tired whipping you.

GEORGE

(Stares at her in disbelief)

You're mad.

MARTHA

For twenty-three years!

GEORGE

You're deluded . . . Martha, you're deluded.

MARTHA

IT'S NOT WHAT I'VE WANTED!

GEORGE

I thought at least you were . . . on to yourself. I didn't know. I . . . didn't know.

MARTHA *(Anger taking over)*

I'm on to myself.

GEORGE

(As if she were some sort of bug)

No . . . no . . . you're . . . sick.

MARTHA *(Rises—screams)*

I'LL SHOW YOU WHO'S SICK!

GEORGE

All right, Martha . . . you're going too far.

MARTHA *(Screams again)*

I'LL SHOW YOU WHO'S SICK. I'LL SHOW YOU.

GEORGE

(He shakes her)

Stop it! *(Pushes her back in her chair)* Now, stop it!

MARTHA *(Calmer)*

I'll show you who's sick. *(Calmer)* Boy, you're really having a field day, hunh? Well, I'm going to finish you . . . before I'm through with you. . . .

GEORGE

. . . you and the quarterback . . . you both gonna finish me . . . ?

MARTHA

. . . before I'm through with you you'll wish you'd died in that automobile, you bastard.

GEORGE
(Emphasizing with his forefinger)
And you'll wish you'd never mentioned our son!

MARTHA *(Dripping contempt)*
You . . .

GEORGE
Now, I said I warned you.

MARTHA
I'm impressed.

GEORGE
I warned you not to go too far.

MARTHA
I'm just beginning.

GEORGE
(Calmly, matter-of-factly)
I'm numbed enough . . . and I don't mean by liquor, though maybe that's been part of the process—a gradual, over-the-years going to sleep of the brain cells—I'm numbed enough, now, to be able to take you when we're alone. I don't listen to you . . . or when I *do* listen to you, I sift everything, I bring everything down to reflex response, so I don't really *hear* you, which is the only way to manage it. But you've taken a new tack, Martha, over the past couple of centuries—or however long it's been I've lived in this house with you—that makes it just too much . . . too much. I don't mind your dirty underthings in public . . . well, I *do* mind, but I've reconciled myself to that . . . but you've moved bag and baggage into your own fantasy world now, and you've started playing variations on your own distortions, and, as a result . . .

MARTHA
Nuts!

GEORGE
Yes . . . you have.

MARTHA
Nuts!

GEORGE
Well, you can go on like that as long as you want to. And, when you're done . . .

MARTHA
Have you ever listened to your sentences, George? Have you ever listened to the way you talk? You're so frigging . . . convoluted . . . that's what you are. You talk like you were writing one of your stupid papers.

GEORGE

Actually, I'm rather worried about you. About your mind.

MARTHA

Don't you worry about my mind, sweetheart!

GEORGE

I think I'll have you committed.

MARTHA

You WHAT?

GEORGE (*Quietly . . . distinctly*)

I think I'll have you committed.

MARTHA

(Breaks into long laughter)
Oh baby, aren't you something!

GEORGE

I've got to find some way to really get at you.

MARTHA

You've got at me, George . . . you don't have to do anything. Twenty-three years of you has been quite enough.

GEORGE

Will you go quietly, then?

MARTHA

You know what's happened, George? You want to know what's *really happened?* (*Snaps her fingers*) It's snapped, finally. Not me . . . *it.* The whole arrangement. You can go along . . . forever, and everything's . . . manageable. You make all sorts of excuses to yourself . . . *you* know . . . this is life . . . the hell with it . . . maybe tomorrow he'll be dead . . . maybe tomorrow *you'll* be dead . . . all sorts of excuses. But then, one day, one night, something happens . . . and SNAP! It breaks. And you just don't give a damn anymore. I've tried with you, baby . . . really, I've tried.

GEORGE

Come off it, Martha.

MARTHA

I've tried . . . I've really tried.

GEORGE (*With some awe*)

You're a monster . . . you *are.*

MARTHA

I'm loud, and I'm vulgar, and I wear the pants in this house because somebody's got to, but I am *not* a monster. I am *not.*

GEORGE

You're a spoiled, self-indulgent, wilful, dirty-minded, liquor-ridden . . .

MARTHA

SNAP! It went snap. Look, I'm not going to try to get through to you any more. . . . I'm not going to try. There was a second back there, maybe, there was a second, just a second, when I could have gotten through to you, when maybe we could have cut through all this crap. But that's past, and now I'm not going to try.

GEORGE

Once a month, Martha! I've gotten used to it . . . once a month and we get misunderstood Martha, the good-hearted girl underneath the barnacles, the little Miss that the touch of kindness'd bring to bloom again. And I've believed it more times than I want to remember, because I don't want to think I'm that much of a sucker. I don't believe you . . . I just don't believe you. There is no moment . . . there is no moment any more when we could . . . come together.

MARTHA *(Armed again)*

Well, maybe you're right, baby. You can't come together with nothing, and you're nothing! SNAP! It went snap tonight at Daddy's party. *(Dripping contempt, but there is fury and loss under it)* I sat there at Daddy's party, and I watched . . . I watched you sitting there, and I watched the younger men around you, the men who were going to go somewhere. And I sat there and I watched you, and *you* weren't *there!* And it snapped! It finally snapped! And I'm going to howl it out, and I'm not going to give a damn what I do, and I'm going to make the damned biggest explosion you ever heard.

GEORGE *(Very pointedly)*

You try it and I'll beat you at your own game.

MARTHA *(Hopefully)*

Is that a threat, George? Hunh?

GEORGE

That's a threat, Martha.

MARTHA *(Fake-spits at him)*

You're going to get it, baby.

GEORGE

Be careful, Martha . . . I'll rip you to pieces.

MARTHA

You aren't man enough . . . you haven't got the guts.

GEORGE

Total war?

MARTHA

Total.

(Silence. They both seem relieved . . . elated. NICK *reenters)*

NICK *(Brushing his hands off)*

Well . . . she's . . . resting.

GEORGE

(Quietly amused at NICK's *calm, off-hand manner)*

Oh?

MARTHA

Yeah? She all right?

NICK

I think so . . . now. I'm . . . terribly sorry . . .

MARTHA

Forget about it.

GEORGE

Happens all the time around here.

NICK

She'll be all right.

MARTHA

She lying down? You put her upstairs? On a bed?

NICK

(Making himself a drink)

Well, no, actually. Uh . . . may I? She's . . . in the bathroom . . . on the bath-room floor . . . she's lying there.

GEORGE *(Considers it)*

Well . . . that's not very nice.

NICK

She likes it. She says it's . . . cool.

GEORGE

Still, I don't think . . .

MARTHA *(Overruling him)*

If she wants to lie on the bathroom floor, let her. *(To* NICK, *seriously)* Maybe she'd be more comfortable in the tub?

NICK *(He, too, seriously)*

No, she says she likes the floor . . . she took up the mat, and she's lying on the tiles. She . . . she lies on the floor a lot . . . she really does.

MARTHA *(Pause)*

Oh.

NICK

She . . . she gets lots of headaches and things, and she always lies on the floor. *(To* GEORGE) Is there . . . ice?

GEORGE

What?

NICK

Ice. Is there ice?

GEORGE

(As if the word were unfamiliar to him)

Ice?

NICK

Ice. Yes.

MARTHA

Ice.

GEORGE

(As if he suddenly understood)

Ice!

MARTHA

Attaboy.

GEORGE *(Without moving)*

Oh, yes . . . I'll get some.

MARTHA

Well, go. *(Mugging . . . to* NICK) Besides, we want to be alone.

GEORGE

(Moving to take the bucket)

I wouldn't be surprised, Martha . . . I wouldn't be surprised.

MARTHA *(As if insulted)*

Oh, you wouldn't, hunh?

GEORGE

Not a bit, Martha.

MARTHA *(Violent)*

NO?

GEORGE *(He too)*

NO! *(Quietly again)* You'll try anything, Martha.

(Picks up the ice bucket)

NICK *(To cover)*

Actually, she's very . . . frail, and . . .

GEORGE

. . . slim-hipped.

NICK *(Remembering)*

Yes . . . exactly.

GEORGE

(At the hallway . . . not kindly)

That why you don't have any kids?

(He exits)

NICK

(To GEORGE's *retreating form)*

Well, I don't know that that's . . . *(Trails off)* . . . if that has anything to do with any . . . thing.

MARTHA

Well, if it does, who cares? Hunh?

NICK

Pardon?

*(*MARTHA *blows him a kiss)*

NICK

(Still concerned with GEORGE's *remark)*

I . . . what? . . . I'm sorry.

MARTHA

I said . . . *(Blows him another kiss)*

NICK *(Uncomfortable)*

Oh . . . yes.

MARTHA

Hey . . . . hand me a cigarette . . . Lover. *(*NICK *fishes in his pocket)* That's a good boy. *(He gives her one)* Unh . . . thanks.

(He lights it for her. As he does, she slips her hand between his legs, somewhere between the knee and the crotch, bringing her hand around to the outside of his leg)

Ummmmmmmm.

(He seems uncertain, but does not move. She smiles, moves her hand a little)

Now, for being such a good boy, you can give me a kiss. C'mon.

NICK *(Nervously)*

Look . . . I don't think we should . . .

MARTHA

C'mon, baby . . . a friendly kiss.

NICK *(Still uncertain)*

Well . . .

MARTHA

. . . you won't get hurt, little boy . . .

NICK

. . . not so little . . .

MARTHA

I'll bet you're not. C'mon . . .

NICK *(Weakening)*

But what if he should come back in, and . . . or . . . ?

MARTHA

(All the while her hand is moving up and down his leg)

George? Don't worry about him. Besides, who could object to a friendly little kiss? It's all in the faculty.

(They both laugh, quietly . . . NICK *a little nervously)*

We're a close-knit family here . . . Daddy always says so. . . . Daddy wants us to get to know each other . . . that's what he had the party for tonight. So c'mon . . . let's get to know each other a little bit.

NICK

It isn't that I don't want to . . . believe me. . . .

MARTHA

You're a scientist, aren't you? C'mon . . . make an experiment . . . make a little experiment. Experiment on old Martha.

NICK *(Giving in)*

. . . not very old. . . .

MARTHA

That's right, not very old, but lots of good experience . . . lots of it.

NICK

I'll . . . I'll bet.

MARTHA

(As they draw slowly closer)

It'll be a nice change for you, too.

NICK

Yes, it would.

MARTHA

And you could go back to your little wife all refreshed.

NICK

(*Closer . . . almost whispering*)
She wouldn't know the difference.

MARTHA

Well, nobody else's going to know, either.

(*They come together. What might have been a joke rapidly becomes serious, with* MARTHA *urging it in that direction. There is no frenetic quality, but rather a slow, continually involving intertwining. Perhaps* MARTHA *is still more or less in her chair, and* NICK *is sort of beside and on the chair.*

(GEORGE *enters . . . stops . . . watches a moment . . . smiles . . . laughs silently, nods his head, turns, exits, without being noticed.*)
(NICK, *who has already had his hand on* MARTHA's *breast, now puts his hand inside her dress*)

MARTHA (*Slowing him down*)

Hey . . . hey. Take it easy, boy. Down, baby. Don't rush it, hunh?

NICK (*His eyes still closed*)

Oh, c'mon, now . . .

MARTHA (*Pushing him away*)

Unh-unh. Later, baby . . . later.

NICK

I told you . . . I'm a biologist.

MARTHA (*Soothing him*)

I know. I can tell. Later, hunh?

(GEORGE *is heard off-stage, singing "Who's afraid of Virginia Woolf?"* MARTHA *and* NICK *go apart,* NICK *wiping his mouth,* MARTHA *checking her clothes. Safely later,* GEORGE *reenters with the ice bucket*)

GEORGE

. . . of Virginia Woolf,
Virginia Woolf,
Virginia . . .
. . . ah! Here we are . . . ice for the lamps of China, Manchuria thrown in. (*To* NICK) You better watch those yellow bastards, my love . . . they aren't amused. Why don't you come on over to our side, and we'll blow the hell out of 'em. Then we can split up the money between us and be on Easy Street. What d'ya say?

NICK

(Not at all sure what is being talked about)

Well . . . sure. Hey! Ice!

GEORGE

(With hideously false enthusiasm)

Right! *(Now to* MARTHA, *purring)* Hello, Martha . . . my dove . . . You look . . . radiant.

MARTHA *(Offhand)*

Thank you.

GEORGE *(Very cheerful)*

Well now, let me see. I've got the ice . . .

MARTHA

. . . gotten . . .

GEORGE

Got, Martha. Got is perfectly correct . . . it's just a little . . . archaic, like you.

MARTHA *(Suspicious)*

What are you so cheerful about?

GEORGE *(Ignoring the remark)*

Let's see now . . . I've got the ice. Can I make someone a drink? Martha, can I make you a drink?

MARTHA *(Bravura)*

Yeah, why not?

GEORGE *(Taking her glass)*

Indeed . . . why not? *(Examines the glass)* Martha! You've been nibbling away at the glass.

MARTHA

I have not!

GEORGE

(To NICK, *who is at the bar)*

I see you're making your own, which is fine . . . fine. I'll just hootch up Martha, here, and then we'll be all set.

MARTHA *(Suspicious)*

All set for what?

GEORGE *(Pause . . . considers)*

Why, I don't know. We're having a party, aren't we? *(To* NICK, *who has moved from the bar)* I passed your wife in the hall. I mean, I passed the john and I looked in on her. Peaceful . . . so peaceful. Sound asleep . . . and she's actually . . . sucking her thumb.

MARTHA

Awwwwww!

GEORGE

Rolled up like a fetus, sucking away.

NICK *(A little uncomfortably)*

I suppose she's all right.

GEORGE *(Expansively)*

Of course she is! *(Hands* MARTHA *her drink)* There you are.

MARTHA *(Still on her guard)*

Thanks.

GEORGE

And now one for me. It's my turn.

MARTHA

Never, baby . . . it's never your turn.

GEORGE *(Too cheerful)*

Oh, now, I wouldn't say that, Martha.

MARTHA

You moving on the principle the worm turns? Well, the worm part's O.K.
. . . cause that fits you fine, but the turning part . . . unh-unh! You're in a
straight line, buddy-boy, and it doesn't lead anywhere . . . *(A vague afterthought)* . . . except maybe the grave.

GEORGE

(Chuckles, takes his drink)

Well, you just hold that thought, Martha . . . hug it close . . . run your hands
over it. Me, I'm going to sit down . . . if you'll excuse me . . . I'm going to
sit down over there and read a book.

*(He moves to a chair facing away from the center of the room, but
not too far from the front door)*

MARTHA

You're gonna do *what?*

GEORGE *(Quietly, distinctly)*

I am going to read a book. Read. Read. Read? You've heard of it? *(Picks
up a book)*

MARTHA *(Standing)*

Whaddya mean you're gonna read? What's the matter with you?

GEORGE *(Too calmly)*

There's nothing the matter with me, Martha. . . . I'm going to read a book.
That's all.

MARTHA *(Oddly furious)*

We've got company!

GEORGE *(Over-patiently)*

I know, my dear . . . *(Looks at his watch)* . . . but . . . it's after four o'clock, and I always read around this time. Now, you . . . *(Dismisses her with a little wave)* . . . go about your business . . . I'll sit here very quietly. . . .

MARTHA

You read in the afternoon! You read at four o'clock in the afternoon . . . you don't read at four o'clock in the morning! Nobody reads at four o'clock in the morning!

GEORGE

(Absorbing himself in his book)

Now, now, now.

MARTHA

(Incredulously, to NICK*)*

He's going to read a book. . . . . The son of a bitch is going to read a book!

NICK *(Smiling a little)*

So it would seem.

(Moves to MARTHA, *puts his arm around her waist.* GEORGE *cannot see this, of course)*

MARTHA *(Getting an idea)*

Well, we can amuse ourselves, can't we?

NICK

I imagine so.

MARTHA

We're going to amuse ourselves, George.

GEORGE *(Not looking up)*

Unh-hunh. That's nice.

MARTHA

You might not like it.

GEORGE *(Never looking up)*

No, no, now . . . you go right ahead . . . you entertain your guests.

MARTHA

I'm going to entertain myself, too.

GEORGE

Good . . . good.

MARTHA

Ha, ha. You're a riot, George.

GEORGE

Unh-hunh.

MARTHA

Well, I'm a riot, too, George.

GEORGE

Yes you are, Martha.

(NICK *takes* MARTHA'*s hand, pulls her to him. They stop for a moment, then kiss, not briefly*)

MARTHA *(After)*

You know what I'm doing, George?

GEORGE

No, Martha . . . what are you doing?

MARTHA

I'm entertaining. I'm entertaining one of the guests. I'm necking with one of the guests.

GEORGE

(Seemingly relaxed and preoccupied, never looking)

Oh, that's nice. Which one?

MARTHA *(Livid)*

Oh, by God you're funny. *(Breaks away from* NICK . . . *moves into* GEORGE'*s side-line of vision by herself. Her balance is none too good, and she bumps into or brushes against the door chimes by the door. They chime)*

GEORGE

Someone at the door, Martha.

MARTHA

Never mind that. I said I was necking with one of the guests.

GEORGE

Good . . . good. You go right on.

MARTHA

(Pauses . . . not knowing quite what to do)

Good?

GEORGE

Yes, good . . . good for you.

MARTHA

(Her eyes narrowing, her voice becoming hard)

Oh, I see what you're up to, you lousy little . . .

GEORGE

I'm up to page a hundred and . . .

MARTHA

Cut it! Just cut it out! *(She hits against the door chimes again; they chime)*
Goddamn bongs.

GEORGE

They're chimes, Martha. Why don't you go back to your necking and stop
bothering me? I want to read.

MARTHA

Why, you miserable . . . I'll show *you*.

GEORGE

(Swings around to face her . . . says, with great loathing)

No . . . show him, Martha . . . he hasn't seen it. *Maybe* he hasn't seen it.
(Turns to NICK*)* You haven't seen it yet, have you?

NICK

(Turning away, a look of disgust on his face)

I . . . I have no respect for you.

GEORGE

And none for yourself, either. . . . *(Indicating* MARTHA*)* I don't know what
the younger generation's coming to.

NICK

You don't . . . you don't even . . .

GEORGE

Care? You're quite right. . . . I couldn't care less. So, you just take this bag
of laundry here, throw her over your shoulder, and . . .

NICK

You're disgusting.

GEORGE *(Incredulous)*

Because *you're* going to hump Martha, *I'm* disgusting?

(He breaks down in ridiculing laughter)

MARTHA *(To* GEORGE*)*

You Mother-Fucker! *(To* NICK*)* Go wait for me, hunh? Go wait for me in
the kitchen. *(But* NICK *does not move.* MARTHA *goes to him, puts her arms
around him)* C'mon, baby . . . please. Wait for me . . . in the kitchen . . . be
a good baby.

*(*NICK *takes her kiss, glares at* GEORGE . . . *who has turned his back
again . . . and exits.*

*(*MARTHA *swings around to* GEORGE*)*

Now you listen to me. . . .

GEORGE

I'd rather read, Martha, if you don't mind. . . .

MARTHA

(Her anger has her close to tears, her frustration to fury)

Well, I do mind. Now, you pay attention to me! You come off this kick you're on, or I swear to God I'll do it. I swear to God I'll follow that guy into the kitchen, and then I'll take him upstairs, and . . .

GEORGE

(Swinging around to her again . . . loud . . . loathing)

SO WHAT, MARTHA?

MARTHA

(Considers him for a moment . . . then, nodding her head, backing off slowly)

O.K. . . . O.K. . . . You asked for it . . . and you're going to get it.

GEORGE *(Softly, sadly)*

Lord, Martha, if you want the boy that much . . . have him . . . but do it honestly, will you? Don't cover it over with all this . . . all this . . . footwork.

MARTHA *(Hopeless)*

I'll make you sorry you made me want to marry you. *(At the hallway)* I'll make you regret the day you ever decided to come to this college. I'll make you sorry you ever let yourself down.

(She exits)

(Silence. GEORGE *sits still, staring straight ahead. Listening . . . but there is no sound. Outwardly calm, he returns to his book, reads a moment, then looks up . . . considers . . .)*

GEORGE

"And the west, encumbered by crippling alliances, and burdened with a morality too rigid to accommodate itself to the swing of events, must . . . eventually . . . fall."

(He laughs, briefly, ruefully . . . rises, with the book in his hand. He stands still . . . then, quickly, he gathers all the fury he has been containing within himself . . . he shakes . . . he looks at the book in his hand and, with a cry that is part growl, part howl, he hurls it at the chimes. They crash against one another, ringing wildly. From off stage comes the sound of MARTHA's *laughter and the crashing of dishes. Yelling.)*

That's right! Go at it! I'm going you get you, Martha. I'm going to get you.

(Exits, leaves the front door open)

CURTAIN

ACT THREE
THE EXORCISM

MARTHA *enters, talking to herself.*

MARTHA

Hey, hey. . . . Where is everybody . . . ? *(It is evident she is not bothered)* So? Drop me; pluck me like a goddamn . . . whatever-it-is . . . creeping vine, and throw me over your shoulder like an old shoe . . . George? *(Looks about her)* George? *(Silence)* George! What are you doing: Hiding, or something? *(Silence)* GEORGE!! *(Silence)* Oh, fa Chri . . . . . . *(Goes to the bar, makes herself a drink and amuses herself with the following performance)* Deserted! Abandon-ed! Left out in the cold like an old pussycat. HA! Can I get you a drink, Martha? Why, thank you, George; that's very kind of you. No, Martha, no; why I'd do anything for you. Would you, George? Why, I'd do anything for you, too. Would you, Martha? Why, certainly, George. Martha, I've misjudged you. And I've misjudged you, too, George. WHERE IS EVERYBODY!!! Hump the Hostess! *(Laughs greatly at this, falls into a chair; calms down, looks defeated, says, softly)* Fat chance. *(Even softer)* Fat chance *(Baby-talk now)* Daddy? Daddy? Martha is abandon-ed. Left to her own vices at . . . *(Peers at a clock)* . . . something o'clock in the old A.M. Daddy White-Mouse; do you really have red eyes? Do you? Let me see. Ohhhhh! You do! You do! Daddy, you have red eyes . . . because you cry all the time, don't you, Daddy. Yes; you do. You cry all-lll the time. I'LL GIVE ALL YOU BASTARDS FIVE TO COME OUT FROM WHERE YOU'RE HIDING!! *(Pause)* I cry all the time too, Daddy. I cry alllll the time; but deep inside, so no one can see me. I cry all the time. And Georgie cries all the time, too. We both cry all the time, and then, what we do, we cry, and we take our tears, and we put 'em in the ice box, in the goddamn ice trays *(Begins to laugh)* until they're all frozen *(Laughs even more)* and then . . . we put them . . . in our . . . drinks. *(More laughter, which is something else, too. After sobering silence)* Up the drain, down the spout, dead, gone and forgotten. . . . Up the spout, not down the spout; *up* the spout: THE POKER NIGHT. Up the spout. . . . *(Sadly)* I've got windshield wipers on my eyes, because I married you . . . baby! . . .

Martha, you'll be a song-writer yet. *(Jiggles the ice in her glass)* CLINK!
(Does it again) CLINK! *(Giggles, repeats it several times)* CLINK! . . .
CLINK! . . . CLINK! . . . CLINK!

> (NICK *enters while* MARTHA *is clinking; he stands in the hall
> entrance and watches her; finally he comes in*)

NICK

My God, you've gone crazy too.

MARTHA

Clink?

NICK

I said, you've gone crazy too.

MARTHA *(Considers it)*

Probably . . . probably.

NICK

You've all gone crazy: I come downstairs, and what happens . . .

MARTHA

What happens?

NICK

. . . my wife's gone into the can with a liquor bottle, and she winks at me
. . . winks at me! . . .

MARTHA *(Sadly)*

She's never wunk at you; what a shame. . . .

NICK

She is lying down on the floor again, the tiles, all curled up, and she starts
peeling the label off the liquor bottle, the brandy bottle . . .

MARTHA

. . . we'll never get the deposit back that way . . .

NICK

. . . and I ask her what she's doing, and she goes: shhhhhh!, nobody knows
I'm here; and I come back in here, and you're sitting there going Clink!,
for God's sake. Clink!

MARTHA

CLINK!

NICK

You've all gone crazy.

MARTHA

Yes. Sad but true.

NICK

Where is your husband?

MARTHA

He is vanish-ed. Pouf!

NICK

You're all crazy: nuts.

MARTHA *(Affects a brogue)*

Awww, 'tis the refuge we take when the unreality of the world weighs too heavy on our tiny heads. *(Normal voice again)* Relax; sink into it; you're no better than anybody else.

NICK *(Defensively)*

I think I am.

MARTHA

(Her glass to her mouth)

You're certainly a flop in some departments.

NICK *(Wincing)*

I beg your pardon . . . ?

MARTHA *(Unnecessarily loud)*

I said, you're certainly a flop in some . . .

NICK *(He, too, too loud)*

I'm sorry you're disappointed.

MARTHA *(Braying)*

I didn't say I was disappointed! Stupid!

NICK

You should try me some time when we haven't been drinking for ten hours, and maybe . . .

MARTHA *(Still braying)*

I wasn't talking about your potential; I was talking about your goddamn performance.

NICK *(Softly)*

Oh.

MARTHA *(She softer, too)*

Your potential's fine. It's dandy. *(Wiggles her eyebrows)* Absolutely dandy. I haven't seen such a dandy potential in a long time. Oh, but baby, you sure are a flop.

NICK *(Snapping it out)*

Everybody's a flop to you! Your husband's a flop, *I'm a* flop. . . .

MARTHA *(Dismissing him)*

You're all flops. I am the Earth Mother, and you're all flops. *(More or less to herself)* I disgust me. I pass my life in crummy, totally pointless infidelities . . . *(Laughs ruefully) would-be* infidelities. Hump the Hostess? That's a laugh. A bunch of boozed-up . . . impotent lunk-heads. Martha makes goo-goo eyes, and the lunk-heads grin, and roll their beautiful, beautiful eyes back, and grin some more, and Martha licks her chops, and the lunk-heads slap over to the bar to pick up a little courage, *and* they pick up a little courage, and they bounce back over to old Martha, who does a little dance for them, which heats them all up . . . mentally . . . and so they slap over to the bar again, and pick up a little more courage, and their wives and sweethearts stick their noses up in the air . . . right through the ceiling, sometimes . . . which sends the lunk-heads back to the soda fountain again where they fuel up some more, while Martha-poo sits there with her dress up over her head . . . suffocating—you don't know how *stuffy* it is with your dress up over your head—suffocating! waiting for the lunk-heads; so, *finally* they get their courage up . . . but that's all, baby! Oh my, there is sometimes some very nice potential, but, oh my! My, my, my. *(Brightly)* But that's how it is in a civilized society. *(To herself again)* All the gorgeous lunk-heads. Poor babies. *(To NICK, now; earnestly)* There is only one man in my life who has ever . . . made me happy. Do you know that? One!

NICK

The . . . the what-do-you-call-it? . . . uh . . . the lawn mower, or something?

MARTHA

No; I'd forgotten him. But when I think about him and me it's almost like being a voyeur. Hunh. No; I didn't mean him; I meant George, of course. *(No response from NICK)* Uh . . . George; my husband.

NICK *(Disbelieving)*

You're kidding.

MARTHA

Am I?

NICK

You must be. Him?

MARTHA

Him.

NICK *(As if in on a joke)*

Sure; sure.

MARTHA

You don't believe it.

NICK *(Mocking)*

Why, of course I do.

MARTHA

You always deal in appearances?

NICK *(Derisively)*

Oh, for God's sake . . .

MARTHA

. . . George who is out somewhere there in the dark. . . . George who is good to me, and whom I revile; who understands me, and whom I push off; who can make me laugh, and I choke it back in my throat; who can hold me, at night, so that it's warm, and whom I will bite so there's blood; who keeps learning the games we play as quickly as I can change the rules; who can make me happy and I do not wish to be happy, and yes I do wish to be happy. George and Martha: sad, sad, sad.

NICK

(Echoing, still not believing)

Sad.

MARTHA

. . . whom I will not forgive for having come to rest; for having seen me and having said: yes; this will do; who has made the hideous, the hurting, the insulting mistake of loving me and must be punished for it. George and Martha: sad, sad, sad.

NICK *(Puzzled)*

Sad.

MARTHA

. . . who tolerates, which is intolerable; who is kind, which is cruel; who understands, which is beyond comprehension. . . .

NICK

George and Martha: sad, sad, sad.

MARTHA

Some day . . . hah! some *night* . . . some stupid, liquor-ridden night . . . I will go too far . . . and I'll either break the man's back . . . or push him off for good . . . which is what I deserve.

NICK

I don't think he's got a vertebra intact.

MARTHA *(Laughing at him)*

You don't, huh? You don't think so. Oh, little boy, you got yourself hunched over that microphone of yours . . .

NICK

Microscope . . .

MARTHA

. . . yes . . . and you don't see anything, do you? You see everything but the goddamn mind; you see all the little specs and crap, but you don't see what goes on, do you?

NICK

I know when a man's had his back broken; I can see that.

MARTHA

Can you!

NICK

You're damn right.

MARTHA

Oh . . . you know so little. And you're going to take over the world, hunh?

NICK

All right, now . . .

MARTHA

You think a man's got his back broken 'cause he makes like a clown and walks bent, hunh? Is that *really* all you know?

NICK

I said, all *right!*

MARTHA

Ohhhh! The stallion's mad, hunh. The gelding's all upset. Ha, ha, ha, HA!

NICK *(Softly; wounded)*

You . . . you swing wild, don't you.

MARTHA *(Triumphant)*

HAH!

NICK

Just . . . anywhere.

MARTHA

HAH! I'm a gattling gun. Hahahahahahahahaha!

NICK *(In wonder)*

Aimless . . . butchery. Pointless.

MARTHA

Aw! You poor little bastard.

NICK

Hit out at everything.
    (The door chimes chime)

MARTHA

Go answer the door.

NICK (*Amazed*)

What did you say?

MARTHA

I said, go answer the door. What are you, deaf?

NICK (*Trying to get it straight*)

You . . . want me . . . to go answer the door?

MARTHA

That's right, lunk-head; answer the door. There must be something you can do well; or, are you too drunk to do that, too? Can't you get the latch up, either?

NICK

Look, there's no need. . . .
(*Door chimes again*)

MARTHA (*Shouting*)

Answer it! (*Softer*) You can be houseboy around here for a while. You can start off being houseboy right now.

NICK

Look, lady, I'm no flunky to you.

MARTHA (*Cheerfully*)

Sure you are! You're ambitious, aren't you, boy? You didn't chase me around the kitchen and up the goddamn stairs out of mad, driven passion, did you now? You were thinking a little bit about your career, weren't you? Well, you can just houseboy your way up the ladder for a while.

NICK

There's no limit to you, is there?
(*Door chimes again*)

MARTHA (*Calmly, surely*)

No, baby; none. Go answer the door. (NICK *hesitates*) Look, boy; once you stick your nose in it, you're not going to pull out just whenever you feel like it. You're in for a while. Now, git!

NICK

Aimless . . . wanton . . . pointless . . .

MARTHA

Now, now, now; just do what you're told; show old Martha there's something you *can* do. Hunh? Atta boy.

NICK
(Considers, gives in, moves toward the door. Chimes again)
I'm coming, for Christ's sake!

MARTHA *(Claps her hands)*
HA HA! Wonderful; marvelous. *(Sings)* "Just a gigolo, everywhere I go, people always say . . ."

NICK
STOP THAT!

MARTHA *(Giggles)*
Sorry, baby; go on now; open the little door.

NICK *(With great rue)*
Christ.
(He flings open the door, and a hand thrusts into the opening a great bunch of snapdragons; they stay there for a moment. NICK strains his eyes to see who is behind them)

MARTHA
Oh, how lovely!

GEORGE
(Appearing in the doorway, the snapdragons covering his face; speaks in a hideously cracked falsetto)
Flores; flores para los muertos. Flores.

MARTHA
Ha, ha, ha HA!

GEORGE
(A step into the room; lowers the flowers; sees NICK; his face becomes gleeful; he opens his arms)
Sonny! You've come home for your birthday! At last!

NICK *(Backing off)*
Stay away from me.

MARTHA
Ha, ha, ha, HA! That's the houseboy, for God's sake.

GEORGE
Really? That's not our own little sonny-Jim? Our own little all-American something-or-other?

MARTHA *(Giggling)*
Well, I certainly hope not; he's been acting awful funny, if he is.

GEORGE *(Almost manic)*

Ohhhh! I'll bet! Chippie-chippie-chippie, hunh? *(Affecting embarrass-ment)* I . . . I brungya dese flowers, Mart'a, 'cause I . . . wull, 'cause you'se . . . awwwwww hell. Gee.

MARTHA

Pansies! Rosemary! Violence! My wedding bouquet!

NICK *(Starting to move away)*

Well, if you two kids don't mind, I think I'll just . . .

MARTHA

Ach! You just stay where you are. Make my hubby a drink.

NICK

I don't think I will.

GEORGE

No, Martha, no; that would be too much; he's your houseboy, baby, not mine.

NICK

I'm nobody's houseboy . . .

GEORGE *and* MARTHA

. . . Now! *(Sing)* I'm nobody's houseboy now . . . *(Both laugh)*

NICK

Vicious . . .

GEORGE *(Finishing it for him)*

. . . children. Hunh? That right? Vicious children, with their oh-so-sad games, hopscotching their way through life, etcetera, etcetera. Is that it?

NICK

Something like it.

GEORGE

Screw, baby.

MARTHA

Him can't. Him too fulla booze.

GEORGE

Weally? *(Handing the snapdragons* to NICK) Here; dump these in some gin. (NICK *takes them, looks at them, drops them on the floor at his feet)*

MARTHA *(Sham dismay)*

Awwwwww.

GEORGE

What a terrible thing to do . . . to Martha's snapdragons.

MARTHA

Is that what they are?

GEORGE

Yup. And here I went out into the moonlight to pick 'em for Martha tonight, and for our sonny-boy tomorrow, for his birfday.

MARTHA

(Passing on information)
There is no moon now. I saw it go down from the bedroom.

GEORGE *(Feigned glee)*
From the bedroom! *(Normal tone)* Well, there was a moon.

MARTHA

(Too patient; laughing a little)
There couldn't have been a moon.

GEORGE

Well, there was. There is.

MARTHA

There is no moon; the moon went down.

GEORGE

There is a moon; the moon is up.

MARTHA

(Straining to keep civil)
I'm afraid you're mistaken.

GEORGE *(Too cheerful)*
No; no.

MARTHA *(Between her teeth)*
There is no goddamn moon.

GEORGE

My dear Martha . . . I did not pick snapdragons in the stony dark. I did not go stumbling around Daddy's greenhouse in the pitch.

MARTHA

Yes . . . you did. You would.

GEORGE

Martha, I do not pick flowers in the blink. I have never robbed a hothouse without there is a light from heaven.

MARTHA *(With finality)*
There is no moon; the moon went down.

GEORGE *(With great logic)*

That may very well be, Chastity; the moon may very well have gone down
. . . but it came back up.

MARTHA

The moon does *not* come back up; when the moon has gone down it stays
down.

GEORGE *(Getting a little ugly)*

You don't know anything. IF the moon went down, then it came back up.

MARTHA

BULLSHIT!

GEORGE

Ignorance! Such . . . ignorance.

MARTHA

Watch who you're calling ignorant!

GEORGE

Once . . . once, when I was sailing past Majorca, drinking on deck with a
correspondent who was talking about Roosevelt, the moon went down,
thought about it for a little . . . considered it, you know what I mean? . . .
and then, POP, came up again. Just like that.

MARTHA

That is not true! That is such a lie!

GEORGE

You must not call everything a lie, Martha. *(To* NICK*)* Must she?

NICK

Hell, I don't know when you people are lying, or what.

MARTHA

You're damned right!

GEORGE

You're not supposed to.

MARTHA

Right!

GEORGE

At any rate, I was sailing past Majorca . . .

MARTHA

You never sailed past Majorca . . .

GEORGE

Martha . . .

MARTHA

You were never in the goddamn Mediterranean at all . . . ever. . . .

GEORGE

I certainly was! My Mommy and Daddy took me there as a college graduation present.

MARTHA

Nuts!

NICK

Was this after you killed them?
    (GEORGE *and* MARTHA *swing around and look at him; there is a
    brief, ugly pause*)

GEORGE (*Defiantly*)

Maybe.

MARTHA

Yeah; maybe not, too.

NICK

Jesus!
    (GEORGE *swoops down, picks up the bunch of snapdragons, shakes
    them like a feather duster in* NICK'S *face, and moves away a little*)

GEORGE

HAH!

NICK

Damn you.

GEORGE (*To* NICK)

Truth and illusion. Who knows the difference, eh, toots? Eh?

MARTHA

You were never in the Mediterranean . . . truth or illusion . . . either way.

GEORGE

If I wasn't in the Mediterranean, how did I get to the Aegean? Hunh?

MARTHA

OVERLAND!

NICK

Yeah!

GEORGE

Don't you side with her, houseboy.

NICK

I am not a houseboy

GEORGE

Look! I know the game! You don't make it in the sack, you're a houseboy.

NICK

I AM NOT A HOUSEBOY!

GEORGE

No? Well then, you must have made it in the sack. Yes? *(He is breathing a little heavy; behaving a little manic)* Yes? Someone's lying around here; somebody isn't playing the game straight. Yes? Come on; come on; who's lying? Martha? Come on!

NICK

(After a pause; to MARTHA, *quietly with intense pleading)*
Tell him I'm not a houseboy.

MARTHA

(After a pause, quietly, lowering her head)
No; you're not a houseboy.

GEORGE *(With great, sad relief)*

So be it.

MARTHA *(Pleading)*

Truth and illusion, George; you don't know the difference.

GEORGE

No; but we must carry on as though we did.

MARTHA

Amen.

GEORGE

(Flourishing the flowers)
SNAP WENT THE DRAGONS!! *(*NICK *and* MARTHA *laugh weakly)*
Hunh? Here we go round the mulberry bush, hunh?

NICK *(Tenderly, to* MARTHA*)*

Thank you.

MARTHA

Skip it.

GEORGE *(Loud)*

I said, here we go round the mulberry bush!

MARTHA *(Impatiently)*

Yeah, yeah; we know; snap go the dragons.

GEORGE

(Taking a snapdragon, throwing it, spear-like, stem-first at MARTHA*)*
SNAP!

MARTHA

Don't, George.

GEORGE *(Throws another)*

SNAP!

NICK

Don't do that.

GEORGE

Shut up, stud.

NICK

I'm not a stud!

GEORGE *(Throws one at* NICK*)*

SNAP! Then you're a houseboy. Which is it? Which are you? Hunh? Make up your mind. Either way . . . *(Throws another at him)* SNAP! . . . *you disgust me.*

MARTHA

Does it matter to you, George!?

GEORGE *(Throws one at her)*

SNAP! No, actually, it doesn't. Either way . . . SNAP!

MARTHA

Stop throwing those goddamn things at me!

GEORGE

Either way. *(Throws another at her)* SNAP! I've had it.

NICK *(To* MARTHA*)*

Do you want me to . . . do something to him?

MARTHA

You leave him alone!

GEORGE

If you're a houseboy, baby, you can pick up after me; if you're a stud, you can go protect your plow. Either way. Either way . . . Everything.

NICK

Oh for God's . . .

MARTHA *(A little afraid)*

Truth or illusion, George. Doesn't it matter to you . . . at all?

GEORGE

(Without throwing anything)

SNAP! *(Silence)* You got your answer, baby?

MARTHA *(Sadly)*

Got it.

GEORGE

You just gird your blue-veined loins, girl. *(Sees* NICK *moving toward the hall)* Now; we got one more game to play. And it's called bringing up baby.

NICK

(More-or-less under his breath)

Oh, for Lord's sake . . .

MARTHA

George . . .

GEORGE

I don't want any fuss. *(To* NICK*)* You don't want any scandal around here, do you, big boy? You don't want to wreck things, do you? Hunh? You want to keep to your timetable, don't you? *(*NICK *sits) (To* MARTHA*)* And you, pretty Miss, you like fun and games, don't you? You're a sport from way back, aren't you?

MARTHA *(Quietly, giving in)*

All right, George; all right.

GEORGE

(Seeing them both cowed; purrs)

Gooooooooood; goooooood. *(Looks about him)* But, we're not all here. *(Snaps his fingers a couple of times at* NICK*)* You; you . . . uh . . . you; your little wifelet isn't here.

NICK

Look; she's had a rough night, now; she's in the can, and she's . . .

GEORGE

Well, we can't play without everyone here. Now that's a fact. We gotta have your little wife. *(Hog-calls toward the hall)* SOOOWWWIIIEEE!! SOOOWWWIIIEEE!!

NICK

(As MARTHA *giggles nervously)*

Cut that!

GEORGE

(Swinging around, facing him)

Then get your butt out of that chair and bring the little dip back in here. *(As* NICK *does not move)* Now be a good puppy. Fetch, good puppy, go fetch.

*(*NICK *rises, opens his mouth to say something, thinks better of it, exits)*

One more game.

MARTHA *(After* NICK *goes)*

I don't like what's going to happen.

GEORGE (*Surprisingly tender*)

Do you know what it is?

MARTHA (*Pathetic*)

No. But I don't like it.

GEORGE

Maybe you will, Martha.

MARTHA

No.

GEORGE

Oh, it's a real fun game, Martha.

MARTHA (*Pleading*)

No more games.

GEORGE (*Quietly triumphant*)

One more, Martha. One more game, and then beddie-bye. Everybody pack up his tools and baggage and stuff and go home. And you and me, well, we gonna climb them well-worn stairs.

MARTHA

No, George; no.

GEORGE

Yes, baby.

MARTHA (*Almost in tears*)

No, George; please?

GEORGE (*Soothing*)

It'll all be done with before you know it.

MARTHA

No, George.

GEORGE

No climb stairs with Georgie?

MARTHA (*A sleepy child*)

No more games . . . please. It's games I don't want. No more games.

GEORGE

Aw, sure you do, Martha . . . original game-girl and all, 'course you do.

MARTHA

Ugly games . . . ugly. And now this new one?

GEORGE (*Stroking her hair*)

You'll love it, baby.

MARTHA

No, George.

GEORGE

You'll have a ball.

MARTHA

(Tenderly; moves to touch him)
Please, George, no more games; I . . .

GEORGE

(Slapping her moving hand with vehemence)
Don't you touch me! You keep your paws clean for the undergraduates!

MARTHA

(A cry of alarm, but faint)

GEORGE

(Grabbing her hair, pulling her head back)
Now, you listen to me, Martha; you have had quite an evening . . . quite a
night for yourself, and you can't just cut it off whenever you've got enough
blood in your mouth. We are going on, and I'm going to have at you, and
it's going to make your performance tonight look like an Easter pageant.
Now I want you to get yourself a little alert. *(Slaps her lightly with his free
hand)* I want a little life in you, baby. *(Again)*

MARTHA *(Struggling)*

Stop it!

GEORGE

(Again) Pull yourself together! *(Again)* I want you on your feet and slug-
ging, sweetheart, because I'm going to knock you around, and I want you
up for it. *(Again; he pulls away, releases her; she rises)*

MARTHA

All right, George. What do you want, George?

GEORGE

An equal battle, baby; that's all.

MARTHA

You'll get it!

GEORGE

I want you mad.

MARTHA

I'M MAD!!

GEORGE

Get madder!

MARTHA

DON'T WORRY ABOUT IT!

GEORGE

Good for you, girl; now, we're going to play this one to the death.

MARTHA

Yours!

GEORGE

You'd be surprised. Now, here come the tots; you be ready for this.

MARTHA

(She paces, actually looks a bit like a fighter)

I'm ready for you.

(NICK *and* HONEY *reenter;* NICK *supporting* HONEY, *who still retains her brandy bottle and glass)*

NICK *(Unhappily)*

Here we are.

HONEY *(Cheerfully)*

Hip, hop. Hip, hop.

NICK

You a bunny, Honey? *(She laughs greatly, sits)*

HONEY

I'm a bunny, Honey.

GEORGE *(To* HONEY*)*

Well, now; how's the bunny?

HONEY

Bunny funny! *(She laughs again)*

NICK *(Under his breath)*

Jesus.

GEORGE

Bunny funny? Good for bunny!

MARTHA

Come on, George!

GEORGE *(To* MARTHA*)*

Honey funny bunny! (HONEY *screams with laughter)*

NICK

Jesus God . . .

GEORGE

(Slaps his hands together, once)

All right! Here we go! Last game! All sit. (NICK *sits*) Sit down, Martha. This is a civilized game.

MARTHA

(Cocks her fist, doesn't swing)
(Sits) Just get on with it.

HONEY

(To NICK*)* Hello, Dear.

MARTHA

It's almost dawn, for God's sake. . . .

HONEY *(Ibid)*

Hello, Dear.

GEORGE *(To* NICK*)*

Well, speak to your little wifelet, your little bunny, for God's sake.

NICK *(Softly, embarrassed)*

Hello, Honey.

GEORGE

Awww, that was nice. I think we've been having a . . . a real good evening . . . all things considered. . . . We've sat around, and got to know each other, and had fun and games . . . curl-up-on-the-floor, for example . . .

HONEY

. . . the tiles . . .

GEORGE

. . . the tiles. . . . Snap the Dragon.

HONEY

. . . peel the label. . . .

GEORGE

. . . peel the . . . what?

MARTHA

Label. Peel the label.

HONEY

(Apologetically, holding up her brandy bottle)
I peel labels.

GEORGE

We all peel labels, sweetie; and when you get through the skin, all three layers, through the muscle, slosh aside the organs *(An aside to* NICK*)* them which is still sloshable—*(Back* to HONEY*)* and get down to bone . . . you know what you do then?

HONEY *(Terribly interested)*

No!

GEORGE

When you get down to bone, you haven't got all the way, yet. There's some thing inside the bone . . . the marrow . . . and that's what you gotta get at. (A *strange smile at* MARTHA)

HONEY

Oh! I see.

GEORGE

The marrow. But bones are pretty resilient, especially in the young. Now, take our son. . . .

HONEY

Who?

GEORGE

Our son. . . . Martha's and my little joy!

NICK *(Moving toward the bar)*

Do you mind if I. . . . ?

GEORGE

No, no; you go right ahead.

MARTHA

George . . .

GEORGE *(Too kindly)*

Yes, Martha?

MARTHA

Just what are you doing?

GEORGE

Why, Love, I was talking about our son.

MARTHA

Don't.

GEORGE

Isn't Martha something? Here we are, on the eve of our boy's homecoming, the eve of his twenty-first birfday, the eve of his majority . . . and Martha says don't talk about him.

MARTHA

Just . . . don't.

GEORGE

But I want to, Martha! It's very important we talk about him. Now bunny and the . . . houseboy or stud here, whichever he is . . . don't know much about junior, and I think they should.

MARTHA

Just . . . don't.

GEORGE

(Snapping his fingers at NICK*)*
You. Hey, you! You want to play bringing up baby, don't you!

NICK *(Hardly civil)*

Were you snapping at me?

GEORGE

That's right. *(Instructing him) You* want to hear about our bouncy boy.

NICK *(Pause; then, shortly)*

Yeah; sure.

GEORGE *(To* HONEY*)*

And you, my dear? You want to hear about him, too, don't you.

HONEY

Whom?

GEORGE

Martha's and my son.

HONEY

Oh, you have a child?
    *(*MARTHA *and* NICK *laugh uncomfortably)*

GEORGE

Oh, indeed; do we ever! Do you want to talk about him, Martha, or shall I?
Hunh?

MARTHA

(A smile that is a sneer)
Don't, George.

GEORGE

All rightie. Well, now; let's see. He's a nice kid, really, in spite of his home
life; I mean, most kids'd grow up neurotic, what with Martha here
carrying on the way she does: sleeping 'til four in the P.M., climbing all
over the poor bastard, trying to break the bathroom door down to wash
him in the tub when he's sixteen, dragging strangers into the house at all
hours. . . .

MARTHA *(Rising)*

O.K. YOU!

GEORGE *(Mock concern)*

Martha!

MARTHA

That's enough!

GEORGE

Well, do you want to take over?

HONEY *(To* NICK*)*

Why would anybody want to wash somebody who's sixteen years old?

NICK

(Slamming his drink down)
Oh, for Christ's sake, Honey!

HONEY *(Stage whisper)*

Well, why?!

GEORGE

Because it's her baby-poo.

MARTHA

ALL RIGHT!!
(By rote; a kind of almost-tearful recitation)
Our son. You want our son? You'll have it.

GEORGE

You want a drink, Martha?

MARTHA *(Pathetically)*

Yes.

NICK *(To* MARTHA *kindly)*

We don't have to hear about it . . . if you don't want to.

GEORGE

Who says so? You in a position to set the rules around here?

NICK *(Pause; tight-lipped)*

No.

GEORGE

Good boy; you'll go far. All right, Martha; your recitation, please.

MARTHA *(From far away)*

What, George?

GEORGE *(Prompting)*

"Our son. . . ."

MARTHA

All right. Our son. Our son was born in a September night, a night not
unlike tonight, though tomorrow, and twenty . . . one . . . years ago.

GEORGE *(Beginning of quiet asides)*

You see? I told you.

MARTHA

It was an easy birth . . .

GEORGE

Oh, Martha; no. You labored . . . how you labored.

MARTHA

It was an easy birth . . . once it had been . . . accepted, relaxed into.

GEORGE

Ah . . . yes. Better.

MARTHA

It was an easy birth, once it had been accepted, and I was young.

GEORGE

And I was younger. . . . *(Laughs quietly to himself)*

MARTHA

And I was young, and he was a healthy child, a red, bawling child, with slippery firm limbs . . .

GEORGE

. . . Martha thinks she saw him at delivery. . . .

MARTHA

. . . with slippery, firm limbs, and a full head of black, fine, fine hair which, oh, later, later, became blond as the sun, our son.

GEORGE

He was a healthy child.

MARTHA

And I had wanted a child . . . oh, I had wanted a child.

GEORGE *(Prodding her)*

A son? A daughter?

MARTHA

A child! *(Quieter)* A child. And I had my child.

GEORGE

Our child.

MARTHA *(With great sadness)*

Our child. And we raised him . . . *(Laughs, briefly, bitterly)* yes, we did; we raised him . . .

GEORGE

With teddy bears and an antique bassinet from Austria . . . and *no nurse*.

MARTHA

. . . with teddy bears and transparent floating goldfish, and a pale blue bed with cane at the headboard when he was older, cane which he wore through . . . finally . . . with his little hands . . . in his . . . sleep. . . .

GEORGE

. . . nightmares . . .

MARTHA

. . . *sleep*. . . . He was a restless child. . . .

GEORGE

. . . *(Soft chuckle, head-shaking of disbelief)* . . . Oh Lord . . .

MARTHA

. . . sleep . . . and a croup tent . . . a pale green croup tent, and the shining kettle hissing in the one light of the room that time he was sick . . . those four days . . . and animal crackers, and the bow and arrow he kept under his bed. . . .

GEORGE

. . . the arrows with rubber cups at their tip . . .

MARTHA

. . . at their tip, which he kept beneath his bed. . . .

GEORGE

Why? Why, Martha?

MARTHA

. . . for fear . . . for fear of . . .

GEORGE

For fear. Just that: for fear.

MARTHA

(Vaguely waving him off; going on)

. . . and . . . and sandwiches on Sunday night, and Saturdays . . . *(Pleased recollection)* . . . and Saturdays the banana boat, the whole peeled banana, scooped out on top, with green grapes for the crew, a double line of green grapes, and along the sides, stuck to the boat with toothpicks, orange slices. . . . SHIELDS.

GEORGE

And for the oar?

MARTHA *(Uncertainly)*

A . . . carrot?

GEORGE

Or a swizzle stick, whatever was easier.

MARTHA

No. A carrot. And his eyes were green . . . green with . . . if you peered so deep into them . . . so deep . . . bronze . . . bronze parentheses around the irises . . . such green eyes!

GEORGE

. . . blue, green, brown . . .

MARTHA

. . . and he loved the sun! . . . He was tan before and after everyone . . . and in the sun his hair . . . became . . . fleece.

GEORGE *(Echoing her)*

. . . fleece . . .

MARTHA

. . . beautiful, beautiful boy.

GEORGE

Absolve, Domine, animas omnium fidelium defunctorum ab omni vinculo delictorum.

MARTHA

. . . and school . . . and summer camp . . . and sledding . . . and swimming. . . .

GEORGE

Et gratia tua illis succurrente, mereantur evadere judicium ultionis.

MARTHA *(Laughing, to herself)*

. . . and how he broke his arm . . . how funny it was . . . oh, no, it hurt him! . . . but, oh, it was funny . . . in a field, his very first cow, the first he'd ever seen . . . and he went into the field, to the cow, where the cow was grazing, head down, busy . . . and he moo'd at it! *(Laughs ibid)* He moo'd at it . . . and the beast, oh, surprised, swung its head up and moo'd at him, all three years of him, and he ran, startled, and he stumbled . . . fell . . . and broke his poor arm. *(Laughs, ibid)* Poor lamb.

GEORGE

Et lucis aeternae beatitudine perfrui.

MARTHA

George cried! Helpless . . . George . . . cried. I carried the poor lamb. George snuffling beside me, I carried the child, having fashioned a sling . . . and across the great fields.

GEORGE

In Paradisum deducant te Angeli.

MARTHA

And as he grew . . . and as he grew . . . oh! so wise! . . . he walked evenly between us . . . *(She spreads her hands)* . . . a hand out to each of us for

what we could offer by way of support, affection, teaching, even love . . .
and these hands, still, to hold us off a bit, for mutual protection, to protect
us all from George's . . . weakness . . . and my necessary greater strength
. . . to protect himself . . . and *us*.

GEORGE

In memoria aeterna erit justus: ab auditione mala non timebit.

MARTHA

So wise; so wise.

NICK (To GEORGE)

What is this? What are you doing?

GEORGE

Shhhhh.

HONEY

Shhhhh.

NICK (Shrugging)

O.K.

MARTHA

So beautiful; so wise.

GEORGE (Laughs quietly)

All truth being relative.

MARTHA

It was true! Beautiful; wise; perfect.

GEORGE

There's a real mother talking.

HONEY

    (Suddenly; almost tearfully)
I want a child.

NICK

Honey . . .

HONEY (More forcefully)

I want a child!

GEORGE

On principle?

HONEY (in tears)

I want a child. I want a baby.

MARTHA

(Waiting out the interruption, not really paying it any mind)
Of course, this state, this perfection . . . couldn't last. Not with George . .
. not with George around.

GEORGE *(To the others)*
There; you see? I knew she'd shift.

HONEY

Be still!

GEORGE *(Mock awe)*
Sorry . . . mother.

NICK

Can't you be still?

GEORGE *(Making a sign at NICK)*
Dominus vobiscum.

MARTHA

Not with George around. A drowning man takes down those nearest.
George tried, but, oh, God, how I fought him. God, how I fought him.

GEORGE *(A satisfied laugh)*
Ahhhhhh.

MARTHA

Lesser states can't stand those above them. Weakness, imperfection cries
out against strength, goodness and innocence. And George tried.

GEORGE

How did I try, Martha? How did I try?

MARTHA

How did you . . . what? . . . No! No . . . he grew . . . our son grew . . . up;
he is grown up; he is away at school, college. He is fine, everything is fine.

GEORGE *(Mocking)*
Oh, come on, Martha!

MARTHA

No. That's all.

GEORGE

Just a minute! You can't cut a story off like that, sweetheart. You started to
say something . . . now you say it!

MARTHA

No!

GEORGE

Well, I will.

MARTHA

No!

GEORGE

You see, Martha, here, stops just when the going gets good . . . just when things start getting a little rough. Now, Martha, here, is a misunderstood little girl; she really is. Not only does she have a husband who is a bog . . . a younger-than-she-is bog albeit . . . not only does she have a husband who is a bog, she has as well a tiny problem with spiritous liquors—like she can't get enough . . .

MARTHA *(Without energy)*

No more, George.

GEORGE

. . . and on top of all that, poor weighed-down girl, PLUS a father who really doesn't give a damn whether she lives or dies, who couldn't care less *what* happens to his only daughter . . . on top of all that she has a *son.* She has a son who fought her every inch of the way, who didn't want to be turned into a weapon against his father, who didn't want to be used as a goddamn club whenever Martha didn't get things like she wanted them!

MARTHA *(Rising to it)*

Lies! Lies!!

GEORGE

Lies? All right. A son who would *not* disown his father, who came to him for advice, for information, for love that wasn't mixed with sickness—and you know what I mean, Martha!—who could not tolerate the slashing, braying residue that called itself his MOTHER. MOTHER? HAH!!

MARTHA *(Cold)*

All right, you. A son who was so ashamed of his father he asked me once if it—possibly—wasn't true, as he had heard, from some cruel boys, maybe, that he was not our child; who could not tolerate the shabby failure his father had become. . . .

GEORGE

Lies!

MARTHA

Lies? Who would not bring his girl friends to the house. . . .

GEORGE

. . . in shame of his mother. . . .

MARTHA

. . . of his father! Who writes letters only to me!

GEORGE

Oh, so you think! To me! At my office!

MARTHA

Liar!

GEORGE

I have a stack of them!

MARTHA

YOU HAVE NO LETTERS!

GEORGE

And you have?

MARTHA

He has no letters. A son . . . a son who spends his summers away . . . away from his family . . . ON ANY PRETEXT . . . because he can't stand the shadow of a man flickering around the edges of a house. . . .

GEORGE

. . . who spends his summers away . . . and he does! . . . who spends his summers away because there isn't room for him in a house full of empty bottles, lies, strange men, and a harridan who . . .

MARTHA

Liar!!

GEORGE

Liar?

MARTHA

. . . A son who I have raised as best I can against . . . vicious odds, against the corruption of weakness and petty revenges. . . .

GEORGE

. . . A son who is, deep in his gut, sorry to have been born. . . .

(BOTH TOGETHER)

MARTHA	GEORGE
I have tried, oh God I have tried; the one thing . . . the one thing I've tried to carry pure and unscathed through the sewer of this marriage; through the sick nights, and the pathetic, stupid days, through the derision and the laughter . . .	Libera me, Domine, de morte aeterna, in die illa tremenda: Quando caeli movendi sunt et terra: Dum veneris judicare saeculum per ignem. Tremens factus sum ego, et timeo, dum discussio venerit, atque ventura ira. Quando
(continued on next page)	*(continued on next page)*

MARTHA	GEORGE
God, the laughter, through one failure after another, one failure compounding another failure, each attempt more sickening, more numbing than the one before; the one thing, the one *person* I have tried to protect, to raise above the mire of this vile, crushing marriage; the one light in all this hopeless . . . *dark*ness . . . *our* SON.	caeli movendi sunt et terra. Dies illa, dies irae, calamitatis et miseriae; dies magna et amara valde. Dum veneris judicare saeculum per ignem. Requiem aeternam dona eis, Domine: et lux perpetua luceat eis. Libera me Domine de morte aeterna in die illa tremenda: quando caeli mo vendi sunt et terra: Dum veneris judicare saeculum per ignem.

(End together)

HONEY *(Her hands to her ears)*
STOP IT!! STOP IT!!

GEORGE *(With a hand sign)*
Kyrie, eleison. Christe, eleison. Kyrie, eleison.

HONEY
JUST STOP IT!!

GEORGE
Why, baby? Don't you like it?

HONEY *(Quite hysterical)*
You . . . can't . . . do . . . this!

GEORGE *(Triumphant)*
Who says!

HONEY
I! Say!

NICK
Is this game over?

HONEY
Yes! Yes, it is.

GEORGE
Ho-ho! Not by a long shot. *(To* MARTHA*)* I've got a little surprise for you, baby. It's about sunny-Jim.

MARTHA
No more, George.

GEORGE
YES!

NICK

Leave her be!

GEORGE

I'M RUNNING THIS SHOW! *(To* MARTHA*)* Sweetheart, I'm afraid I've got some bad news for you . . . for us, of course. Some rather sad news.
  (HONEY *begins weeping, head in hands*)

MARTHA *(Afraid, suspicious)*

What is this?

GEORGE *(Oh, so patiently)*

Well, Martha, while you were out of the room, while the . . . two of you were out of the room . . . I mean, I don't know where, hell, you both must have been somewhere *(Little laugh)*. . . . While you were out of the room, for a while . . . well, the doorbell chimed . . . and . . . well, it's hard to tell you, Martha . . .

MARTHA *(A strange throaty voice)*

Tell me.

GEORGE

. . . and . . . what it was . . . it was good old Western Union, some little boy about seventy.

MARTHA *(Involved)*

Crazy Billy?

GEORGE

Yes, Martha, that's right . . . crazy Billy . . . and he had a telegram, and it was for us, and I have to tell you about it.

MARTHA

  (As if from a distance)
Why didn't they phone it? Why did they bring it; why didn't they telephone it?

GEORGE

Some telegrams you have to deliver, Martha; some telegrams you can't phone.

MARTHA *(Rising)*

What do you mean?

GEORGE

Martha . . . I can hardly bring myself to say it. . . . *(Sighing heavily)* Well, Martha . . . I'm afraid our boy isn't coming home for his birthday.

MARTHA

Of course he is.

GEORGE

No, Martha.

MARTHA

Of course he is. I say he is!

GEORGE

He . . . can't.

MARTHA

He is! I say so!

GEORGE

Martha . . . *(Long pause)* . . . our son is . . . dead.
   (Silence)
He was . . . killed . . . late in the afternoon . . .
   (Silence)
(A *tiny chuckle*) on a country road, with his learner's permit in his pocket,
he swerved, to avoid a porcupine, and drove straight into a . . .

MARTHA *(Rigid fury)*

YOU . . . CAN'T . . . DO . . . THAT!

GEORGE

. . . large tree.

MARTHA

YOU CANNOT DO THAT!

NICK *(Softly)*

Oh my God. (HONEY *is weeping louder*)

GEORGE *(Quietly, dispassionately)*

I thought you should know.

NICK

Oh my God; no.

MARTHA

   (Quivering with rage and loss)
NO! NO! YOU CANNOT DO THAT! YOU CAN'T DECIDE THAT
FOR YOURSELF! I WILL NOT LET YOU DO THAT!

GEORGE

We'll have to leave around noon, I suppose . . .

MARTHA

I WILL NOT LET YOU DECIDE THESE THINGS!

GEORGE

. . . because there are matters of identification, naturally, and arrangements to be made. . . .

MARTHA

(*Leaping at* GEORGE, *but ineffectual*)
YOU CAN'T DO THIS!
(NICK *rises, grabs hold of* MARTHA, *pins her arms behind her back*)
I WON'T LET YOU DO THIS, GET YOUR HANDS OFF ME!

GEORGE

(*As* NICK *holds on; right in* MARTHA's *face*)
You don't seem to understand, Martha; I haven't done anything. Now, pull yourself together. Our son is DEAD! Can you get that into your head?

MARTHA

YOU CAN'T DECIDE THESE THINGS.

NICK

Lady, please.

MARTHA

LET ME GO!

GEORGE

Now listen, Martha; listen carefully. We got a telegram; there was a car accident, and he's dead. POUF! Just like that! Now, how do you like it?

MARTHA

(*A howl which weakens into a moan*)
NOOOOOOoooooo.

GEORGE (*To* NICK)

Let her go. (MARTHA *slumps to the floor in a sitting position*) She'll be all right now.

MARTHA (*Pathetic*)
No; no, he is *not* dead; he is not *dead*.

GEORGE

He is dead. Kyrie, eleison. Christe, eleison. Kyrie, eleison.

MARTHA

You can*not*. You may not decide these things.

NICK

(*Leaning over her; tenderly*)
He hasn't decided anything, lady. It's not his doing. He doesn't have the power . . .

GEORGE

That's right, Martha; I'm not a god. I don't have the power over life and death, do I?

MARTHA

YOU CAN'T KILL HIM! YOU CAN'T HAVE HIM DIE!

NICK

Lady . . . please . . .

MARTHA

YOU CAN'T!

GEORGE

There was a telegram, Martha.

MARTHA *(Up; facing him)*

Show it to me! Show me the telegram!

GEORGE

(Long pause; then, with a straight face)

I ate it.

MARTHA

(A pause; then with the greatest disbelief possible, tinged with hysteria)

What did you just say to me?

GEORGE

(Barely able to stop exploding with laughter)

I . . . ate . . . it.

(MARTHA *stares at him for a long moment, then spits in his face)*

GEORGE *(With a smile)*

Good for you, Martha.

NICK *(To* GEORGE*)*

Do you think that's the way to treat her at a time like this? Making an ugly goddamn joke like that? Hunh?

MARTHA *(To* GEORGE, *coldly)*

You're not going to get away with this.

GEORGE *(With disgust)*

YOU KNOW THE RULES, MARTHA! FOR CHRIST'S SAKE, YOU KNOW THE RULES!!

MARTHA

NO!

NICK
(With the beginnings of a knowledge he cannot face)
What are you two talking about?

GEORGE
I can kill him, Martha, if I want to.

MARTHA
HE IS OUR CHILD!

GEORGE
Oh yes, and you bore him, and it was a good delivery . . .

MARTHA
HE IS OUR CHILD!

GEORGE
AND I HAVE KILLED HIM!

MARTHA
NO!

GEORGE
YES!
(Long silence)

NICK *(Very quietly)*
I think I understand this.

GEORGE *(Ibid)*
Do you?

NICK *(Ibid)*
Jesus Christ, I think I understand this.

GEORGE *(Ibid)*
Good for you, buster.

NICK *(Violently)*
JESUS CHRIST I THINK I UNDERSTAND THIS!

MARTHA *(Great sadness and loss)*
You have no right . . . you have no right at all . . .

GEORGE *(Tenderly)*
I have the right, Martha. We never spoke of it; that's all. I could kill him any time I wanted to.

MARTHA
But why? Why?

GEORGE
You broke our rule, baby. You mentioned him . . . you mentioned him to someone else.

MARTHA *(Tearfully)*

I did *not*. I never did.

GEORGE

Yes, you did.

MARTHA

Who? WHO?!

HONEY *(Crying)*

To me. You mentioned him to me.

MARTHA *(Crying)*

I FORGET! Sometimes . . . sometimes when it's night, when it's late, and . . . and everybody else is . . . talking . . . I forget and I . . . want to mention him . . . but I . . . HOLD ON . . . I hold on . . . but I've wanted to . . . so often . . . oh, George, you've *pushed* it . . . there was no need . . . there was no need for *this*. I *men*tioned him . . . all right . . . but you didn't have to push it over the EDGE. You didn't have to . . . kill him.

GEORGE

Requiescat in pace.

HONEY

Amen.

MARTHA

You didn't have to have him die, George.

GEORGE

Requiem aeternam dona eis, Domine.

HONEY

Et lux perpetua luceat eis.

MARTHA

That wasn't . . . needed.
   (A long silence)

GEORGE *(Softly)*

It will be dawn soon. I think the party's over.

NICK *(To* GEORGE; *quietly)*

You couldn't have . . . any?

GEORGE

We couldn't.

MARTHA

   (A hint of communion in this)
We couldn't.

GEORGE *(To* NICK *and* HONEY)

Home to bed, children; it's way past your bedtime.

NICK *(His hand out to* HONEY)

Honey?

HONEY *(Rising, moving to him)*

Yes.

GEORGE

(MARTHA *is sitting on the floor by a chair now)*

You two go now.

NICK

Yes.

HONEY

Yes.

NICK

I'd like to . . .

GEORGE

Good night.

NICK *(Pause)*

Good night.

(NICK *and* HONEY *exit;* GEORGE *closes the door after them; looks around the room; sighs, picks up a glass or two, takes it to the bar)*

(This whole last section very softly, very slowly)

GEORGE

Do you want anything, Martha?

MARTHA *(Still looking away)*

No . . . nothing.

GEORGE

All right. *(Pause)* Time for bed.

MARTHA

Yes.

GEORGE

Are you tired?

MARTHA

Yes.

GEORGE

I am.

MARTHA

Yes.

GEORGE

Sunday tomorrow; all day.

MARTHA

Yes.

(A long silence between them)
Did you . . . did you . . . have to?

GEORGE *(Pause)*

Yes.

MARTHA

It was . . . ? You had to?

GEORGE *(Pause)*

Yes.

MARTHA

I don't know.

GEORGE

It was . . . time.

MARTHA

Was it?

GEORGE

Yes.

MARTHA *(Pause)*

I'm cold.

GEORGE

It's late.

MARTHA

Yes.

GEORGE *(Long silence)*

It will be better.

MARTHA *(Long silence)*

I don't . . . know.

GEORGE

It will be . . . maybe.

MARTHA

I'm . . . not . . . sure.

GEORGE

No.

MARTHA

Just . . . us?

GEORGE

Yes.

MARTHA

I don't suppose, maybe, we could . . .

GEORGE

No, Martha.

MARTHA

Yes. No.

GEORGE

Are you all right?

MARTHA

Yes. No.

GEORGE

(Puts his hand gently on her shoulder; she puts her head back, and he sings to her, very softly)
Who's afraid of Virginia Woolf
                    Virginia Woolf
                    Virginia Woolf,

MARTHA

I . . . am . . . George. . . .

GEORGE

Who's afraid of Virginia Woolf . . .

MARTHA

I . . . am . . . George. . . . I . . . am. . . .
       (GEORGE *nods, slowly)*
       (Silence; tableau)

CURTAIN

The Ballad of the Sad Cafe

FROM THE NOVELLA BY
CARSON McCULLERS

This adaptation to the stage of
THE BALLAD OF THE SAD CAFE
is dedicated to Carson McCullers,
of course, with great love.

EDWARD ALBEE

FIRST PERFORMANCE

October 30, 1963. New York City.
Martin Beck Theater

THE NARRATOR	*Roscoe Lee Browne*
RAINEY 1	*Louis W. Waldon*
RAINEY 2	*Deane Selmier*
STUMPY MAC PHAIL	*John C. Becher*
HENRY MACY	*William Prince*
MISS AMELIA EVANS	*Colleen Dewhurst*
COUSIN LYMON	*Michael Dunn*
EMMA HALE	*Enid Markey*
MRS. PETERSON	*Jenny Egan*
MERLIE RYAN	*Roberts Blossom*
HORACE WELLS	*William Duell*
HENRY FORD CRIMP	*David Clarke*
ROSSER CLINE	*Griff Evans*
LUCY WILLINS	*Nell Harrison*
MRS. HASTY MALONE	*Bette Henritze*
MARVIN MACY	*Lou Antonio*
HENRIETTA FORD CRIMP, JR.	*Susan Dunfee*
TOWNSPEOPLE	*Ernest Austin*
	Alice Drummond
	Jack Kehoe

Directed by ALAN SCHNEIDER
Set by BEN EDWARDS
Lighting by JEAN ROSENTHAL
Music by WILLIAM FLANAGAN
Production Stage Manager, JOHN MAXTONE-GRAHAM

THE SET

One set: MISS AMELIA's *house (later the cafe) taking most of the stage, not centered, though, but tending to stage-right, leaving a playing area, stage-left, for the battle, which will take place out-of -doors.* MISS AMELIA's *house must be practical, in the sense that its interior will be used, both upstairs and down, and, as well, we must be able to see its exterior without entering it. The main street of the town runs before the porch of the house, parallel to the apron of the stage.*

THE BALLAD OF THE SAD CAFE
is meant to be played without an intermission

Noon sun; street deserted; house boarded up; nothing moves, no one is to be seen; heat; quiet. Music: under all or some of the following.

THE NARRATOR

The Ballad of the Sad Cafe. The Beginning.

This building here—this boarded-up house—is twice distinguished; it is the oldest building in town . . . and the largest. Of course, the town is not very old—nor is it very large. There isn't much to it, except the cotton mill, the two-room houses where the workers live, a few peach trees, a church with two water-colored windows, and a miserable main street only a hundred yards long. The town is lonesome—sad—like a place that is far off and estranged from all other places in the world. The winters here are short and raw . . . the summers—white with glare, and fiery hot. If you walk along the main street on an August afternoon, there is nothing whatever to do. *(Pause)* There is heat . . . and silence. *(Pause)* Notice that window up there; notice that second-story window; notice that shuttered window. There's someone living up there. *(Short pause)* These August afternoons there is absolutely nothing to do; you might as well walk down to the Fork Falls Road and watch the chain gang . . . listen to the men sing. Though . . .

(Here, the upstairs window mentioned before slowly opens, and MISS AMELIA's *appearance at the window is described as it occurs)*

. . . look now; watch the window. *(Pause)* Sometimes, in the late afternoon, when the heat is at its worst, a hand will slowly open the shutter there, and a face will look down at the town . . . a terrible, dim face . . . like the faces known in dreams. The face will linger at the window for an hour or so,

(Silence for a moment or two, then, as the shutters are slowly closed)

. . . then the shutters will be closed once more, and as likely as not there will not be another soul to be seen along the main street.

(Silence; a lighting change begins)

But once . . . once, this building—this boarded-up house—was a cafe. Oh, there were tables with paper napkins, colored streamers hanging from the lamps, and great gatherings on Saturday nights.

(Perhaps an echo of such sounds here)

It was the center of the town! And this cafe . . . this cafe was run by a Miss Amelia Evans . . . who lives up there even now . . . whose face, in the late afternoons, sometimes, when the heat is at its worst, can be seen peering out from that shuttered window.

(Now we are shifting to an April evening, eight years previous. The boarded-up house will become a general store, its interior and exterior both visible)

We are going back in time now, back even before the opening of the cafe, for there are two stories to be told: How the cafe came into being . . . for there was not always a cafe . . . and how the cafe . . . died. How we came to . . . silence.

(By now it is night; the lights are dim in the general store, the interior of which is visible. During the following paragraph, three townsmen saunter onstage, move to the porch in front of the store; two sit on the steps, one leans against a porch post or the building itself)

It is toward midnight; April . . . eight years ago. Most people are in bed, but several men of the town, for reasons we shall see directly, prefer the front steps of Miss Amelia's general store. It is the kind of night when it is good to hear from far away, across the dark fields, the slow song of a field hand on his way to make love; or when it is pleasant to sit quietly and pick a guitar, or simply to rest alone, and think of nothing at all. Talk . . . or stay silent.

(The focus of the scene is now on the general store. Brief tableau, held chord under it)

The men are STUMPY MACPHAIL, *and the* RAINEY TWINS, RAINEY 1 *and* RAINEY 2. *They are silent; then a figure is seen coming in the shadows from stage-right.*

MACPHAIL

Who is that? *(The figure continues advancing)* I said, who is that there?

RAINEY 1 *(A high, giggly voice)*

Why, it's Henry Macy; that's who it is.

RAINEY 2 *(He, too)*

Henry Macy; Henry Macy.

MACPHAIL

Henry?

HENRY MACY
(In view now, by the porch. Nods)
Stumpy; evening. *(Then, to the twins)* Boys?

RAINEY 2
How you, Henry? And how is Marvin, Henry? How is your brother?
    (RAINEY 1 *giggles*)

MACPHAIL
Now, now.

RAINEY 1
How is he enjoying his stay, Henry? How is he enjoying the penitentiary?

MACPHAIL
Quiet, you!

HENRY MACY *(Placating)*
Now, Stumpy . . .

MACPHAIL
You got no sense at all? You *all* foolish in the head? Talk about Marvin
Macy, Miss Amelia nearby, maybe, God knows?
    (RAINEY 2 *giggles*)
Miss Amelia hear that name, she knock you clear to Society City.
    (Both RAINEYS *giggle)*

HENRY MACY *(A weary sigh)*
That true, Lord knows.

MACPHAIL
Knock you clear to Society City.

RAINEY 2
Miss Amelia ain't back. She at the still.

MACPHAIL
It don't matter.

RAINEY 1
You here for liquor, Henry?

HENRY MACY *(Distant)*
I just come by; just . . . by.

RAINEY 2
You not waiting on liquor, Henry?

MACPHAIL
He said he come by.

HENRY MACY (*To* MACPHAIL)

Miss Amelia digging up a barrel?

RAINEY 2 (*Giggling*)

He just come by.

HENRY MACY

I thirst for good liquor like any man; I thirst for Miss Amelia's liquor.

RAINEY 1 (*To* RAINEY 2)

We all waiting on liquor

(RAINEY 2 *giggles.*

A door in the rear of the general store opens; MISS AMELIA *enters, carrying several dark glass bottles. She is dressed in Levis and a cotton work shirt (red?), boots. She kicks the door shut with a foot. The sound is heard)*

MACPHAIL

Hm?

RAINEY 1

It Miss Amelia; it Miss Amelia back.

HENRY MACY (*Rising*)

That so?

RAINEY 2

Why, sure, less we got prowlers . . . thieves, people breaking in t'houses like some people . . .

(*Both* RAINEYS *go into smothered giggles.* MISS AMELIA *carries the bottles to the store counter, puts them down, comes out onto the porch)*

HENRY MACY

Evening, Miss Amelia.

MACPHAIL

Miss Amelia.

RAINEY 1 & 2

Evening, Miss Amelia.

MISS AMELIA

(*Nods; grunts. Not unpleasantly, though; it is her way)*

HENRY MACY

I come by. I thought . . . I come by.

RAINEY 1

. . . We said you been to the still.

MISS AMELIA *(Very deliberately)*

I been *thinking.*

RAINEY 2

*(*MISS AMELIA'*s remark is a known quantity)*

Oh-oh.

*(*RAINEY 1 *giggles)*

You been thinking on a new medicine? You making improvements on your Croup Cure?

MISS AMELIA *(Shakes her head)*

No.

RAINEY 1

You figuring on someone to sue, Miss Amelia? You found somebody you can bring suit against, Miss Amelia?

MISS AMELIA

No. *(Pause)* I been thinking on some way to get some silence out of you; I been figuring up a nice batch of poison to stop your foolish mouth.

(The RAINEY TWINS *giggle, laugh.* MACPHAIL *roars,* HENRY MACY *shakes his head, smiles)*

MISS AMELIA

(Pushing RAINEY 1 *roughly, but not angrily with her boot)*

That's what I been doing.

RAINEY 1

Oh, Miss Amelia, you wouldn't do that with me.

MACPHAIL

Best thing ever happen round here.

RAINEY 2

Poison me; you poison my brother, you poison me.

MISS AMELIA

Oblige you both.

MACPHAIL

Better idea yet.

(A chuckle or two; a silence)

MISS AMELIA

(A silence. To them all)

You come to buy liquor?

MACPHAIL

If you'd be so kind . . .

RAINEY 1

We all thirsty from the lack of rain.

(RAINEY 2 *giggles*)

MISS AMELIA (*After a long pause*)

I'll get some liquor.

HENRY MACY

(*Just as* MISS AMELIA *starts to turn, halting her*)

I see something coming.

(*They all look off, stage-left, where nothing is yet to be seen*)

RAINEY 1

It's a calf got loose.

(*They keep looking*)

MACPHAIL

No; no it ain't.

(*They keep looking*)

RAINEY 2

No; it's somebody's youngun.

(*They keep looking*)

HENRY MACY

(*As a figure emerges from stage-left*)

No . . . no.

MISS AMELIA (*Squinting*)

What is it then?

(COUSIN LYMON *moves into the lighted area near the porch; his clothes are dusty; he carries a tiny battered suitcase tied with a rope. He is a dwarf; a hunchback. He stops, suitcase still in hand; he is out of breath*)

COUSIN LYMON

Evening. I am hunting for Miss Amelia Evans.

(*The group neither replies nor nods; merely stares*)

MISS AMELIA (*After a long pause*)

How come?

COUSIN LYMON

Because I am kin to her.

(*The group looks at* MISS AMELIA *to see her reaction*)

MISS AMELIA (*After a long pause*)

You lookin' for me. How do you mean "kin"?

COUSIN LYMON

Because . . . (*Uneasily, as if he is about to cry, setting the suitcase down, but keeping hold of the handle*) Because my mother was Fanny Jesup and she came from Cheehaw. She left Cheehaw some thirty years ago when she married her first husband.

(RAINEY 1 *giggles*)

. . . and I am the son of Fanny's first husband. So that would make you and I . . . (*His voice trails off. With quick, bird-like gestures he bends down, opens the suitcase*) I have a . . . (*Brings out a photograph*) . . . this is a picture of my mother and her half-sister.

(*He holds it out to* MISS AMELIA, *who does not take it.* MACPHAIL *does, examines it in the light*)

MACPHAIL

(*After squinting at the photograph*)

Why . . . what is this supposed to be! What are those . . . baby children? And so fuzzy you can't tell night from day. (*He hands it towards* MISS AMELIA, *who refuses it, keeping her gaze on* COUSIN LYMON. *He hands the photograph back to the hunchback*) Where you come from?

COUSIN LYMON (*Uncertainly*)

I was . . . traveling.

(RAINEY 2 *giggles contemptuously.* HENRY MACY *gets up, starts to leave*)

HENRY MACY

Night, Miss Amelia.

RAINEY 1

Where you going, Henry? Ain't you going to wait on your liquor?

RAINEY 2

Oh, no; Henry will sacrifice his thirst cause he is too squeamish; he don't want to be here when Miss Amelia boot this kind off her property. He don't want to be here for that.

HENRY MACY (*As he exits*)

Night, Miss Amelia.

RAINEY 1

That right, Henry? You don't want to see Miss Amelia send this one flying?

(HENRY MACY *exits, without commenting or turning;* COUSIN LYMON, *who has been waiting, apprehensively, finally sits down on the steps and suddenly begins to cry. No one moves; they watch him*)

RAINEY 2 (*Finally*)

Well, I'll be damned if he ain't a . . . look at him go! . . . I'll be damned if he ain't a regular crybaby.

RAINEY 1

He is a poor little thing.

MACPHAIL

Well, he is afflicted. There is some cause.

(RAINEY 2 *loudly imitates* COUSIN LYMON's *crying.* MISS AMELIA *crosses the porch slowly but deliberately. She reaches* COUSIN LYMON *and stops, looking thoughtfully at him. Then, gingerly, with her right forefinger, she touches the hump on his back. She keeps her finger there until his crying lessens. Then, she removes her finger from his hump, takes a bottle from her hip pocket, wipes the top with the palm of her other hand, and offers it to him to drink*)

MISS AMELIA

Drink. (*Brief pause*) It will liven your gizzard.

RAINEY 1 (*To* COUSIN LYMON)

Hey there, you; better get your money up; Miss Amelia don't give liquor free. Unh-unh, you get your money up.

MISS AMELIA (*To* COUSIN LYMON)

Drink.

(COUSIN LYMON *stops crying and, rather like a snuffling child, puts the bottle to his mouth and drinks. When he is done,* MISS AMELIA *takes the bottle, washes her mouth with a small swallow, spits it out, and then drinks. This done, she hands the bottle back to* COUSIN LYMON. *He takes it enthusiastically. To the others, as she moves to the store door*)

You want liquor? *You* get your money up.

(*She goes inside, takes three bottles from the counter. The three men watch* COUSIN LYMON *as he drinks.* MISS AMELIA *returns with the liquor, gives a bottle to each of the men, takes money. The men open the bottles—which are corked—and take long, slow swallows.* MISS AMELIA *near to* COUSIN LYMON)

MACPHAIL (*Music beginning*)

It is smooth liquor, Miss Amelia; I have never known you to fail.

RAINEY 1

Yeah.

RAINEY 2

Yeah, sure is.

THE NARRATOR

(Music under this speech. Maybe the lighting on the scene alters slightly. The players drink, laugh, ad lib, but softly under the following paragraph)

The whiskey they drank that evening is important. Otherwise, it would be hard to account for what followed. Perhaps without it there would never have been a cafe. For the liquor of Miss Amelia has a special quality of its own. It is clean and sharp on the tongue, but once down a man, it glows inside him for a long time afterward. And that is not all. Things that have gone unnoticed, thoughts that have been harbored far back in the dark mind, are suddenly recognized and comprehended.

(Laughter from the group here, more noticeable than usual)

A man may suffer, or he may be spent with joy—but he has warmed his soul and seen the message hidden there.

(Music ending; focus now back on porch scene)

RAINEY 1

(Leaning back; a quiet sound of deep satisfaction)
Ohhhh—Whooooooo . . .

MACPHAIL *(After a pause)*
Yes; that *is* good.

MISS AMELIA

(To COUSIN LYMON, *after a pause)*
I don't know your name.

COUSIN LYMON
I'm Lymon Willis.

RAINEY 2 *(Softly, to no one)*
I am warm and dreamy.

MISS AMELIA

(Rising, to COUSIN LYMON*)*
Well, come on in. Some supper was left in the stove and you can eat.
(The three TOWNSMEN *look at* MISS AMELIA *and* COUSIN LYMON. RAINEY 1 *nudges* RAINEY 2. COUSIN LYMON *does not move)*

MISS AMELIA
I'll just warm up what's there.
(As before, more or less)
There is fried chicken; there are rootabeggars, collards and sweet potatoes.

COUSIN LYMON

(Stirring, shy and coy, almost like a young girl)
I am partial to collards—if they be cooked with sausage.

MISS AMELIA *(Pause)*

They be.

(RAINEY 2 *giggles softly*)

COUSIN LYMON

(Rising, facing MISS AMELIA*)*

I am partial to collards.

MISS AMELIA

(Moving toward the door)

Then bring your stuff.

(COUSIN LYMON *closes his suitcase, picks it up, stands on a step, looking at* MISS AMELIA, *still hesitant*)

COUSIN LYMON

(Softly, as if describing a glory)

. . . with sausages.

MISS AMELIA

There is a room for you upstairs . . . where you can sleep . . . when you are done eating.

(COUSIN LYMON *follows* MISS AMELIA *into the store, the interior of which fades; the front wall of the building takes its place.*

The three townsmen sit for a moment. Music, softly)

MACPHAIL *(Stirring)*

Well . . . *(Pause)* . . . home *(Rises)*

RAINEY 1

(To MACPHAIL *in some awe)*

I never seen nothing like that in my life. What she up to? Miss Amelia never invite people into her house . . . eat from her table. What she up to?

MACPHAIL *(Puzzled)*

Don't know.

(Begins to cross, stage-left. The RAINEY TWINS *follow after)*

RAINEY 1

What is she up to, Stumpy? Hunh?

MACPHAIL *(Speeding up, exiting)*

Don't know.

(The twins stop, toward stage-left, look back to the building)

RAINEY 1

What is she up to? She never done a thing like that since . . .

RAINEY 2

Shhh! *(Giggles)* Can't talk about that.

RAINEY 1

Maybe . . . maybe she think there something in that suitcase of his. *(With some excitement)* Maybe she going to rob him! And then . . . and then kill him!

RAINEY 2 *(Giggles)*

Oh . . . hush. *(Giggles again)*

RAINEY 1

(As they move off, stage-left)
I don't know . . . I don't know what she up to.

RAINEY 2 *(Expansively)*

I am warm and dreamy!

RAINEY 1 *(Shaking his head)*

I don't know.

(Lights slowly down to black, music under. Black for five seconds, chord held under, then lights up to bright day; brief, brisk morning music)

HENRY MACY *enters, stage-left, stays there.* MISS AMELIA *comes out from the building, looks at the sky, goes to the pump in front of the building, washes her head, arms; does not dry—shakes off her arms; spies* HENRY MACY, *pauses; does not speak or nod.*

HENRY MACY

(A greeting that is a question)
Morning, Miss Amelia?
(She nods, waits. He takes a step or two closer)
You . . . you opening the store?

MISS AMELIA *(Squinting)*

You here to buy?

HENRY MACY

Why, not now; I just . . .

MISS AMELIA

Then I am closed.

HENRY MACY

Well . . . I just . . .

MISS AMELIA *(Fixing a sleeve)*

I am off to tend to some land I bought . . . up near Fork Falls Road.

HENRY MACY *(Shyly)*

Land, Miss Amelia?

MISS AMELIA

Cotton. *(Pause)* You don't want nothing?

(Pause. HENRY MACY *shakes his head)*

MISS AMELIA

Then I am off.

(She turns, moves stage-right. Two townsladies, EMMA *and* MRS. PETERSON, *enter from stage-right)*

EMMA *(In a portentous way)*

Morning, Miss Amelia.

MRS. PETERSON

(Timid; breathless)

Morning, Miss Amelia.

(They stand; MISS AMELIA *stands. The two ladies cannot help but steal glances toward the building. They stand silently;* MISS AMELIA *scratches her leg)*

MISS AMELIA

(Not unfriendly, but not friendly)

You two want something?

MRS. PETERSON

Why . . . why whatever do you mean?

EMMA *(Significantly again)*

Just passing the time of day, Miss Amelia.

MISS AMELIA

You here to buy?

EMMA *(As before)*

Why, are you open today, Miss Amelia?

MISS AMELIA

Yes . . . or no?

MRS. PETERSON *(Flustered)*

Why . . . no; no.

MISS AMELIA

(Striding past them exiting)

I got business to tend to.

EMMA

(After her, but so she cannot hear; really for MRS. PETERSON *and* HENRY MACY)

Oh! I'll bet you do. Have you foreclosed on someone, Miss Amelia? You grabbed some more property on a debt? You drove another poor, luckless soul out of his land?

(MRS. PETERSON *tsks, rapidly, softly*)
Bet that's what she done.

HENRY MACY

Morning, ladies.

(The three meet toward center stage)

EMMA

Henry Macy! Is it true? Is it true what I hear?

HENRY MACY *(Drawled)*

Why, I don't know, Emma. What is it you hear?

EMMA

Don't you sport with me! You know perfectly well what I hear . . . what the whole town hear.

HENRY MACY *(A small smile)*

Well, now, people hear a lot.

EMMA

Two nights ago? Here? You all sitting around, late, you men?

HENRY MACY

Well that is true; yes; we was sitting.

MRS. PETERSON *(Exasperated)*

Ohhhhhhhhh.

EMMA

. . . and then up the road, out of the dark, come this broke-back, this runt? Some tiny thing claim to be kin to Miss Amelia?

HENRY MACY

Now is that what you hear?

EMMA

. . . and this twisted thing claim to be kin?

MRS. PETERSON

(Almost whispered)
. . . and he was took upstairs . . . and he ain't been seen since?

(HENRY MACY shakes his head; laughs softly)

EMMA *(Officiously)*

Well?

HENRY MACY *(Calmly; slowly)*

A brokeback come by . . . two nights ago . . . he claim to be kin to Miss Amelia . . . Miss Amelia take him in . . . feed him . . . offer him a bed.

(MRS. PETERSON gasps with enthusiasm)

EMMA *(To nail it down)*

And he ain't been seen since.

MRS. PETERSON

I knew it; I knew it.

HENRY MACY

You knew what?

MRS. PETERSON *(Helplessly)*

I . . . knew it.

(STUMPY MACPHAIL *enters, from stage-left, carrying a lunch pail)*

EMMA *(To* MACPHAIL*)*

. . . And he ain't been seen since; morning.

MACPHAIL

Morning. Who ain't? Morning, Henry.

EMMA

Why, you know . . .

HENRY MACY

Morning, Stumpy.

MACPHAIL *(To* MRS. PETERSON*)*

Morning. *(To* EMMA*)* Who ain't?

EMMA *(Exasperated)*

Why, you know! That brokeback . . . that kind claim to be kin to Miss
Amelia.

MACPHAIL

(Scratching his head, looking toward building)

Oh . . . yeah, yeah.

MRS. PETERSON *(Proudly)*

And he ain't been seen since.

EMMA

Two days . . . no sign of . . . whatever it is.

HENRY MACY *(Weary)*

Oh, Emma . . .

MACPHAIL

Well, now; he may have took ill. He is afflicted.

EMMA *(Mysteriously)*

May. May not.

MRS. PETERSON

May not.

MACPHAIL

It ain't natural.

EMMA

It sure ain't.

HENRY MACY

He say he is kin.

EMMA

Miss Amelia got no kin!

MACPHAIL

Who can have kin like what come 't'other night? That be kin to no one.

EMMA

Whatever he be, Miss Amelia been took in.

HENRY MACY

Miss Amelia ain't known to be soft-hearted.

EMMA *(Triumphantly)*

In the head, then!

MACPHAIL

I say she fed him, sent him on.

HENRY MACY

You told me she give him a bed.

MACPHAIL

She *say.* That don't mean nothing.
(*Enter* RAINEY 1, *he, too, with a lunch pail. Trailing behind him,* MERLIE RYAN.

To RAINEY 1)
That don't mean nothing; do it?

RAINEY 1

What don't mean nothing?

MACPHAIL

Miss Amelia *say* she give the brokeback a bed don't mean he stay.

RAINEY 1 *(With great relish)*

Ain't nobody seen him, hunh? Well now, where could he be?

EMMA

(*To* MRS. PETERSON, *who breathes agreement*)
Just what I *say.*

MERLIE RYAN

I know what Miss Amelia done.

EMMA *(Dismissing him)*

Hunh, you—you queer-headed old thing.

MACPHAIL

(With a gesture to quiet EMMA: *very interested)*

What; what she done?

*(*RAINEY 1 *giggles)*

MERLIE RYAN

I know what Miss Amelia done.

*(*RAINEY 1 *giggles again)*

EMMA

Well, what?

MRS. PETERSON

What?

MERLIE RYAN

(As if remembering a message to be given)

I know what Miss Amelia done: She murdered that man for something in that suitcase.

*(*HENRY MACY *snorts dismissal;* RAINEY 1 *giggles;* MACPHAIL *whistles; the ladies gasp)*

She murdered that man for something in that suitcase. She cut his body up, and she bury him in the swamp. *(As before from the others)* I know what Miss Amelia done?

(Maybe the ladies stare at the building, move back from it)

HENRY MACY

(Ridiculing the idea)

Oh, now . . .

MRS. PETERSON

I knew it; I knew it . . .

EMMA

(With great, slow nods of her head)

So that what she done.

MERLIE RYAN *(Sing-song)*

That what she done; that what she done.

*(*RAINEY 1 *giggles)*

HENRY MACY *(To* RAINEY 1*)*

You tell him this? You put these things in his head?

RAINEY 1

(So we do not know if he is serious or not)

Me? Tell a thing like that to Crazy Merlie here? Why, Henry; you know me better'n that.

EMMA

Buried him in the swamp.

MACPHAIL

It ain't beyond reason.

HENRY MACY *(Angry)*

It ain't likely!

MERLIE RYAN

I know what Miss Amelia done.

(RAINEY 1 *giggles*)

(Barely audible chatter from those on stage during the following)

THE NARRATOR *(Music under it)*

And so it went that whole day. A midnight burial in the swamp, the dragging of Miss Amelia through the streets of the town on the way to prison . . .

(Three other TOWNSMEN *enter, join in)*

. . . the squabbles over what would happen to her property—all told in hushed voices and repeated with some fresh and weird detail.

(Lighting moves toward evening: MISS AMELIA *enters, stage-right, takes brief note of the townspeople, moves into the building)*

And when it came toward evening, and Miss Amelia returned from her business, and they saw that there were no bloodstains on her anywhere, the consternation grew.

MISS AMELIA

Well, quite a gathering.

*(It becomes dark, now. The townsmen—*HENRY MACY, MACPHAIL, *the* RAINEY TWINS, MERLIE RYAN *and the* THREE TOWNSMEN, RAINEY 2 *having entered from stage-left at the beginning of this lighting change—have moved to the porch of the building, are sitting or standing with* HENRY MACY *off to one side of the group . . . stage-right.* EMMA *and* MRS. PETERSON *have been joined by two other women, and are in a group, stage-left, watching the porch, watching the men)*

THE NARRATOR

And dark came on. It was just past eight o'clock, and still nothing had happened. But there was silent agreement among the men that this night would not pass with the mystery still unsolved. There is a time beyond which questions may not stay unanswered. So, the men had gathered on Miss Amelia's porch, and Miss Amelia had gone into the room she kept as an office.

(*Lights on* MISS AMELIA *in the office*)

FIRST TOWNSMAN (To SECOND)

What she doin'?

SECOND TOWNSMAN

Don't know. I don't know.

MERLIE RYAN

I know what she done. She murdered that man for somethin' . . .

MACPHAIL

Shhh.

HENRY MACY

Hush, Merlie!

(*Both* RAINEYS *giggle*)

FIRST TOWNSMAN

What we gonna do?

RAINEY 1

We goin' in?

MACPHAIL (Rising portentously)

Yup; we goin' in. Henry?

HENRY MACY (After a pause)

All right.

(*The men rise, file slowly into the store; the women, taking this as a sign, move, with sotto voce comments, toward the porch. The men move silently, keeping fairly close to the walls, keeping a distance from both* MISS AMELIA's *office and from the stairs, stage-center-rear.*

Maybe there is a high, soft sustained chord of music here, ending abruptly with a sound from the top of the stairs. The men turn toward the sound.

COUSIN LYMON *descends the stairs, slowly, one at a time—imperiously, like a great hostess. He is no longer ragged; he is clean; he wears his little coat, but neat and mended, a red and black checkered shirt, knee breeches, black stockings, shoes laced up over the ankles, and a great lime green shawl, with fringe, which almost touches the ground. The effect is somehow regal . . . or papal. The room is as still as death.* COUSIN LYMON *walks to the center of the room; the men move back a little. He stares at them, one after*

the other, down to up, slowly, craning his neck to see their faces.
RAINEY 2 *giggles, but there is some terror in it)*

COUSIN LYMON

(After he has examined the men; as if he had heard some piece of unimportant news, which he dismisses)
Evenin'.
(He seats himself on a barrel, quite center, and takes from a pocket a snuff-box. There is an intake of breath from some of the men)

MACPHAIL

(Daring to move a step closer)
What is it you have there?

FIRST TOWNSMAN

Yeah; what is that, Peanut?

SECOND TOWNSMAN

Why, that is Miss Amelia's snuffbox . . . belonged to her father.

MACPHAIL

What is it you have there?

COUSIN LYMON

(Sharply; mischievously)
What is this? Why, this is a lay-low . . . to catch meddlers.

SECOND TOWNSMAN

It *is* her snuff box. Belonged to her father.

COUSIN LYMON *(After taking snuff)*
This is not proper snuff; this is sugar and cocoa.
(Silence from the men; MISS AMELIA *can be heard whistling softly to herself)*
The very teeth in my head have always tasted sour to me; that is the reason why I take this kind of sweet snuff.

MACPHAIL *(To get it straight)*
It *is* Miss Amelia's snuff box.

COUSIN LYMON *(Almost arrogantly)*
Yes?

HENRY MACY

It is natural enough.

COUSIN LYMON

(Swinging on him; not unfriendly—objective)
Who are you?

HENRY MACY *(Kindly)*

I am Henry Macy.

COUSIN LYMON

I remember; when I come. How old are you?
   (An exchange of glances among the other men; one or two words)

HENRY MACY

I am forty-seven.

COUSIN LYMON *(Swinging his legs)*

Where you work?

HENRY MACY

The mill.

COUSIN LYMON *(To* MACPHAIL*)*

And you!

MACPHAIL

I . . .

COUSIN LYMON

Who are *you?*

RAINEY 2

That Stumpy MacPhail.
   (Giggles)

COUSIN LYMON

How old are you?

MACPHAIL

I am . . . thirty-eight.

RAINEY 1

He work in the mill, too.

COUSIN LYMON

   (Ignoring RAINEY 1; *to* MACPHAIL*)*
You married, Stumpy MacPhail?

RAINEY 2

Oh, is he!
   (A couple of the men laugh gently)

MACPHAIL *(Retaining his dignity)*

I am married. Yes.

COUSIN LYMON

   (A small, pleased child)
Is your wife fat?

(Whoops of laughter from the men, which bring the women hovering to the door)

MACPHAIL

(Embarrassed, but by the attention, not the fact)

She is . . . ample.

(More laughter)

COUSIN LYMON *(To* RAINEY TWINS*)*

And you two giggling things . . . who are *you?*

FIRST TOWNSMAN

Them is the Rainey twins . . .

SECOND TOWNSMAN

(Indicating MERLIE RYAN*)*

And this here is Merlie Ryan . . .

COUSIN LYMON

(With a sweep of his hand)

Come in, ladies!

(The TOWNSWOMEN *enter, the introductions become general, simultaneous. The* THREE TOWNSMEN *use names such as* HASTY MALONE, ROSSER CLINE, *and* HENRY FORD CRIMP. EMMA *is* EMMA HALE. *The chatter is general; and while there is a lot of talk and some laughter, there is still tension, and people tend to look at* COUSIN LYMON *out of the corners of their eyes and keep a formal distance—as if he were a Martian, a friendly Martian, but still a Martian. There are now twelve* TOWNSPEOPLE *in the store. Through the general chatter we hear, specifically, things like the following)*

RAINEY 1

When you come up the road t'other night . . . I swore it were a calf got loose.

RAINEY 2 *(Qualifying)*

It were so dark.

HENRY MACY

It is a pleasure to have you visiting.

EMMA

This lime green scarf is pretty.

MRS. PETERSON

Oh, yes; yes, it look well on you.

COUSIN LYMON

(To MRS. PETERSON*)*

I will not bite you. *(Snaps his teeth at her)* Grrr!

MRS. PETERSON *(Almost fainting)*

Oh! Oh!

MERLIE RYAN

Know what I thought she done? . . . Know what I thought happened to the brokeback? . . .

HENRY MACY & MACPHAIL

Hush. You be still.

RAINEY 2

. . . and I thought it were someone's youngun . . .

RAINEY 1

It were so dark.

COUSIN LYMON

Well, it were not.

RAINEY 2

No; it were not.

(Giggles)

RAINEY 1

It were dark.

(Groups have formed, and the conversation does not hinge solely on COUSIN LYMON. *Perhaps music has been used judiciously throughout this ad lib scene. The door to the office swings open, and* MISS AMELIA *enters the store. As the* TOWNSPEOPLE *see her, their conversation trails off, until there is silence.* MISS AMELIA *stands for a moment, taking everything in, glances at* COUSIN LYMON *and smiles, briefly, shyly, then leans her elbows back on the counter)*

MISS AMELIA *(Quietly)*

Does anyone want waiting on?

(A brief pause, which HENRY MACY *breaks)*

HENRY MACY

Why, yes, Miss Amelia . . . if you have some liquor . . .

(This serves as a dam-break, and several of the men ad lib agreement, and the general chatter starts again.

Music from now until the end of the scene.

MISS AMELIA *turns, goes behind the counter, gets bottles, serves the men, takes money)*

THE NARRATOR (*Over the talk*)

What happened at this moment was not ordinary. While the men of the town could count on Miss Amelia for their liquor, it was a rule she had that they must drink it outside her premises—and there was no feeling of joy in the transaction: after getting his liquor, a man would have to drink it on the porch, or guzzle it on the street, or walk off into the night. But at this moment, Miss Amelia broke her rule, and the men could drink in her store. More than that, she furnished glasses and opened two boxes of crackers so that they were there hospitably in a platter on the counter and anyone who wished could take one free.

(*Suitable action under the above, general chatter continuing*)

Now, this was the beginning of the cafe. It was as simple as that. There was a certain timidness, for people in this town were unused to gathering together in any number for the sake of pleasure. But, it was the beginning.

(*The sounds continue.* MISS AMELIA *moves to where* COUSIN LYMON *is sitting*)

MISS AMELIA

Cousin Lymon, will you have your liquor straight, or warmed in a pan with water on the stove?

(*A slight lessening in the general conversation in attention to this*)

COUSIN LYMON

If you please, Amelia . . . if you please, I'll have it warmed.

(*Some general consternation*)

EMMA

(*A half-whisper, to anyone, as* MISS AMELIA, *smiling secretly, moves off to do* COUSIN LYMON'S *bidding*)

Did you hear that? He called her *Amelia!* He said *Amelia!*

MRS. PETERSON

(*Breathless, as usual*)

Why, it is *Miss* Amelia to . . . to everyone.

EMMA

And *he* called her *Amelia.*

THIRD TOWNSMAN

Her Daddy called her . . . Little. He called her Little.

(RAINEY 2 *giggles*)

RAINEY 1

Some Little!

EMMA (*Unable to get over it*)

Did you hear it? He called her Amelia.

(In another area, HENRY MACY, MACPHAIL *and* MERLIE RYAN *are gathered)*

MACPHAIL

I ain't see Miss Amelia like this. There is something puzzling to her face.

HENRY MACY

(Looking at her; she is oblivious to all but COUSIN LYMON*)*
Well . . . it may be she is happy.

MACPHAIL *(Uncertain)*

It may be.

MERLIE RYAN

I know; I know what it is.

HENRY MACY

Oh, now, Merlie . . .

MERLIE RYAN

I know what it is . . . Miss Amelia in love. That what it is.
(Only HENRY MACY *and* MACPHAIL *have heard this)*

MACPHAIL

(As if he is being joshed)
Ohhhhhhhh . . .

HENRY MACY

Hush, now, Merlie . . .

MERLIE RYAN

Miss Amelia in love. Miss Amelia in love.
(Music and crowd louder, general party. Interior of the store dims, becomes invisible during the next speech, the exterior becoming visible, in the darkness and moonlight)

THE NARRATOR

And so it went. This opening of the cafe came to an end at midnight. Everyone said goodbye to everyone else in a friendly fashion . . . and soon, everything—all the town, in fact— was dark and silent. And so ended three days and nights in which had come the arrival of a stranger, an unholy holiday, and the start of the cafe.
(Dim to blackness. MUSIC holds)

Daylight—toward evening—comes up; only the exterior of the cafe is visible save directly below, as indicated. No one, narrator excepted, is on stage. Music up and under.

THE NARRATOR

Now time must pass. Four years . . . Time passes quickly in this section of the country; you breathe in and it is summer; out, and it is autumn; in again, out, and a year has gone by. Only the seasons change, but they are so regular in their turning that four years can pass . . . *(Pause)* . . . like that. The hunchback continued to live with Miss Amelia. The cafe expanded in a gradual way, and Miss Amelia began to sell her liquor by the drink, and some tables were brought into the store, and there were customers every evening, and on Saturday nights a great crowd. The place was a store no longer but had become a proper cafe, and was open every evening from six until twelve o'clock. Things once done were accepted.

(MISS AMELIA *and* COUSIN LYMON *emerge, sit on the steps)*

And Cousin Lymon's presence in Miss Amelia's house, his sleeping in her dead father's room, was passed by, save by a few, women mostly, whose minds had darker corners than they dared dream of. And the cafe was welcomed by everyone but the minister's wife, who was a secret drinker and felt more alone than ever. Four years have passed . . .

COUSIN LYMON

(As MISS AMELIA *massages his shoulders)*

Slowly, Amelia, slowly.

MISS AMELIA *(Amused tolerance)*

Yes, Cousin Lymon.

COUSIN LYMON

That do feel good, Amelia.

MISS AMELIA

You have not grown stronger; you are still so pitiful.

COUSIN LYMON

I am not a big person, Amelia.

MISS AMELIA

Now, I think your head *has* got bigger . . . and your hunch, too . . .

COUSIN LYMON *(Pulls away; surly)*

Leave me be.

MISS AMELIA

But your legs, as thin as ever . . . grasshopper . . .

COUSIN LYMON

(A tone of command)

Amelia! *(A sudden giggle)* Course, you could always figger up a new medicine for me . . . one turn me into a giant; you could do that.

MISS AMELIA *(Affectionately)*

You enough trouble big as you are. Don't know what I'd do with you normal size.

COUSIN LYMON *(Greatly amused)*

Though there be a danger you make me a growin' medicine, since you so particular with your remedies you try 'em out on yourself first . . .

MISS AMELIA *(Laughs)*

Hush, you.

COUSIN LYMON

. . . you make me a growin' medicine, an' it work we gonna have you in the treetops, birds nestin' in you, an' . . .

MISS AMELIA *(Gently)*

Ain't no medicine gonna make you grow, Cousin Lymon.

COUSIN LYMON *(Briefly serious)*

I know that, Amelia. *(Giggling again)* Only thing happen, you make up a new remedy be you try it out on yourself an' you spend the next two days hustlin' to the privy . . .

MISS AMELIA *(To stop him)*

Well, you gotta try your medicine on yourself first, you be any good at doctorin'.

COUSIN LYMON *(Giggles)*

I know . . . but it's funny.

MISS AMELIA

An' all ailments is centered in the bowel.

COUSIN LYMON

Oh?

MISS AMELIA

Yes.

COUSIN LYMON

(Mischievous scoffing)

Do that be so, Amelia?

MISS AMELIA

Yes.

COUSIN LYMON

Well, your remedies *do* affect the bowel, no doubt there. Surprisin' anyone die in these parts.

MISS AMELIA

People die here same as anywhere.

COUSIN LYMON *(Still mischievous)*

What do they die of, Amelia? Ain't your medicine, now . . .

MISS AMELIA

People die of natural causes. Like anywhere.

COUSIN LYMON

What is the natural cause, Amelia?

MISS AMELIA

(At a loss first; then . . .)

. . . dyin'.

COUSIN LYMON

(As if a great truth has been revealed)

Oh.

(A tone of command)

Amelia! *(A small silence, then he continues in a cajoling tone)* As tomorrow is Sunday, Amelia, you gonna drive us into Cheehaw to the movie show? Or, maybe we can go to the fair. There is a fair which is out beyond . . .

MISS AMELIA

We will go . . . we will go . . . somewhere.

COUSIN LYMON

To the fair, Amelia.

MISS AMELIA

We will go . . . somewhere.

(COUSIN LYMON pulls away again, dead-spoiled, pouting, moves a few feet away)

Cousin Lymon?

COUSIN LYMON *(Imperiously)*

Your father's bed is too big for my size, Amelia; I am not comfortable in a bed that size.

MISS AMELIA *(Laughing)*

Oh, now . . .

COUSIN LYMON *(Greatly petulant)*

I said I am not at ease in a ten acre bed. Have one made for me; have a bed made for me that I can sleep comfortable in.

MISS AMELIA

(Attempting a light tone)

I will have a bed made for you, Cousin Lymon, just to your size, and it can be used for you as a coffin some day.

COUSIN LYMON

(Rising; furious; screaming)

I AM SLEEPING IN A COFFIN NOW! I AM SLEEPING IN YOUR
FATHER'S COFFIN. *(Softer, whining again)* I want a small bed, Amelia.
I want a bed my size.

MISS AMELIA *(Placating)*

Yes; yes.

COUSIN LYMON

And . . . and I want to go in the Ford tomorrow . . . to Cheehaw . . . to the
movie show, and . . .

MISS AMELIA

(Quietly correcting him)

You want to go to the *fair.*

COUSIN LYMON *(Imperious again)*

Either way; don't matter.

MISS AMELIA *(A slightly sad smile)*

No; don't matter.

COUSIN LYMON

(Mysterious and intensely curious)

Amelia . . . in the parlor upstairs there is that curio cabinet that had that
snuff-box you gave me I admired so when I first came.

MISS AMELIA *(Affirming this)*

Yes, Cousin Lymon, there be.

COUSIN LYMON

Well, that cabinet has in it some *other* things that I have become curious
about, and I would like to ask you about them.

MISS AMELIA

(Suddenly defensive, her eyes narrowing)

You go in there? You rummage about in that curio cabinet?

COUSIN LYMON

(His eyes narrowing, too)

Why, Amelia, it is a curio cabinet, and I am a curious little person; besides,
Amelia, you got no secrets from me. You got secrets from me, Amelia?

MISS AMELIA

No.

(Music out)

COUSIN LYMON

No. Well Amelia, I have found something I would like to ask you about *(He fishes into a pocket and brings up an acorn)* I found this: an acorn. What does it signify?

MISS AMELIA

Why, it's just an acorn, just an acorn I picked up on the afternoon Papa died.

COUSIN LYMON

How do you mean?

MISS AMELIA

I mean it's just an acorn I spied on the ground that day. I picked it up and put it in my pocket. But I don't know why.

COUSIN LYMON

What a peculiar reason to keep it.

MISS AMELIA

Do you want *it,* Cousin Lymon?

COUSIN LYMON

(After a brief, almost unkind hesitation; gifting her)

Why no, Amelia, you may have it. It were your father's and he were dear to you.

MISS AMELIA

(With a remembering smile)

He were. Law, I remember when I were little, I slept and slept. I'd go to bed just as the lamp was turned on and sleep—why, I'd sleep like I was drowned in warm axle grease. Then come daybreak Papa would walk in and put his hand down on my shoulder. "Get stirring, Little," he would say. Then later he would holler up the stairs from the kitchen when the stove was hot. "Fried grits," he would holler. "White meat and gravy. Ham and eggs." And I'd run down the stairs and dress by the hot stove while he was washing up out at the pump. Then off we'd go to the still, or maybe . . .

COUSIN LYMON

The grits we had this morning was poor; fried too quick so that the inside never heated.

MISS AMELIA

And when Papa would run off the liquor in those days . . .

COUSIN LYMON

You know I don't like grits lest they be done exactly right. You know I have told you many times, Amelia . . .

MISS AMELIA

. . . or when he would take me with him when he buried the barrels . . .

COUSIN LYMON

I say: the grits we had this morning was poor.

MISS AMELIA

. . . an' we would go, an' . . . all right, Cousin Lymon; I will take more care
with them.

COUSIN LYMON

You loved your poppa, didn't you, Amelia?

MISS AMELIA

I . . .

COUSIN LYMON

You can say it.

MISS AMELIA *(Finally)*

Course I loved my poppa. Momma dyin' as she did, birthin' me . . .

COUSIN LYMON

You were normal size, Amelia? You a regular baby size when you born?

MISS AMELIA

(Laughing amazement)
Course I was, Cousin Lymon.

COUSIN LYMON

Course you were.

MISS AMELIA

. . . an' . . . an' poppa an' me, we'd take long trips together . . .

COUSIN LYMON

Into Cheehaw? Or to the fair sometimes?

MISS AMELIA

Yes . . . an' sometimes beyond. Way beyond. We'd take long trips.

COUSIN LYMON

And I found this, Amelia—
*(He goes into a pocket, takes out a small velvet box, at the sight of
which* MISS AMELIA *makes a half grab, but* COUSIN LYMON *moves
away)*
I have found this tiny velvet box, and if I open it up . . . *(Does so)* . . . what
do I see?

MISS AMELIA *(Blushing)*

You give that here.

COUSIN LYMON

What do I see? *(Pause)* Hmm? What do I see?

(Looks to MISS AMELIA, *who still blushes and will not look at either him or the box)*

I see two small little grey stones, and I wonder to myself "What do they be? Why has Amelia kept these stones?" What do they be, Amelia?

*(*MISS AMELIA *mumbles something at last, which we cannot hear)*

Hmm? I did not hear you, Amelia.

MISS AMELIA *(Shyer than ever)*

They be . . .

COUSIN LYMON *(Enjoying it greatly)*

Yes? Yes?

MISS AMELIA *(Finally)*

They be . . . I were in great pain, years back, and I went into Cheehaw, to the doctor there—I couldn't figure the pain, and none of my remedies worked for it—and I went to the doctor there and . . . *(In great embarrassment)* . . . those be my kidney stones. *(A fair silence)* Now, give 'em here.

COUSIN LYMON

(Examining the stones)

So that is what they be.

MISS AMELIA

Give them here, now.

COUSIN LYMON

I admire these, Amelia. You ain't given me a present in the longest time now. You give me these as a present. Yes?

MISS AMELIA

(Can't help but laugh)

But what would you do with them, Cousin Lymon?

COUSIN LYMON

I have always admired . . . I have always wanted a great gold chain across my vest, and you could get me a great gold chain for across my vest, and you could have these hung from it. Oh, Amelia, I would love that so. I would so love that.

*(*MISS AMELIA *laughs blushingly)*

Oh, I would.

MISS AMELIA

Unh-hunh; yes, if you want it, Cousin Lymon.

COUSIN LYMON

(Quite coldly)
Oh, Amelia, I do love you so.

MISS AMELIA

(With some awkward gesture: kicking the dirt off a boot, maybe)
Humf! Those are words I don't wanna hear. *(Pause)* Understand?

COUSIN LYMON

(A too-eager schoolboy)
Yes, Amelia!

MISS AMELIA *(After a silence)*
I am fond of you, Cousin Lymon.
(Music begins here, softly)

THE NARRATOR

Ah, Amelia, I do love you so. Now, was that true? Well, we will find out.
But it is true that Miss Amelia loved Cousin Lymon, for he was kin to her,
and Miss Amelia had, for many years, before the arrival of Cousin Lymon,
lived a solitary life. And, too, there are many kinds of love . . . as we shall
find out. But this is how they talked, and was one of the ways in which Miss
Amelia showed her love for Cousin Lymon . . . her fondness. In fact, there
was only one part of her life that she did not want Cousin Lymon to share
with her . . . to know about; and it concerned a man named Marvin Macy.
It was a name that never crossed her lips . . . a name that no one in the
town dared mention in her presence . . . the name Marvin Macy.

The scene changes slowly to dark. MISS AMELIA *and* COUSIN LYMON
rise, go indoors. Under THE NARRATOR's *next speech the lights rise
on the interior of the cafe, revealing it full of* TOWNSPEOPLE, *sitting
around tables, drinking, or standing, buying, etc. Saturday night
is in full swing. Everyone is there.* STUMPY MACPHAIL *and one of
the* TOWNSMEN *are playing checkers; the* RAINEY TWINS *are at separate places, and they glower at each other occasionally.* HENRY
MACY *is at a table by himself, downstage; he is drinking and he
does not look happy.*

Music continues.

THE NARRATOR

We come now to a night of terrible importance, the beginning of a series
of events which will result in calamity and great sadness. It looks to be a
Saturday night like any other since the cafe has opened, but the great and

terrible events of a person's life occur most often in the most common-place of circumstances.

(*Music out.*

Cafe scene up full, general chatter. COUSIN LYMON *mills around the guests.* MISS AMELIA *enters, from the kitchen, bearing a handwritten sign with the legend "Chicken dinner tonite—twenty cents")*

MISS AMELIA

(*Tacking the sign up*)

For them of you as can't read . . . Chicken dinner tonight . . . twenty cents.

(*General approval; some people move to the kitchen to be served. It must be understood that there is ad lib conversation all throughout this scene*)

It's in the kitchen. Pay on the bar and get it yourselves.

(*She moves to where* HENRY MACY *sits*)

What ails you?

HENRY MACY (*Half rising*)

Miss Amelia?

MISS AMELIA

What ails you tonight, Henry?

HENRY MACY (*Obviously lying*)

Why . . . why, nothing, Miss Amelia. Nothing.

MISS AMELIA

Then you better eat.

HENRY MACY

No, no; I got a drink here, Miss Amelia; I will sit with it.

MISS AMELIA

(*Still sits, regarding him*)

Suit yourself.

COUSIN LYMON

(*To* STUMPY MACPHAIL)

And I walked to Rotten Lake today to fish, and on the way I stepped over what appeared at first to be a big fallen tree. But then as I stepped over I felt something stir and I taken this second look and there I was straddling this here alligator long as from the front door to the kitchen and thicker than a hog.

(STUMPY MACPHAIL *and several of the others laugh good-naturedly*)

STUMPY MACPHAIL

Sure you did, peanut. Sure.

COUSIN LYMON

I did. I did. And . . . and I looked down at him, and I . . .

MACPHAIL

. . . and you picked him up by his big ugly tail, and you swung him around your shoulder, and you flung him over the . . .

COUSIN LYMON *(Superior)*

All right, you just go look over at Rotten Lake sometime, smarty!

MISS AMELIA

(Smiling over to COUSIN LYMON*)*

You tell 'em.

(Now back to HENRY MACY*)*

Still not talkin'? Not eating? An' nothin' ails you, and you're just gonna sit there drinkin'. Right?

HENRY MACY

That's right, Miss Amelia.

MISS AMELIA

(Nods knowingly again)

All right.

COUSIN LYMON

(Having moved to where RAINEY 1 *is sitting)*

And how are you tonight?

RAINEY 1

(Glowering at RAINEY 2, *who returns his glower)*

Just dandy.

COUSIN LYMON

(Determined to make mischief)

Ohhhhh, and I see your brother is just dandy, too.

RAINEY 1

I don't know who you mean.

COUSIN LYMON

Why, I mean your lookalike.

RAINEY 1 *(Greatly indignant)*

Humf! That one!

RAINEY 2

(To COUSIN LYMON; *he too indignant)*

Don't you go talkin' to that no-account. He rob the hump off your back quick as look at you.

COUSIN LYMON

(Marches over to RAINEY 2; *swipes at him, snarls, almost)*

You mean to say your brother is some kind of wizard? That what you mean to say?

MISS AMELIA

(Still sitting, but concerned)

Cousin Lymon . . . ?

COUSIN LYMON

(Stamping back to RAINEY 1)

That what he mean to say? That what your no-account brother saying? He some kind of wizard?

RAINEY 2 *(So all will hear)*

I don't mean that. I mean that thievin' no-good over there'll steal you blind before you know it.

RAINEY 1 *(Rising)*

I ain't no thief!

COUSIN LYMON

(Mischief again, coming between the brothers)

Oh, now now now. You talked to him; I caught you: you talked to your own brother.

RAINEY 1 *(Angry)*

I talked *on* him; I said I ain't no thief. I didn't talk *to* him.

COUSIN LYMON

My, my; two years now you two ain't spoke a word to each other; not a word in two whole years.

RAINEY 2

HE STOLE MY KNIFE!

RAINEY 1

I NEVER STOLE NOBODY'S KNIFE!

(They glare, subside. COUSIN LYMON *moves to* MISS AMELIA)

COUSIN LYMON

Now, ain't that something, Amelia: These two not speaking to one another for more'n two years now over six inches of sharp steel? Ain't that something?

MISS AMELIA

Some people been killed for less.

*(*COUSIN LYMON *chases* HENRIETTA FORD CRIMP JR. *around a table)*

MISS AMELIA

Leave that kid be. She been sick. (*Rises*) I'm eatin'. Cousin Lymon, can I bring you your dinner?

COUSIN LYMON

My appetite is poor tonight; there is a sourness in my mouth.

MISS AMELIA

Just a pick: the breast, the liver and the heart.

COUSIN LYMON

(*Sweet-spoiled; sitting at the table with* HENRY MACY)
All right, Amelia, if you will do that for me.

MISS AMELIA

Henry?

HENRY MACY

No, Miss Amelia . . . thank you. I will stay with your good liquor.

MISS AMELIA

(*Walking to the kitchen*)
Ain't like you, Henry.

COUSIN LYMON

(*Imitating* MISS AMELIA)
Ain't like you, Henry. What ails you, Henry Macy?

HENRY MACY

Nothin'! Now don't you start in, too!

COUSIN LYMON

Oooohhhh . . . Law!

HENRY MACY

Just . . . leave it be.

COUSIN LYMON

Now, that ain't polite, Henry . . .

HENRY MACY

(*A quiet warning; a little drunk*)
Look, runt; go pick on someone your own size, hear?

MACPHAIL

Yeah, go back fight another flock o' alligators or whatever they was.

COUSIN LYMON

(*To* STUMPY MACPHAIL)
You go on out to Rotten Lake now, and you see!

(EMMA *and* MRS. PETERSON *emerge from the kitchen, carrying plates; call back to* MISS AMELIA *in the kitchen*)

EMMA *(Her mouth full)*
Real fine chicken, Miss Amelia!

MRS. PETERSON
Oh, yes, a good bird . . . it is, Miss Amelia.

EMMA *(Still shouting)*
Real fine. *(Then sotto voce, to* MRS. PETERSON*)* Probably stole them chickens off some poor tenant farmer out near . . .

MRS. PETERSON
Oooooohhhh, *Emma* . . .

EMMA
. . . or maybe somebody behind on a loan to her, she walk in an say, "I'll take all your birds." That's what. Somethin' like that.

MRS. PETERSON *(Whispering)*
Emma.

EMMA *(Loud)*
Wouldn't put it past her.

COUSIN LYMON
(As they pass him, barks at EMMA*)*
WARF! WARF!
(Several people laugh)

EMMA
(As MRS. PETERSON *squeals, jumps)*
You stop that, runt. I'll knock you clear into next week!

COUSIN LYMON
(Raises his hands like a puppy's paws, whimpers a moment; then)
FATTY! You fat thing!

EMMA
(Looming above COUSIN LYMON, *as* MISS AMELIA *emerges from the kitchen with two plates)*
FAT: Well, fat is better'n twisted, you miserable little runt. . . !

MISS AMELIA *(A command)*
EMMA HALE!
(EMMA subsides, moves to a table)

EMMA

(Not to MISS AMELIA, *but for her ears)*

They is some good cafes in these parts, I hear, where they is not monkeys crawling around the floor; where the owners' pets is not . . .

MISS AMELIA

(Setting a plate down before COUSIN LYMON *and one at her own place)*

That'll do now.

MRS. PETERSON

(Whispered, breathless)

Emma, you *know* you mustn't . . .

MISS AMELIA

Them people oughta go to them cafes; if they ain't careful they won't be welcome no more in *this* cafe.

(To COUSIN LYMON)

Eat.

COUSIN LYMON

(Sweet in victory and vindication, looking toward EMMA)

Thank you, Amelia. And they is *some* cafes, I hear, where they do not allow just *any*body to come in an' . . .

MISS AMELIA

(Silencing him, too, but kindly)

All right now. Eat.

(They fall to; the general cafe conversation continues, lessens a bit, perhaps, for our attention should move outside, stage-left, where the figure of a man appears. It is MARVIN MACY. *He stands, gazing at the cafe, begins whittling, all the while staring at the cafe, and whistling softly.*

(To COUSIN LYMON)

You was hungry after all.

COUSIN LYMON

(Shovelling food into his mouth)

It would seem. But only for the delicacies. Like you choose 'em.

(HENRY MACY clears his throat, makes as if to speak of something difficult, but stops)

MISS AMELIA

Henry Macy, if you gonna sit here all night, and drink liquor, and . . .

COUSIN LYMON (*Gleefully*)

Bet he got a secret.

(*Throughout the following, the cafe conversations grow quiet; eventually, when indicated, cease entirely*)

MISS AMELIA

You got a secret, Henry?

COUSIN LYMON

Bet he do.

HENRY MACY (*Finally*)

I . . . I got a letter last week, Miss Amelia.

MISS AMELIA

(*After a brief pause; unsurprised at the news*)

Yeah?

HENRY MACY

It were . . . it were a letter from my brother.

(*Noticeable lessening in the cafe conversation*)

MISS AMELIA

(*After a silence, leaning to* HENRY MACY, *saying, with great force*)

You are welcome to it. (*Pause*) You hear?

HENRY MACY

He . . . he is on parole. He is out of the penitentiary. I got this letter last week, an' he is on parole.

(*The cafe is very quiet now.* COUSIN LYMON *senses something extraordinary; he gets up, moves about, speaks to the others*)

COUSIN LYMON

Who? . . . Who? . . . What?

MISS AMELIA

(*Slamming her fist down on the table*)

You are welcome to any letter you get from him, because your brother is a . . . because he belong to be in that penitentiary the balance of his life!

COUSIN LYMON

Who? . . . Who is this about?

MERLIE RYAN

Marvin Macy comin' back? Is Marvin Macy . . .

MACPHAIL

Hush, you!

COUSIN LYMON *(To* HENRY MACY*)*

You got a brother? Hunh? What is all this?

MISS AMELIA

Marvin Macy belong to be in that penitentiary the balance of his life!

COUSIN LYMON

(Beside himself with curiosity and a strange excitement)

WHO IS MARVIN MACY? Parole? What . . . what did he do?

MISS AMELIA

(Still to HENRY MACY*)*

You hear me?

COUSIN LYMON

(To STUMPY MACPHAIL*)*

What did he do?

MACPHAIL

(With embarrassment, not looking up)

Well, he . . . well, he robbed three filling stations . . . for one . . .

MERLIE RYAN

Do Miss Amelia know Marvin Macy comin' back?

(Several quiet him)

HENRY MACY

(With great difficulty)

He don't say much . . . his letter don't say much . . . 'cept . . .

(He stops)

MISS AMELIA *(Her fists clenched)*

. . . 'Cept?

(Dead silence)

HENRY MACY *(Finally)*

'Cept he is comin' back here.

(Flurry of excitement)

MISS AMELIA

(A commandment)

He will never set his split hoof on my premises! Never. That is all!

(Swings around to the others)

Get back to your drinkin', all of you!

(Self-conscious and half-hearted return to normalcy. But COUSIN LYMON *will not be put by)*

COUSIN LYMON

(Turning to FIRST TOWNSMAN*)*
Tell me about Marvin Macy; tell me what he done!

FIRST TOWNSMAN *(Moving away)*

Let it be.

COUSIN LYMON

Who is Marvin Macy?

SECOND TOWNSMAN

Go on about your business, now.

COUSIN LYMON

(To no one; to the center of the room)
Who is . . . who is . . .
(Sees MISS AMELIA *moving to the porch; runs after her)*
Who is he? Amelia, who is Marvin Macy?

MISS AMELIA

(Going on to the porch)
Finish your dinner.

COUSIN LYMON

(Following her on to the porch)
Amelia, who is Marvin Macy? I want to know who this man is! Who
is . . . ?
*(*MISS AMELIA *and* COUSIN LYMON *see* MARVIN MACY *simultaneously. Tense silence)*

MISS AMELIA

(As COUSIN LYMON *takes a couple of tentative steps toward*
MARVIN MACY, *stops)*
You clear outa here! You get on!
(Silence for a second, then MARVIN MACY *laughs, turns, exits.* MISS
AMELIA *stares after him, turns to go in, goes, leaving* COUSIN
LYMON *alone on the porch)*

COUSIN LYMON *(Alone)*

WHO IS MARVIN MACY?
(Stays where he is)

THE NARRATOR

Who is Marvin Macy? Who is Marvin Macy? Now, while no one would tell
Cousin Lymon about Marvin Macy that night in the cafe . . . *(Lighting shift
to day here)* . . . people are braver in the daylight, and the next day it was

not hard at all for him to learn what he wanted to know. And what he found out was this . . . that many years ago, back when Miss Amelia was nineteen years old, there occurred in her life a singular and awesome event: Miss Amelia had been married. Back when Miss Amelia was nineteen years old there were, at the same time, two brothers, the living remainder of a brood of seven children. The brothers were Marvin and Henry Macy, and Marvin was ten years younger than his brother, Henry. And Marvin Macy was a loom-fixer at the mill, and he was the handsomest man in the region . . . and the wildest.

(COUSIN LYMON *stays on stage, way to one side.*

Music out.

MARVIN *and* HENRY MACY *come on*)

HENRY MACY

The Tanner girl . . .

MARVIN MACY

What about the Tanner girl?

HENRY MACY

She gone off to Society City.

MARVIN MACY (Challenging)

So?

(*No response from* HENRY)

So, let her go; she be happy there, give her some free space to run about in.

HENRY MACY

(*Sitting;* MARVIN *stays standing*)

I hear she left on account of you.

MARVIN MACY

Who says? . . . Hunh?

HENRY MACY

Mrs. Tanner. She stops me comin' back from the mill . . . yesterday . . . she say Laura go off to Society City on account of you . . .

MARVIN MACY

On account of me *what* . . . ?

HENRY MACY

Land, Marvin, *you* know.

MARVIN MACY

(*Intentionally transparent pretense of innocence*)

I don't know.

HENRY MACY

Ain't the first young girl you take out to the woods with you, ain't the first young girl you forced to leave home . . . you ruined. Ain't the first . . .

MARVIN MACY *(Bored impatience)*

I know what I *do*. *(Leers)* I know who I take walkin' in the moonlight with me, goes out little girls comes back women . . .

HENRY MACY

It ain't right!

MARVIN MACY *(Suddenly ugly)*

Don't you tell me what's right! God damn, for a brother you act one hell of a lot like you was my father!

HENRY MACY

(Softer, but still to the point)
It ain't right.

MARVIN MACY

Them young girls . . . ? Them young girls you talk about . . . *(Cruel imitation)* . . . "it ain't right" . . . *(His face close to* HENRY's) . . . you know what they want? Hunh? How you know what they do out there in the woods, drive a man half out of his mind; what d' you know about that? *(Sneers)* The kinda moonlight walks *you* take, Henry, them solitary walks at night, that . . . *(Chuckles)* . . . that ain't the same thing . . . ain't, at all. *(An afterthought; still not kind)* 'Sides, don't think a walk in the woods with Laura Tanner do you any harm . . . might do you some good!

HENRY MACY *(To avoid)*

She ain't the first you take out there! They ain't all pressing theirselves up against you, free for all. They be a legal word for what you do out there, Marvin!

MARVIN MACY *(Quietly amused)*

Yeah? What be it?

HENRY MACY

Never . . . never mind.

MARVIN MACY

They be a word for what you do out there in them woods, too, Henry.

HENRY MACY

(Embarrassed, but still brother)
You . . . you gonna get yourself in big trouble one day.

MARVIN MACY *(Sneering bravura)*

I been in trouble. Oooh, I am evil, Henry.

HENRY MACY

Carryin' marijuana around with you, and . . .

MARVIN MACY

(Pretending to fish into a pocket)

Want some, Henry? Want some marijuana?

HENRY MACY *(Vacant)*

It is for them who are discouraged and drawn toward death.

MARVIN MACY *(A great laugh)*

And you ain't? *(Pause)* It is also for little girls who would be women; makes their heads whirl, gives 'em that floating feelin' . . .

(Laughs again, softer)

HENRY MACY

And aside from that, all your drinkin', and you not savin' any money, an' . . .

MARVIN MACY *(Angry)*

I got steady work, an' I make good money! I spend it as I like! I don't need you tellin' me . . .

HENRY MACY *(Softly)*

All right. *(Loud)* ALL RIGHT!

MARVIN MACY *(Muttering)*

I don't need you tellin' me anything 'bout how to go about livin'. I make good money . . .

HENRY MACY *(Weary impatience)*

. . . you make good money, an' you don't need me . . . yeah, I know all about it.

MARVIN MACY

Yeah.

HENRY MACY

Yeah. Don't change nothin', though.

MARVIN MACY *(Almost whining)*

Oh, Henry.

HENRY MACY

Man like you oughta settle down, oughta get married, raise some kids.

MARVIN MACY *(Suddenly furious)*

For what! Raise kids, have 'em a life like what we had? For what!

HENRY MACY

They is no need for kids to grow up like we had to; they is . . .

*(*MISS AMELIA *enters, near them; she wears a dress. She looks younger —maybe her hair is down. They do not see her)*

MARVIN MACY

For what!

HENRY MACY

All right now.

MARVIN MACY

Kids better off not born!

HENRY MACY

All right.

MARVIN MACY

Damn fool idea!

MISS AMELIA *(Irony)*

Afternoon.

    *(*HENRY MACY *rises;* MARVIN MACY *does not)*

HENRY MACY

Afternoon, Miss Amelia.

MARVIN MACY

Afternoon, Miss Amelia.

MISS AMELIA *(To* MARVIN MACY*)*

Your legs broke?

MARVIN MACY

Miss Amelia?

MISS AMELIA

I say: your legs broke?

MARVIN MACY *(Lazily)*

Why, no, Miss Amelia; my legs fine.

MISS AMELIA *(Snorts)*

I wondered. *(Purposefully, to* HENRY MACY*)* Whyn't you sit on back down, Henry?

HENRY MACY *(Resits)*

Thank you, Miss Amelia.

MARVIN MACY

Ohhhhhh.

    (Slowly rises, mock-bows to MISS AMELIA*)*

Half the time I forget you're a girl, Miss Amelia . . . you so big; you more like a man.

MISS AMELIA

Yeah?

(*She swings backhand at* MARVIN MACY, *who ducks, laughs, sits again*)

MARVIN MACY

Temper, Miss Amelia.

MISS AMELIA (*Only half a joke*)

Don't you worry about temper. I'll knock you across the road.

MARVIN MACY

Bet you'd try.

MISS AMELIA

Bet I would. Do it, too.

MARVIN MACY

Well, you might *try*, Miss Amelia . . .

MISS AMELIA

Stand back up; I'll give you a sample.

HENRY MACY

Now, why don't you two just . . .

MISS AMELIA (*Smiling*)

Stand back up.

MARVIN MACY (*Gently*)

I don't go 'round hittin' girls, now.

MISS AMELIA

I didn't say nothin' about you hittin' me; I said I knock you across the road, an' I could do it.

MARVIN MACY (*Pleased*)

Well, maybe you could, Miss Amelia; maybe you could, at that.

MISS AMELIA

'Course, you could always pull a razor on me, like I hear you done to that man over in Cheehaw you fought.

MARVIN MACY (*Mock shock*)

Miss Amelia!

MISS AMELIA

I hear about it.

MARVIN MACY

Now, what did you hear?

MISS AMELIA

I hear. I hear you take a razor to that man, an' you cut his ear off.

HENRY MACY

Oh, now.

MISS AMELIA

An' you know what else I hear?

MARVIN MACY *(Greatly amused)*

No. What else you hear?

MISS AMELIA

I hear you got that man's ear salted and dried an' you carry it around with you.

HENRY MACY *(Dogmatically)*

That ain't true.

MARVIN MACY

Now, do you think I'd do a thing like that?

HENRY MACY

That ain't *true*.

MISS AMELIA *(To* HENRY MACY*)*

You know? You got proof it ain't?

(To MARVIN MACY*)*

You got proof you ain't got that man's ear?

MARVIN MACY

(Leans back lazily)

You want proof, Miss Amelia? You wanna search me? I'll lay back real quiet and let you go through my pockets, if you have a mind to. I'll lay back real quiet.

MISS AMELIA

(Finally, after a moment's noticeable embarrassment and confusion)

Clear across the road! I'll knock you clear across the road.

*(*MARVIN MACY *laughs;* HENRY *joins in)*

MARVIN MACY

Uhhh-*huh*!

MISS AMELIA

(Embarrassment back a little, begins to move toward her house)

I'll . . . I'll let you two go on back to whatever caused all that shoutin' you two were at . . . yellin' at each other . . .

MARVIN MACY

Why, you know what we were talkin' about, Miss Amelia? Shoutin', you say? We were talkin' about how it time for me to get a wife, that's what.

MISS AMELIA *(Snorts)*

Who marry you?

MARVIN MACY *(Mock seriousness)*

Why, Miss Amelia, I thought you would. Don't you want to marry me, Miss Amelia?

MISS AMELIA

(Confused for a moment, then)

In a pig's ear!

(Strides to and into her house)

MARVIN MACY

(To her retreating form)

Why, I thought you'd like that, Miss Amelia.

HENRY MACY

Bye, Miss Amelia.

MARVIN MACY

Thought you'd like that.

HENRY MACY *(After* MISS AMELIA *has gone)*

Some jokes ain't in the best taste, Marvin.

MARVIN MACY

Hm?

HENRY MACY

Some jokes ain't in the best taste.

MARVIN MACY

(After momentary puzzlement)

Oh . . . no . . . that be a point, Henry . . . some jokes ain't.

HENRY MACY

No; they ain't.

MARVIN MACY

Hey, you know I be right about somethin': Miss Amelia ain't no girl; she be a woman already.

HENRY MACY

Yes, she be. Sure ain't right for you, Marvin; she be grown up.

MARVIN MACY

(Gets up, wanders toward the door to the house)

No. Sure ain't.

HENRY MACY

(Gets up, prepares to leave)

Well . . .

MARVIN MACY

Hey, Henry . . . ?

HENRY MACY

Yeah?

MARVIN MACY

A real grown-up woman.

HENRY MACY

Marvin . . .

MARVIN MACY

Hey, Henry . . . if I *was* gonna get a wife . . .

HENRY MACY

You crazy?

MARVIN MACY

Some say.

HENRY MACY

You ain't serious, Marvin. She laugh in your face.

MARVIN MACY

Hmmm? Oh, yeah, bet you right.

HENRY MACY

You ain't serious, Marvin.

MARVIN MACY

(After a moment; smiles at HENRY MACY*)*

No. I ain't serious.

(They hold positions)

THE NARRATOR

Oh, but he was; Marvin Macy was dead serious. He had, at that moment, without knowing it, chosen Miss Amelia Evans to be his bride. He had chosen her to be his bride, and when he realized that astonishing fact he was dismayed. For while he knew he loved her, had probably loved her for some time without knowing it, he also knew he did not deserve her. He was sick with dismay at his unworthiness. So, for two full years, Marvin Macy did not speak to Miss Amelia of his love for her, but spent that time in bettering himself in her eyes. No man in the town ever reversed his character more fully. And finally, one Sunday evening, at the end of two years, Marvin Macy returned to Miss Amelia and plighted his troth.

(MARVIN MACY *enters from stage-left, bearing a sack of chitterlins, a bunch of swamp flowers and, in the pocket of his dressy suit, a silver ring. He approaches slowly, his eyes on the ground; he stops a number of feet from where* MISS AMELIA *is sitting*)

MARVIN MACY

(Still not looking at her)

Evenin' Miss Amelia. *(No response)* Sure is hot.

MISS AMELIA *(After a pause)*

It so hot, what you all dressed up for a funeral for?

MARVIN MACY

(After a blushing laugh)

Oh, I . . . I am come callin'.

(*Let it be understood here that there are, unless otherwise stated, varying pauses between speeches in this scene*)

MISS AMELIA

Yeah? On who?

MARVIN MACY

Oh . . . on you . . . Miss Amelia.

MISS AMELIA *(Restating a fact)*

On me.

MARVIN MACY *(Laughs briefly)*

Yep . . . on you.

MISS AMELIA *(Considers it; then)*

Somethin' wrong?

MARVIN MACY

I . . .

(*He makes a sudden decision, hurriedly brings the bag of chitterlins and the flowers over to where* MISS AMELIA *is, puts them on the ground below where she is sitting, the flowers on top of the bag, and returns to his position*)

. . . I brought you these.

MISS AMELIA *(Stares at them)*

What be these?

MARVIN MACY *(Terribly shy)*

Flowers.

MISS AMELIA

I can see that. What be in the bag?

MARVIN MACY *(As before)*

They be . . . chitterlins.

MISS AMELIA *(Mild surprise)*

Chitterlins.

MARVIN MACY

Yep.

> (MISS AMELIA *descends the stairs, picks up the flowers as though they were a duster)*

MISS AMELIA *(Reseating herself)*

What for?

MARVIN MACY

Miss Amelia?

MISS AMELIA

I say: what for? Why you bring me chitterlins and flowers?

MARVIN MACY

(Bravely taking one or two steps forward)

Miss Amelia, I am . . . I am a reformed person. I have mended my ways, and . . .

MISS AMELIA

If you are come to call, sit down. Don't stand there in the road.

MARVIN MACY

Thank . . . Thank you, Miss Amelia.

> (He comes onto the porch and seats himself, but four or five feet from MISS AMELIA)

I have mended my ways; I am, like I said, a reformed person, Miss Amelia . . .

MISS AMELIA

(Looking at the flowers)

What are these called?

MARVIN MACY

Hunh? . . . Oh, they . . . they be swamp flowers.

MISS AMELIA

But what are they *called?*

MARVIN MACY *(Shrugs, helplessly)*

Swamp flowers.

MISS AMELIA

They got a name.

MARVIN MACY

I . . . I don't know.

MISS AMELIA

I don't neither. *(Pause)* They got a name in some *language;* all flowers do.

MARVIN MACY

I don't know, Miss Amelia.

MISS AMELIA

I don't neither. *(Smells them)* They don't smell none.

MARVIN MACY

I'm . . . sorry.

MISS AMELIA

Don't have to smell; they pretty.

MARVIN MACY *(Blurting)*

Miss Amelia, I have mended my ways; I go to church regular, and I have . . .

MISS AMELIA

I see it. You go to church now, services an' meetings . . .

MARVIN MACY

. . . yes, an' I have learned to put money aside . . .

MISS AMELIA

. . . you have learned thrift; that good . . .

MARVIN MACY

. . . an' I have bought me some land, I have bought me ten acres of timber over by . . .

MISS AMELIA

. . . I hear so; timber is good land . . .

MARVIN MACY

. . . an', an' I don't drink none no more . . .

MISS AMELIA

. . . don't drink? . . .

MARVIN MACY *(Blushes)*

. . . well, you know what I mean . . .

MISS AMELIA

Man don't drink none ain't natural.

MARVIN MACY

Well, I don't squander my wages away on drink an' all that I used to . . .

MISS AMELIA
Uh-huuh.

MARVIN MACY
. . . an' . . . Miss Amelia? . . . an' I am less sportin' with the girls now . . . I
have reformed my character in that way, too . . .

MISS AMELIA *(Nods slowly)*
I know; I hear.

MARVIN MACY
. . . an'; an' I have stopped pickin' fights with folks . . .

MISS AMELIA
You still got that ear? You still got that ear you cut off that man in Cheehaw
you fight? . . .

MARVIN MACY *(Embarrassed)*
Oh, Miss Amelia, I never done that.

MISS AMELIA *(Disbelieving)*
I *hear.*

MARVIN MACY
Oh, no, Miss Amelia, I never done that. I . . . I let that story pass 'round
. . . but I never done that.

MISS AMELIA
(The slightest tinge of disappointment)
Oh. That so.

MARVIN MACY
So, you see, I have reformed my character.

MISS AMELIA *(Nods)*
Would seem.
(A long pause between them)

MARVIN MACY
Yes.

MISS AMELIA
Land is good to have. I been dickerin' over near Society City to pick up
thirty-five acres . . . timber, too . . . man there near broke, an' he wanna
sell to me.

MARVIN MACY
Miss . . . Miss Amelia . . . *(Brings the ring from his pocket)* I brought somethin' else with me, too . . .

MISS AMELIA *(Curious)*
Yeah?

MARVIN MACY

I. . .

(Shows it to her)

. . . I brought this silver ring.

MISS AMELIA

(Looks at it; hands it back)

It silver?

MARVIN MACY

Yep, it silver. Miss Amelia, will you . . .

MISS AMELIA

Bet it cost some.

MARVIN MACY

(Determined to get it out)

Miss Amelia, will you marry me?

MISS AMELIA

(After an interminable pause, during which she scratches her head, then her arm, then very offhand)

Sure.

MARVIN MACY

(Almost not having heard)

You . . . Yes?! . . . You will?

MISS AMELIA

(Narrowing her eyes, almost unfriendly)

I said sure.

MARVIN MACY

(Not rising, begins sliding himself across the step to her)

Oh, Amelia . . .

MISS AMELIA *(Sharply)*

What?

MARVIN MACY

(In a split second studies what he has said wrong, realizes it, keeps sliding)

Oh, *Miss* Amelia . . .

(He reaches her, begins the gesture of putting one arm behind her back, the other in front, preparatory to kissing her. MISS AMELIA *reacts swiftly, leans back a bit, swings her right arm back, with a fist, ready to hit him)*

MISS AMELIA

Whoa there, you!

MARVIN MACY

(Retreats some, slides back a few feet)

Wait 'til I tell Henry; wait 'til I tell *everybody*. *(Very happy)* Oh, Miss Amelia.

MISS AMELIA *(Rises, stretches)*

Well . . . g'night.

*(MARVIN MACY, momentarily confused, but too happy to worry
about it, rises, also, backs down the porch steps, begins backing
off, stage-left)*

MARVIN MACY

G' . . . G' . . . G'night, Miss Amelia.

*(Reaches the far side of the stage, then just before turning to run
off, shouts)*

G'night, Miss Amelia.

(Exits)

MISS AMELIA

(Standing on the porch, alone; long pause)

G'night . . .

(Pause)

Marvin Macy.

(MISS AMELIA goes indoors)

NARRATOR

And the very next Sunday they were married. It was a proper church wedding, performed by the Reverend Potter, and Miss Amelia had held a bouquet of flowers, and Henry was there to give Marvin away, and it was,
indeed, a proper wedding. Now it is true that some of the townspeople had
misgivings about the match, but no one—not even the most evil-minded—
had foreseen what was to happen: for the marriage of Marvin Macy and
Miss Amelia Evans lasted only ten days . . . ten unholy days which became
a legend, a whispered legend in the town.

(Interior of store visible. MISS AMELIA *and* MARVIN MACY *alone.*
MISS AMELIA *wears a wedding dress, carries a wedding bouquet.*
MARVIN MACY *has a flower in his coat)*

MARVIN MACY *(Shyly)*

Well, Miss Amelia . . .

MISS AMELIA

(Picking at her dress)

Don't know why a person's supposed to get all up in this stuff . . . just to
get married.

MARVIN MACY

I think it look . . . nice.

MISS AMELIA *(Studying the dress)*

Belong to my mother.

MARVIN MACY

It look . . . nice.

MISS AMELIA

Too short.

MARVIN MACY

It look . . . nice. You . . . you pass it on down to . . .

MISS AMELIA

Hm?

MARVIN MACY

You pass it on down to our kids . . . our daughters.

MISS AMELIA

(Looks at him, snorts)
Hunh! *(Laughs briefly, sardonically)* If you hungry, go eat.

MARVIN MACY

I ain't hungry, Miss Amelia.

MISS AMELIA

No? Suit yourself. I got some figgerin' to do.

MARVIN MACY *(Shyly)*

Figgerin' . . . Miss Amelia?

MISS AMELIA

(Totally oblivious of his surprise)
Yeah, I got a bargain goin' on some kindlin' I want, an' I gotta figger. I
think I figgered a way to get that kindlin' good an' cheap. That farmer
owe me a favor: once I fixed boils for him, an' he ain't never paid a bill
he owed papa when he were alive. I kin get it good an' cheap. What you
think?

MARVIN MACY

I think . . . I think it be time . . . ain't it time for bed, Miss Amelia?

MISS AMELIA

Ain't ten. You tired?

MARVIN MACY

(Sitting gently, to wait)
No. I . . . ain't tired.

MISS AMELIA

You wanna smoke a pipe? Before sleep? Ain't no pockets in this dress. Thought I had my clothes on.

MARVIN MACY

No, I don't need a pipe. Miss Amelia, it . . . time for bed.

MISS AMELIA

(Stretching; off-hand)

Yeah . . . well, c'mon . . . I'll show you where your room is.

MARVIN MACY

My . . . room . . . Miss Amelia?

MISS AMELIA

(Going toward the stairs)

C'mon.

MARVIN MACY *(Moving to her)*

Kin I . . . kin I take your arm?

MISS AMELIA

(Looks at him as though he were crazy. Laughs in his face)

What for?

MARVIN MACY

Well, it is . . . proper for a groom . . . to take his bride by the hand, an' . . .

MISS AMELIA

(Annoyed by the impracticality of his suggestion)

I got a lamp. You want it to spill?

*(*MISS AMELIA, *followed by* MARVIN MACY, *climb the stairs, disappear. It becomes dark in the store, but the interior stays visible)*

THE NARRATOR

And what happened next, what happened that wedding night of Miss Amelia and Marvin Macy, no one will ever truly know. But part of it—part of it—was witnessed by Emma Hale, who had watched it, her nose pressed against the downstairs window of the store. And she could not wait to tell what she had seen.

EMMA HALE *(To* HENRY MACY*)*

An' it weren't no more'n a half hour after they'd gone upstairs, him followin' after her . . .

(Pantomime from MISS AMELIA *and* MARVIN MACY *to this)*

Miss Amelia come thumpin' back down those stairs, her face black with anger? An' she'd changed outa that dress o' hers, an' she were got up like she usually be now, an' she went into her office . . .

(Pauses for effect)

. . . and she stayed there 'till *dawn*. She stay there the whole night! He stayed up *there*, an' she stayed down *there*, in her office. *(Proudly)* An' how do you like that for a weddin' night?

HENRY MACY

I . . . I . . . didn't know.

EMMA HALE

All I can say is: a groom is in a sorry fix when he is unable to bring his well-beloved bride to bed with him. An' the whole town know it. There is some question there—specially a man like Marvin, his reputation: up-ending girls from here to Cheehaw an' back. Somethin' funny there.

HENRY MACY

Marvin?

MARVIN MACY

(His attention only on HENRY*)*

Henry . . . she . . .

HENRY MACY *(Gently)*

I know; I know.

MARVIN MACY *(A child)*

Henry, she don't like me . . . she don't . . . want me.

HENRY MACY

Well, now, Marvin, sometime it takes a while to . . .

MARVIN MACY

What'd I do wrong, Henry? She don't want me.

HENRY MACY *(Helplessly)*

Well, Marvin . . .

MARVIN MACY

We get upstairs, an' . . .

HENRY MACY

It take time, Marvin.

MARVIN MACY

I don't know; I don't know, Henry.

HENRY MACY *(Vaguely)*

Well . . .

MARVIN MACY

(An idea coming to him, enthusiasm growing)

Hey! Henry, maybe . . . maybe it 'cause I didn't give her no . . . no weddin' gifts . . . you know, women like to have them things. Hey, Henry? Maybe that it, huh?

HENRY MACY *(Cautious)*

Well, now . . .

MARVIN MACY

That's what I'll do, Henry: I'll go in to Society City an' . . . an' I'll get her a bunch of stuff.

(He leaves the porch, heads off)

That'll do it, Henry! I bet!

(He exits, happily)

HENRY MACY *(After him)*

Maybe . . . might be.

(Stays on stage)

THE NARRATOR

And off he went to Society City, and he brought her back all kinds of things; a huge box of chocolates which cost two dollars and a half, an enamel brooch, an opal ring, and a silver bracelet which had, hanging from it, two silver lovebirds. And he gave these presents to her . . . and she put them up for sale . . . all save the chocolates . . . which she ate. And, sad to tell, these presents did not soften her heart toward him.

MISS AMELIA

Oh, by the way, I gonna drag a mattress down from upstairs; you can sleep on *it*, in front of the stove, down here in the store.

(She waits for some reaction, gets none, goes inside)

MARVIN MACY

(By himself; the night has deepened a little. In a soft, plaintive voice)

Henry? . . . Henry?

IIENRY MACY

(From far off to one side)

Yes, Marvin.

MARVIN MACY

(To the night, not to HENRY's *voice)*

Henry, I don't know what to do.

HENRY MACY *(Helpless himself)*

Well, now, Marvin . . .

MARVIN MACY

I love her, Henry. I don't know what to do.

HENRY MACY

Time, Marvin. Time?

MARVIN MACY *(Pause)*

Yeah. *(Pause)* Sure, Henry.

(It comes up to daylight again now, MARVIN MACY *staying where he is)*

MARVIN MACY

(Gets up, shouts at the upstairs of the house, both a threat and a promise)

I be back!

HENRY MACY

(As MARVIN MACY *passes him, exiting)*

Marvin? Marvin, where you . . .

MARVIN MACY *(Pushing past)*

I goin' into Cheehaw; I be back.

(Exits)

THE NARRATOR

There was, of course, speculation in the town on the reason Miss Amelia had married Marvin Macy in the first place. No one doubted that *he* loved *her*, but as to why she had accepted his proposal in the first place there were myriad opinions. And while some people were . . . confused by the course of events, no one could honestly say he was surprised.

MARVIN MACY

(Reenters, moves inside to MISS AMELIA; *she looks up at him with a cool curiosity)*

Miss Amelia?

MISS AMELIA

You doin' a lot of travelin', I notice.

MARVIN MACY

I . . . I been to Cheehaw today.

MISS AMELIA *(Indifferent)*

Yeah? What you do there?

MARVIN MACY

I went into Cheehaw, an' . . . an' I saw a lawyer.

MISS AMELIA

(Suddenly on her guard)

Yeah? What you seein' a lawyer about?

MARVIN MACY *(Shy; embarrassed)*

Well, now. . .

MISS AMELIA *(Smelling trouble)*

What you know about lawyers?

MARVIN MACY

Well, I got me a lawyer . . . *(Takes out the paper)* . . . an' I got this paper drawn up . . .

MISS AMELIA *(Belligerently)*

Yeah, an'? . . .

MARVIN MACY

(Shy, but enthusiastic)

An' what I done, I got this paper drawn up, an' I had the deed to my timber land . . . the . . . the ten acres of timber land I bought with my savin's the past couple years . . . an' I had the deed to my timber land turned over to you, Miss Amelia. I had it put in your name; it all yours.

(He eagerly holds the paper out to MISS AMELIA*)*

MISS AMELIA

(She looks at him for a moment, no expression on her face, then she takes the paper from him, not snatching it, but not taking a gift, either. She studies it)

Hm!

MARVIN MACY

It all legal, Miss Amelia; I seen to that.

MISS AMELIA *(Still studying it)*

Hm.

MARVIN MACY

Them ten acres all yours now.

MISS AMELIA *(Still studying)*

Unh-hunh.

MARVIN MACY *(Shy)*

I . . . I thought you'd be pleased . . . Miss Amelia.

MISS AMELIA

(Folding the paper, putting it in her jeans, rising)

Yeah; it all legal.

MARVIN MACY

It is everything I have in the world.

MISS AMELIA

(Moving toward the door)

It legal.

MARVIN MACY

It is everything I have in the world, an' . . . I thought it would please you to have it.

MISS AMELIA

It adjoin *my* timber land, *my* acres; it make a nice spread.

MARVIN MACY *(Bewildered)*

Miss Amelia . . .

MISS AMELIA *(Daring him)*

Yeah?

MARVIN MACY

(His eyes on his feet)

I am not . . . as comfortable as I might be, sleepin' down in the store, in front of the stove, like I am.

MISS AMELIA *(No compassion)*

Oh no?

MARVIN MACY

No, I am not too comfortable sleepin' there.
(There is a pleading in this)

MISS AMELIA *(Considers it)*

Oh. *(Then)* Well, in that case then, why don't you pull your mattress out onto the porch, sleep there, or move over into the smoke house? Plenty of places you can sleep.
(She waits, challengingly, for his reply)

MARVIN MACY

(Too pitiable to be pitied)

I'd . . . you know where I'd rather sleep, Miss Amelia.

MISS AMELIA

Or why don't you just move back with your brother Henry?
(She turns, goes indoors)

MARVIN MACY

(Sits for a moment, contemplates his hopelessness; speaks to himself, gathering resolve)

I am your husband; you are married to me, *Miss* Amelia Evans.
(He gets up, follows her into the store, says to her with firmness and bravura)

Where is your likker?

MISS AMELIA *(Preoccupied)*

Hm?

MARVIN MACY

Gimme some likker!

MISS AMELIA

(With some distaste)
You takin' up drinkin' again? High noon drinkin'?

MARVIN MACY

Gimme some likker!

MISS AMELIA

(Her eyes narrowing)
You want some likker, you get your money up like anybody else.

MARVIN MACY

(Digging into his pocket)
I got my money; you give me that likker!
(He slams the money down on the counter)
(She reaches under the counter, brings up a bottle and slams it down on the counter. The two glower at each other)
(Murderously)
Thank you.

MISS AMELIA *(The same)*

You welcome.

MARVIN MACY

(Taking the bottle)
Now, I think I'll just take me off into the swamp an' have me a few drinks, an' then I think I'll just come back here an . . .

MISS AMELIA

You get yourself full of likker you don't set your foot in my house!

MARVIN MACY

We see about that . . . *Mrs. Macy!*

MISS AMELIA *(A threat)*

You come back here drunk you wish you never born.

MARVIN MACY

We see about that! I love you, Miss Amelia.

MISS AMELIA

OUTA HERE!!

MARVIN MACY

(Still coming toward her)
You my bride, an' I gonna make you my wife.

MISS AMELIA

(Her fist cocked)

One step more, you!

MARVIN MACY

(At her now, tries to embrace her)

I love you, Miss Amelia.

(At this, MISS AMELIA *swings at him, cracks him right in the jaw, with such force that he staggers back and crashes, hard, against a wall; slumps there a little, one hand to his mouth)*

MISS AMELIA

(Her fists still cocked)

OUT! OUT!

MARVIN MACY

(Surprised and hurt)

You . . . you broke my tooth; you . . . you broke one of my teeth.

MISS AMELIA

(Beginning to advance on him)

I break your head you don't get outa here!

MARVIN MACY

(Scrambling to get out, keeping as far from her advancing form as he can)

You . . . you broke my tooth.

MISS AMELIA *(Advancing)*

OUT!

MARVIN MACY

(Backs out onto the porch, down the steps)

You . . . you hit me.

MISS AMELIA

(Towering above him)

You stay out, an' don't you never come back!

MARVIN MACY

(Still unable to believe it)

You hit me.

MISS AMELIA

You hear me? Don't you never come back! (MISS AMELIA *goes back into the store)*

*(*MARVIN MACY *gets up, moves front and center, broods at the foot-lights.)*

(He reconsiders, marches up the steps, pauses momentarily, then, with renewed resolve, gets to the door. Forcefully:)

Miss Amelia?

(She turns around where she is, behind the counter, perhaps, looks at him)

Miss Amelia, I comin' back in.

(She moves to another area of the store)

You hear me? I got rights to be in here, as you is my wife an' what's yours is mine, too. So, I comin' in!

(MISS AMELIA picks up her shotgun, breaks it, reaches for shells, loads it, begins to walk toward MARVIN MACY)

I got my rights now, an' I'm comin' in there, an' I'm gonna . . . *(He sees the gun in her hand)*

(She keeps advancing, pointing the gun at him, holding it at hip level)

You . . . you can't do that, now . . . you . . .

(He retreats from the door, as MISS AMELIA keeps advancing)

I got my rights, an'

(He backs down the steps as MISS AMELIA comes out on the porch, stony-faced, the shotgun still pointed at him)

You . . . you keep that thing off me!

(He keeps backing off, finally stops)

Miss Amelia . . .

(So plaintively)

I love you.

MISS AMELIA

(Sits on the porch, the gun is still on him)

You come one step closer, I blast your head off. You step one foot on my property again, I shoot you.

MARVIN MACY

(Stands stock still for a moment, then breaks, moves off past HENRY MACY)

I'm leavin', Henry, I can't take no more; I can't take no more of this, Henry. *(Exits)*

HENRY MACY

(Moving to where MISS AMELIA is)

Miss . . . Miss Amelia?

MISS AMELIA

(In a rage, but abstracted)

Yeah? Whadda ya want?

HENRY MACY

Miss Amelia, Marvin say he leavin'.

(She does not react)

He say he gonna take off from you.

MISS AMELIA

(Finally)

What this I hear 'bout a bridge gonna be built . . . ten mile up, or so. What about that? I hear they gonna have prison labor put it up. Gonna have the chain gang work on it.

HENRY MACY

He say he gonna . . . leave town.

MISS AMELIA

Been thinkin' . . . been thinkin' of havin' the prison farm bring some trusties work my cotton. It cheap labor.

HENRY MACY

I . . . You could do that, Miss Amelia.

MISS AMELIA

(Belligerently, almost a dare)

I know I could.

HENRY MACY

I . . .

(Decides to say nothing, moves away)

Well . . .

(Touches two fingers to his forehead)

Miss Amelia.

MISS AMELIA

Henry.

(Dusk begins to fall now. MISS AMELIA *stays sitting on her porch, the gun across her knees.* MARVIN MACY *comes back on stage, carrying his tin suitcase.* NOTE: *While it is true that on stage the* MACY BROTHERS *and* MISS AMELIA *will be in fairly close proximity, the following scene must give the impression that* MISS AMELIA *cannot overhear what is being said)*

MARVIN MACY *(Quietly)*

I'm leavin', Henry.

HENRY MACY

Are you, Marvin?

MARVIN MACY

Yep.
    (Almost tearful)
I can't take no more.

HENRY MACY

No. I don't figger so.

MARVIN MACY

So I'm takin' off.

HENRY MACY

Where you goin', Marvin?

MARVIN MACY

I don't *know.* I go somewhere; I get away from *here.*

HENRY MACY

It best . . . I suppose.

MARVIN MACY

You write me a letter?

HENRY MACY

Why, sure I write you, Marvin, you tell me where you are . . .

MARVIN MACY

No. I don't mean that.
    (Takes paper and a pencil from his pocket)
You write a letter *for* me, you put down what I tell you.

HENRY MACY

Oh!
    (Takes the paper and pencil from MARVIN MACY, *takes the tin suitcase to use as a writing table)*
All right, Marvin; I ready.

MARVIN MACY

You take down just what I tell you.

HENRY MACY *(Quietly, patiently)*

Yes, Marvin.

MARVIN MACY

    (HENRY MACY *always writing)*
Dear Miss Amelia, my wife. Underline wife.

HENRY MACY

Yes, Marvin.

MARVIN MACY

Dear Miss Amelia, my *wife*. I hate you.

HENRY MACY

Marvin . . .

MARVIN MACY

Put it down! I hate you. I love you.

HENRY MACY

Marvin . . .

MARVIN MACY

Do what I tell you! I love you. I have loved you for two years, an' I have reformed my ways to be worthy of you. I hate you. You gettin' all this?

HENRY MACY

Yes, Marvin.

MARVIN MACY

I . . . I hate you with all the power of my love for you. I woulda been a good husband to you, an' I loved you for two years 'fore I even dared speak my love for you, you . . . you no-good rotten . . .

HENRY MACY

Slow down, Marvin . . . you no-good rotten . . .

MARVIN MACY

. . . you no-good rotten cross-eyed ugly lump!

HENRY MACY

Miss Amelia's eyes don't cross . . .

MARVIN MACY

When she mad! When she mad one eye bang right into her nose. Yes.

HENRY MACY

I . . . I never noticed.

MARVIN MACY

I . . . I reformed my character, an' I made myself worthy of you, an' the night you said yes you marry me no man ever been happier . . . ever. I gonna come back some day an' kill you!

HENRY MACY

Marvin, you don't mean that, now . . .

MARVIN MACY

You put it down! I gonna come back some day an' kill you. I gonna . . . I gonna bust your face open, I gonna . . . I gonna tear your arms outa your body like they bug wings.

HENRY MACY

Slow down, now.

MARVIN MACY

Write fast!

HENRY MACY

I writin' fast. You want it readable, don't you?

MARVIN MACY

Yes. No. I don't care.

HENRY MACY

I doin' the best I can.

MARVIN MACY

I . . . I give you my land, land I worked hard for, 'cause I thought it'd please you; I . . . I bought you jewels, I bought you jewelry, an' you put it up for *sale*. You treated me like nothin', an' I *loved* you. I . . . I love you, Miss Amelia; I love you. An' . . .

HENRY MACY

(*As* MARVIN MACY *pauses*)

Go on, Marvin.

MARVIN MACY (*Almost tearfully*)

An' I goin' away now, I goin' away an' I never comin' back. (*A rush*) An' when I come back I gonna fix you, I gonna kill you!

HENRY MACY

(*As* MARVIN MACY *pauses again*)

Yeah?

MARVIN MACY

(*In a sort of disgusted, sad rush*)

With all my love very truly yours your husband Marvin Macy.

HENRY MACY (*As he finishes*)

You . . . you wanna sign it?

MARVIN MACY

No, you write my name down, but I gonna sign it special.

(*He takes out his knife and gingerly jabs his thumb, drawing blood*)

Here, gimme that.

(*He bends down, bloods the bottom of the letter with his thumb*)

That make it all official.

HENRY MACY

You . . . you want me give her this?

MARVIN MACY

After I go; I goin' now.
(He picks up his tin suitcase)

HENRY MACY *(Gets up)*

I take care of it.

MARVIN MACY

(Almost not wanting to go)
Well, Henry . . .

HENRY MACY

Marvin, you take care now.

MARVIN MACY

I'll . . . *(Shrugs)* take care of myself.

HENRY MACY

Don't go . . . gettin' in any trouble.

MARVIN MACY

(A brief, rueful laugh)
You know, Henry? I wouldn't be surprised one bit if I did? Wouldn't surprise me I turned into one of the worst people you ever saw?

HENRY MACY

You . . . stay good now.

MARVIN MACY

(A sudden, sick violence)
WHY?

HENRY MACY

You . . . you take care.

MARVIN MACY

Well . . . *(Pause)* . . . Goodbye, Henry.

HENRY MACY

(As MARVIN MACY exits)
Goodbye . . . Marvin.
(HENRY MACY watches after MARVIN MACY for a moment, looks at the letter in his hand, turns, slowly walks to the foot of the steps, where MISS AMELIA is sitting)

HENRY MACY *(Quietly)*

Miss Amelia.

MISS AMELIA

That loom-fixer take off? Your brother finally clear out?

HENRY MACY *(As before)*

Yeah. He gone.

MISS AMELIA

(After a brief silence)
Good riddance.

HENRY MACY

He . . .

(Hands her the letter)
. . . He want you to have this.

MISS AMELIA

(Glances at it only long enough to realize it is a letter)
Good riddance.

HENRY MACY

Well . . . 'night, Miss Amelia.

MISS AMELIA *(Pause)*

'Night, Henry.

(HENRY MACY *exits,* MISS AMELIA, *left alone on stage, begins to read the letter.*

(Music up, if not used throughout so far)

THE NARRATOR

And so ended the ten days of marriage of Miss Amelia Evans and Marvin Macy and answers the question that Cousin Lymon asked some years later. Who is Marvin Macy? Who is Marvin Macy?

(MISS AMELIA *and* COUSIN LYMON *alone on the porch.*)

COUSIN LYMON

Amelia!

MISS AMELIA

Yeah?

COUSIN LYMON

I been learnin' some things, Amelia.

MISS AMELIA

Yeah? What?

COUSIN LYMON

(After a long pause; quietly, seriously, with no trace of sport in it)
Amelia? Why you never tell me you married?

(This startles MISS AMELIA; *maybe she rises, walks a few steps, kicks a post, does not look at* COUSIN LYMON)

MISS AMELIA

(Finally; hoarsely, angrily)

I ain't!

COUSIN LYMON

(Quietly, persistently)

Yes, you be. You married Marvin Macy, years an' years ago. You married.

MISS AMELIA (A *pretense*)

No!

COUSIN LYMON

Why you never tell me that?

MISS AMELIA

(Convincing herself)

I ain't married!

COUSIN LYMON

Why you never tell me you married, Amelia?

MISS AMELIA

(Finally turning, facing him)

I *were* married. I were married, to that no-account loom-fixer . . . but that is past . . . over! . . . done!

COUSIN LYMON

(The same quiet insistence)

You ever divorce from him?

MISS AMELIA

He run off; he run off years ago; I ain't married to him no more!

COUSIN LYMON

You ever divorce from him?

MISS AMELIA (*Furious*)

HE RUN OFF!! (*Then, finally, softer*) I ain't married no more.

COUSIN LYMON

(Quietly, logically)

Oh, yes you be. You still married to him. Why you never tell me about that, Amelia?

MISS AMELIA

(Returning to him, sitting, quieter)

It . . . it long ago; it . . . it way in the past.

(As COUSIN LYMON *just looks at her)*

It . . . It don't have nothin' to do with . . . nothin'.

COUSIN LYMON

I find it mighty strange you never tell me about that, Amelia.

MISS AMELIA

(Strangely shy)

Ain't . . . weren't nothin' to tell. I . . . I married him . . . he run off. (Almost pleading) He . . . he no good, Cousin Lymon. He never were a good man.

COUSIN LYMON

You married him.

MISS AMELIA (Shyer yet)

We were . . . we never really . . . married.

COUSIN LYMON

You promise you never have secrets from me, Amelia. Give me a real funny feelin', . . . knowin' you keep things from me; give me a feelin' I don't like.

MISS AMELIA

It weren't no real secret, Cousin Lymon. I don't . . . I don't like you to worry none about things; I like you to be comfortable, an' . . . an' happy.

COUSIN LYMON

It give me a feelin' I don't like.

MISS AMELIA

It were nothin' for you to know.

COUSIN LYMON

(Turning on her; almost savage; yes, savage)

It were nothin' for me to know!?!

MISS AMELIA

I . . . I don't keep much from you, Cousin Lymon; you know my business, my . . . my accounts; I told you all about my poppa, an' all . . .

COUSIN LYMON (Accusing)

All 'cept Marvin Macy.

MISS AMELIA (Acquiescing)

All 'cept Marvin Macy.

COUSIN LYMON

(A change begins to come over him; he is through chastising MISS AMELIA: an excitement has come into his voice)

An' Marvin Macy, he . . . he is, what I hear tell, such a man!

MISS AMELIA

(Still wrapped in thought)

Huuh! A no-good.

COUSIN LYMON

You . . . you keep from me the most . . . the most excitin' thing in your life.

MISS AMELIA *(Still half-hearing)*

Never been no good, that one.

COUSIN LYMON

An' you keep the fact of him from me, the most important fact of all in your whole life . . .

MISS AMELIA

(Becoming aware of what he is saying)

Cousin Lymon . . .

COUSIN LYMON

(Caught up with it now)

. . . a man like Marvin Macy, who has been *everywhere*, who has seen things no other man never seen, who . . .

MISS AMELIA *(Disbelief)*

Cousin Lymon!

(Music begins here)

COUSIN LYMON

. . . who has . . . who has *(Wonder comes into his voice)* been to *Atlanta!*

MISS AMELIA

(Trying to gather what is going on)

Atlanta ain't much.

COUSIN LYMON

Who has been to *Atlanta,* an' . . . *(Religious awe enters his voice now)* an' who has had to do with the *law* . . . an' *(This is the ecstasy)* who has spent time in the *penitentiary.* Oh, Amelia! You have kept this from me!

MISS AMELIA

(Anger coming through)

He is a common criminal, that's all!

COUSIN LYMON

Oh, Amelia, he has been in the penitentiary, an' . . . an' I bet he spent time on the chain gang. Oh, Amelia!

MISS AMELIA *(Confused)*

You . . . you seen the chain gang, Cousin Lymon.

COUSIN LYMON

Yes!

MISS AMELIA

A bunch of common criminals, chained together by the ankle, workin' on the roads in the broilin' sun, a guard standin' over 'em with a gun.

COUSIN LYMON

Yes! Yes! Yes! Amelia!

MISS AMELIA *(Pleading)*

Cousin Lymon . . . they common criminals, they . . . they got no freedom.

COUSIN LYMON

I know, Amelia . . . but they *together.*

MISS AMELIA

(After a long pause; shyly)
We together . . . Cousin Lymon.

COUSIN LYMON *(Dismissing it)*

Yes, Amelia, we together.

MISS AMELIA

An' . . . an' we got a good life together.

COUSIN LYMON *(Same)*

Oh, yes, of course, Amelia. *(The ecstasy returns)* An' they are together, those men, an' . . . an' how they *sing*, Amelia! You hear them sing, Amelia?

MISS AMELIA

(Retreating into her mind)
Yes, I hear them sing.

COUSIN LYMON

An' . . . an' they . . . *together. (Silence.*

Music stops abruptly. MARVIN MACY *enters from stage-left, stays there, leans against the proscenium, maybe, whittling on a piece of wood.* MISS AMELIA *and* COUSIN LYMON *see him simultaneously.* MISS AMELIA *rises, stiffens, her fists clenched.* MARVIN MACY *stays lounging.* COUSIN LYMON *gets up, moves slowly, cautiously toward* MARVIN MACY)

MISS AMELIA *(To* MARVIN MACY)

You clear outa here!

(COUSIN LYMON *continues his slow move toward* MARVIN MACY)

MARVIN MACY

(Throws his head back, laughs contemptuously at MISS AMELIA. COUSIN LYMON *continues moving toward him, is quite near him now.*

To COUSIN LYMON, *contemptuously)*
Whatta you want, bug?

MISS AMELIA

Cousin Lymon!

COUSIN LYMON *(Waving her off)*

Leave it be, Amelia.

(Approaches MARVIN MACY*)*

You . . . you be Marvin Macy.

(With this, COUSIN LYMON *begins small, involuntary spasms of excitement, little jumps from the ground, strange jerks of his hands)*

You be Marvin Macy.

MARVIN MACY

(To MISS AMELIA, *but staring at* COUSIN LYMON*)*

What ails this brokeback?

MISS AMELIA *(Not moving)*

You clear out!

COUSIN LYMON

(His spasms continuing)

You been . . . you been to Atlanta, an' . . . an' . . . an' . . .

MARVIN MACY

Is the runt throwin' a fit?

COUSIN LYMON *(As before)*

An' . . . an' . . . an' you been to the penitentiary?

*(*MARVIN MACY *backhands* COUSIN LYMON *a sharp cuff on the ear which sends him sprawling backwards toward center-stage. He falls, scrambles up)*

MARVIN MACY

That'll learn you, brokeback, starin' at me!

COUSIN LYMON

(On his feet, staring at MARVIN MACY, *but with a hand-stopping signal to* MISS AMELIA *who has taken a step down the porch steps)*

Leave it be, Miss Amelia . . . just . . . leave . . . it . . . be. . .

MISS AMELIA

I'll fix that no-good!

COUSIN LYMON

(His eyes firmly on MARVIN MACY: *a command to* MISS AMELIA*)*

Leave me alone, Amelia! Just leave it be!

MISS AMELIA *(A hopeless call)*

Cousin Lymon!

COUSIN LYMON

Leave off, Amelia; leave off.

MARVIN MACY *(Laughs, turns)*

Bye . . . Mrs. Macy.
    (Exits)

COUSIN LYMON

Marvin Macy!

MISS AMELIA

(As COUSIN LYMON *follows* MARVIN MACY *off-stage)*
Cousin Lymon?

COUSIN LYMON *(From off-stage)*

Marvin Macy! Marvin Macy! Marvin Macy!

*(*MISS AMELIA *is left alone on stage in the deepening night . . .*

Music holds)

Music begins.

Tableau: MISS AMELIA *on the porch, one step down.*

THE NARRATOR

The time has come to speak about love. Now consider three people who were subject to that condition. Miss Amelia, Cousin Lymon, and Marvin Macy.

But what sort of thing is love? First of all, it is a joint experience between two persons, but that fact does not mean that it is a similar experience to the two people involved. There are the lover and the beloved, but these two come from different countries. Often the beloved is only the stimulus for all the stored-up love which has lain quiet within the lover for a long time hitherto. And somehow every lover knows this. He feels in his soul that his love is a solitary thing. He comes to know a new, strange loneliness. Now, the beloved can also be of any description: the most outlandish people can be the stimulus for love. Yes, and the lover may see this as clearly as anyone else—but that does not affect the evolution of his love one whit. Therefore, the quality and value of any love is determined solely by the lover himself.

It is for this reason that most of us would rather love than be loved; and the curt truth is that, in a deep secret way, the state of being beloved is intolerable to many; for the lover craves any possible relation with the beloved, even if this experience can cause them both only pain.

But though the outward facts of love are often sad and ridiculous, it must be remembered that no one can know what really takes place in the soul of the lover himself. So, who but God can be the final judge of any love? But one thing can be said about these three people—all of whom, Miss Amelia,

Cousin Lymon, and Marvin Macy, all of whom were subject to the condition of love. The thing that can be said is this: No good will come of it.

Music still holding.

MISS AMELIA *rises right at the end of* THE NARRATOR's *speech, goes indoors, leaving the stage momentarily empty. It is still evening.*

Music out; MISS AMELIA *has gone inside.* MARVIN MACY *and* HENRY MACY *come on stage together, with* COUSIN LYMON *trailing after them, peripheral, but hovering.*

MARVIN MACY

(To COUSIN LYMON*: ugly)*
You quit followin' me!? You hear!?

HENRY MACY

Oh, let him be. He don't do no harm.

MARVIN MACY *(To* HENRY MACY*)*

Followin' me around like some damn dog . . . yippin' at my heels. *(Falsetto)* "Marvin Macy; hello there, Marvin Macy; Marvin Macy, Marvin Macy." *(Natural voice again)* Drive a man crazy.

(Back to COUSIN LYMON*)*
Whyn't you get on back to your friend . . . jabber at her?

COUSIN LYMON

(Shy, but almost flirtatious)
Oh, now, I ain't no trouble.

HENRY MACY

Marvin, he don't do no harm.

MARVIN MACY

Damn brokeback, trailin' after me.
(To COUSIN LYMON, *loud)*
What you want, anyway!?

COUSIN LYMON *(Shy)*

Oh . . . I, I don't want nothin'.

MARVIN MACY *(To himself)*

Damn bug.

HENRY MACY

You . . . you passin' through, Marvin? You on your way somewhere?

MARVIN MACY

(With a mean grin)
Oh, I don't know, Henry; don't got no plans. I, uh . . . I might settle a spell.

HENRY MACY *(Sorry)*

Oh, I thought you might be on your way through.

MARVIN MACY *(Ugly)*

Whatsa matter, Henry, don't you want me 'round here?

COUSIN LYMON

Stay, Marvin Macy. Don't go on nowhere.

MARVIN MACY *(To* COUSIN LYMON*)*

You shut up, you damn little . . .

(Switches his attention to HENRY MACY*)*

You see? You see? That brokeback want me to stay. Whatsa matter with you, Henry? Why you so eager to have me move on?

HENRY MACY *(Hesitant)*

It just . . . it just that things all settled down now, now you been gone so long, an' . . . I figgered you might be plannin' to stir up . . . you know . . . some trouble.

MARVIN MACY

(After a great laugh)

Me? Stir up trouble? Why, whatever could you mean?

*(*COUSIN LYMON *giggles in support of* MARVIN MACY*)*

Look you!

(This to COUSIN LYMON*)*

You been followin' me around near a week now, wigglin' your ears at me, flappin' around, dancin' . . . you don't go home 'cept for your eats an' bed. What you expectin' me to do . . . *adopt* you?

COUSIN LYMON

(With exaggerated longing)

Oh, Marvin Macy . . . *would* you? Would you do that?

MARVIN MACY

(Takes a swipe at him which COUSIN LYMON *ducks expertly, laughs)*

Damn little lap dog.

(But there is kindness in the contempt)

HENRY MACY

An' . . . an' I hoped you wasn't plannin' to stir up no trouble.

MARVIN MACY

Maybe just you tired of havin' me move in on you. That house of yours half mine, just like this place here, half mine you know, but I 'spect you got so used to livin' there all by yourself you got a little selfish in your middle-age.

HENRY MACY (*Quietly*)

You welcome to stay long as you like.

MARVIN MACY (*Unrelenting*)

Or maybe you don't want no ex-convict hangin' around you. Well, I tell you somethin', Henry: I ain't quite sure why I come back, not that there ain't no scores to settle, but I ain't quite sure *why* I come back; just thought I'd have a look around.

HENRY MACY

Miss Amelia is . . .

MARVIN MACY (*Suddenly harsh*)

Who said anythin' bout *her?* Hunh? I bring her up?

HENRY MACY

Miss Amelia is . . . settled down, now; she is . . . she have Cousin Lymon with her.

(COUSIN LYMON *giggles*)

. . . an' she got her cafe, an' . . . an' everythin' is quiet an' settled.

MARVIN MACY

Yeah, she got quite a business goin' for herself, hunh? She takin' in good money, I bet, hunh?

HENRY MACY (*Defensively*)

Miss Amelia run the cafe for . . . us, for all of *us:* it be . . . it be a good place to come. It be a special place for us. Important.

MARVIN MACY

Yeah, an' it half mine, ain't it?

HENRY MACY

(*Disappointed in his brother*)

Oh, Marvin!

MARVIN MACY

She still my wife; don't you forget that!

HENRY MACY

Oh, Marvin! That were years ago.

MARVIN MACY

I know how long ago it were; I had lots of time to think about it! Lots of time rottin' in that penitentiary . . . all on account of her! On account of that one!!!

HENRY MACY

That . . . that kinda thing you can't blame on no one person, Marvin.

MARVIN MACY

The hell I can't!! Who says?!

HENRY MACY (*Weakly*)

It . . . it all long past now.

MARVIN MACY

Yeah, but you got a lotta time to think on things when you in the penitentiary, Henry.

(COUSIN LYMON *giggles*)

Ain't that right, peanut?

COUSIN LYMON (*Hopefully*)

Oh, I ain't never been in the penitentiary.

MARVIN MACY (*Ironically*)

Well, maybe you will be someday, peanut.

(*Back to* HENRY MACY)

Yeah, you get a lotta time to brood on things, Henry. An' . . . you know? You start makin' *plans?* Oh, all kindsa plans.

HENRY MACY

Leave . . . leave everythin' be, Marvin. Let it all rest.

MARVIN MACY

(*Concluding an interview*)

Well, you just keep to your own business, Henry, an' you let me worry on mine. All right?

(*He rises*)

HENRY MACY (*Still sitting*)

You . . . you always done what you wanted, Marvin.

MARVIN MACY (*Proudly*)

Damn right, Henry; so you just let me go about my business.

(*Looks at* COUSIN LYMON, *smiles at him*)

You just let *us* go about *our* business. Right, peanut?

COUSIN LYMON (*Beside himself*)

Oh, yes, yes; oh, yes.

THE NARRATOR

It was the beginning of the destruction. And the things that happened next were beyond imagination.

(MARVIN MACY *and* COUSIN LYMON *move off-stage,* COUSIN LYMON *second, leaving* HENRY MACY *alone on stage.*

The interior of the cafe becomes visible; a usual evening is in progress. Most of the TOWNSPEOPLE *are there.* HENRY MACY

*remains stationary where he was, to one side of the stage.
Drinking and general conversation in the cafe, though there seems
to be a curious expectant quietness which* EMMA HALE *feels she
must comment on from time to time, by talking too loud)*

EMMA *(Too loud)*

My, it sure is cheerful in here tonight . . . considerin' everythin'.

MACPHAIL

Oh, Emma.

EMMA *(Undaunted)*

Well, it do seem strange to me.

MISS AMELIA *(No nonsense)*

What seem strange to you, Emma?

(The group becomes quieter at this)

MRS. PETERSON

(A whispered warning)

Now, Emma, watch yourself now.

MISS AMELIA *(Louder; sterner)*

What seem strange to you, Emma?

EMMA

(Flustered at first, but regaining her composure as she goes on)

Why, it seem strange to me that . . . uh, that everybody sittin' here so
cheerful . . .

MISS AMELIA

Why! Why that strange?

EMMA

Why . . . uh . . . *(Her eyes narrowing)* . . . it seem strange to have everybody
here save *one*. *(Murderously solicitous)* I mean when poor Cousin Lymon ain't
here to join in the merriment, an' have his little supper, an' be such an enter-
tainment for us all, an' to keep you *company*, Miss Amelia? *(Transparently
false innocence)* Where is Cousin Lymon, Miss Amelia? Why, I hardly don't
see him *ever* no more. Where do he keep himself these days, Miss Amelia?

MRS. PETERSON *(Whispered again)*

Emma!

MISS AMELIA *(Clenching her fists)*

Emma!? *(Pause as the cafe falls silent)* You shut your mouth!!

EMMA *(Feigned shock)*

But, Miss Amelia, I was just askin' to find out the whereabouts of poor
Cousin . . .

MISS AMELIA

SHUT IT I SAID!!

EMMA

(Her face back to her dinner plate, mortally offended)

Well, of course if you gonna talk *that* way I . . . I just won't bother myself about the little runt no more, that's all.

MISS AMELIA

Eat an' get out, Emma.

MRS. PETERSON

Oh, now, Miss Amelia, all she meant was . . .

MISS AMELIA

You, too. Both of you. Eat an' git.

EMMA *(Great dignity)*

We will do that, Miss Amelia, lest we choke to death first on whatever this is you servin'.

MISS AMELIA

Better'n your cookin'. My pigs wouldn't eat the slop you set before yourself in your own kitchen.

MACPHAIL

(A little drunk; genial)

Ladies. Now, *please.*

MISS AMELIA *(Grumpily)*

She can't talk that way about the food in this cafe.

(HENRY MACY enters)

Evenin', Henry.

HENRY MACY

(As several say evening to him, chooses his solitary table)

Evenin', Miss Amelia.

MISS AMELIA

(Comes up to him, tries to take care none of the others overhear)

You, uh . . . have you, uh . . . seen Cousin Lymon?

HENRY MACY

(Not looking at her)

Yeah, I have, Miss Amelia. He with Marvin. He with Marvin again.

MISS AMELIA *(After a pause)*

Eats, or likker?

HENRY MACY *(Very polite)*

I . . . I think I will just have a bottle, Miss Amelia.

MISS AMELIA *(Preoccupied)*

Suit yourself.

HENRY MACY

They not far off, I wouldn't guess; they somewhere near here together.

MISS AMELIA

(A stab at unconcern)

Huuh; couldn't care less. Don't make no matter to me.

(MARVIN MACY and COUSIN LYMON reappear on stage, stay lurking to one side until it is time for them to enter the cafe)

HENRY MACY *(Embarrassed)*

I . . . I know.

EMMA *(Loud)*

What I find so remarkable is the way no one ain't allowed to talk about nothin' in this cafe, which is a public gatherin' place.

FIRST TOWNSWOMAN

(Weary of it all)

Oh, Lord.

MACPHAIL

Emma Hale, you been told to eat up an' get out.

EMMA

(With the speed of a copperhead)

Stumpy MacPhail, you go back to your boozin, an' keep outa this. *(Same loud tone)* What I find so remarkable is that now Marvin Macy back in town our little Cousin Lymon spend all his time with *him* . . . 'stead of with Miss Amelia.

(Dead silence in the cafe)

MISS AMELIA

Emma? You remember that lawyer cheated me six—seven years back? The one tried to cheat me outa some land on a deed? You remember what I did to him?

EMMA *(Pretending forgetfulness)*

Why, now . . .

MACPHAIL *(To EMMA: helpful)*

Why, you remember, Emma. Miss Amelia went at him, beat him up within an inch of his life. Broke his arm? An' he were big; an' he were a *man*.

MISS AMELIA (*To* EMMA)

Don't let it be said I wouldn't take my fists to a woman, either . . . if she didn't keep her place.

(MARVIN MACY *and* COUSIN LYMON *start moving toward the steps,* COUSIN LYMON *leading the way*)

MERLIE RYAN (*Cheerfully*)

Miss Amelia gonna kill Emma? She gonna kill her?

SECOND TOWNSMAN

No, Merlie; 'course not.

MERLIE RYAN (*Disappointed*)

Don't see why not.

EMMA

(*To* MISS AMELIA; *uncertainly*)

I . . . I ain't afraid of you.

(COUSIN LYMON *and* MARVIN MACY *are up the steps now*)

MACPHAIL (*Great slow wisdom*)

Why don't you all simmer down.

EMMA

(*To* MRS. PETERSON *and one of the* TOWNSWOMEN)

I ain't afraid of her.

MRS. PETERSON

You crazy if you ain't.

TOWNSWOMAN

That sure.

EMMA

I put my faith in God!

MRS. PETERSON (*Very unsure*)

Well . . . Amen.

MERLIE RYAN (*Waving a glass*)

Amen! Amen!

(COUSIN LYMON, *having waved* MARVIN MACY *out of the light from the door, enters.* MISS AMELIA *smiles to see him*)

EMMA (*Her assurance back*)

Well, here the little cockatoo now.

MACPHAIL

Evenin', Cousin Lymon.

HENRY MACY

Cousin Lymon.

(And, as well, a chorus of greeting. COUSIN LYMON *ignores them all, marches directly up to* MISS AMELIA*)*

COUSIN LYMON

(Mockingly formal)

Evenin', Amelia.

MISS AMELIA

Well, where you been, Cousin Lymon; I about give you up.

COUSIN LYMON

Ooohhh . . . been about; been wanderin' around. Havin' a little stroll an' a talk.

(Waits very briefly to see if MISS AMELIA *reacts to this; she does not)*

My! Supper do smell good! What we havin'?

MISS AMELIA *(Preoccupied)*

Uh . . . what, Cousin Lymon?

COUSIN LYMON

I say: what we havin' for supper!

MISS AMELIA

Oh! Oh, well, there be ham, an' winter peas, an' hominy grits, an' I brung out the peach preserves.

RAINEY 1 *(His mouth full)*

It be good.

RAINEY 2 *(The same)*

Yeah, it awful good.

COUSIN LYMON

Well, ain't that nice.

MISS AMELIA

You . . . you hungry now, Cousin Lymon?

COUSIN LYMON

I mean ain't that nice . . . since we have a guest for dinner tonight.

(The cafe becomes silent)

I have invited a special guest for dinner tonight.

(He can hardly keep still waiting for MISS AMELIA'S *reaction)*

MISS AMELIA

(Her reaction is slow in coming; finally, tonelessly)

Yeah?

COUSIN LYMON

Yeah.

(Calls to outside)

C'mon in, now; Miss Amelia waitin' on you.

(Absolute silence as MARVIN MACY *enters, silence except an audible intake of breath here and there.* MARVIN MACY *surveys the scene briefly, smiles wickedly at* MISS AMELIA, *who is immobile, moves to an empty table, kicks the chair out, sits down. Still silence)*

MARVIN MACY

Hey! Brokeback! Bring me my dinner.

MERLIE RYAN

Hey, Miss Amelia; Marvin Macy back. Miss Amelia!

MACPHAIL

Shut up, you damn fool!

EMMA

(As MISS AMELIA *is still silent, immobile)*

I never thought I'd live to see it. I tell you, I never thought I'd live to see it.

MERLIE RYAN

Miss Amelia? Marvin Macy back.

*(*RAINEY 1 *chokes on his food, has a brief choking fit;* RAINEY 2 *slaps his back.* MISS AMELIA *doesn't move)*

MARVIN MACY

Hey, brokeback! My dinner!

COUSIN LYMON

(Moving to do his bidding)

Yes; yes, Marvin.

MISS AMELIA *(Barring his way)*

Keep outa there.

COUSIN LYMON

Marvin want his dinner!

MARVIN MACY *(To* MISS AMELIA)

Let him through!!

MISS AMELIA

(Advancing on MARVIN MACY)

Look you!

MARVIN MACY

Yeah?

(They face each other, MARVIN MACY *having risen; perhaps his chair has fallen over. They both clench their fists, but near their sides; they begin to circle each other. The tension is immense)*

COUSIN LYMON

(From behind the counter)

You like grits, Marvin?

MARVIN MACY

(His eyes never off MISS AMELIA*)*

Pile 'em on.

MISS AMELIA

(To COUSIN LYMON, *her eyes never off* MARVIN MACY*)*

There some rat poison under the counter while you at it; put a little on for flavor.

MRS. PETERSON

I gonna faint.

EMMA

Hush!

MARVIN MACY

(As they continue circling each other)

I found that trap you set for me in the woods where I hunt. That woulda killed me good, wouldn't it?

MISS AMELIA

It woulda done the job.

MARVIN MACY *(Murderously)*

You watch yourself.

COUSIN LYMON

(Appearing with a heaping plate)

Dinner! Dinner!

*(*MISS AMELIA *suddenly swings around and stalks out of the cafe to the porch steps, sits. Action continues inside, though maybe the interior lights dim a little; certainly the interior conversation, such as it is, lessens in volume.* HENRY MACY *waits a moment, then follows* MISS AMELIA *out on to the porch)*

HENRY MACY

Miss Amelia? *(No reply)* Miss Amelia?

MISS AMELIA *(Finally)*

Leave me be.

HENRY MACY

He . . . he gonna move on soon. I know it.

MISS AMELIA *(Doubting)*

Yeah?

HENRY MACY *(Soothing)*

Sure, he move on; ain't no place for him here.

MISS AMELIA *(With deepest irony)*

You sure, huuh?

HENRY MACY *(Unsure)*

Sure.

(Music up.

During THE NARRATOR's *speech,* MISS AMELIA *and* HENRY MACY *return inside the cafe, where life goes on,* COUSIN LYMON *waiting on* MARVIN MACY, MISS AMELIA *staying off to one side. Maybe there is barely audible conversation under this speech)*

THE NARRATOR

Oh, but Henry Macy was wrong, for Marvin did not move on. He stayed in the town, and every night the cafe was open he would arrive for dinner, and Cousin Lymon would wait on him, and bring him liquor for which he never paid a cent. And during these nights, which stretched into weeks, Miss Amelia did nothing. She did nothing at all, except to stand to one side and watch.

(Appropriate action for the following)

But every night one thing would be sure to happen. Once every night, sometimes for no reason at all that anyone could see, Miss Amelia and Marvin Macy would approach each other, their fists clenched, and they would circle one another, and it was during these rituals that the towns-people expected blows to be struck . . . but it never happened. All that ever happened was they would circle one another, and then move apart. Everyone knew that one time they would finally come to blows, that soon-er or later Marvin Macy and Miss Amelia would fight, would set upon one another in a battle that would leave one of them brutally beaten or dead. But everyone also knew that it was not yet time.

One night, though, nearly three months after Marvin Macy returned to town, there occurred an event which set the sure course to calamity.

(Music out.

Cafe scene back)

MISS AMELIA

You finally movin' on.

MARVIN MACY

Yeah?

MISS AMELIA

Well, you all packed.

COUSIN LYMON

(From his throne on the barrel)

Amelia!

(Brief silence; she looks to him)

Marvin Macy is goin' to visit a spell with us.

MISS AMELIA

(After quite a pause, shakes her head as if to clear it)

I don't understand you, Cousin Lymon.

COUSIN LYMON

I said: Marvin Macy is goin' to visit a spell with us. *(Slowly, distinctly)* He is goin' to move in here. *(Pause, as nothing seems to have registered)* He is gonna live here. With us.

(A stock-still silence, broken by)

MISS AMELIA

(Finally: to MARVIN MACY*)*

Ain't no room.

MARVIN MACY *(Mocking)*

Ain't no room, huuh?

MISS AMELIA

This ain't no flop house . . . for convicts.

MARVIN MACY

(His eyes still on MISS AMELIA*)*

Cousin Lymon? They ain't no room for me?

COUSIN LYMON *(Imperious)*

Amelia!

(She turns her sad attention to him)

Amelia, I think I told you Marvin Macy is gonna live here with us.

MISS AMELIA

(Surprisingly helpless before his tone)

But . . . but, Cousin Lymon . . .

COUSIN LYMON

(Giving orders, but taking a childish pleasure in the power of it)

Marvin Macy will sleep in your Papa's big bed, an' we will move what you have referred to as my coffin—my tiny bed— into your room . . . an' you . . .

(He pauses here for full effect)

. . . an you, Amelia . . . well, you can pull up a mattress, an' sleep by the stove down here.

(More silence, broken only by MARVIN MACY's *soft, throaty chuckle)*

HENRY MACY

(Quietly, to the bottle in front of him on the table)

Lord God in heaven.

MISS AMELIA

(Tries to speak, but all that emerges is)

Arrggh . . . uh, uh, arrggh.

COUSIN LYMON

(Oblivious to her attempted reply)

So, you see, Amelia, there *is* room, after all. It merely a question of makin' space.

MACPHAIL

(Rises, but does not move)

I think I goin' home.

MRS. PETERSON

(Not moving at all)

Yes; me, too.

SECOND TOWNSWOMAN

Think you right.

COUSIN LYMON

(Jumping off the barrel)

So! Now I think Marvin an' I move upstairs an' get things arranged comfortable. Marvin?

MARVIN MACY

(Picking up his tin suitcase)

Comin'.

*(*MISS AMELIA *has not moved; will not look at anyone.* MARVIN MACY *follows* COUSIN LYMON *up the stairs; they vanish. All the* TOWNSPEOPLE, *save* HENRY MACY, *slowly exit now, all of them, save* MERLIE RYAN, *who just sort of drifts out, pausing briefly by* MISS AMELIA, *either to say goodnight, or touch her by the elbow, or just stop, then move on. When they have all left the cafe and are nearly off-stage,* MISS AMELIA *rouses herself slightly from her lethargy, looks slowly around the cafe, and moves out on to the porch, where she sits, staring vacantly off.*

Music here, maybe a move back.

The lights go down on the cafe, its interior vanishes, and then HENRY MACY *comes out the door and sits fairly near* MISS AMELIA)

MISS AMELIA *(After a pause)*

Henry?

HENRY MACY

Yes, Miss Amelia.

(All the speeches slowly responded to now)

MISS AMELIA

I gotta do it now.

HENRY MACY

Do . . . what, Miss Amelia?

MISS AMELIA

I gotta get your brother.

HENRY MACY

Yes.

MISS AMELIA

I gotta drive him off, or kill him, or . . .

HENRY MACY

I know.

MISS AMELIA

But if I do that . . .

HENRY MACY

If you do that, what?

MISS AMELIA

If I drive him off then . . . then Cousin Lymon go off with him.

HENRY MACY

Oh, Miss Amelia . . .

MISS AMELIA

He would! I'd 'a done it long before now . . . 'cept . . .

HENRY MACY

'Cept you think Cousin Lymon go off too; go off with him?

MISS AMELIA

Unh-hunh.

HENRY MACY

But . . . but do it matter that much?

MISS AMELIA
(Looking at him finally)
Cousin Lymon go off . . . I all alone.

HENRY MACY
He ain't . . . much comfort, Cousin Lymon.

MISS AMELIA
He some. He been some. I gonna get your brother, Henry.

HENRY MACY
(Thinks; acquiesces to it)
All right. *(Pause)* Night, Miss Amelia.

MISS AMELIA
Night, Henry.

HENRY MACY
(Starting to walk off; stops, makes a statement)
Ain't nothin' I can do, is there.

MISS AMELIA
(Rising, starting to go indoors)
No. Ain't nothin', Henry.

HENRY MACY
No. Well . . . night.
(He moves off exits)

MISS AMELIA
Night, Henry.
(She goes indoors)
Music up.
Lights up to daylight. Only the outside of the cafe is seen.

THE NARRATOR
And the fight, which everybody had expected but nobody had known exactly when it would happen, took place, when it finally occurred, on Ground Hog's Day.
(Appropriate action for the following)
And it was at the same time both a solemn and a festive occasion. Bets had been placed—with Emma Hale's money going on Marvin Macy, of course. And Miss Amelia had lay flat down on her porch to rest her strength for the fight, and Marvin Macy sat nearby with a tin can of hog fat between his knees and carefully greased his arms and legs. Everybody knew, and they did not need Cousin Lymon as their clarion—though of course they could not stop him.

COUSIN LYMON *(To* MARVIN MACY*)*

You grease up good, now; you be real slippery she can't get a good grip on you.

MARVIN MACY *(Greasing his arm)*

That what I doin'; don't you worry.

COUSIN LYMON

(To some of the TOWNSPEOPLE *who are beginning to saunter in)*

Today! It gonna be today!

MACPHAIL

Yeah, we know; we know.

THIRD TOWNSMAN

Yeah, don't worry, now; we know.

COUSIN LYMON

(Beside himself with excitement, stops briefly at MARVIN MACY*)*

You grease real good now.

(Darts off toward MISS AMELIA*)*

MARVIN MACY

(As he greases the other arm)

Yeeessssss!!

COUSIN LYMON

(On his way to MISS AMELIA, *spies other* TOWNSPEOPLE *entering from the other side)*

The fight startin'! It about to begin.

(Moves toward MISS AMELIA *again)*

HENRY MACY *(Sadly; impatiently)*

We *know!* We know!

EMMA

An' I gonna win me a dollar today, too.

MRS. PETERSON *(Stuck-up)*

Don't see how that can be, since *I* gonna win one.

EMMA *(A gay laugh)*

You see.

COUSIN LYMON

(Now by where MISS AMELIA *is lying)*

Amelia?

MISS AMELIA

(Not moving; staring at the sky; little expression in her voice)
Yes, Cousin Lymon?

COUSIN LYMON *(All excitement)*
You . . . you restin' for the fight, huuh?

MISS AMELIA
Yes, Cousin Lymon.

COUSIN LYMON
An' . . . an' . . . you eat good?

MISS AMELIA
Yes, Cousin Lymon; I had me three helpings of rare roast.

COUSIN LYMON
Marvin ate *four.*

MISS AMELIA
Good for him.

COUSIN LYMON
(A tentative finger out to touch her)
He . . . Marvin all greased up. You . . . you greased, Amelia?

MISS AMELIA
Yes, Cousin Lymon.

COUSIN LYMON
(Takes a step or two back, looks around the crowd, seems to be pleading)
Then . . . then you both about ready, I . . . I'd say.
(To STUMPY MACPHAIL*)*
I'd say they both about ready.
(Everybody is on stage, now, the TOWNSPEOPLE *still peripheral)*

MACPHAIL *(Piqued)*
I'll decide on that.

COUSIN LYMON
(Moving to one side, a curved smile on his lips)
I just tryin' to be helpful.

HENRY MACY
You be more help you go hide under a log, or somethin'.

MACPHAIL
(Moves over to MARVIN MACY*)*
You all fixed an' ready, Marvin?

MARVIN MACY

(Rises, rubs a little more grease into his arms)
Never be readier!

MACPHAIL

(Moving toward where MISS AMELIA *is lying; she sits up)*
You . . . you all ready, Miss Amelia?

MISS AMELIA

I been ready for years.

MACPHAIL

(Moves front and center)
Well, then, you two c'mere.

MERLIE RYAN

What . . . what gonna happen?
    *(*MISS AMELIA *and* MARVIN MACY *slowly approach front and center)*

EMMA *(Answering* MERLIE RYAN*)*
Marvin Macy gonna kill Miss Amelia, Merlie; that what gonna happen.

MRS. PETERSON

Other way 'round!

MERLIE RYAN

Why . . . why they gonna fight?

SECOND TOWNSMAN

Hush, you.

MERLIE RYAN *(A lonely child)*
I wanna know why. I wanna know why Marvin an' Miss Amelia gonna
kill t'other.

THIRD TOWNSMAN *(Laughing)*
'Cause they know each other, Merlie.
    (A couple of people laugh at this, but mostly there is tense silence)

MERLIE RYAN *(Same)*
'T'ain't no good reason.

EMMA

It gonna have to do.

MACPHAIL

(To MARVIN MACY *and* MISS AMELIA, *who come and stand, one to
either side of him.* MARVIN MACY *is stripped to the waist, his
trouser legs folded up to above the knees;* MISS AMELIA *has her*

sleeves rolled up to the tops of her shoulders, her jean legs pulled up, too)

Got knives, either of you?

MISS AMELIA & MARVIN MACY

Nope.

MACPHAIL

I gotta check anyway. (*He feels into* MARVIN's *back pockets*) You clean.

MARVIN MACY (*Vicious*)

What you think I be . . . a liar?

MACPHAIL (*Stony*)

Knives has a way of slippin' into pockets sometimes without a person knowin' about 'em, Marvin. You musta seen a lot of that in your time.

MARVIN MACY

(*Ugly, but not about to argue further*)

Yeah?

MISS AMELIA (*Impatiently*)

Come on!

MARVIN MACY

(*At* MISS AMELIA; *soft and wicked*)

Oh, I can't wait.

MACPHAIL (*To quiet them*)

All right! All right, now.

(*Tense silence from everyone;* MISS AMELIA *and* MARVIN MACY *move a bit apart, stand in boxing poses, ready*)

All right! Begin!

(THE FIGHT: *They circle for a moment, and then both strike out simultaneously, without warning. Both blows land well and stun both fighters for a little. They circle more, then they join and mix in vicious in-fighting.* MISS AMELIA *gets hit, staggers backwards, almost falls, rights herself. They in-fight again.* MARVIN MACY *gets struck a hard blow, staggers back. They in-fight again. Suddenly the fight shifts from boxing to wrestling. At this, the crowd comes in closer. The fighters battle muscle to muscle, hipbones braced against each other; gradually* MISS AMELIA *gains the advantage, and inch by inch she bends* MARVIN MACY *over backwards, forcing him to the ground.* COUSIN LYMON *is extremely agitated. Finally,* MISS AMELIA *has* MARVIN MACY *to the ground, and straddles him, her hands on his throat. The crowd presses closer, to watch the kill)*

MRS. PETERSON (*Shrieking*)

Kill him! Kill him!

MERLIE RYAN (*Taking it up*)

Kill him! Kill him!

COUSIN LYMON

(*Half a shriek, half a word, howled*)

NNNNNNOOOOOOOOOOOOO!

(COUSIN LYMON *races from where he has been standing, mounts* MISS AMELIA*'s back and begins choking her from behind*)

HENRY MACY

Stop him!

EMMA

Get her; get her!

(COUSIN LYMON *continues choking* MISS AMELIA, *and this is enough to shift the balance of the fight.* MARVIN MACY *manages to get* MISS AMELIA*'s hands from his throat, forces her down.* COUSIN LYMON *backs off a few steps.* MARVIN MACY *straddles* MISS AMELIA, *beats her senseless, furiously, excessively, as the crowd gasps, yells.*

All becomes silence. Music stops. The crowd moves back a bit. MARVIN MACY *rises from the prostrate form of* MISS AMELIA; *he breathes heavily, stands over her, barely able to stand, himself*)

HENRY MACY (*Very quietly*)

Oh, Lord, no.

(*All is very still, the loudest sound* MARVIN MACY*'s breathing. Some of the* TOWNSPEOPLE *begin to wander dreamily off*)

EMMA

(*Moving toward* MISS AMELIA; *great solicitude*)

Oh, poor Miss Amelia, poor . . .

HENRY MACY

Leave her be.

(EMMA *obeys, exits, leaving, finally, only* MISS AMELIA, MARVIN MACY, COUSIN LYMON *and* HENRY MACY *on stage.*

MISS AMELIA *slowly pulls herself up on one arm, crawls slowly, painfully from where she has been lying to the steps, up them, collapses again on the porch.*

COUSIN LYMON *walks slowly, shyly over to* MARVIN MACY, *who puts his arm around him, still breathing hard, still looking at* MISS AMELIA.

HENRY MACY *takes a few tentative steps toward* MISS AMELIA, *changes his mind, begins to exit)*

MARVIN MACY

'Bye, Henry.

HENRY MACY *(Continuing out)*

'Bye Marvin.

COUSIN LYMON

'Bye, Henry.

(HENRY MACY *exits, as if he had not heard* COUSIN LYMON)

(Music up)

THE NARRATOR

(Tableau, with MARVIN MACY, COUSIN LYMON *together,* MISS AMELIA *sprawled on the porch)*

Marvin Macy and Cousin Lymon left town that night, but before they went away, they did their best to wreck the store. They took what money there was in the cafe, and the few curios and pieces of jewelry Miss Amelia kept upstairs; and they carved vile words on the cafe tables. After they had done all this . . . they left town . . . together.

(MARVIN MACY *and* COUSIN LYMON *stand for a moment,* MARVIN MACY *breathing a little less hard, laughing a little)*

MARVIN MACY

(With a small chuckle)

C'mon, peanut; let's go.

(The two exit, MARVIN MACY's *arm still over* COUSIN LYMON's *shoulder.* MISS AMELIA *is left alone on stage)*

She rights herself to a sitting position, howls once, becomes silent.

Music continues to the end of the play.

THE NARRATOR

And every night thereafter, for three years, Miss Amelia sat out on the front steps, alone and silent, looking down the road and waiting. But Cousin Lymon never returned. Nothing more was ever heard of Marvin Macy or Cousin Lymon. The cafe, of course, never reopened, and life in the town was that much drearier.

(MRS. PETERSON *comes on, timidly, advances to where* MISS AMELIA *is sitting*)

And Miss Amelia closed the general store, as well, or it would be more correct to say that she discouraged anyone from coming there anymore.

MRS. PETERSON (*Quietly*)

Miss Amelia?

(MISS AMELIA *looks at her after a moment, says nothing*)

I . . . I wondered . . . I thought I would buy a coke.

MISS AMELIA

(*No expression, save some vague loss*)

Sure. (*Not moving*) That will be a dollar and five cents.

MRS. PETERSON

(*Still quiet, but flustered*)

But . . . but a coke be a nickel.

MISS AMELIA

(*Looking steadily at her; blank voice*)

Yes. (*Pause*) Five cents for the coke, and a dollar for seein' me. A dollar for lookin' at the freak.

MRS. PETERSON

(*Moving away, slowly at first, then fleeing*)

Oh . . . Miss Amelia . . .

(MISS AMELIA *alone on stage. Gets up, goes indoors, closes the door after her. Lights up to opening of the play*)

THE NARRATOR

And at the end of three years Miss Amelia went indoors one night, climbed the stairs, and never again left her upstairs rooms.

The town is dreary. On August afternoons the road is empty, white with dust, and the sky above is bright as glass. If you walk along the main street there is nothing whatsoever to do. Nothing moves—there are no children's voices, only the hum of the mill.

(*The upstairs window opens and closes as in the beginning of the play, accompanying the below*)

Though sometimes, in the late afternoon, when the heat is at its worst, a hand will slowly open the shutter of the window up there, and a face will look down at the town . . . a terrible, dim face . . . like the faces known in dreams. The face will linger at the window for an hour or so, then the shutters will be closed once more, and as likely as not there will not be another soul to be seen along the main street. Heat . . . and silence. There is nothing whatsoever to do. You might as well walk down to the Fork Falls Road and watch the chain gang. The twelve mortal men . . . who are together.

The Ballad of the Sad Cafe . . . the end.

(Music holds for four seconds, stops. Silence for four seconds)

CURTAIN

Tiny Alice

For
Noel Farrand

AUTHOR'S NOTE

It has been the expressed hope of many that I would write a preface to the published text of *Tiny Alice,* clarifying obscure points in the play—explaining my intention, in other words. I have decided against creating such a guide because I find—after reading the play over—that I share the view of even more people: that the play is quite clear. I will confess, though, that *Tiny Alice* is less opaque in reading than it would be in any single viewing.

EDWARD ALBEE

FIRST PERFORMANCE

December 29, 1964, New York City,
Billy Rose Theatre

LAWYER   *William Hutt*
CARDINAL   *Eric Berry*
JULIAN   *John Gielgud*
BUTLER   *John Heffernan*
MISS ALICE   *Irene Worth*

Directed by ALAN SCHNEIDER
Sets by WILLIAM RITMAN
Gowns by MAINBOCHER
Lighting by MARTIN ARONSTEIN

ACT ONE

SCENE ONE

(The CARDINAL's *garden. What is needed . . . ? Ivy climbing a partial wall of huge stones? An iron gate? Certainly two chairs—one, the larger, obviously for His Eminence; the other, smaller—and certainly an elaborate birdcage, to stage-left, with some foliage in it, and two birds, cardinals . . . which need not be real. At rise, the* LAWYER *is at the birdcage, talking to the birds)*

LAWYER

Oomm, yoom, yoom, um? Tick-tick-tick-tick-tick. Um? You do-do-do-do-do-um? Tick-tick-tick-tick-tick-tick-tick-um? *(He raises his fingers to the bars)* Do-do-do-do-do-do-do? Aaaaaawwwww! Oomm, yoom, yoom, um?

(The CARDINAL *enters from stage-right—through the iron gates?—unseen by the* LAWYER, *who repeats some of the above as the* CARDINAL *moves toward center)*

CARDINAL

(Finally. Quietly amused)

Saint Francis?

LAWYER

(Swinging around; flustered; perhaps more annoyed than embarrassed at being discovered)

Your Eminence!

CARDINAL

Our dear Saint Francis, who wandered in the fields and forests, talked to all the . . .

LAWYER

(Moving to kiss the ring)

Your Eminence, we appreciate your kindness in taking the time to see us; we know how heavy a schedule you . . .

CARDINAL

(Silencing him by waving his ring at him. The lawyer kneels, kisses the ring, rises)

We are pleased . . . *we* are pleased to be your servant *(Trailing off)* . . . if . . . we can be your servant. We addressed you as Saint Francis . . .

LAWYER *(Properly mumbling)*

Oh, but surely . . .

CARDINAL

. . . as Saint Francis . . . who did talk to the birds so, did he not. And here we find *you*, who talk not only to the birds but to *(With a wave at the cage)*—you must forgive us—to cardinals as well. *(Waits for reaction, gets none, tries again)* . . . To cardinals? As well?

LAWYER *(A tight smile)*

We . . . we understood.

CARDINAL *(He, too)*

Did we.

(A brief silence, as both smiles hold)

LAWYER

(To break it, moving back toward the cage)

We find it droll—if altogether appropriate in this setting— that there should be two cardinals . . . uh, together . . . *(Almost a sneer)* . . . in conversation, as it were.

CARDINAL *(The smile again)*

Ah, well, they are a comfort to each other . . . companionship. And they have so much to say. They . . . understand each other so much better than they would . . . uh, *other* birds.

LAWYER

Indeed. And so much better than they would understand saints?

CARDINAL

(Daring him to repeat it, but still amused)

Sir?

LAWYER *(Right in)*

That cardinals understand each *other* better than they understand saints.

CARDINAL *(Not rising to it)*
Who is to say? Will you sit?

LAWYER *(Peering into the cage)*
They are extraordinary birds . . . cardinals, if I may say so. . . .

CARDINAL *(Through with it)*
You push it too far, sir. Will you join us?
(He moves to his chair, sits in it)

LAWYER

(Brief pause, then surrender; moves to the other chair)
Of course. *(Looks around. Indicates a back wall.)* Such a . . . corporate setting.

CARDINAL
(Smug) Well . . . you know. *(A deep sigh)* What should we do now? *(Pause)* Should we clap our hands *(Does so, twice)* . . . twice, and have a monk appear? A very old monk? With just a ring of white hair around the base of his head, stooped, fast-shuffling, his hands deep in his sleeves? Eh? And should we send him for wine? Um? Should we offer you wine, and should we send him scurrying off after it? Yes? Is that the scene you expect now?

LAWYER

(Very relaxed, but pointed)
It's so difficult to know what to expect in a Cardinal's garden, Your Eminence. An old monk would do . . . or—who is to say?—perhaps some good-looking young novice, all freshly scrubbed, with big working-class hands, who would . . .

CARDINAL *(Magnanimous)*
We have both in our service; if a boy is more to your pleasure . . .

LAWYER
I don't drink in the afternoon, so there is need for neither . . . unless Your Eminence . . . ?

CARDINAL
(His eyes sparkling with the joke to come about his nature)
We are known to be . . . ascetic, so we will have none of it. Just . . . three cardinals . . . and Saint Francis.

LAWYER
Oh, not Saint Francis, not a saint. Closer to a king; closer to Croesus. That was gibberish I was speaking to the cardinals—and it's certainly not accepted that Saint Francis spoke gibberish to his . . . parishioners . . . intentional gibberish or otherwise.

CARDINAL

It is not accepted; no.

LAWYER

No. May I smoke?

CARDINAL

Do.

LAWYER *(Lights up)*

Closer to Croesus; to gold; closer to wealth.

CARDINAL *(A heavy, weary sigh)*

Aahhhh, you *do* want to talk business, don't you?

LAWYER *(Surprisingly tough)*

Oh, come on, Your Eminence: *(Softer)* Do you want to spend the afternoon with me, making small talk? Shall we . . . shall we talk about . . . times gone by?

CARDINAL

(Thinks about it with some distaste)

No. No no; we don't think so. It wouldn't do. It's not charitable of us to say so, but when we were at school we did loathe you so.

(Both laugh slightly)

LAWYER

Your Eminence was not . . . beloved of everyone himself.

CARDINAL

(Thinking back, a bit smugly)

Ah, no; a bit out of place; out of step.

LAWYER

A swine, I thought.

CARDINAL

And we you.

(Both laugh a little again)

LAWYER

Do you ever slip?

CARDINAL

Sir?

LAWYER

Mightn't you—if you're not careful—*(Tiny pause)* lapse . . . and say *I* to me . . . not we?

CARDINAL

(Pretending sudden understanding)

Ah *ha!* Yes, we under*stand*.

LAWYER

Do we, do we.

CARDINAL

We do. We—and here we speak of our*selves* and not of our station—we . . . *we* reserve the first-person singular for intimates . . . and equals.

LAWYER

. . . And your superiors.

CARDINAL

(Brushing away a gnat)
The case does not apply.

LAWYER

(Matter-of-factly; the vengeance is underneath) You'll grovel, Buddy. *(Slaps his hip hard)* As automatically and naturally as people slobber on that ring of yours. As naturally as that, I'll have you do your obeisance. *(Sweetly)* As you used to, old friend.

CARDINAL

We . . . *(Thinks better of what he was about to say)* You *were* a swine at school. *(More matter-of-factly)* A cheat in your examinations, a liar in all things of any matter, vile in your personal habits—unwashed and indecent, a bully to those you could intimidate and a sycophant to everyone else. We remember you more clearly each moment. It is law you practice, is it not? We find it fitting.

LAWYER

(A mock bow, head only)
We are of the same school, Your Eminence.

CARDINAL

And in the same class . . . but not *of.* You have come far—in a worldly sense . . . from so little, we mean. *(Musing)* The law.

LAWYER

I speak plainly.

CARDINAL

You are plain. As from your beginnings.

LAWYER *(Quietly)*

Overstuffed, arrogant, pompous son of a profiteer. And a whore. You are in the Church, are you not? We find it fitting.

CARDINAL

(A burst of appreciative laughter)
You're *good!* You *are! Still!* Gutter, but good. But, in law . . . *(Leaves it unfinished with a gesture)* Ah! It comes back to us; it begins to. What

did we call you at school? What name, what nickname did we have for you . . . all of us? What term of simple honesty and . . . rough affection did we have for you? *(Tapping his head impatiently)* It comes back to us.

LAWYER *(Almost a snarl)*

We had a name for you, too.

CARDINAL *(Dismissing it)*

Yes, yes, but we forget it.

LAWYER

Your Eminence was not always so . . . eminent.

CARDINAL *(Remembering)*

Hy-e . . . *(Relishing each syllable)* Hy-e-na. Hy. E. Na. We recall.

LAWYER

(Close to break-through anger)

We are close to Croesus, Your Eminence. I've brought gold with me . . . *(Leans forward)* money, Your Eminence.

CARDINAL *(Brushing it off)*

Yes, yes; later. Hy-e-na.

LAWYER *(A threat, but quiet)*

A great deal of money, Your Eminence.

CARDINAL

We hear you, and we will discuss your business shortly. And why did we call you hyena . . . ?

LAWYER *(Quiet threat again)*

If Croesus goes, he takes the gold away.

CARDINAL *(Outgoing)*

But, Hyena, you are not Croesus; you are Croesus' emissary. You will wait; the gold will wait.

LAWYER

Are you certain?

CARDINAL *(Ignoring the last)*

Ah, yes, it was in natural-science class, was it not? *(The* LAWYER *rises, moves away a little)* Was it not?

LAWYER

Considering your mother's vagaries, you were never certain of your true father . . . were you?

CARDINAL

Correct, my child: considering one's mother's vagaries, one was never certain of one's true father . . . was one? But then, my child, we embraced the

Church; and we *know* our true father. *(Pause; the* LAWYER *is silent)* It was in natural-science class, eleven-five until noon, and did we not discover about the hyena . . .

LAWYER

More money than you've ever seen!

CARDINAL *(Parody; cool)*

Yum-yum. *(Back to former tone)* Did we not discover about the hyena that it was a most resourceful scavenger? That, failing all other food, it would dine on offal . . .

LAWYER *(Angrier)*

Millions!

CARDINAL *(Pressing on)*

. . . and that it devoured the wounded and the dead? We found that last the most shocking: the dead. But we were young. And what horrified us most—and, indeed, what gave us all the thought that the name was most fitting for yourself—

LAWYER *(Ibid.)*

Money!

CARDINAL

. . . was that to devour its dead, scavenged prey, it would often chew into it . . .

LAWYER

MONEY, YOU SWINE!

CARDINAL

(Each word rising in pitch and volume)
. . . chew into it THROUGH THE ANUS????
(Both silent, breathing a little hard)

LAWYER *(Finally; softly)*

Bastard.

CARDINAL *(Quietly, too)*

And now that we have brought the past to mind, and remembered what we could not exactly, shall we . . . talk business?

LAWYER *(Softly; sadly)*

Robes the color of your mother's vice.

CARDINAL *(Kindly)*

Come. Let us talk business. You are a businessman.

LAWYER *(Sadly again)*

As are you.

CARDINAL
(As if reminding a child of something)
We are a Prince of the Church. Do you forget?

LAWYER
(Suddenly pointing to the cage; too offhand) Are those two lovers? Do they
mate?

CARDINAL
(Patronizing; through with games)
Come; let us talk business.

LAWYER *(Persisting)*
Is it true? Do they? Even cardinals?

CARDINAL *(A command)*
If you have money to give us . . . sit down and give it.

LAWYER
To the lay mind—to the cognoscenti it may be fact, accepted and put out
of the head—but to the lay mind it's speculation . . . voyeuristic, perhaps,
and certainly anti-Rome . . . mere speculation, but whispered about, even
by the school children—indeed, as you must recall, the more . . . urbane
of us wondered about the Fathers at school . . .

CARDINAL
. . . the more wicked . . .

LAWYER
. . . about their vaunted celibacy . . . among one another. Of course, we
were at an age when everyone diddled everyone else . . .

CARDINAL
Some.

LAWYER
Yes, and I suppose it was natural enough for us to assume that the priests
did too.

CARDINAL
(As if changing the subject)
You have . . . fallen away from the Church.

LAWYER
And into the arms of reason.

CARDINAL
(Almost thinking of something else)
An unsanctified union: not a marriage: a whore's bed.

LAWYER

A common-law marriage, for I am at law and, as you say, common. But it is quite respectable these days.

CARDINAL

(Tough; bored with the church play-acting; heavy and tired)
All right; that's enough. What's your business?

LAWYER

(Pacing a little, after an appreciative smile)
My employer . . . wants to give some of her money to the Church.

CARDINAL

(Enthusiastic, but guarded)
Does she!

LAWYER

Gradually.

CARDINAL *(Understanding)*

Ah-ha.

LAWYER *(Offhand)*

A billion now.

CARDINAL

(Happy) A million now.

LAWYER

No. A billion.

CARDINAL

A billion?!

LAWYER

Yes, a billion. B, as in boy, as in "oh, boy!" A billion now.

CARDINAL

I see . . . And the rest gradually.

LAWYER

And the same amount each year for the next twenty—a billion a year. She is not ill; she has no intention of dying; she is quite young, youngish; there is no . . . rush.

CARDINAL

Indeed not.

LAWYER

It is that she is . . . overburdened with wealth.

CARDINAL

And it weighs on her soul.

LAWYER

Her soul is in excellent repair. If it were not, I doubt she'd be making the gesture. It is, as I said, that she is overburdened with wealth, and it . . . uh . . .

CARDINAL

(Finding the words for him)

. . . piles up.

LAWYER *(A small smile)*

. . . and it is . . . wasted . . . lying about. It is one of several bequests— arrangements—she is making at the moment.

CARDINAL

(Not astonishment, but unconcealed curiosity)

One of several?

LAWYER

Yes. The Protestants as well, the Jews . . . hospitals, universities, orchestras, revolutions here and there . . .

CARDINAL

Well, we think it is a . . . responsible action. She is well, as you say.

LAWYER

Oh, yes; very.

CARDINAL

We are . . . glad. *(Amused fascination)* How did you become her . . . lawyer, if we're not intruding upon . . . ?

LAWYER *(Brief pause; tight smile)*

She had a dossier on me, I suppose.

CARDINAL

It must be a great deal less revealing than ours . . . than our dossier on you.

LAWYER

Or a great deal *more* revealing.

CARDINAL

For her sake, and yours, we hope so.

LAWYER

To answer your question: I am a very good lawyer. It is as simple as that.

CARDINAL *(Speculating on it)*

You *have* escaped prison.

LAWYER

I've done nothing to be imprisoned for.

CARDINAL

Pure. You're pure. You're ringed by stench, but you're pure. There's an odor that precedes you, and follows after you're gone, but you walk in the eye of it . . . pure.

LAWYER *(Contemptuous)*

Look, pig, I don't enjoy you.

CARDINAL

(Mockingly; his arms wide as if for an embrace)
School chum!

LAWYER

If it were not my job to . . .

CARDINAL *(Abruptly)*

Well, it is! Do it!

LAWYER

(A smile to a hated but respected adversary)
I've given you the facts: a billion a year for twenty years.

CARDINAL

But . . .?

LAWYER *(Shrugs)*

That's all.

CARDINAL

(Stuttering with quiet excitement)
Y-y-y-y-yes, b-b-but shall I just go to the *house* and pick it up in a *truck?*

LAWYER *(Great, heavy relief)*

AAAAAAAHHHHHHHhhhhhhhhh.

CARDINAL *(Caught up short)*

Hm? (No *reply*) HM???

LAWYER

Say it again. Say it once again for me.

CARDINAL *(Puzzled; suspicious)*

What? Say what?

LAWYER *(Leaning over him)*

Say it again; repeat what you said. It was a sweet sound.

CARDINAL *(Shouting)*

SAY WHAT!

LAWYER *(Cooing into his ear)*
"Yes, but shall I just go to the house and pick it up in a truck?"

CARDINAL
(Thinks on it a moment)
Well, perhaps there was a bit . . . perhaps there was too much levity there
. . . uh, if one did not know one . . .

LAWYER *(Coos again)*
. . . "But shall *I* just go to the house . . ."

CARDINAL
Wh . . . NO!

LAWYER *(Sings it out)*
Shall IIIIIIII just go!

CARDINAL *(Cross)*
No! We . . . we did not say that!

LAWYER
IIIIIIIIIIIII.

CARDINAL *(A threat)*
We did not say "I."

LAWYER *(Almost baby talk)*
We said I. Yes, we did; we said I. *(Suddenly loud and tough)* We said I, and
we said it straight. I! I! I! By God, we picked up our skirts and lunged for
it! IIIIIII! Me! Me! Gimme!

CARDINAL *(Full shout)*
WE SAID NO SUCH THING!

LAWYER *(Oily imitation)*
We reserve the first-person singular, do we not, for . . . for intimates,
equals . . . or superiors. *(Harsher)* Well, my dear, you found all three apply-
ing. Intimate. How close would we rub to someone for all that wealth? As
close as we once did?

CARDINAL
(Not wanting to hear, but weak)
Leave . . . leave off.

LAWYER *(Pressing)*
Equals? Oh, money equals anything you want. Levels! LEVELS THE
EARTH! AND THE HEAVENS!

CARDINAL
ENOUGH!!

LAWYER *(The final thrust)*

... Or superiors. Who is superior, the one who stands on the mount of heaven? We think not! We have come down off our plural ... when the stakes are high enough ... and the hand, the kissed hand palsies out ... FOR THE LOOT!!

CARDINAL *(Hissed)*

Satan!

LAWYER *(After a pause)*

Satan? You would believe it ... if you believed in God. *(Breaks into—for lack of a better word—Satanic laughter, subsides. Patronizing now)* No, poor Eminence, you don't have to drive a truck around to the back door for it. We'll get the money to you ... to your ... people. Fact, I don't want you coming 'round ... at all. Clacketing through the great corridors of the place, sizing it up, not content with enough wealth to buy off the first two hundred saints picked out of a bag, but wondering if *it* mightn't get thrown into the bargain as a ... summer residence, perhaps ... uh, after she dies and scoots up to heaven.

CARDINAL

(On his feet, but shaky, uncertain)

This ... uh ...

LAWYER

... interview is terminated?

CARDINAL *(Quietly)*

This is unseemly talk.

LAWYER *(Vastly, wryly amused)*

Oh? Is it?

CARDINAL

(A mechanical toy breaking down)

We will ... we will forgive your presumption, your ... excess ... ex*cuse*, yes ... excuse? ... We will ... overlook your ... *(A plea is underneath)* Let us have no more of this talk. It *is* unseemly.

LAWYER

(Businesslike; as if the preceding speech had not happened)

As I said, I don't want you coming 'round ... bothering her.

CARDINAL *(Humble)*

I would not bother the lady; I have not met her. Of course, I would very much like to have the pleasure of ...

LAWYER

We slip often now, don't we.

CARDINAL *(Very soul-weary)*

Pardon?

LAWYER

The plural is gone out of us, I see.

CARDINAL

Ah. Well. Perhaps.

LAWYER

Regird yourself. We *are* about terminated. *(Quick, insulting finger-snaps)* Come! Come! Back up; back on your majesty! Hup!

CARDINAL

(Slowly, wearily coming back into shape)

Uh . . . yes . . . of—of course. We, uh, we shall make any arrangements you wish . . . naturally. We . . . we have no desire to intrude ourselves upon . . . uh . . . upon . . .

LAWYER

Miss Alice.

CARDINAL

Yes; upon Miss Alice. If she . . . if Miss Alice desires privacy, certainly her generosity has earned it for her. We . . . would not intrude.

LAWYER

You *are* kind. *(Fishing in a pocket for a notebook)* What . . . is . . . your . . . secretary's . . . name . . . I think I have it . . . right . . . *(Finds notebook)*

CARDINAL

Brother . . .

LAWYER

Julian! Is that not right?

CARDINAL

Yes, Brother Julian. He is an old friend of ours; we . . .

LAWYER

Rather daring of you, wasn't it? Choosing a lay brother as your private secretary?

CARDINAL

(A combination of apology and defiance)

He is an old friend of ours, and he has served the . . .

LAWYER *(Praising a puppy)*

You are adventurous, are you not?

CARDINAL

He has been assigned many years to the . . .

LAWYER

(Waving his notebook a little)

We have it; all down; we know.

CARDINAL *(A little sadly)*

Ah-ha.

LAWYER

Yes. Well, we will send for your . . . Brother Julian. . . . To clear up odds and ends. Every bank has its runners. We don't ask vice presidents to . . . fetch and carry. Inform Your Brother Julian. We will send for him.

(LAWYER exits)

CARDINAL *(To the exiting figure)*

Yes, we . . . will.

(Stands still, looks at the ground, tired, looks at his sleeves, his fingernails, his ring, up, out, over. Sighs, looks at the cage. Smiles slightly, moves to the cage, the fingers of his left hand fluttering at it)

Do . . . do you . . . do you have much to say to one another, my dears? Do you? You find it comforting? Hmmmmmmm? Do you? Hmmmmn? Do-do-do-do-do-do-do-do? Hmmmmmm? Do?

CURTAIN

SCENE TWO

(The library of a mansion—a castle. Pillared walls, floor-to-ceiling leather-bound books. A great arched doorway, rear-center. A huge reading table to stage-left—practical. A phrenological head on it. To stage-right, jutting out of the wings, a huge doll's-house model of the building of which the present room is a part. It is as tall as a man, and a good deal of it must be visible from all parts of the audience. An alternative—and perhaps more practical—would be for the arched doorway to be either left or right, with bookshelves to both sides of the set, coming toward the center, and to have the entire doll's house in the rear wall, in which case it could be smaller—say, twelve feet long and proportionately high. At any rate, it is essential. At rise, JULIAN is alone on stage, looking at the house)

JULIAN

(After a few moments of head-shaking concentration)
Extraordinary . . . extraordinary.

BUTLER

(After entering, observing JULIAN, *not having heard him)*
Extraordinary, isn't it?

JULIAN *(Mildly startled)*
Uh . . . yes, unbelievable . . . *(Agreeing)* Extraordinary.

BUTLER

(Who moves about with a kind of unbutlerlike ease)
I never cease to wonder at the . . . the fact of it, I suppose.

JULIAN

The workmanship . . .

BUTLER *(A mild correction)*
That someone would do it.

JULIAN *(Seeing)*
Yes, yes.

BUTLER

That someone would . . . well, for heaven's sake, that someone would
build . . . *(Refers to the set)* . . . this . . . castle? . . . and then . . . dupli-
cate it in such precise miniature, so exactly. Have you looked through the
windows?

JULIAN

No, I . . .

BUTLER

It is exact. Look and see.

JULIAN

(Moves even closer to the model, peers through a tiny window)
Why . . . why, YES. I . . . there's a great . . . baronial dining room, even with
tiny candlesticks on the tables!

BUTLER

(Nodding his head, a thumb back over his shoulder)
It's down the hall, off the hallway to the right.

JULIAN

(The proper words won't come)
It's . . . it's . . .

BUTLER

Look over here. There; right there.

JULIAN *(Peers)*

It's . . . it's this *room!* This room we're *in!*

BUTLER

Yes.

JULIAN

Extraordinary.

BUTLER

Is there anyone there? Are we there?

JULIAN

(Briefly startled, then laughs, looks back into the model)

Uh . . . no. It seems to be quite . . . empty.

BUTLER *(A quiet smile)*

One feels one should see one's self . . . almost.

JULIAN

(Looks back to him; after a brief, thoughtful pause)

Yes. That would be rather a shock, wouldn't it?

BUTLER

Did you notice . . . did you notice that there is a model within that room in the castle? A model of the model?

JULIAN

I . . . I did. But . . . I didn't register it, it seemed so . . . continual.

BUTLER *(A shy smile)*

You don't suppose that within that tiny model in the model there, there is . . . another room like this, with yet a tinier model within it, and within . . .

JULIAN *(Laughs)*

. . . and within and within and within and . . . ? No, I . . . rather doubt it. It's remarkable craftsmanship, though. Remarkable.

BUTLER

Hell to clean.

JULIAN

(Conversational enthusiasm)

Yes! I should think so! Does it open from . . .

BUTLER

It's sealed. Tight. There is no dust.

JULIAN

(Disappointed at being joked with)

Oh.

BUTLER

I was sporting.

JULIAN

Oh.

BUTLER *(Straight curiosity)*

Did you mind?

JULIAN *(Too free)*

I? No!

BUTLER *(Doctrine, no sarcasm)*

It would almost be taken for granted—one would think— that if a person or a person's surrogate went to the trouble, *and* expense, of having such a dream toy made, that the person *would* have it sealed, so that there'd be no dust. Wouldn't one think.

JULIAN

(Sarcasm and embarrassment together)
One would think.

BUTLER *(After a pause, some rue)*

I have enough to do as it is.

JULIAN

(Eager to move on to something else)
Yes, yes!

BUTLER

It's enormous . . . *(A sudden thought)* even for a castle, I suppose. *(Points to the model)* Not that. *(Now to the room)* This.

JULIAN

Endless! You . . . certainly you don't work alone.

BUTLER

Oh, Christ, no.

JULIAN *(Reaffirming)*

I would have *thought.*

BUTLER

(Almost daring him to disagree)
Still, there's enough work.

JULIAN *(Slightly testy)*

I'm *sure.*
(A pause between them)

BUTLER

(For no reason, a sort of "Oh, what the hell")
Heigh-ho.

JULIAN

Will there be . . . someone? . . . to see me? . . . soon?

BUTLER

Hm?

JULIAN

Will there be someone to see me soon! *(After a blank stare from the other)*
You announced me? I trust?

BUTLER *(Snapping to)*

Oh! Yes! *(Laughs)* Sorry. Uh . . . yes, there will be someone to see you
soon.

JULIAN

(Attempt at good-fellowship)
Ah, good!

BUTLER

Are you a priest?

JULIAN *(Self-demeaning)*

I? No, no . . .

BUTLER

If not Catholic, Episcopal.

JULIAN

No . . .

BUTLER

What, then?

JULIAN

I am a lay brother. I am not ordained.

BUTLER

You are *of* the cloth but have not taken it.

JULIAN *(None too happy)*

You *could* say that.

BUTLER *(No trifling)*

One *could* say it, and quite accurately. May I get you some ice water?

JULIAN *(Put off and confused)*

No!

BUTLER *(Feigns apology)*

Sorry.

JULIAN

You must forgive me. *(Almost childlike enthusiasm)* This is rather a big day for me.

BUTLER *(Nods understandingly)*

Iced *tea.*

JULIAN *(Laughs)*

No . . . nothing, thank you . . . uh . . . I don't have your name.

BUTLER

Fortunate.

JULIAN

No, I meant that . . .

BUTLER

Butler.

JULIAN

Pardon?

BUTLER

Butler.

JULIAN

Yes. You. . . you *are* the butler, are you not, but . . .

BUTLER

Butler. My name is Butler.

JULIAN *(Innocent pleasure)*

How extraordinary!

BUTLER *(Putting it aside)*

No, not really. Appropriate: Butler . . . butler. If my name were Carpenter, and I were a butler . . . or if I *were* a carpenter, and my name were Butler . . .

JULIAN

But *still* . . .

BUTLER

. . . it would not be so appropriate. And think: if I were a woman, and had become a chambermaid, say, and my name were Butler . . .

JULIAN *(Anticipating)*

. . . you would be in for some rather tiresome exchanges.

BUTLER *(Cutting, but light)*

None more than this.

JULIAN *(Sadly)*

Aha.

BUTLER *(Forgiving)*

Coffee, then.

JULIAN *(As if he can't explain)*

No. Nothing.

BUTLER *(Semi-serious bow)*

I am at your service.
    *(*LAWYER *enters)*

LAWYER

I, too.

JULIAN

Ah!

LAWYER

I'm sorry to have kept you waiting, but . . .

JULIAN

Oh, no, no . . .

LAWYER

. . . I was conferring with Miss Alice.

JULIAN

Yes.

LAWYER *(To* BUTLER; *no fondness)*

Dearest.

BUTLER *(To* LAWYER; *same)*

Darling.

LAWYER *(To* JULIAN*)*

Doubtless, though, you two have . . . *(Waves a hand about)*

JULIAN

Oh, we've had a most . . . unusual . . .

LAWYER

(To BUTLER, *ignoring* JULIAN's *answer)*
You've offered our guest refreshments?

JULIAN

Brother Julian.

BUTLER

Ice water, iced tea, and coffee—hot assumed, I imagine—none taken.

LAWYER

Gracious! *(Back to* JULIAN*)* Port, perhaps. Removed people take port, I've noticed.

JULIAN

(More to please than anything)
Yes. Port. Please.

LAWYER *(To* BUTLER*)*

Port for . . .

JULIAN

Julian—Brother Julian.

LAWYER *(Slightly patronizing)*
I *know.* (BUTLER *goes to a sideboard)* I would join you, but it is not my habit to drink before sundown. Not a condemnation, you understand. One of my minor disciplines.

BUTLER

(Generally, looking at the bottle)
The port is eighteen-oh-six. *(To the* LAWYER*)* How do they fortify wines, again?

JULIAN

Alcohol is added, more alcohol . . . at the time of casking. Fortify . . . strengthen.

BUTLER

Ah, yes.

LAWYER *(To* JULIAN*)*
Of course, your grandfather was a vintner, was he not.

JULIAN

Goodness, you . . . you have my history.

LAWYER

Oh, we do. Such a mild life . . . save those six years in your thirties which are . . . blank . . . in our report on you.

JULIAN *(A good covering laugh)*
Oh, they were . . . mild, in their own way. Blank, but not black.

LAWYER

Will you fill them for us? The blank years?

JULIAN

(Taking the glass from BUTLER*)*
Thank you. *(The laugh again)* They were nothing.

LAWYER *(Steelier)*

Still, you will fill them for us.

JULIAN *(Pleasant, but very firm)*

No.

BUTLER

Gracious!

LAWYER

Recalcitrance, yes . . . well, we must have our people dig further.

JULIAN

You'll find nothing interesting. You'll find some . . . upheaval, but . . . waste, mostly. Dull waste.

LAWYER

The look of most of our vices in retrospect, eh?

BUTLER *(Light)*

I have fleshpot visions: carousals, thighs and heavy perfume. . . .

LAWYER *(To BUTLER)*

It's in your mind, fitting, a mind worthy of your name. *(To JULIAN)* Did you two . . . did he tell you his name, and did you two have a veritable badminton over it? Puns and chuckles?

JULIAN

We . . . labored it a bit, I more than . . . Butler, it would appear.

BUTLER

I was churlish, I'm sorry. If there weren't so many of *you* and only one of *me* . . .

JULIAN

Oh, now . . .

LAWYER *(Still on it)*

You're not going to tell me about those six years, eh?

JULIAN

(Stares at him for a moment, then says it clearly, enunciating)

No.

(LAWYER shrugs)

BUTLER

May I have some port?

LAWYER *(Slightly incredulous)*

Do you *like* port?

BUTLER

Not very, but I thought I'd keep him company while you play police.

LAWYER *(Shrugs again)*

It's not my house. *(Turns to* JULIAN*)* One can't say, "It's not my castle," can one? *(Back to* BUTLER*)* If you think it's proper.

BUTLER *(Getting himself some)*

Well, with the wine cellar stacked like a munitions dump, and you "never having any" until the barn swallows start screeping around . . .

LAWYER

There's no such word as screep.

BUTLER *(Shrugs)*

Fit.

JULIAN

I think it has a nice onomatopoetic ring about it . . .

LAWYER

(Down to business, rather rudely)
Your buddy told you why we sent for you?

JULIAN

(Offended, but pretending confusion)
My . . . buddy?

LAWYER

Mine, really. We were at school together. Did he tell you that? *(As* JULIAN *intentionally looks blank)* His Eminence.

JULIAN

Ah!

LAWYER *(Imitation)*

Ah! *(Snapped)* Well? Did he?

JULIAN

(Choosing his words carefully, precisely)
His Eminence informed me . . . generally. He called me into his . . .

LAWYER

. . . garden . . .

JULIAN

. . . garden . . . which is a comfortable office in summer . . .

BUTLER

Ninety-six today.

JULIAN *(Interested)*

Indeed!

BUTLER

More tomorrow.

LAWYER *(Impatiently)*

Called you into his garden.

JULIAN

And—sorry—and . . . told me of the high honor which he had chosen for me.

LAWYER *(Scoffing)*

He. Chosen. You.

JULIAN

Of . . . your lady's most . . .

LAWYER

Miss Alice.

JULIAN

Of Miss Alice's—sorry, I've not met the lady yet, and first names—of her overwhelming bequest to the Church . . .

LAWYER

Not a bequest; a bequest is made in a will; Miss Alice is not dead.

JULIAN

Uh . . . grant?

LAWYER

Grant.

JULIAN *(Taking a deep breath)*

Of her overwhelming grant to the Church, and of my assignment to come here, to take care of . . .

LAWYER

Odds and ends.

JULIAN *(Shrugs one shoulder)*

. . . if you like. "A few questions and answers" was how it was put to me.

BUTLER *(To LAWYER, impressed)*

He's a lay brother.

LAWYER *(Bored)*

We *know.* (For JULIAN's *benefit)* His Eminence—buddy . . .

JULIAN *(Natural, sincere)*

Tch—tch—tch—tch—tch . . .

LAWYER

He was my buddy at school . . . if you don't mind. *(Beginning, now, to* BUT-LER, *but quickly becoming general)* His Eminence—though you have

never met him, Butler, seen him, perhaps—is a most . . . eminent man; and
bold, very bold; behind—or, underneath—what would seem to be a solid
rock of . . . pomposity, sham, peacocking, there is a . . . flows a secret river
. . . of . . .

BUTLER (*For* JULIAN's *benefit*)

This is an endless metaphor.

LAWYER

. . . of unconventionality, defiance, even. Simple sentences? Is that all you
want? Did you know that Brother Julian here is the only lay brother in the
history of Christendom assigned, chosen, as secretary and confidant to a
Prince of the Church? Ever?

JULIAN (*Mildly*)

That is not known as fact.

LAWYER

Name others!

JULIAN

I say it is not known as fact. I grant it is not usual—my appointment as secretary to His Eminence. . . .

LAWYER (*Faint disgust*)

An honor, at any rate, an unusual honor for a lay brother, an honor accorded
by a most unusual Prince of the Church—a prince of a man, in fact—a
prince whose still waters . . . well, you finish it.

BUTLER

(*Pretending puzzlement as to how to finish it*)

. . . whose still waters . . .

JULIAN

His Eminence is, indeed, a most unusual man.

LAWYER (*Sourly*)

I said he was a prince.

BUTLER

(*Pretending to be talking to himself*)

. . . run quiet? Run deep? Run *deep! That's* good!

LAWYER

Weren't there a few eyebrows raised at your appointment?

JULIAN

There . . . I was not informed of it . . . if there were. His Eminence would
not burden me. . . .

LAWYER

(Still to JULIAN, *patronizing)*
He is really Santa Claus; we know.

JULIAN *(Rising to it)*
Your animosity toward His Eminence must make your task very difficult
for you. I must say I . . .

LAWYER
I have learned . . . *(Brief pause before he says the name with some distaste)*
Brother Julian . . . never to confuse the representative of a . . . thing with
the thing itself.

BUTLER
. . . though I wonder if you'd intended to get involved in *two* watery
metaphors there: underground river, and still waters.

LAWYER *(To* BUTLER)
No, I had not. *(Back to* JULIAN) A thing with its representative. Your
Cardinal and I loathe one another, and I find him unworthy of
contempt. (A *hand up to stop any coming objection)* A cynic and a
hypocrite, a posturer, but all the same the representative of an august
and revered . . . body.

JULIAN *(Murmured)*
You are most unjust.

LAWYER

(As if he were continuing a prepared speech)
Uh . . . revered body. And Rome, in its perhaps wily—though *certainly*
inscrutable—wisdom, Rome has found reason to appoint that wreckage as
its representative.

JULIAN
Really, I can't permit you to talk that way.

LAWYER
You will permit it, you're under instructions, you have a job to do. In fact,
you have this present job *because* I cannot stand your Cardinal.

JULIAN
He . . . he did not tell me so.

LAWYER
We tell you so.

(JULIAN *dips his head to one side in a "perhaps it is true" gesture)*
And it is so.

JULIAN
I will not . . . I will not concern myself with . . . all this.

BUTLER *(Quite to himself)*

I don't *like* port.

LAWYER *(To* BUTLER*)*

Then don't drink it. *(To* JULIAN*)* You're quite right: bow your head, stop up your ears and do what you're told.

JULIAN

Obedience is not a fault.

LAWYER

Nor always a virtue. See Fascism.

JULIAN *(Rather strong for him)*

Perhaps we can get on with our business. . . .

LAWYER *(He, too)*

You don't want to take up my time, or your own.

JULIAN

Yes.

BUTLER *(Putting down glass)*

Then I won't drink it.

LAWYER

(To JULIAN, *briskly, as to a servant)*

All right! I shall tell Miss Alice you've come—that the drab fledgling is pecking away in the library, impatient for . . . food for the Church.

JULIAN

(A tight smile, a tiny formal bow)

If you would be so kind.

LAWYER *(Twisting the knife)*

I'll find out if she cares to see you today.

JULIAN *(Ibid.)*

Please.

LAWYER

(Moving toward the archway)

And, if she cares to, I will have you brought up.

JULIAN

(Mild surprise, but not a question)

Up.

LAWYER

(Almost challenging him)

Up. *(Pause)* You will not tell us about the six years—those years blank but not black . . . the waste, the dull waste.

JULIAN *(Small smile)*

No.

LAWYER *(He, too)*

You will . . . in time. *(To* BUTLER*)* Won't he, Butler? Time? The great revealer?

*(*LAWYER *exits)*

JULIAN

(After the LAWYER *is gone; no indignation)*
Well.

BUTLER *(Offhand)*

Nasty man.

JULIAN

(Intentionally feigning surprise)
Oh? *(He and* BUTLER *laugh)* Up.

BUTLER

Sir?

JULIAN

Up.

BUTLER

Oh! Yes! She . . . *(Moves to the model)* has her apartments up . . . here. *(He points to a tower area)* Here.

JULIAN

A-ha.

BUTLER

(Straightening things up)
About those six years . . .

JULIAN

(Not unfriendly, very matter-of-fact)
What of them?

BUTLER

Yes, what of them?

JULIAN

Oh . . . *(Pause)* I . . . I lost my faith. *(Pause)* In God.

BUTLER

Ah. *(Then a questioning look)*

JULIAN

Is there more?

BUTLER

Is there more?

JULIAN

Well, nothing . . . of matter. I . . . declined. I . . . shriveled into myself;
a glass dome . . . descended, and it seemed I was out of reach, unreach-
able, finally unreaching, in this . . . paralysis, of sorts. I . . . put myself
in a mental home.

BUTLER

(Curiously noncommittal)

Ah.

JULIAN

I could not reconcile myself to the chasm between the nature of God and
the use to which men put . . . God.

BUTLER

Between your God and others', your view and theirs.

JULIAN

I said what I intended: *(Weighs the opposites in each hand)* It is God the
mover, not God the puppet; God the creator, not the God created by man.

BUTLER *(Almost pitying)*

Six years in the loony bin for semantics?

JULIAN *(Slightly flustered, heat)*

It is not semantics! Men create a false God in their own image, it is easier
for them! . . . It is not . . .

BUTLER

Levity! Forget it!

JULIAN

I . . . yes.

(A chime sounds)

BUTLER

Miss Alice will see you. I will take you up.

JULIAN

Forgive me . . . I . . .

BUTLER *(Moves toward archway)*

Let me show you up.

JULIAN

You *did* ask me.

BUTLER *(Level)*

Yes, and you told me.

JULIAN

(An explanation, not an apology)
My faith and my sanity . . . they are one and the same.

BUTLER

Yes? *(Considers it)* A-ha. *(Smiles noncommittally)* We must not keep the lady waiting.

    (They begin exiting, BUTLER *preceding* JULIAN*)*

CURTAIN

SCENE THREE

(An upstairs sitting room of the castle. Feminine, but not frilly. Blues instead of pinks. Fireplace in keeping with the castle. A door to the bedroom in the rear wall, stage-left; a door from the hallway in the side wall, stage-left.

At rise, MISS ALICE *is seated in a wing chair, facing windows, its back to the audience; the* LAWYER *is to one side, facing her)*

LAWYER

(Clear that he expects JULIAN *to overhear. He has finished one sentence, is pondering another)*
. . . Nor is it as simple as all that. The instinct of giving may die out in our time—if you'll grant that giving is an instinct. The government is far more interested in taking, in regulated taking, than in promoting spontaneous generosity. Remember what I told you—what we discussed—in reference to the charitable foundations, and how . . . *(A knock on the hall door)* That will be our bird of prey. Pray. P-R-A-Y. What a pun I could make on that; bird of pray. Come in.

    (The hall door opens; BUTLER *precedes* JULIAN *into the room)*

BUTLER

Brother Julian, who *was* in the library, is now here.

LAWYER

So he is. *(To* JULIAN, *impatiently) Come* in, *come* in.

JULIAN *(Advancing a little)*

Yes . . . certainly.

BUTLER

May I go? I'm tired.

LAWYER *(Grandly)*

By all means.

BUTLER *(Turns to go)*

Thank you. *(To* JULIAN*)* Goodbye.

JULIAN

Goodb . . . I'll . . . we'll see one another again?

BUTLER

Oh. Yes, probably. *(As he exits)* Goodbye, everybody.

LAWYER

(After BUTLER *exits, chuckles)*

What is it the nouveaux riches are always saying? "You can't get good servants nowadays"?

JULIAN

He seems . . .

LAWYER *(Curt)*

He is very good. *(Turns to the chair)* Miss Alice, our Brother Julian is here. *(Repeats it, louder)* OUR BROTHER JULIAN IS HERE. *(To* JULIAN*)* She's terribly hard of hearing. *(To* MISS ALICE*)* DO YOU WANT TO SEE HIM? *(To* JULIAN*)* I think she's responding. Sometimes . . . well, at her age and condition . . . twenty minutes can go by . . . for her to assimilate a sentence and reply to it.

JULIAN

But I thought . . . His Eminence said she was . . . young.

LAWYER

SHHHHHHHH! She's moving.

> (MISS ALICE *slowly rises from her chair and comes around it. Her face is that of a withered crone, her hair gray and white and matted; she is bent; she moves with two canes)*

MISS ALICE

(Finally, with a cracked and ancient voice, to JULIAN*)*

Hello there, young man.

LAWYER

(As JULIAN *takes a step forward)*

Hah! Don't come too close, you'll unnerve her.

JULIAN

But I'm terribly puzzled. I was led to believe that she was a young woman, and . . .

MISS ALICE

Hello there, young man.

LAWYER

Speak to her.

JULIAN

Miss . . . Miss Alice, how do you do?

LAWYER

Louder.

JULIAN

HOW DO YOU DO?

MISS ALICE *(To* LAWYER*)*

How do I do *what?*

LAWYER

It's a formality.

MISS ALICE

WHAT!?

LAWYER

IT IS A FORMALITY, AN OPENING GAMBIT.

MISS ALICE

Oh. *(To* JULIAN*)* How do *you* do?

JULIAN

Very well . . . thank you.

MISS ALICE

WHAT!?

JULIAN

VERY WELL, THANK YOU.

MISS ALICE

Don't you scream at me!

JULIAN *(Mumbled)*

Sorry.

MISS ALICE

WHAT!?

JULIAN

SORRY!

MISS ALICE *(Almost a pout)*

Oh.

LAWYER *(Who has enjoyed this)*

Well, I think I'll leave you two now . . . for your business. I'm sure you'll have a . . .

JULIAN

(An attempted urgent aside to the LAWYER*)*

Do you think you . . . shouldn't you be here? You've . . . you've had more experience with her, and . . .

LAWYER *(Laughing)*

No, no, you'll get along fine. *(To* MISS ALICE*)* I'LL LEAVE YOU TWO TOGETHER NOW. *(*MISS ALICE *nods vigorously)* HIS NAME IS BROTHER JULIAN, AND THERE ARE SIX YEARS MISSING FROM HIS LIFE. *(She nods again)* I'LL BE DOWNSTAIRS. *(Begins to leave)*

MISS ALICE

(When the LAWYER *is at the door)*

Don't steal anything.

LAWYER *(Exiting)*

ALL RIGHT!

JULIAN

(After a pause, begins bravely, taking a step forward)

Perhaps you should sit down. Let me . . .

MISS ALICE

WHAT!?

JULIAN

PERHAPS YOU SHOULD SIT DOWN!

MISS ALICE

(Not fear; malevolence)

Keep away from me!

JULIAN

Sorry. *(To himself)* Oh, really, this is impossible.

MISS ALICE

WHAT!?

JULIAN

I SAID THIS WAS IMPOSSIBLE.

MISS ALICE

(Thinks about that for a moment, then)

If you're a defrocked priest, what're you doing in all that? *(Pointing to* JULIAN's *garb)*

JULIAN

I AM NOT A DEFROCKED PRIEST, I AM A LAY BROTHER. I HAVE NEVER BEEN A PRIEST.

MISS ALICE

What did you drink downstairs?

JULIAN

I had a glass of port . . . PORT!

MISS ALICE

(A spoiled, crafty child)
You didn't bring *me* one.

JULIAN

I had no idea you . . .

MISS ALICE

WHAT!?

JULIAN

SHALL I GET YOU A GLASS?

MISS ALICE

A glass of *what.*

JULIAN

PORT. A GLASS OF PORT.

MISS ALICE *(As if he were crazy)*

What for?

JULIAN

BECAUSE YOU . . . *(To himself again)* Really, this *won't* do.

MISS ALICE

(Straightening up, ridding herself of the canes, assuming a normal voice)
I agree with you, it won't do, really.

JULIAN *(Astonishment)*

I beg your pardon?

MISS ALICE

I said it won't do at all.
(She unfastens and removes her wig, unties and takes off her mask, becomes herself, as JULIAN *watches, openmouthed)*
There. Is that better? And you needn't yell at me any more; if anything, my hearing is *too* good.

JULIAN (*Slightly put out*)

I . . . I don't understand.

MISS ALICE

Are you annoyed?

JULIAN

I suspect I will be . . . might be . . . after the surprise leaves me.

MISS ALICE (*Smiling*)

Don't be; it's only a little game.

JULIAN

Yes, doubtless. But why?

MISS ALICE

Oh, indulge us, please.

JULIAN

Well, of course, it would be my pleasure . . . but, considering the importance of our meeting . . .

MISS ALICE

Exactly. Considering the importance of our meeting.

JULIAN

A . . . a test for me.

MISS ALICE (*Laughs*)

No, not at all, a little lightness to counter the weight. (*Mock seriousness*) For we are involved in weighty matters . . . the transfer of billions, the rocking of empires. (*Normal, light tone again*) Let's be comfortable, shall we? Swing my chair around. (JULIAN *moves to do so*) As you can see—you *can*, I trust—I'm *not* a hundred and thirteen years old, but I *do* have my crotchets, even now: I have chairs everywhere that are mine—in each room . . . a chair that is mine, that I alone use.

JULIAN (*Moving the chair*)

Where would you . . .

MISS ALICE (*Lightly*)

Just . . . swing it . . . around. You needn't move it. Good. Now, sit with me. (*They sit*) Fine. In the dining room, of course, there is no question— I sit at the head of the table. But, in the drawing rooms, or the library, or whatever room you wish to mention, I have a chair that I consider my possession.

JULIAN

But you possess the entire . . . (*Thinks of a word*) establishment.

MISS ALICE

Of course, but it is such a large . . . establishment that one needs the feel of specific possession in every . . . area.

JULIAN

(Rather shy, but pleasant)

Do you become . . . cross if someone accidentally assumes your chair, one of your chairs?

MISS ALICE

(Thinks about it, then)

How odd! Curiously, it has never happened, so I cannot say. Tell me about yourself.

JULIAN

Well, there isn't much to say . . . much that isn't already known. Your lawyer would seem to have assembled a case book on me, and . . .

MISS ALICE

Yes, yes, but not the things that would interest him, the things that would interest me.

JULIAN *(Genuine interest)*

And what are they?

MISS ALICE *(Laughs again)*

Let me see. Ah! Do I terrify you?

JULIAN

You *did,* and you are still . . . awesome.

MISS ALICE *(Sweetly)*

Thank you. Did my lawyer intimidate you?

JULIAN

It would seem to be his nature—or his pleasure—to intimidate, and . . . well, I am, perhaps, more easily intimidated than some.

MISS ALICE

Perhaps you are, but he *is* a professional. And how did you find Butler?

JULIAN

A gentle man, quick . . . but mostly gentle.

MISS ALICE

Gentle, yes. He was my lover at one time. *(As* JULIAN *averts his head)* Oh! Perhaps I shouldn't have told you.

JULIAN

No, forgive me. Things sometimes . . . are so unexpected.

MISS ALICE

Yes, they are. I am presently mistress to my lawyer—the gentleman who intimidated you so. He is a pig.

JULIAN *(Embarrassed)*

Yes, yes. You have . . . never married.

MISS ALICE *(Quiet amusement)*

Alas.

JULIAN

You are . . . not Catholic.

MISS ALICE *(The same)*

Again, alas.

JULIAN

No, it is fortunate you are not.

MISS ALICE

I am bored with my present lover.

JULIAN

I . . . *(Shrugs)*

MISS ALICE

I was not soliciting advice.

JULIAN *(Quiet laugh)*

Good, for I have none.

MISS ALICE

These six years of yours.

JULIAN

(Says it all in one deep breath)

There is no mystery to it, my faith in God left me, and I committed myself to an asylum. *(Pause)* You see? Nothing to it.

MISS ALICE

What an odd place to go to look for one's faith.

JULIAN

You misunderstand me. I did not go there to *look* for my faith, but because *it* had left me.

MISS ALICE

You tell it so easily.

JULIAN *(Shrugs)*

It is easy to tell.

MISS ALICE

Ah.

JULIAN *(Giggles a little)*

However, I would not tell your present . . . uh, your lawyer. And that made him quite angry.

MISS ALICE

Have you slept with many women?

JULIAN *(Carefully)*

I am not certain.

MISS ALICE *(Tiny laugh)*

It is an easy enough thing to determine.

JULIAN

Not so. For one, I am celibate. A lay brother—you must know—while not a priest, while not ordained, is still required to take vows. And chastity is one of them.

MISS ALICE

A dedicated gesture, to be sure, celibacy without priesthood . . . but a melancholy one, for you're a handsome man . . . in your way.

JULIAN

You're kind.

MISS ALICE

But, tell me: why did you not become a priest? Having gone so far, I should think . . .

JULIAN

A lay brother serves.

MISS ALICE

. . . but is not ordained, is more a servant.

JULIAN

The house of God is so grand . . . *(Sweet apologetic smile)* it needs many servants.

MISS ALICE

How humble. But is that the only reason?

JULIAN

I am not wholly reconciled. Man's God and mine are not . . . close friends.

MISS ALICE

Indeed. But, tell me, how are you not certain that you have slept with a woman?

JULIAN *(With curiosity)*

Shall I tell you? We have many more important matters. . . .

MISS ALICE

Tell me, please. The money will not run off. Great wealth is patient.

JULIAN

I would not know. Very well. It's good for me, I think, to talk about it. The institution . . . to which I committed myself—it was deep inland, by the way—was a good one, good enough, and had, as I am told most do, sections—buildings, or floors of buildings—for patients in various conditions . . . some for violent cases, for example, others for children. . . .

MISS ALICE

How sad.

JULIAN

Yes. Well, at any rate . . . sections. Mine . . . my section was for people who were . . . mildly troubled—which I found ironic, for I have never considered the fleeing of faith a mild matter. Nonetheless, for the mildly troubled. The windows were not barred; one was allowed utensils, and one's own clothes. You see, escape was not a matter of urgency, for it was a section for mildly troubled people who had committed themselves, and should escape occur, it was not a danger for the world outside.

MISS ALICE

I understand.

JULIAN

There was a period during my stay, however, when I began to . . . hallucinate, and to withdraw, to a point where I was not entirely certain when my mind was tricking me, or when it was not. I believe one would say—how is it said?—that my grasp on reality was . . . tenuous—occasionally. There was, at the same time, in my section, a woman who, on very infrequent occasions, believed that she was the Virgin Mary.

MISS ALICE *(Mild surprise)*

My goodness.

JULIAN

A quiet woman, plain, but soft features, not hard; at forty, or a year either side, married, her husband the owner of a dry-goods store, if my memory is correct; childless . . . the sort of woman, in short, that one is not aware of passing on the street, or in a hallway . . . unlike you—if you will permit me.

MISS ALICE *(Smiles)*

It may be I am . . . noticeable, but almost never identified.

JULIAN

You shun publicity.

MISS ALICE

Oh, indeed. And I have few friends . . . that, too, by choice. *(Urges him on with a gesture)* But please . . .

JULIAN

Of course. My hallucinations . . . were saddening to me. I suspect I should
have been frightened of them—as well as by them—most people are, or
would be . . . by hallucinations. But I was . . . saddened. They were, after
all, provoked, brought on by the departure of my faith, and this in turn was
brought on by the manner in which people mock God. . . .

MISS ALICE

I notice you do not say you lost your faith, but that it abandoned you.

JULIAN

Do I. Perhaps at bottom I had lost it, but I think more that I was confused
. . . *and* intimidated . . . by the world about me, and let slip contact with it
. . . with my faith. So, I was *sad*dened.

MISS ALICE

Yes.

JULIAN

The periods of hallucination would be announced by a ringing in the ears,
which produced, or was accompanied by, a loss of hearing. I would hear
people's voices from a great distance and through the roaring of . . . surf.
And my body would feel light, and not mine, and I would float—no, glide.

MISS ALICE

There was no feeling of terror in this? I would be beside myself.

JULIAN

No, as I said, sadness. Aaaaahhh, I would think, I am going from myself
again. How very, very sad . . . everything. Loss, great loss.

MISS ALICE

I understand.

JULIAN

And when I was away from myself—never far enough, you know, to . . .
blank, just to . . . fog over—when I was away from myself I could not sort
out my imaginings from what was real. Oh, sometimes I would say to a
nurse or one of the attendants, "Could you tell me, did I preach last night?
To the patients? A fire-and-brimstone lesson. Did I do that, or did I imagine it?" And they would tell me, if they knew.

MISS ALICE

And did you?

JULIAN

Hm? . . . No, it would seem I did not . . . to their knowledge. But I was
never sure, you see.

MISS ALICE *(Nodding)*

No.

JULIAN *(A brief, rueful laugh)*

I imagined so many things, or . . did so many things I thought I had imagined. The uncertainty . . . you know?

MISS ALICE *(Smiles)*

Are you sure you're not describing what passes for sanity?

JULIAN *(Laughs briefly, ruefully)*

Perhaps. But one night . . . now, there! You see? I said "one night," and I'm not sure, even now, whether or not this thing happened or, if it did not happen, it did or did not happen at noon, or in the morning, much less at night . . . yet I say night. Doubtless one will do as well as another. So. One *night* the following either happened or did not happen. I was walking in the gardens—or I imagined I was walking in the gardens—walking in the gardens, and I heard a sound . . . sounds from near where a small pool stood, with rosebushes, rather overgrown, a formal garden once, the . . . the place had been an estate, I remember being told. Sounds . . . sobbing? Low cries. And there was, as well, the ringing in my ears, and . . . and fog, a . . . a milkiness, between myself and . . . everything. I went toward the cries, the sounds, and . . . I, I fear my description will become rather . . . vivid now. . . .

MISS ALICE

I am a grown woman.

JULIAN *(Nods)*

Yes. *(A deep breath)* The . . . the woman, the woman I told you about, who hallucinated, herself, that she was the Virgin . . .

MISS ALICE

Yes, yes.

JULIAN

. . . was . . . was on a grassy space by the pool—or this is what I imagined—on the ground, and she was in her . . . a nightdress, a . . . gossamer, filmy thing, or perhaps she was not, but there she was, on the ground, on an incline, a slight incline, and when she saw me—or sensed me there— she raised her head, and put her arms . . . *(Demonstrates)* . . . out, in a . . . supplication, and cried, "Help me, help me . . . help me, oh God, God, help me . . . oh, help, help." This, over and over, and with the sounds in her throat between. I . . . I came closer, and the sounds, her sounds, her words, the roaring in my ears, the gossamer and the milk film, I . . . a ROAR, AN OCEAN! Saliva, perfume, sweat, the taste of blood and rich earth in the mouth, sweet sweaty slipping . . . *(Looks to her apologetically, nods)* . . . ejaculation. *(She nods)* The sound cascading away, the rhythms breaking, everything slowly, limpid, quieter, damper, soft . . . soft, quiet . . . done.

(They are both silent. MISS ALICE *is gripping the arms of her chair;* JULIAN *continues softly)*

I have described it to you, as best I can, as it . . . happened, or did not happen.

MISS ALICE

(Curiously . . . dispassionately)

I . . . am a very beautiful woman.

JULIAN

(After a pause which serves as reply to her statement)

I must tell you more, though. You *have* asked me for an entirety.

MISS ALICE

And a very rich one.

JULIAN *(Brief pause, nods)*

As I mentioned to you, the woman was given to hallucinations as well, but perhaps I should have said that being the Virgin Mary was merely the strongest of her . . . delusions; she . . . hallucinated . . . as well as the next person, about perfectly mundane matters, too. So it may be that now we come to coincidence, or it may not. Shortly—several days—after the encounter I have described to you—the encounter which did or did not happen—the woman . . . I do not know which word to use here, either descended or ascended into an ecstasy, the substance of which was that she was with child . . . that she was pregnant with the Son of God.

MISS ALICE

And I live here, in all these rooms.

JULIAN

You don't laugh? Well, perhaps you will, at *me.* I was . . . beside myself, for I assumed the piling of delusion upon delusion, though the chance of there being fact, happening, there somewhere . . . I went to my . . . doctor and told him of my hallucination—if indeed that is what it was. He told me, then . . . that the woman had been examined, that she was suffering from cancer of the womb, that it was advanced, had spread. In a month, she died.

MISS ALICE

Did you believe it?

JULIAN *(Small smile)*

That she died?

MISS ALICE

That you spoke with your doctor.

JULIAN *(Pause)*

It has never occurred to me until this moment to doubt it. He has informed me many times.

MISS ALICE

Ah?

JULIAN

I *do see* him . . . in reality. We have become friends, we talk from time to time. Socially.

MISS ALICE

Ah. And was it he who discharged you from . . . your asylum?

JULIAN

I was persuaded, eventually, that perhaps I was . . . over-concerned by hallucination; that some was inevitable, and a portion of that—even desirable.

MISS ALICE

Of course.

JULIAN *(Looking at his hands)*

Have I answered your question? That I am not . . . sure that I have slept with a woman.

MISS ALICE

(Puzzling . . . slowly)

I don't . . . know. Is the memory of something having happened the same as it having happened?

JULIAN

It is not the nicest of . . . occurrences—to have described to you.

MISS ALICE *(Kindly)*

It was many years ago. *(Then, an afterthought)* Was it not?

JULIAN

Yes, yes, quite a while ago.

MISS ALICE *(Vaguely amused)*

I am rich and I am beautiful and I live here in all these rooms . . . without relatives, with a . . . *(Wry)* companion, from time to time . . . *(Leans forward, whispers, but still amused)* . . . and with a secret.

JULIAN

Oh? *(Trying to be light, too)* And may I know it? The secret?

MISS ALICE

I don't know yet.

JULIAN *(Relaxing)*

Ah-ha.

MISS ALICE

(Sudden change of mood, to brisk, official, cool)
Well then. You're here on business, not for idle conversation, I believe.

JULIAN

(Confused, even a little hurt)
Oh . . . yes, that's . . . that's right.

MISS ALICE

You have instruction to give me—not formal, I'm not about to settle in your faith. Information, facts, questions and answers.

JULIAN *(Slightly sour)*
Odds and ends, I believe.

MISS ALICE *(Sharp)*
To you, perhaps. But important if you're to succeed, if you're not to queer the whole business, if you're not to . . .

JULIAN

Yes, yes!

MISS ALICE

So you'll be coming back here . . . when I wish to see you.

JULIAN

Yes.

MISS ALICE

Several times. It might be better if you were to move in. I'll decide it.

JULIAN

Oh . . . well, of course, if you think . . .

MISS ALICE

I think. (JULIAN *nods acquiescence*) Very good. *(She rises)* No more today, no more now.

JULIAN

(Up, maybe retreating a little)
Well, if you'll let me know when . . .

MISS ALICE

Come here.
(JULIAN goes to her; she takes his head in her hands, kisses him on the forehead, he registers embarrassment, she laughs, a slightly mocking, unnerving laugh)
Little recluse. *(Laughs again)*

JULIAN

If you'll . . . advise me, or His Eminence, when you'd like me to . . .

MISS ALICE

Little bird, pecking away in the library. *(Laughs again)*

JULIAN

I'm . . . disappointed you find me so . . . humorous.

MISS ALICE

(Cheerful, but not contrite)

Oh, forgive me, I live so alone, the oddest things cheer me up. You . . . cheer me up. *(Holds out her hand to be kissed)* Here. (JULIAN *hesitates)* Ah-ah-ah, he who hesitates loses all.

> (JULIAN *hesitates again, momentarily, then kisses her hand, but kneeling, as he would kiss a Cardinal's ring.* MISS ALICE *laughs at this)*

Do you think I am a Cardinal? Do I look like a Prince? Have you never even kissed a woman's hand?

JULIAN *(Back on his feet, evenly)*

No. I have not.

MISS ALICE *(Kindlier now)*

I'll send for you, we'll have . . . pleasant afternoons, you and I. Goodbye.

> (MISS ALICE *turns away from* JULIAN, *gazes out a window, her back to the audience.* JULIAN *exits. The* LAWYER *enters the set from the bedroom door)*

LAWYER

(To MISS ALICE, *a bit abruptly)*

How did it go, eh?

MISS ALICE

(Turns around, matter-of-factly)

Not badly.

LAWYER

You took long enough.

> (MISS ALICE *shrugs)*

When are you having him again?

MISS ALICE *(Very wickedly)*

On business, or privately?

LAWYER

Don't be childish.

MISS ALICE

Whenever you like, whenever you say. *(Seriously)* Tell me honestly, do you really think we're wise?

LAWYER

Wise? Well, we'll see. If we prove not, I can't think of anything standing in the way that can't be destroyed. *(Pause)* Can you?

MISS ALICE *(Rather sadly)*

No. Nothing.

CURTAIN

ACT TWO

SCENE ONE

(The library—as of Act One, Scene Two. No one on stage. Evening. MISS ALICE *hurtles through the archway, half running, half backing, with the* LAWYER *after her. It is not a chase; she has just broken from him, and her hurtling is the result of sudden freeing)*

MISS ALICE

(Just before and as she is entering; her tone is neither hysterical nor frightened; she is furious and has been mildly hurt)
KEEP . . . GO! GET YOUR . . . LET GO OF ME! *(She is in the room)* KEEP OFF! KEEP OFF ME!

LAWYER

(Excited, ruffled, but trying to maintain decorum)
Don't be hysterical, now.

MISS ALICE

(Still moving away from him, as he comes on)
KEEP . . . AWAY. JUST STAY AWAY FROM ME.

LAWYER

I said don't be hysterical.

MISS ALICE

I'll *show* you hysteria. I'll give you *fireworks!* KEEP! Keep away.

LAWYER

(Soothing, but always moving in on her)
A simple touch, an affectionate hand on you; nothing more . . .

MISS ALICE (*Quiet loathing*)

You're degenerate.

LAWYER (*Steely*)

An affectionate hand, in the privacy of a hallway . . .

MISS ALICE (*Almost a shriek*)

THERE ARE PEOPLE!!

LAWYER

Where? There are no people.

MISS ALICE (*Between her teeth*)

There are people.

LAWYER (*Feigning surprise*)

There are no people. (*To a child*) Ahh! (*Walks toward the model, indicates it*) Unless you mean all the little people running around inside here. Is that what you mean?

MISS ALICE

(*A mirthless, don't-you-know-it laugh*)

Hunh-hunh-hunh-hunh.

LAWYER

Is that who you mean? All the little people in here? (*Change of tone to normal, if sarcastic*) Why don't we show them a few of your tricks, hunh?

MISS ALICE

(*Moving away, clenched teeth again*)

Keep . . . away . . . from . . . me.

LAWYER (*Without affection*)

To love is to possess, and since I desire to possess you, that must mean conversely that I love you, must it not. Come here.

MISS ALICE (*With great force*)

PEOPLE!

LAWYER

Your little priest? Your little Julian? He is not . . .

MISS ALICE

He is not a priest!

LAWYER

No. And he is not nearby—momentarily! (*Hissed*) I am sick of him here day after day, sick of the time you're taking. Will you get it done with!

MISS ALICE

No! He will be *up*.

LAWYER

Oh, for Christ's sake, he's a connoisseur; he'll be nosing around the god-damn wine cellar for hours!

MISS ALICE

He will be *up*. (*Afterthought*) Butler!

LAWYER (*Advancing*)

Butler? Let him watch. (*A sneer*) Which is something I've been meaning to discuss with you for the longest time now. . . .

MISS ALICE

(*Calm, quivering hatred; almost laughing with it*)
I have a loathing for you that I can't des*cribe*.

LAWYER

You were never one with words. (*Suddenly brutal*) NOW COME HERE.

MISS ALICE (*Shrugs*)

All right. I won't react, I promise you.

LAWYER

(*Beginning to fondle her*)
Won't react . . . indeed.
(*During this next,* MISS ALICE *is backed up against something, and the* LAWYER *is calmly at her, kissing her neck, fondling her. She is calm, and at first he seems amused*)

MISS ALICE

What causes this loathing I have for you? It's the *way* you have, I suppose; the clinical way; methodical, slow . . .

LAWYER

. . . thorough . . .

MISS ALICE

. . . uninvolved . . .

LAWYER

. . . oh, very involved . . .

MISS ALICE

. . . impersonality in the most personal things . . .

LAWYER

. . . your passivity is exciting . . .

MISS ALICE

. . . passive only to some people . . . (*He nips her*) OW.

LAWYER

A little passion; good.

MISS ALICE

(*As he continues fondling her; perhaps by the end he has her dress off her shoulders*)

With so much . . . many things to loathe, I must choose carefully, to impress you most with it.

LAWYER

Um-humh.

MISS ALICE

Is it the hair? Is it the hair on your back I loathe most? Where the fat lies, on your shoulderblades, the hair on your back . . . black, ugly? . . .

LAWYER

But too short to get a hold on, eh?

MISS ALICE

Is it that—the back hair? It could be; it would be enough. Is it your . . . what is the polite word for it . . . your sex?

LAWYER (*Mocking*)

Careful now, with a man's pride.

MISS ALICE

Ugly; that too—ugly.

LAWYER (*Unruffled*)

Better than most, if you care for a *man* . . .

MISS ALICE

. . . ugly coarse uncut ragged . . . PUSH!

LAWYER

Push . . . yes . . .

MISS ALICE

. . . selfish, hurtful, ALWAYS! OVER AND OVER!

LAWYER

You like it; it feels good.

MISS ALICE

(*Very calm and analytical*)

But is that what I loathe most? It could be; that would be enough, too.

LAWYER

. . . oh, what a list . . .

MISS ALICE

But I think it is most the feel of your skin . . . *(Hard)* that you can't sweat. *(He stiffens some)* That your body is as impersonal as your . . . self—dry, uncaring, rubbery . . . dead. Ah . . . there . . . that is what I loathe about you most: you're dead. Moving pushing selfish dry dead. *(Brief pause)* Does that hurt? Does something finally, beautifully hurt? *(Self-mocking laugh)* Have I finally gotten . . . into you?

LAWYER

(A little away from her now)

Insensitive, still, aren't you, after all this time. Does it hurt? Does something finally hurt?

MISS ALICE

. . . deep, gouging hurt?

LAWYER

Everything! Everything in the day and night, eating, resting, walking, rutting, everything! Everything *hurts.*

MISS ALICE

Awwwwww.

LAWYER

Inside the . . . sensibility, everything hurts. Deeply.

MISS ALICE *(Ridiculing)*

And is that why I loathe you?

LAWYER *(A quiet, rueful laugh)*

Probably. *(Quickly back to himself)* But you, little playmate, you're what I want now. GIVE!

MISS ALICE

If Julian comes in here . . .

LAWYER *(Shoves her)*

Are you playing it straight, hunh? Or do you like your work a little bit, hunh? *(Again)* Do you enjoy spreading your legs for the clergy? *(Again)* Hunh?

MISS ALICE

STOP! . . . YOU!

LAWYER

Is that our private donation to the Church? Our own grant? YES? *(Begins to hurt her arm)* Are we planning to turn into a charitable, educational foundation?

MISS ALICE (In pain)

My arm!

(BUTLER enters, unnoticed; watches)

LAWYER (Hard and very serious)

Don't you dare mess this thing up. You behave the way I've told you; you PLAY-ACT. You do your part; STRAIGHT.

BUTLER (Calmly)

Brother Julian . . .

MISS ALICE

Butler! Help me!

BUTLER

(As the LAWYER releases her)

. . . has now examined the wine cellar, with awe and much murmuring, and will be with us presently. He's peeing. So I suggest—unless you're doing this for his benefit—uh, you stop.

MISS ALICE

(As she and the LAWYER pull themselves together)

He hurt me, Butler.

BUTLER

(Calmly, as if reminding her)

Often. (To the LAWYER, with mock friendliness) Up to your old tricks, eh?

LAWYER (Dusting himself off)

She is . . . not behaving.

BUTLER (Very noncommittal)

Ah me.

MISS ALICE

(Under her breath, to the LAWYER)

Savage! (Realizes) Both of you!

LAWYER (Laughs)

The maiden in the shark pond.

MISS ALICE

He thinks I'm sleeping with Julian. (To LAWYER) You poor jealous . . .

BUTLER

Are you?

MISS ALICE (Indignant)

No! (Almost sad about it) No, I am not.

LAWYER

She is!

MISS ALICE

I said I am not!

BUTLER

Are you going to?

MISS ALICE

(*After a pause; to* LAWYER)

Am I going to? Am I going to . . . spread my legs for the clergy? Enjoy my work a little? Isn't that what you'd have me do? To not mess it up? To play my part straight? Isn't that what you'll HAVE ME DO?

LAWYER

You don't need urging! . . .

BUTLER

Now, children . . .

MISS ALICE

When the time comes? Won't you have me at him? Like it or not? Well . . . I will like it!

(*A little hard breathing from* MISS ALICE *and the* LAWYER)

BUTLER

Something *should* be done about the wine cellar. I've noticed it—as a passerby would—but Brother Julian pointed out the extent of it to me: bottles have burst, are bursting, corks rotting . . . something to do with the temperature or the dampness. It's a shame, you know.

MISS ALICE (*Surprisingly shrill*)

Well, fix it!

BUTLER (*Ignoring her tone*)

Some great years, popping, dribbling away, going to vinegar under our feet. There is a Mouton Rothschild—one I'm especially fond of— that's . . .

LAWYER (*Pacifying*)

Do. Do . . . fix it.

BUTLER (*Shakes his head*)

Going. All of it. Great shame.

LAWYER

Yes, yes.

BUTLER (*Brightly*)

Nice thing about having Julian here so much . . . he's helpful. Wines, plants

. . . do you know, he told me some astonishing things about ferns. We were
in the solarium . . .

MISS ALICE *(Quiet pleading)*

Please . . . stop.

BUTLER

Oh. Well, it's nice having him about.

LAWYER *(Sour)*

Oh, we'll be a foursome very soon.

MISS ALICE *(Brightly)*

Yes.

LAWYER *(With a mirthless smile)*

Warning.

BUTLER *(Cheerful again)*

It *would* be a great deal more sensible than . . . puttering out here every
day. We could put him over the chapel! Now, that's a splendid idea. He
likes the chapel, he said, not resonant, too small or something, wrong
angles, but he likes it . . .

MISS ALICE

When he moves here . . .

LAWYER

He will move here when I say—and as I say.

MISS ALICE *(Fake smile)*

We shall see.

LAWYER *(Still offhand)*

We shall not see.

JULIAN *(Offstage)*

Halloo!

BUTLER

In . . . in here.

MISS ALICE

(Sotto voce to the LAWYER*)*
You say we shall not see? *Shall* we?

LAWYER *(As above)*

Warning.

*(*JULIAN *enters)*

JULIAN

An! There you all are.

LAWYER

We had wondered where *you* were.

MISS ALICE *(Reminding a child)*

You usually find us here after dinner.

JULIAN

Yes, and a superb dinner.

LAWYER

. . . and then Butler reminded us that you were in the cellar.

JULIAN *(Sincere, but prepared)*

Miss Alice, your . . . home possesses two things that, were I a designer of houses—for the very wealthy, of course—I would put in all my designs.

MISS ALICE *(Smiling)*

And what are they?

LAWYER

(To MISS ALICE, *mildly mocking* JULIAN*)*

Can't you guess?

MISS ALICE *(Charmingly)*

Of course I can guess, but I want Julian to have the pleasure of saying it.

JULIAN

A chapel and a wine cellar.

MISS ALICE

(Agreeing, but is she making light fun?)

Yes.

LAWYER

We hear, though, that the wine cellar is a wreck. And aren't there cobwebs in the chapel, too?

JULIAN

(Light but standing up to him)

One or two spiders have been busy around the altar, and the organ is . . . in need of use . . .

LAWYER *(Very funny to him)*

HUNH!

JULIAN *(Choosing to ignore it)*

. . . but it *is* a chapel, a good one. The wine cellar, however . . . *(Shakes his head)* . . . great, great shame.

BUTLER

Exactly my words.

MISS ALICE

Well, we must have it tended to—and especially since you are our guest so
frequently these days, and enjoy good wines.

JULIAN

I would call someone in, a specialist, if I were you.

LAWYER *(Patronizing)*

Why? Can't you take care of it? Your domain?

JULIAN *(Quietly)*

The chapel, more, I should think.

BUTLER

Where does the Church get its wine . . . for Communion and the like?

JULIAN

Oh, it is grown, *made* . . . grown, the grapes, harvested, pressed . . . by,
by monks.

LAWYER *(False heartiness)*

A regular profit-making setup, the Church.

JULIAN *(Quietly, as usual)*

Self-sustaining . . . in some areas.

LAWYER

But not in others, eh? Sometimes the old beggar bell comes out, doesn't
it? Priest as leper.

MISS ALICE

(Mildly to the LAWYER*)*
It *is* true: you are not fit for God's sight.

BUTLER

(To the LAWYER; *cheerfully interested)*
Is that *so!* I wasn't sure.

LAWYER

(To MISS ALICE, *feigning curiosity and surprise)*
Who whispered it to you?

MISS ALICE

(Indicating JULIAN. *Semi-serious)*
My confessor.

LAWYER *(A Sneer; to* JULIAN*)*

Did you? And so *you* object, as well? To my mention of the Church as
solicitor.

JULIAN

In England I believe *you* would be referred to as solicitor.

LAWYER

No, I would not. And we are not in England . . . are we?

BUTLER

This *place* was . . . in England.

MISS ALICE

    (As if suddenly remembering)
Yes, it was! Every stone, marked and shipped. *(Indicates entire room)*
Well, and a few eccentric additions.

JULIAN

Oh; I had thought it was a replica.

LAWYER

Oh no; that would have been too simple. Though it *is* a replica . . . in its
way.

JULIAN

Of?

LAWYER

    (Pointing to the model)
Of that.
    *(*JULIAN *laughs a little; the* LAWYER *shrugs)*
Ah well.

JULIAN *(To* MISS ALICE*)*

Did your . . . did your father have it . . . put up?

MISS ALICE

That my father put it up? No. Let us not say that.

BUTLER

    (To JULIAN, *pointing first to the model, then to the room)*
Do you mean the model . . . or the replica?

JULIAN

I mean the . . . I mean . . . what we are in.

BUTLER

Ah-ha. And which is that?

JULIAN

That we are in?

BUTLER

Yes.

LAWYER *(To* JULIAN*)*

You are clearly not a Jesuit. *(Turning)* Butler, you've put him in a clumsy trap.

BUTLER *(Shrugging)*

I'm only a servant.

LAWYER

(To JULIAN, *too sweetly)*

You needn't accept his alternative . . . that since we are clearly not in a model we must be in a replica.

BUTLER *(Vaguely annoyed)*

Why must he not accept that?

MISS ALICE

Yes. Why not?

LAWYER

I said he did not *need* to accept it; the problem is only semantic.

BUTLER *(Perhaps too consoling)*

Well, yes; that's what I would have thought.

LAWYER

Not necessarily, though. Depends, doesn't it, on your concept of reality, on the limit of possibilities. . . .

MISS ALICE *(Genuinely put off)*

Oh, Lord!

LAWYER

There are no limits to possibi . . . *(Suddenly embarrassed)* I'm . . . I'm sorry.

MISS ALICE

(To JULIAN, *but at the* LAWYER*)*

He starts in, he *will;* give him the most sophomoric conundrum, and he'll bore you to death.

LAWYER *(Violently)*

I! Will! Not!

JULIAN *(To break the silence)*

Well . . . perhaps I'm at fault here.

MISS ALICE *(Quietly, kindly)*

How could you be? . . . Dear Julian.

LAWYER

(To MISS ALICE; *burning)*

I thought I had educated you; I thought I had drilled you sufficiently in matters of consequence; *(Growing louder)* I thought I had made it clear to you the way you were to behave.

JULIAN

Perhaps I should leave now; I think that . . .

LAWYER

DON'T INTERRUPT ME!

(Glares at JULIAN, *who moves off to the model)*

MISS ALICE

(To the LAWYER; *calmly)*

You forget your place.

LAWYER

(Clearly trying to get hold of himself)

I . . . you . . . are quite right . . . Miss Alice, and abstractions *are* upsetting.

MISS ALICE

(To the LAWYER; *patiently)*

Perhaps you'll go home now.

BUTLER *(Cheerfully)*

Shall I have your car brought around?

LAWYER

(Trying to be private in public)

I . . . I thought that with so much to attend to, I might . . . spend the night. Of course, if you'd rather I didn't . . .

(Leaves it unfinished. MISS ALICE *smiles enigmatically)*

BUTLER

(Pretending to think the remark was for him)

I don't *mind* whether you do or not.

JULIAN

(Peering at the model, rather amazed)

Can it . . . can it be?

LAWYER

In the heat of . . . I, I forgot myself.

MISS ALICE *(Patronizingly sweet)*

Yes.

LAWYER *(Matter-of-fact)*

You will forgive me.

MISS ALICE *(Toying)*

Oh?

BUTLER

Shall I have his car brought around?

LAWYER *(Sudden softening)*

Let me stay.

JULIAN

(Shy attempt at getting attention)

Please . . .

MISS ALICE

(Malicious pleasure in it)

I don't know . . .

JULIAN *(More urgently)*

Please!

LAWYER *(Bitter)*

As you wish, of course.

(Swings his hand back as if to strike her; she flinches)

JULIAN

PLEASE!

BUTLER

(Patiently amused curiosity)

What *is* it, for heaven's sake?

JULIAN *(Pointing to the model)*

The model is . . . on fire; it's on fire!

BUTLER

(Urgent dropping of butlerish attitudes)

Where!

LAWYER

Good Christ!

MISS ALICE

Quick!

(The LAWYER *and* BUTLER *rush to the model)*

BUTLER

Where, for Christ's sake!

JULIAN *(Jostled)*

In the . . . over the . . .

LAWYER

Find it!

BUTLER

(Peering into various windows with great agitation)

It's . . . it's the . . . where the hell is it! . . . It's the . . . chapel! The chapel's burning!

MISS ALICE

Hurry!

BUTLER

Come on! Let's get to it! *(Begins to run out of the room)* Are you coming? Julian!

JULIAN

(Confused, but following)

But I . . . but . . . yes, of course.

(JULIAN and BUTLER run out)

MISS ALICE

(To the LAWYER as he hangs back)

We're burning down! Hurry!

LAWYER

(Comes up to her, grabs her by the wrist, forces her to the ground, keeps hold)

Burning down? Consumed? WHY NOT! Remember what I told you. Watch . . . your . . . step!

(He runs out after the others. MISS ALICE is left alone; maybe we hear one or two diminishing shouts from the others, offstage. Finally, silence. MISS ALICE doesn't rise from the floor, but gradually assumes a more natural position on it)

MISS ALICE

(She alternates between a kind of incantation-prayer and a natural tone)

(Prayer)

Let the fire be put out. Let the chapel be saved; let the fire not spread; let us not be consumed.

(Natural)

He hurt me. My wrist hurts. Who was the boy when I was little hurt my wrist? I don't remember.

(Prayer)

Let the fire not spread; let them be quick.

(Natural)

YOU PIG!

(Softly, almost a whine)

You hurt my wrist.

(Imitates the LAWYER's *tone)*

Watch . . . your . . . step.

(Prayer)

Oh God, I have watched my step. I have . . . trod . . . so carefully.

(Natural and weary)

Let it all come down—let the whole place . . . go.

(She must now, when using a natural tone, almost give the suggestion of talking to someone in the model. Natural)

I don't mean that. I don't remember his name . . . or his face; merely the hurt . . . and that continues, the hurt the same, the name and the face changing, but it doesn't matter. Let them save it.

(Prayer)

Let them save it. Don't . . . destroy. Let them save the resonance.

(Natural)

Increase it. Julian says there is no resonance, that it's not right.

(Prayer)

Let the resonance increase.

(Natural; a little-girl tone)

I have tried very hard to be careful, to obey, to withhold my . . . nature? I have tried so hard to be good, but I'm . . . such a stranger . . . here.

(Prayer)

I have tried to obey what I have not understood, understanding that I must obey. Don't destroy! I have tried! TRIED.

(Natural)

Is that the way about hurt? That *it* does not change . . . but merely its agents?

*(*JULIAN *appears, unseen by* MISS ALICE*)*

(Natural, still)

I will hold on.

(Sweetly, apologetically)

I will try to hold on.

(Prayer)

I will try to hold on!

(Natural)

Please, please . . . if you *do* . . . be generous and gentle with me, or . . . just gentle.

JULIAN *(Softly, a little sadly)*

I don't understand anything. The chapel was in flames.

MISS ALICE

Yes.

JULIAN

. . . and yet . . . I saw the fire here in the model . . . and yet . . . the real chapel was in flames. We put it out. And now the fire here is out as well.

MISS ALICE

(Preceded by a brief, hysterical laugh)

. . . yes.

JULIAN

(Underneath the wonder, some fear)

I don't understand.

MISS ALICE

(She is shivering a little)

It's very hard. Is the chapel saved?

JULIAN

(His attention on the model)

Hm? Oh, yes . . . partially, mostly. The . . . the boards, floorboards, around the altar were . . . gave way, were burned through. The altar . . . sank, some, angled down into the burned-through floor. Marble.

MISS ALICE *(Almost a whisper)*

But the fire is out.

JULIAN

Yes. Out. The spiders, burned to a crisp, I should say, curled-up, burned balls. *(Asking the same question)* I . . . I don't understand.

MISS ALICE

(Vaguely to the model)

It is all well. We are not . . . consumed.

JULIAN

Miss Alice? Why, why did it happen that way—in both dimensions?

MISS ALICE

(Her arms out to him)

Help me.

(JULIAN *goes to her, lifts her by the arms; they stand, at arm's length, holding hands, facing each other*)

JULIAN

Will you . . . tell me anything?

MISS ALICE

(*A helpless laugh, though sad*)
I don't know anything.

JULIAN

But you were . . . (*Stops*)

MISS ALICE (*Pleading*)

I don't *know* anything.

JULIAN (*Gently, to placate*)

Very well.

MISS ALICE

(*Coming closer to him*)
Come stay.

JULIAN

Miss Alice?

MISS ALICE

Come stay here. It will . . . be easier. For you.

JULIAN (*Concern, not anger*)

Did he hurt you?

MISS ALICE

Easier than going back and forth. And for me, too.

JULIAN

Did he?

MISS ALICE

(*After a pause and a sad smile*)
Some. You're shivering, Julian.

JULIAN

No, Miss Alice, it is *you* . . . you are shivering.

MISS ALICE

The Cardinal will agree to it.

JULIAN

(*Looking toward the model*)
Yes, I . . . suppose so.

MISS ALICE

Are you frightened, Julian?

JULIAN

Why, no, I . . . I *am* shivering, am I not?

MISS ALICE

Yes.

JULIAN

But I am not . . . yes, I suppose I am . . . frightened.

MISS ALICE

Of what, Julian?

JULIAN

(Looks toward the model again)
But there is . . . *(Back)* . . . of what.

MISS ALICE

Yes.

JULIAN *(Knowing there is)*
Is there anything to be frightened of, Miss Alice?

MISS ALICE *(After a long pause)*
Always.

CURTAIN

SCENE TWO

(The library—as of Act One, Scene Two. The BUTLER *is on stage. The* LAWYER *enters immediately, angry, impatient)*

LAWYER

Well, where are they today?

BUTLER *(Calm, uninvolved)*
Hm? Who?

LAWYER

WHERE IS SHE! Where is she off to now?

BUTLER

Miss Alice? Well, I don't really know. *(Thinks about it)* You look around?

LAWYER

They're not here.

BUTLER

You don't think they've eloped, do you?

LAWYER

Do you know!

BUTLER

They're moving together nicely; the fire in the chapel helped, I thought, though maybe it was intended to . . . brought them closer.

LAWYER

Where are they!

BUTLER

They spend so much time together now; everything on schedule.

LAWYER

Where have they gone!

BUTLER

I don't *know;* really. Out walking? In the gardens? Driving somewhere? Picnicking, maybe? Cold chicken, cheese, a Montrachet under an elm? I don't *know* where they are.

LAWYER

Don't you watch them?

BUTLER

Keep one eye peeled? Can't she take care of herself? She knows her business. *(Pause; then, quietly meaningful)* Doesn't she. *(No answer)* Doesn't she.

LAWYER

You should watch them. We don't want . . . error. She *is* . . .

BUTLER

Human? Yes, and clever, too . . . isn't she. *Good* at it, wrapping around fingers, enticing. I recall.

LAWYER

Too human; not playing it straight.

BUTLER

Enjoying her work a little? They're not sleeping together yet.

LAWYER

NO! NOT YET!

BUTLER *(A quiet warning)*

Well, it won't bother you when they do . . . will it.

LAWYER *(Matter-of-factly)*

I, too: human.

BUTLER

Human, but dedicated.

LAWYER *(Quiet, sick loathing)*

He doesn't deserve her.

BUTLER *(Kindly)*

Well, he'll not have her long.

LAWYER *(Weary)*

No; not long.

BUTLER

On . . . and on . . . we go.

LAWYER *(Sad)*

Yes.

BUTLER *(Too offhand, maybe)*

I've noticed, you've let your feelings loose lately; too much: possessiveness, jealousy.

LAWYER

I'm *sorry.*

BUTLER

You used to be so good.

LAWYER

I'm SORRY!

BUTLER

It's all right; just watch it.

LAWYER

Attrition: the toll time takes.

BUTLER

I watch you carefully—you, too—and it's the oddest thing: you're a cruel person, straight through; it's not cover; you're hard and cold, saved by dedication; just that.

LAWYER *(Soft sarcasm)*

Thank you.

BUTLER

You're welcome, but what's happened is you're acting like the man you wish you were.

LAWYER

Yes?

BUTLER

Feeling things you can't feel. Why don't you mourn for what you are? There's lament enough there.

LAWYER *(A sad discovery)*

I've never liked you.

BUTLER *(A little sad, too)*

I don't mind. We get along. The three of us.

LAWYER

She's *using* Julian! To humiliate me.

BUTLER *(Nodding)*

Of course. Humiliate; not hurt. Well, let her do her job the way she wants; she'll lead him, bring him around to it.

LAWYER

But she *cares* for him.

BUTLER

Of course; human, a woman. Cares, but it won't get in the way. Let her use what she can. It will be done. Don't you think it's time you went to see His Holiness again?

LAWYER

Eminence, not Holiness. You think it's time I went again? Yes; well, it *is* time. You come, too.

BUTLER *(Mildly taunting)*

But shouldn't I stay here . . . to watch? To fill you in on the goings-on? To let you be the last to know?

LAWYER

YOU COME! To back me up, when I want emphasis.

BUTLER

In the sense that my father used the word? Wants emphasis: lacks emphasis?

LAWYER

No. The touch of the proletarian: your simplicity, guilelessness . . .

BUTLER

Aw . . .

LAWYER

His Eminence is a pompous ass.

BUTLER

Stupid? I doubt *that*.

LAWYER

Not stupid; an ass.

BUTLER

Cardinals aren't stupid; takes brains to get there; no jokes in the Church.

LAWYER

Pompous!

BUTLER

Well, in front of you, maybe. Maybe has to wear a face; you're not easy. What will you tell him?

LAWYER

What will I tell him? Tell me.

BUTLER

All right. You play Cardinal, I'll play you.

LAWYER

(Goes into it eagerly; with a laugh)

Ah, two of you. We are doubly honored. Will you not sit?

BUTLER

Really? Like that?

LAWYER

And how is our Brother Julian faring . . . in the world of the moneyed and the powerful?

BUTLER

No. Really?

LAWYER

Really! And can we be of service to you, further service?

BUTLER

Maybe.

LAWYER

Maybe? Ah?

BUTLER

Yes, your Brother Julian is going to be taken from you.

LAWYER

Our Brother Julian? Taken? From us?

BUTLER

Come on, Your Eminence.

LAWYER

This is a . . . preposterous . . . We . . . we don't understand you.

BUTLER

Isn't the grant enough? Isn't a billion a year for twenty years enough? For one man? He's not even a priest.

LAWYER *(As the* CARDINAL*)*

A man's soul, Sir! *(Himself)* Not his soul, mustn't say that to him.

BUTLER *(Musing)*

Shall we be dishonest? Well, then, I suppose you'll have to tell him more. Tell him the whole thing.

LAWYER *(Himself)*

I will like that. It will blanch his goddamn robes . . . turn 'em white.

BUTLER *(Chuckles)*

Nice when you can enjoy your work, isn't it? Tell him that Julian is leaving him. That Julian has found what he's after. *(Walks to the model, indicates it.)* And I suppose you'd better tell him about . . . this, too.

LAWYER

The wonders of the world?

BUTLER

I think he'd better know . . . about this.

LAWYER

Shatter.

BUTLER

And, you know what I think would be a lovely touch?

LAWYER

(A quiet smile that is also a grimace)

Tell me.

BUTLER

How eager you are. I think it would be a lovely touch were the Cardinal to marry them, to perform the wedding, to marry Julian to . . .

LAWYER

Alice.

BUTLER

Miss Alice.

LAWYER

Alice!

BUTLER

Have him marry them.

LAWYER *(Smiles a little)*

It would be nice.

BUTLER

I thought so.

LAWYER

But *shall* we tell him the whole thing? The Cardinal? What is happening?

BUTLER

How much can he take?

LAWYER

He is a man of God, however much he simplifies.

BUTLER

Like everyone.

LAWYER

Like most.

BUTLER

Julian can't stand that; he told me so: men make God in their own image, he said. Those six years I told you about.

LAWYER

Yes. When he went into an asylum. YES.

BUTLER

It was—because he could not stand it, wasn't it? The use men put God to.

LAWYER

It's perfect; wonderful.

BUTLER

Could not reconcile.

LAWYER

No.

BUTLER

God as older brother, scout leader, couldn't take that.

LAWYER

And still not reconciled.

BUTLER

Has pardoned men, I think. Is walking on the edge of an abyss, but is balancing. Can be pushed . . . over, back to the asylums.

LAWYER

Or over . . . to the Truth *(Addressing* JULIAN, *as if he were there; some thunder in the voice)* God, Julian? Yes? God? *Whose* God? Have you pardoned men their blasphemy, Julian? Have you forgiven them?

BUTLER

(Quiet echoing answers; being JULIAN*)*
No, I have not, have not really; have *let* them, but cannot accept.

LAWYER

Have not forgiven. No, Julian. Could you ever?

BUTLER *(Ibid.)*

It is their comfort; my agony.

LAWYER

Soft God? The servant? Gingerbread God with the raisin eyes?

BUTLER *(Ibid.)*

I cannot accept it.

LAWYER

Then don't accept it, Julian.

BUTLER

But there is *some*thing. There is a *true* God.

LAWYER

There is an abstraction, Julian, but it cannot be understood. You cannot worship it.

BUTLER *(Ibid.)*

There is more.

LAWYER

There is Alice, Julian. That can be understood. Only the mouse in the model. Just that.

BUTLER *(Ibid.)*

There must be more.

LAWYER

The mouse. Believe it. Don't personify the abstraction, Julian, limit it, demean it. Only the mouse, the toy. And that does not exist . . . but is all that can be worshiped . . . Cut off from it, Julian, ease yourself, ease off. No trouble now; accept it.

BUTLER

(Talking to JULIAN *now)*
Accept it, Julian; ease off. Worship it . . .

LAWYER

Accept it.

BUTLER

(After a pause; normal again)

Poor, poor Julian.

LAWYER *(Normal, too)*

He can make it.

BUTLER

I hope he can.

LAWYER

If not? *(Shrugs) Out* with him.

BUTLER *(Pause)*

You cannot tell the Cardinal . . . that.

LAWYER *(Weary)*

The benefits to the Church.

BUTLER

Not simply that.

LAWYER

And a man's soul. If it be saved . . . what matter how?

BUTLER

Then we'd best go to him.

LAWYER

Yes.

BUTLER

Leave Julian to Miss Alice; he is in good hands.

LAWYER *(Quiet, sick rage rising)*

But his hands . . . on her.

BUTLER *(Soothing)*

Temporary . . . temporal. You'll have her back.

LAWYER *(Rises)*

All right.

BUTLER

Let's go.

LAWYER

(Walks to the model, addresses it; quietly, but forcefully; no sar-casm)

Rest easy; you'll have him . . . Hum; purr; breathe; rest. You will have your Julian. Wait for him. He will be yours.

CURTAIN

SCENE THREE

(MISS ALICE's *sitting room, as of Act One, Scene Three.* JULIAN *is on stage, near the fireplace, carries a riding crop; the door to the bedroom is ajar)*

JULIAN
(After a moment; over his shoulder)
It was fun, Miss Alice; it was fun.

MISS ALICE
(From behind the door)
What, Julian?

JULIAN *(Turns)*
It was . . . I enjoyed it; very much.

MISS ALICE
(Her head appearing from behind the door)
Enjoyed what?

JULIAN
Riding; it was . . . exhilarating.

MISS ALICE
I would never have thought you rode. You were good. *(Disappears)*

JULIAN
(A small, self-deprecating laugh)
Oh. Yes. When I was young—a child—I knew a family who . . . kept horses, as a pastime, not as a business. They were moneyed—well, had *some*. It was one of their sons who was my playmate . . . and we would ride.

MISS ALICE
(Still behind the door)
Yes.

JULIAN
You remember, you know how seriously children talk, the cabalas we have . . . had. My friend and I would take two hunters, and we would go off for hours, and talk ourselves into quite a state—mutually mesmerizing, almost an hysteria. We would forget the time, and bring the animals back quite lathered. *(Laughs)* We would be scolded—no: cursed *out*—by one groom

or another; usually by a great dark Welshman—a young fellow who always scowled and had—I remember it clearly, for I found it remarkable—the hairiest hands I have ever seen, with hair—and this is what I found most remarkable—tufts of coarse black hair on his thumbs. (*Looks at his own thumbs*) Not down, or a few hairs, which many of us have, but tufts. This Welshman.

MISS ALICE

(*Head appearing again*)
D. H. Lawrence.

JULIAN

Pardon?

MISS ALICE

(*Appearing, wearing a black negligee with great sleeves*)
"Love on the Farm." Don't you know it?
(*Circles him as she recites it; mock-stalks him*)
"I hear his hand on the latch, and rise from my chair
Watching the door open . . .
He flings the rabbit soft on the table board
And comes toward me: he! the uplifted sword
Of his hand against my bosom! . . .
. . . With his hand he turns my face to him
And caresses me with his fingers that still smell grim
Of rabbit's fur! . . .
And down his mouth comes on my mouth! and down
His bright dark eyes over me . . .
. . . his lips meet mine, and a flood
Of sweet fire sweeps across me, so I drown
Against him, die and find death good!"
(*Cocks her head, smiles*)
No?

JULIAN (*Embarrassed*)
That was . . . not quite my reaction.

MISS ALICE

(*A great, crystal laugh*)
No! Silly Julian! No. (*Conspiratorial*) That was a verse I knew at school, that I memorized. "And down his mouth comes on my mouth." Oh! That would excite us so . . . at school; things like that. (*Normal tone; a shrug, a smile*) Early eroticism; mental sex play.

JULIAN (*Still embarrassed*)
Yes.

MISS ALICE

I've embarrassed you!

JULIAN

No! No!

MISS ALICE

Poor Julian; I have. And you were telling me about horseback riding.

JULIAN

No, I was telling you about the groom, as far as that goes. And I suppose .
. . yes, I suppose . . . those thumbs were . . . erotic for *me*—at that time, if
you think about it; mental sex play. Unconscious.

MISS ALICE

(Sweetly, to divert him)
It *was* fun riding. *Today.*

JULIAN

Yes!

MISS ALICE

I am fond of hair—man's body hair, except that on the back. *(Very offhand)*
Are you hairy, Julian?

JULIAN

I . . . my chest is rather nice, but my arms are . . . surprisingly hairless.

MISS ALICE

And you have no back hair.

JULIAN

Well . . . do you really wish to know?

MISS ALICE *(With a laugh)*

Yes!

JULIAN *(Nods in acquiescence)*
I have no . . . back hair, in the usual sense—of the shoulders . . .
    (MISS ALICE nods)
. . . but there is hair, at the small of the back . . . rising.

MISS ALICE

Yes, yes, well, *that* is nice. *(Laughs, points to the crop)* You're carrying the
crop. Are you still in the saddle?

JULIAN

(Laughing; shyly brandishing the crop)
Are you one of Mr. Lawrence's ladies? Do you like the smell of saddle
soap, and shall I take my crop to you?

MISS ALICE

(Briefest pause; testing)
Would you?

JULIAN *(Half-hearted laugh)*
MISS ALICE!

MISS ALICE
Nobody does things naturally any more—so few people have the grace. A
man takes a whip to you—a loving whip, you understand—and you *know,*
deep and sadly, that it's imitation—literary, seen. *(Intentionally too much)*
No one has the natural graces any more.

JULIAN

(Putting the crop down; quietly)
I have . . . not whipped . . .

MISS ALICE
But surely you have.

JULIAN *(An apology)*
I do not recall.

MISS ALICE *(Expansive)*
Oh, my Julian! How many layers! Yes?

JULIAN
We . . . simplify our life . . . as we grow older.

MISS ALICE *(Teasing him)*
But from understanding and acceptance; not from . . . emptying ourselves.

JULIAN
There are many ways.

MISS ALICE *(Showing her outfit)*
Do you like this?

JULIAN
It is most . . . becoming.

MISS ALICE *(Giggles)*
We're dressed quite alike.

JULIAN *(He, too)*
But the effect is not the same.

MISS ALICE
No. It is easier for you living here . . . isn't it?

JULIAN
It's . . . more than a person could want—or *should* want, which is something we must discuss.

MISS ALICE
(Sensing a coming disappointment)

Oh . . .

JULIAN

Really.

MISS ALICE *(Not pleasantly)*

What do we do wrong?

JULIAN

One of the sins is gluttony . . .

MISS ALICE

Are you getting a belly?

JULIAN
(Smiles, but won't be put off)

. . . and it has many faces—or many bellies, if you wish. It's a common-place that we can have too much of things, and I have too much . . . of comfort, of surroundings, of ease, of kindness . . . of happiness. I am filled to bursting.

MISS ALICE *(Hard)*

I think perhaps you misunderstand why you're here. You're *not* here to . . . to indulge yourself, to . . .

JULIAN *(Tight-lipped)*

I'm aware of that.

MISS ALICE

. . . to . . . to ease in. You're here in service to your *Church*.

JULIAN

I've not lost sight of my function.

MISS ALICE

I wonder!

JULIAN *(Really quite angry)*

And *I* wonder! What's being *done* to me. Am I . . . am I being temp—test-ed in some fashion?

MISS ALICE *(Jumping on it)*

Tempted?

JULIAN

Tested in some fashion?

MISS ALICE

TEMPTED?

JULIAN

BOTH! Tested! What! My . . . my sincerity, my . . . my other cheek? You have allowed that . . . that *man,* your . . . your lover, to . . . ridicule me. You have per*mit*ted it.

MISS ALICE

I? Permit?

JULIAN

You have allowed him to abuse me, my position, his, the Church; you have tolerated it, and *smiled.*

MISS ALICE

Tolerate!

JULIAN

And smiled. WHY AM I BEING TESTED! . . . And why am I being tempted? By luxury, by ease, by . . . content . . . by things I do not care to discuss.

MISS ALICE *(Unsympathetic)*

You're answerable to your own temptations.

JULIAN

Yes?

MISS ALICE

(Singsong and patronizing)
Or God is.
    *(*JULIAN *snorts)*
No? God is not? Is not answerable?

JULIAN

Knows. But is not answerable. I.

MISS ALICE *(Softening some)*

Then *be* answerable.

JULIAN

To my temptations, I am. *(To himself more than to her)* It would be so easy to . . . fall in, to . . . accept these surroundings. Oh, life would speed by!

MISS ALICE

With all the ridicule?

JULIAN

That aside.

MISS ALICE

You *have* a friend here . . . as they put it.

JULIAN (*Smiles*)

Butler. Yes; he's nice.

MISS ALICE (*A little laugh*)

I meant me.

JULIAN

Well, of *course*. . . .

MISS ALICE

Or, do you think of me otherwise? Do *I* tempt you?

JULIAN

You, Miss Alice?

MISS ALICE

Or, is it merely the fact of temptation that upsets you so?

JULIAN

I have longed . . . to be of great service. When I was young—and very prideful—I was filled with a self-importance that was . . . well disguised. Serve. That was the active word: I would serve! (*Clenches his fist*) I would serve, and damn anyone or anything that stood in my way. I would shout my humility from the roof and break whatever rules impeded my headlong rush toward obedience. I suspect that had I joined the Trappist order, where silence is the law, I would have chattered about it endlessly. I was impatient with God's agents, and with God, too, I see it now. A . . . novice porter, ripping suitcases from patrons' hands, cursing those who preferred to carry some small parcel for their own. And I was blind to my pride, and intolerant of any who did not see me as the humblest of men.

MISS ALICE (*A little malice*)

You phrase it so; I suspect you've said it before.

JULIAN

Doubtless I have. Articulate men often carry set paragraphs.

MISS ALICE

Pride still.

JULIAN

Some.

MISS ALICE

And how did your ambition sit?

JULIAN

Ambition? Was it?

(MISS ALICE *displays a knee casually;* JULIAN *jumps*)

What are you doing!

MISS ALICE *(Vague flirting)*

I'm . . . sorry.

JULIAN

Well. Ambition, yes, I suppose—ambition to be nothing, to be least. Most obedient, humblest. How did it sit? For some, patiently, but not well. For me? Even less well. But I . . . learned.

MISS ALICE

To . . . subside. Is that the simplification you mentioned before? Of your life. To subside . . . and vanish; to leave no memory.

JULIAN

No; I wish to leave a . . . memory—of work, of things done. I've told you; I wish to be of great service, to move great events; but when it's all time for crediting, I'd like someone to say no more than "Ah, wasn't there someone involved in this, who brought it all about? A priest? Ah-*ha*, a *lay* brother—was that it." *(Smiles)* Like that. The memory of someone who helped.

MISS ALICE

(Pauses, then laughs)

You're lying!

JULIAN

I?

(Then they both laugh, like conspiratorial children)

MISS ALICE

Every monster was a man first, Julian; every dictator was a colonel who vowed to retire once the revolution was done; it's so easy to postpone elections, little brother.

JULIAN

The history of the Church . . .

MISS ALICE

The history of the Church shows half its saints were martyrs, martyred either for the Church, or by it. The chronology is jammed with death-seekers and hysterics: the bloodbath to immortality, Julian. Joan was only one of the suicides.

JULIAN

(Quivering with intensity)

I WISH TO SERVE AND . . . BE FORGOTTEN.

MISS ALICE

(Comes over, strokes his cheek)

Perhaps you will, Julian.

(He takes her hand, kisses it, puts it back on his cheek)
Yes?

JULIAN *(Guiltily)*
I wish to be of service. *(A little giggle)* I do.

MISS ALICE
And be forgotten.

JULIAN
Yes.

MISS ALICE *(Stroking his head)*
Not even remembered a little? By some? As a gentle man, gentle Julian . . .

JULIAN
Per . . . perhaps.

MISS ALICE
. . . my little lay brother and expert on wines; my little horseback rider and
crop switcher . . .

JULIAN *(As she ruffles his hair)*
Don't . . . do that.

MISS ALICE *(Ruffles harder)*
My little whipper, and RAPIST?

JULIAN *(Rising, moving away)*
DON'T!

MISS ALICE *(Pouting, advancing)*
Julian . . .

JULIAN
No, now; no.

MISS ALICE *(Still pouting)*
Julian, come kiss me.

JULIAN
Please!

MISS ALICE *(Singsong)*
Come kiss.

JULIAN *(A plea)*
Miss Alice . . . Just . . . let me do my service, and let me go.

MISS ALICE
(Abruptly to business; not curt, though)
But you're doing great service. Not many people have been put in the position you've been graced by—not many. Who knows—had some lesser man
than you come, some bishop, all dried and salted, clacketing phrases from

memory, or . . . one of those insinuating super-salesmen your Church uses, had one of them come . . . who knows? Perhaps the whole deal would have gone out the window.

JULIAN

Surely, Miss Alice, you haven't been playing games with . . . so monumental a matter.

MISS ALICE

The rich are said to be quixotic, the very wealthy cruel, overbearing; who is to say—might not vast wealth, the insulation of it, make one quite mad? Games? Oh, no, my little Julian, there are no games played here; this is for keeps, and in dead earnest. There *are* cruelties, for the insulation breeds a strange kind of voyeurism; and there is impatience, too, over the need to accomplish what should not be explained; and, at the end of it, a madness of sorts . . . but a triumph.

JULIAN *(Hands apart)*

Use me, then . . . for the triumph.

MISS ALICE

(Moving on him again)

You are *being* used, my little Julian. *I* am being used . . . my little Julian. You want to be . . . employed, do you not? Sacrificed, even?

JULIAN

I have . . . there are no secrets from you, Miss Alice . . . I have . . . dreamed of sacrifice.

MISS ALICE

(She touches his neck)

Tell me.

JULIAN

You mustn't do . . . it is not wise . . .

MISS ALICE

Tell me.

(She will circle him, touch him occasionally, kiss the back of his neck once during the next speech)

JULIAN

Still my pride . . . a vestige of it.

(He becomes quite by himself during this; unaware of her)

Oh, when I was still a child, and read of the Romans, how they used the saints as playthings—enraged children gutting their teddy bears, dashing the head of their doll against the bedpost, I could . . . I could entrance myself, and see the gladiator on me, his trident fork against my neck, and hear, even hear, as much as feel, the prongs as they entered me; the . . . the beast's saliva dripping from the yellow teeth, the slack sides of the mouth, the . . . sweet, warm breath of the lion; great paws on my spread arms . . . even the rough leather of the pads; and to the point of . . . as the great mouth opened, the breath no longer warm but hot, the fangs on my jaw and forehead, positioned . . . IN. And as the fangs sank in, the great tongue on my cheek and eye, the splitting of the bone, and the *blood* . . . just before the great sound, the coming dark and the silence. I could . . . experience it all. And was . . . engulfed. (*A brief laugh, but not breaking the trance*) Oh, martyrdom. To be that. To be able . . . to be that.

MISS ALICE

(*Softly, into his ear; he does not hear it*)
Marry me, Julian.

JULIAN

The . . . death of the saints . . . was always the beginning of their lives. To go bloodstained and worthy . . . upward. I could feel the blood on my robes as I went; the smell of the blood, as intense as paint . . . and warm . . . and painless.

MISS ALICE

Marry me.

JULIAN

"Here. I have come. You see my robes? They're red, are they not? Warm? And are not the folds caught together . . . as the blood coagulates? The . . . fingers of my left hand—of both!—are . . . are hard to move apart, as the blood holds finger to finger. And there is a wound in me, the warm dark flow . . . runs down my belly . . . to . . . bathing my groin. You see? I have come . . . bloodstained and worthy."

MISS ALICE

Marry me.

JULIAN (*Still self-tranced*)

Bathed . . . my groin. And as the thumbs of the gladiator pressed . . . against . . . my neck, I . . . as the lion's belly pressed on my chest, I . . . as the . . . I . . . or as the woman sank . . . on the mossy hillock by the roses, and the roar is the crunching growl is the moan is the sweat-breathing is the . . .

MISS ALICE

(*Behind him, her arms around his neck, on his chest*)
. . . sweat-breathing on the mossy hillock and the white mist in the perfumes . . .

JULIAN

. . . fumes . . . lying . . . on the moss hill in the white filmy gladiator's belly

pressing on the chest fanged and the soft hard tongue and the *blood* . . .
ENTERS . . . *(Lurches from the chair)* . . . STOP! . . . THAT!

MISS ALICE

(Coming at him slowly)
Come to Alice, Julian, in your sacrifice . . .

JULIAN

(Moving away, but helpless)
Stay . . . away . . . stay.

MISS ALICE
. . . give yourself to her, Julian . . .

JULIAN
. . . a . . . away . . .

MISS ALICE *(Sweetly singsong)*
Come marry Alice, she wants you so; she says she wants you so, come give
yourself to Alice; oh, Alice needs you and your sacrifice . . .

JULIAN
. . . no . . . no . . .

MISS ALICE
. . . Alice says she wants you, come to Alice, Alice tells me so, she wants
you, come to Alice . . .

JULIAN
. . . no . . . sacrifice . . .

MISS ALICE
Alice tells me so, instructs me, come to her.
   (MISS ALICE *has her back to the audience,* JULIAN *facing her, but at
   a distance; she takes her gown and, spreading her arms slowly,
   opens the gown wide; it is the unfurling of great wings)*

JULIAN
(Shaking, staring at her body)
. . . and . . . sacrifice . . . on the altar of . . .

MISS ALICE
Come . . . come . . .

JULIAN
. . . the . . . Lord . . . God . . in . . . . Heaven . . .

MISS ALICE
Come . . .

(JULIAN *utters a sort of dying cry and moves, his arms in front of him, to* MISS ALICE; *when he reaches her, she enfolds him in her great wings*)

MISS ALICE (*Soothing*)
You will be hers; you will sacrifice yourself to her . . .

JULIAN (*Muffled*)
Oh my God in heaven . . .

MISS ALICE
(*Her head going back, calling out*)
Alice! . . . Alice? . . .

JULIAN
(*Slowly kneeling within the great wings*)
. . . in . . . my . . . sacrifice . . .

MISS ALICE (*Still calling out*)
He will be yours! He will be yours! AAAAALLLLLIIIIICCCCCEEEEE!

CURTAIN

ACT THREE

(The library, as of Act One, Scene Two. No one on stage. After a moment or so, BUTLER *enters, carrying what looks to be a pile of gray sheets. They are clearly quite heavy. He sets them down on a table, straightens his shoulders from the effort, looks at various chairs, turns to counting the pile.* JULIAN *enters, at more than a casual pace, dressed in a suit)*

JULIAN

Butler!

BUTLER

(Deliberate pause; then)
. . . four . . . five . . . six . . . *(Pretending suddenly to see* JULIAN*)* Oh! Hello there.

JULIAN

Where . . . I . . . I feel quite *lost*.

BUTLER *(No comment)*

Why?

JULIAN *(Agitation underneath)*

Well, uh . . . I will confess I haven't participated in . . . been married before, but . . . I can't imagine it's usual for everyone to disap*pear*.

BUTLER

Has everyone?

JULIAN

Yes! *(Quieter)* Yes, I . . . per—perhaps His Eminence is occupied, or has *business*—that's it!—has business with . . . but—but why *she* should . . . There I was . . . one moment married, flooded with white, and . . . then . . . the next, alone. Quite alone, in the . . . echoes.

BUTLER

There is an echo, sometimes, all through it, down every long hall, up in the huge beams . . .

JULIAN

But to be left alone!

BUTLER

Aren't you used to that?

JULIAN

Suddenly!

BUTLER *(Sad smile)*

Like a little boy? When the closet door swings shut after him? Locking him in the dark?

JULIAN

Hm? Yes . . . yes, like that. *(Shudders a little)* Terrifying.

BUTLER

And it's always remote, an attic closet, where one should not have been, where no one can hear, and is not likely to come . . . for a very long time.

JULIAN *(Asking him to stop)*

Yes!

BUTLER

(To the sheets again, counting them)

We learn so early . . . are *told,* where not to go, the things we should not do. And there's often a reason.

JULIAN

And *she* vanished as well.

BUTLER

Who?

JULIAN

My . . . my wife.

BUTLER

And who is that?

JULIAN

(As if BUTLER *had forgotten everything)*

Miss Alice!

BUTLER

Ah. Really?

JULIAN

Butler, you saw the wedding!

BUTLER *(Puzzles it a moment)*

Quite so; I did. We . . . Well. Perhaps Miss Alice is changing.

JULIAN

She *must* be; of course. But . . . for everyone to . . . vanish, as if I'd turned my back for a *moment,* and an hour elapsed, or a . . . dimension had . . .

BUTLER *(Passing it over)*

Yes, a dimension—well, that happens.

JULIAN *(Still preoccupied)*

Yes, she must be . . . upstairs. What . . . what are you doing?

BUTLER

What?

JULIAN

What are those?

BUTLER

These? *(Looks at them)* Uh . . . sheets, or covers, more accurately.

JULIAN

(Still quite nervous, staying away)

What are they for?

BUTLER

To . . . cover.

JULIAN *(Ibid.)*

Cover *what!*

BUTLER

Oh . . . nothing; no matter. Housework, that's all. One of my labors.

JULIAN

I . . . I would have thought you'd have champagne . . . ready, that you'd be busy with the party. . . .

BUTLER

One does *many* things. You'll have your champagne, sir, never fear.

JULIAN

I'm sorry; I . . . I was so upset.

BUTLER

Yes.

JULIAN *(Attempting a joke)*

After all, I've not been married before.

BUTLER

No.

JULIAN

And the procedures are a little . . . well, you know.

BUTLER

Yes.

JULIAN

. . . still . . .

BUTLER

Yes.

JULIAN

It all *does* seem odd.

BUTLER

Marriage is a confusing business.

JULIAN

Have . . . have you been . . . married?

(BUTLER *gives a noncommittal laugh as answer*)

I . . . I don't know if marriage is, but certainly the circumstances surrounding this *wedding* are rather . . .

BUTLER (*A fairly chilling smile*)

Special people, special problems.

JULIAN (*Hurt*)

Oh. Well . . . yes.

BUTLER (*Disdainful curiosity*)

Do you . . . *feel* married?

JULIAN (*Withdrawn*)

Not having been, I cannot say. (*Pause*) Can I?

BUTLER

(*Takes one of the sheets, opens it with a cracking sound, holds it in front of him, a hand on each shoulder*)

No. (*Puts it to one side*) I suppose not.

JULIAN

No. I wonder if . . . I wonder if you could go upstairs, perhaps, and see if Miss Alice . . . my *wife* . . . is . . .

BUTLER

No. (*Then, rather stern*) I have much too much work to do. (*Cheerful*) I'll get you some champagne, though.

JULIAN (*Rather removed*)

No, I'll . . . wait for the others, if they haven't all . . . disappeared.

BUTLER *(Noncommittal)*
To leave you alone with your bride, on your wedding night? No; not yet.

JULIAN
(For something to say, as much as anything, yet hopeful of an answer, or an explanation)
Miss Alice . . . chose not to invite . . . friends . . . to the ceremony.

BUTLER *(Chuckle)*
Ah, no. Alice . . . *Miss* Alice does not have friends; admirers, yes. Worshipers . . . but not buddies.

JULIAN *(Puzzled)*
I asked her why she had not, and she replied . . .

BUTLER *(Improvising)*
. . . it is you, Julian, who are being married . . . ?

JULIAN
(Too self-absorbed to be surprised)
Yes; something like that.

BUTLER
Your wife is . . . something of a recluse.

JULIAN *(Hopeful)*
But so outgoing!

BUTLER
Yes? Well, then; you will indeed have fun. *(Mock instructions)* Uncover the chandeliers in the ballroom! Lay on some footmen! Unplug the fountains! Trim the maze!

JULIAN *(More or less to himself)*
She *must* have friends . . . *(Unsure)* must she not?

BUTLER *(Stage whisper)*
I don't know; no one has ever asked her.

JULIAN *(Laughing nervously)*
Oh, indeed!

(MISS ALICE comes hurriedly into the room; she has on a suit. She sees only BUTLER first)

MISS ALICE
Butler! Have you seen . . . ? *(Sees JULIAN)* Oh, I'm . . . sorry. *(She begins to leave)*

JULIAN

There you are. No, wait; wait!

(But MISS ALICE *has left the room. In need of help)*

I find everything today puzzling.

BUTLER *(About to give advice)*

Look . . . *(Thinks better of it)*

JULIAN

Yes?

BUTLER

When you're locked in the attic, Julian, in the attic closet, in the dark, do you care who comes?

JULIAN

No. But . . .

BUTLER *(Starts to leave)*

Let me get the champagne.

JULIAN

Please!

BUTLER

So that we all can toast.

(As BUTLER *leaves, the* CARDINAL *enters)*

Ah! Here comes the Church.

JULIAN

(Going to the CARDINAL, *kneeling before him, kissing his ring, holding the ring hand afterward, staying kneeling)*

Your Eminence.

CARDINAL

Julian. Our dear Julian.

BUTLER

Have you caught the bride?

CARDINAL

No. No. Not seen her since the . . . since we married her.

JULIAN

It was good of you. I suspect she will be here soon. Butler, would you . . . go see? If she will come here? His Eminence would . . . Now do be good and go.

*(*BUTLER *exits)*

He has been a great help. At times when my service has . . . perplexed me, till I grew despondent, and wondered if perhaps you'd not been mistaken in putting such a burden . . .

CARDINAL

(Not wanting to get into it)
Yes, yes, Julian. We have *resolved* it.

JULIAN

But then I judge it is God's doing, this . . . wrenching of my life from one light to another . . .

CARDINAL

. . . Julian . . .

JULIAN

. . . though not losing God's light, joining it with . . . my new. *(He is like a bubbling little boy)* I can't tell you, the . . . radiance, humming, and the witchcraft, I think it must be, the ecstasy of this light, as *God's* exactly; the transport the same, the lifting, the . . . the sense of service, and the EXPANSION . . .

CARDINAL

. . . Julian . . .

JULIAN

. . . the blessed wonder of service with a renewing, not an ending joy—that joy I thought possible only through martyrdom, now, now the sunlight is no longer the hope for glare and choking in the dust and plummeting, but with cool and green and yellow dappled . . . perfumes . . .

CARDINAL *(Sharply)*

Julian!

JULIAN *(Little-boy smile)*

Sir.

CARDINAL

(Evading JULIAN's *eyes)*
We sign the papers today, Julian. It's all arranged, the grant is accomplished; through your marriage . . . your service.

JULIAN *(Puzzlement)*

Father?

CARDINAL

(Barely keeping pleasure in his voice)
And isn't it wonderful: that you have . . . found yourself such great service and such . . . exceeding happiness, too; that God's way has brought such gifts to his servant, and to his servant's servant as well.

JULIAN *(Puzzled)*

Thank you . . . Your Eminence.

CARDINAL *(Sadly)*

It is your wedding day, Julian!

JULIAN

(Smiles, throws off his mood)

Yes, it is! It's my wedding day. And a day of glory to God, that His Church has been blessed with great wealth, for the suffering of the world, conversion and the pronouncement of His Glory.

CARDINAL

(Embarrassed; perfunctory)

Praise God.

JULIAN

That God has seen fit to let me be His instrument in this undertaking, that God . . .

CARDINAL

Julian. *(Pause)* As you have accepted what has happened . . . removed, so far removed from . . . any thought . . . accept what . . . *will* happen, *may* happen, with the same humility and . . .

JULIAN *(Happily)*

It is my service.

CARDINAL *(Nods)*

Accept what may come . . . as God's will.

JULIAN

Don't . . . don't frighten me. Bless me, Father.

CARDINAL *(Embarrassed)*

Julian, please . . .

JULIAN

(On his knees before the CARDINAL)

Bless me?

CARDINAL

(Reluctantly; appropriate gestures)

In the name of the Father and of the Son and the Holy Ghost . . .

JULIAN

. . . Amen . . .

CARDINAL

. . . Amen. You *have* . . . confessed, Julian?

JULIAN

(Blushing, but childishly pleased)

I . . . I have, Father; I have . . . confessed, and finally, to sins more real than imagined, but . . . but they are not sins, are they, in God's name, done in God's name, Father?

CARDINAL

May the presence of our Lord, Jesus Christ be with you always . . .

JULIAN

. . . to . . . to shield my eyes from too much light, that I may be always worthy . . .

CARDINAL

. . . to light your way for you in the darkness . . .

JULIAN

. . . dark, darkness, Father? . . .

CARDINAL

. . . that you may be worthy of whatever sacrifice, unto death itself . . .

JULIAN

. . . in all this light! . . .

CARDINAL

. . . is asked of you; that you may accept what you do not understand . . .

JULIAN *(A mild argument)*

But, Father . . .

CARDINAL

. . . and that the Lord may have mercy on your soul . . . as, indeed, may He have on us all . . . all our souls.

JULIAN

. . . A . . . Amen?

CARDINAL *(Nodding)*

Amen.

LAWYER *(Entering)*

Well, well. Your Eminence. Julian. Well, you are indeed a fortunate man, today. What more cheering sight can there be than Frank Fearnought, clean-living, healthy farm lad, come from the heartland of the country, from the asylums—you see, I know—in search of fame, and true love— never fortune, of course.

JULIAN

. . . Please . . .

LAWYER

And see what has happened to brave and handsome Frank: he has found what he sought . . . true . . . love; *and* fortune—to his surprise, for wealth had never crossed his pure mind; and fame? . . . Oooooh, there will be a private fame, perhaps.

CARDINAL

Very pretty.

LAWYER

And we are dressed in city ways, too, are we not? No longer the simple gown of the farm lad, the hems trailing in the dung; no; now we are in city clothes . . . banker's clothes.

JULIAN

These are proper clothes.

LAWYER

As you will discover, poor priestlet, poor former priestlet. Dressed differently for the sacrifice, eh?

JULIAN

I . . . think I'll . . . look for Miss . . . for my wife.

LAWYER

Do.

CARDINAL

Oh, yes, Julian; please.

JULIAN

(Kneels, kisses the ring again)
Your Eminence. *(To the* LAWYER, *mildly)* We are both far too old . . . are we not . . . for all that?
*(*JULIAN *exits)*

CARDINAL *(After* JULIAN *leaves)*
Is cruelty a lesson you learned at your mother's knee? One of the songs you were taught?

LAWYER

One learns by growing, as they say. I have fine instructors behind me . . . yourself amongst them. *(A dismissing gesture)* We have no time. *(Raises his briefcase, then throws it on a table)* All here. *(Great cheerfulness)* Twenty billion, kid. Twenty years of grace for no work at all; no labor . . . at least not yours.

CARDINAL

We do not . . . fetch and carry.

LAWYER

Not God's errand boy?

CARDINAL

God's; not yours.

LAWYER

Who are the gods? *(Normal tone again)* I must say, your Church lawyers are picky men.

CARDINAL

Thorough.

LAWYER

Picky. Humorless on small matters, great wits on the major ones; ribald over the whole proposition.

CARDINAL *(Mumbling)*

. . . hardly a subject for ribaldry . . .

LAWYER

Oh, quite a dowry, greatest marriage settlement in history, *mother* church indeed . . . things like that.

CARDINAL *(Unhappily)*

Well, it's all over now . . .

LAWYER

Almost.

CARDINAL

Yes.

LAWYER

Cheer up; the price was high enough.

CARDINAL

Then it is . . . really true? About . . . *this?* *(Points at the model)*

LAWYER

I haven't time to lie to you.

CARDINAL

Really . . . true.

LAWYER

(Moving to the model)

Really. Can't you accept the wonders of the world? Why not of this one, as well as the other?

CARDINAL

We should be . . . getting on.

LAWYER

Yes. *(Points to a place in the model)* Since the wedding was . . . *here* . . . and we are *(Indicates the room they are in)* here . . . we have come quite a . . . dimension, have we not?

(The LAWYER *moves away from the model to a table, as the* CARDINAL *stays at the model)*

CARDINAL *(Abstracted)*

Yes. A distance.

(Turns, sees the LAWYER *open a drawer, take out a pistol and check its cartridges)*

What . . . what are you doing? *(Moves toward the* LAWYER, *slowly)*

LAWYER

House pistol.

CARDINAL

But what are you doing?

LAWYER

(Looking it over carefully)

I've never shot one of these things . . . pistols. *(Then, to answer)* I'm looking at it . . . to be sure the cartridges are there, to see that it is oiled, or whatever is done to it . . . to see how it functions.

CARDINAL

But . . .

LAWYER *(Calmly)*

You know we may have to shoot him; you know that may be necessary.

CARDINAL *(Sadly and softly)*

Dear God, no.

LAWYER *(Looking at the gun)*

I suppose all you do is . . . pull. *(Looks at the* CARDINAL) If the great machinery threatens . . . to come to a halt . . . the great axis on which all turns . . . if it needs oil . . . well, we lubricate it, do we not? And if blood is the only oil handy . . . what is a little blood?

CARDINAL *(False bravura)*

But that will not be necessary. *(Great empty, quiet loss)* Dear God, let that not be necessary.

LAWYER

Better off dead, perhaps. You know? Eh?

CARDINAL

The making of a martyr? A saint?

LAWYER
Well, let's make that saint when we come to him.

CARDINAL
Dear God, let that not be necessary.

LAWYER
Why not? Give me *any* person . . . a martyr, if you wish . . . a saint . . . He'll take what he gets for . . . what he wishes it to be. AH, it is what I have always wanted, he'll say, looking terror and betrayal straight in the eye. Why not: face the inevitable and call it what you have always wanted. How to come out on top, going under.
(JULIAN *enters*)

LAWYER
Ah! There you are. Still not with Miss Alice!

JULIAN
I seem not to be with anyone.

LAWYER (*Smile*)
Isn't that odd?

JULIAN
(*Turning away, more to himself*)
I would have thought it so.

CARDINAL
(*Hearty, but ill at ease*)
One would have thought to have it all now—corks popping, glasses splintering in the fireplace . . .

LAWYER
When Christ told Peter—so legends tell—that he would found his church upon that rock, He must have had in mind an island in a sea of wine. How firm a foundation in the vintage years . . .
(*We hear voices from without; they do, too*)

MISS ALICE (*Offstage*)
I don't *want* to go in there . . .

BUTLER (*Offstage*)
You *have* to come in, now . . .

MISS ALICE (*Offstage*)
I won't go *in* there . . .

BUTLER (*Offstage*)
Come along now; don't be a child . . .

MISS ALICE (*Offstage*)

I . . . won't . . . go. . .

(BUTLER *appears; two champagne bottles in one hand, pulling* MISS ALICE *with the other*)

BUTLER

Come along!

MISS ALICE

(*As she enters; sotto voce*)

I don't want to . . .

(*As she sees the others see her, she stops talking, smiles, tries to save the entrance*)

BUTLER

Lurking in the gallery, talking to the ancestral wall, but I found her.

MISS ALICE

Don't be silly; I was . . . (*Shrugs*)

BUTLER (*Shrugs, too*)

Suit yourself. Champagne, everybody!

JULIAN

Ah! Good. (*Moving toward* MISS ALICE) Are you all right?

MISS ALICE

(*Moves away from him; rather impatiently*)

Yes.

CARDINAL

But you've changed your clothes, and your wedding gown was . . .

MISS ALICE

. . . two hundred years old . . .

LAWYER

. . . fragile.

CARDINAL

Ah!

(*Something of a silence falls. The other characters are away from* JULIAN; *unless otherwise specified, they will keep a distance, surrounding him, but more than at arm's length. They will observe him, rather clinically, and while this shift of attitude must be subtle, it must also be evident.* JULIAN *will grow to knowledge of it, will aid us, though we will be aware of it before he is*)

JULIAN (*To break the silence*)

Well, shall we have the champagne?

BUTLER

Stay there! *(Pause)* I'll bring it.

CARDINAL

Once, when we were in France, we toured the champagne country . . .

LAWYER *(No interest)*

Really.

CARDINAL

Saw the . . . mechanics, so to speak, of how it was done. . . .

LAWYER

Peasants? Treading?

CARDINAL *(Laughs)*

No, no. That is for woodcuts.

    (The cork pops)

Ah!

BUTLER

Nobody move! I'll bring it to you all.

    (Starts pouring into glasses already placed to the side)

MISS ALICE *(To the LAWYER)*

The ceremony.

    (He does not reply)

The ceremony!

LAWYER *(Overly sweet smile)*

Yes. *(To them all)* The ceremony.

CARDINAL

Another? Must we officiate?

LAWYER

No need.

JULIAN *(A little apprehensive)*

What . . . ceremony is this?

BUTLER *(His back to them)*

There's never as much in a champagne bottle as I expect there to be; I never learn. Or, perhaps the glasses are larger than they seem.

LAWYER *(Ironic)*

When the lights go on all over the world . . . the true world. The ceremony of Alice.

JULIAN *(To* MISS ALICE*)*

What is this about?

(She nods toward the LAWYER*)*

LAWYER

Butler? Are you poured?

BUTLER

(Finishing; squeezing the bottle)

Yeeeeesssss . . .

LAWYER

Pass.

BUTLER

(Starts passing the tray of glasses)

Miss Alice.

MISS ALICE *(Strained)*

Thank you.

BUTLER

(Starts toward JULIAN, *changes his mind, goes to the* CARDINAL*)*

Your Eminence?

CARDINAL

Ahhh.

BUTLER

(Starts toward JULIAN *again, changes his mind goes to the* LAWYER*)*

Sweetheart?

LAWYER

Thank you.

BUTLER

(Finally goes to JULIAN, *holds the tray at arm's length; speaks, not unkindly)*

Our Brother Julian.

JULIAN *(Shy friendliness)*

Thank you, Butler.

LAWYER

And now . . .

BUTLER

(Moving back to the table with the tray)

Hold on; I haven't got mine yet. It's over here.

JULIAN

Yes! Butler must drink with us. (*To* MISS ALICE) Don't you think so?

MISS ALICE (*Curiously weary*)

Why not? He's family.

LAWYER

(*Moving toward the model*)

Yes; what a large family you have.

(*The* LAWYER *would naturally have to pass near* JULIAN; *pauses, detours*)

JULIAN

I'm sorry; am . . . am I in your way?

LAWYER

(*Continues to the model*)

Large family, years of adding. The ceremony, children. The ceremony of Alice.

(*The others have turned, are facing the model. The* LAWYER *raises his glass*)

To Julian and his bride.

CARDINAL

Hear, hear.

JULIAN (*Blushing*)

Oh, my goodness.

LAWYER

To Julian and his bride; to Alice's wisdom, wealth and whatever.

BUTLER (*Quietly, seriously*)

To Alice.

MISS ALICE

To Alice.

(*Brief pause; only* JULIAN *turns his head, is about to speak, but*)

LAWYER

To their marriage. To their binding together, acceptance and worship . . . received; accepted.

BUTLER

To Alice.

LAWYER

To the marriage vow between them, which has brought joy to them both, and great benefit to the Church.

CARDINAL

Amen.

MISS ALICE

To Alice.

(Again only JULIAN *responds to this; a half turn of the head)*

LAWYER

To their house.

BUTLER, MISS ALICE and CARDINAL

(Not quite together)

To their house.

JULIAN *(After them)*

To their house.

LAWYER

To the chapel wherein they were bound in wedlock.

(A light goes on in a room in the model. JULIAN *makes sounds of amazement; the others are silent)*

To their quarters.

(Light goes on upstairs in the model)

To the private rooms where marriage lives.

BUTLER

To Alice.

MISS ALICE

To Alice.

(To which JULIAN *does not respond this time)*

LAWYER

And to this room . . .

(Another light goes on in the model)

in which they are met, in which we are met . . . to celebrate their coming together.

BUTLER

Amen.

LAWYER

A union whose spiritual values shall be uppermost . . .

MISS ALICE

That's enough. . . .

LAWYER

. . . whose carnal side shall . . .

MISS ALICE

That's enough!

JULIAN

May . . . May I?

(*It is important that he stay facing the model, not* MISS ALICE. BUT-
LER, *who is behind him, may look at him; the* CARDINAL *will look
to the floor*)

May I . . . propose. To the wonders . . . which may befall a man . . . least
where he is looking, least that he would have thought; to the clear plan of
that which we call chance, to what we see as accident till our humility
returns to us when we are faced with the mysteries. To all that which we
really want, until our guile and pride . . .

CARDINAL

(*Still looking at the floor*)
. . . Julian . . .

JULIAN

. . . betray us? (*Looks at the* CARDINAL; *pauses, goes on, smiling sweetly*)
My gratitude . . . my wonder . . . and my love.

LAWYER (*Pause*)

Amen?

JULIAN

Amen.

LAWYER (*Abruptly turning*)

Then, if we're packed, let us go.

BUTLER (*Not moving*)

Dust covers.

JULIAN (*Still smiling*)

Go?

MISS ALICE

I am packed.

JULIAN (*Still off by himself*)

Packed? . . . Miss Alice?

MISS ALICE

(*To the* LAWYER; *cold*)
May we leave soon?

JULIAN

Miss . . . Alice?

MISS ALICE

May we?

LAWYER *(Pause)*

Fairly.

JULIAN *(Sharp)*

Miss Alice!

MISS ALICE

(Turns toward him; flat tone; a recitation)
I'm very happy for you, Julian, you've done well.

JULIAN

(Backing away from everyone a little)
What is . . . going on . . . here? *(To* MISS ALICE*)* Tell me!

MISS ALICE

(As if she is not interested)
I am packed. We are going.

JULIAN *(Sudden understanding)*
Ah! *(Points to himself)* We are going. But where? You . . . didn't tell me we
. . . we were . . .

MISS ALICE

(To the LAWYER*, moving away)*
Tell him.

JULIAN

. . . going somewhere. . . .

MISS ALICE *(Quite furious)*

Tell him!

LAWYER

(About to make a speech)
Brother Julian . . .

JULIAN *(Strained)*

I am no longer Brother.

LAWYER *(Oily)*

Oh, are we not all brothers?

JULIAN

(To MISS ALICE*; with a half-hearted gesture)*
Come stand by me.

MISS ALICE

(Surprisingly little-girl fright)

No!

LAWYER

Now. Julian.

CARDINAL

Order yourself, Julian.

JULIAN *(To the* CARDINAL*)*

Sir?

LAWYER

(Sarcasm is gone; all is gone, save fact)

Dear Julian; we all serve, do we not? Each of us his own priesthood; publicly, some, others . . . within only; but we all do—what's-his-name's special trumpet, or clear lonely bell. Predestination, fate, the will of God, accident . . . All swirled up in it, no matter what the name. And being man, we have invented choice, and have, indeed, gone further, and have catalogued the underpinnings of choice. But we do not know. Anything. End prologue.

MISS ALICE

Tell him.

LAWYER

No matter. We are leaving you now, Julian; going. We are leaving you . . . to your accomplishment: your marriage, your wife, your . . . special priesthood.

JULIAN

(Apprehension and great suspicion)

I . . . don't know what you're talking about.

LAWYER *(Unperturbed)*

What is so amazing is the . . . coming together . . . of disparates . . . left-fielding, out of the most unlikely. Who would have thought, Julian? Who would have thought? You have brought us to the end of our service here. We go on; you stay.

BUTLER

May I begin to cover?

MISS ALICE

Not yet. *(Kindly)* Do you understand, Julian?

JULIAN *(Barely in control)*

Of course not!

MISS ALICE

Julian, I have tried to be . . . *her.* No; I have tried to be . . . what I thought
she might, what might make you happy, what you might use, as a . . . what?

BUTLER

Play God; go on.

MISS ALICE

We must . . . represent, draw pictures, reduce or enlarge to . . . to what we
can understand.

JULIAN *(Sad, mild)*

But I have fought against it . . . all my life. When they said, "Bring the
wonders down to me, closer; I cannot see them, touch; nor can I believe."
I have fought against it . . . all my life.

BUTLER *(To* MISS ALICE; *softly)*

You see? No good.

MISS ALICE *(Shrugs)*

I have done what I can with it.

JULIAN

All my life. In and out of . . . confinement, fought against the symbol.

MISS ALICE

Then you should be happy now.

CARDINAL

Julian, it has been your desire always to serve; your sense of mission . . .

LAWYER

We are surrogates; *our* task is done now.

MISS ALICE

Stay with her.

JULIAN

(Horror behind it; disbelieving)

Stay . . . with . . . her?

MISS ALICE

Stay with her. Accept it.

LAWYER *(At the model)*

Her rooms are lighted. It is warm, there is enough.

MISS ALICE

Be content with it. Stay with her.

JULIAN

(Refusing to accept what he is hearing)

Miss Alice . . . I have married *you.*

MISS ALICE *(Kind, still)*

No, Julian; you have married *her* . . . through me.

JULIAN

(Pointing to the model)

There is nothing there! We are *here!* There is no one *there!*

LAWYER

She is there . . . we believe.

JULIAN *(To* MISS ALICE*)*

I have *been* with *you!*

MISS ALICE

(Not explaining; sort of dreamy)

You have felt her warmth through me, touched her lips through my lips, held hands, through mine, my breasts, hers, lain on her bed, through mine, wrapped yourself in her wings, your hands on the small of her back, your mouth on her hair, the voice in your ear, hers not mine, all hers; her. You are hers.

CARDINAL

Accept.

BUTLER

Accept.

LAWYER

Accept.

JULIAN

THERE IS NO ONE THERE!

MISS ALICE

She is there.

JULIAN

(Rushes to the model, shouts at it)

THERE IS NOTHING THERE! *(Turns to them all)* THERE IS NOTH-ING THERE!

CARDINAL *(Softly)*

Accept it, Julian.

JULIAN *(All the power he has)*

ACCEPT IT!

LAWYER *(Quietly)*

All legal, all accomplished, all satisfied, that which we believe.

JULIAN

ACCEPT!

BUTLER

. . . that which is done, and may not be revoked.

CARDINAL *(With some difficulty)*

. . . yes.

JULIAN

WHAT AM I TO ACCEPT!

LAWYER

An act of faith.

JULIAN *(Slow, incredulous)*

An . . . act . . . of . . . faith!

LAWYER

(Snaps his fingers at the cardinal)
Buddy?

CARDINAL

An act of faith, Julian, however we must . . .

JULIAN *(Horror)*

FAITH!?

CARDINAL

. . . in God's will . . .

JULIAN

GOD'S! WILL!

CARDINAL

(Moving toward him a little)
Julian . . .

JULIAN

Stay back! I have not come this long way . . . have not—in all sweet obedience—walked in these . . . *(Realizes he is differently dressed)* those robes . . . to be MOCKED.

LAWYER

Accept it, Julian.

JULIAN

I have not come this long *way!*

BUTLER

Yes; oh, yes.

JULIAN

I HAVE NOT!

MISS ALICE

Julian . . . dear Julian; accept.

JULIAN

(Turns toward her, supplicating)

I have not worn and given up for . . . for mockery; I have not stretched out
the path of my life before me, to walk on straight, to be . . .

MISS ALICE

Accept.

JULIAN

I have not fought the nightmares—and the waking demons, yes—and the
years of despair, those, too . . . I have not accepted *half,* for *nothing.*

CARDINAL

For everything.

MISS ALICE

Dear Julian; accept. Allow us all to rest.

JULIAN

(A child's terror of being alone)

NO!

MISS ALICE *(Still kind)*

You must.

BUTLER

No choice.

JULIAN

I have . . . have . . . given up everything to gain everything, for the sake of
my faith and my peace; I have allowed and followed, and sworn and cher-
ished, but I have *not,* have *not* . . .

MISS ALICE

Be with her. Please.

JULIAN

For halluci*nation?* I HAVE DONE WITH HALLUCINATION.

MISS ALICE

Then have done with forgery, Julian; accept what's real.

JULIAN *(Retreating)*

No . . . no no no, oh no.

LAWYER *(Quietly)*

All legal, all accomplished, all satisfied, that which we believe.

MISS ALICE

All done.

JULIAN *(Quite frightened)*

I . . . choose . . . *not.*

CARDINAL

There is no choice here, Julian. . . .

LAWYER

No choice at all.

MISS ALICE *(Hands apart)*

All done.

>   (JULIAN *begins backing toward the model; the* LAWYER *begins crossing to the desk wherein he has put the gun)*

BUTLER *(Quietly)*

I *must* cover now; the cars are waiting.

JULIAN

No . . . no . . . I WILL NOT ACCEPT THIS.

LAWYER

>   *(Snaps for the* CARDINAL *again)*

Buddy . . .

CARDINAL

We . . . *(Harder tone)* I *order* you.

LAWYER *(Smile)*

There. Now will you accept?

JULIAN

I . . . cannot be so mistaken, to have . . . I cannot have so misunderstood my life; I cannot have . . . was I sane *then?* Those *years?* My time in the *asylum?* WAS THAT WHEN I WAS RATIONAL? THEN?

CARDINAL

Julian . . .

LAWYER

>   *(Taking the gun from the drawer, checking it; to the* CARDINAL*)*

Don't you teach your people anything? Do you let them improvise? *Make* their Gods? *Make* them as they *see* them?

JULIAN *(Rage in the terror)*

I HAVE ACCEPTED GOD.

LAWYER

>   *(Turns to* JULIAN, *gun in hand)*

Then accept his works. Resign yourself to the mysteries . . .

MISS ALICE

. . . to greater wisdom.

LAWYER

Take it! Accept what you're given.

MISS ALICE

Your priesthood, Julian—full, at last. Stay with her. Accept your service.

JULIAN

I . . . cannot . . . accept . . . this.

LAWYER *(Aims)*

Very well, then.

JULIAN

I have not come this . . . given up so much for . . .

BUTLER

Accept it, Julian.

MISS ALICE

Stay with her.

JULIAN

No, no, I will . . . I will go *back!* I will . . . go *back* to it. *(Starts backing toward the stairs)* To . . . to . . . I will go back to the asylum.

LAWYER

Last chance.

MISS ALICE

Accept it, Julian.

JULIAN

To . . . my asylum. MY! ASYLUM! My . . . my refuge . . . in the world, from all the demons waking, my . . . REFUGE!

LAWYER

Very well then.
   (Shoots. Then silence. JULIAN *does not cry out, but clutches his belly, stumbles forward a few steps, sinks to the floor in front of the model)*

MISS ALICE

   (Softly, with compassion)
Oh, Julian. *(To the* LAWYER; *calm)* He would have stayed.

LAWYER

   (To MISS ALICE, *shrugging)*
It was an accident.

JULIAN

Fa . . . ther?

MISS ALICE

Poor Julian. (*To the* LAWYER) You did not have to do that; I could have made him stay.

LAWYER

Perhaps. But what does it matter . . . one man . . . in the face of so much.

JULIAN

Fa . . . ther?

BUTLER (*Going to* JULIAN)

Let me look.

MISS ALICE

(*Starting to go to him*)

Oh, poor Julian . . .

LAWYER (*Stopping her*)

Stay where you are.

(BUTLER *goes to* JULIAN *while the others keep their places.* BUTLER *bends over him, maybe pulling his head back*)

BUTLER

Do you want a doctor for him?

LAWYER (*After a tiny pause*)

Why?

BUTLER (*Straightening up*)

Because . . .

LAWYER

Yes?

BUTLER (*Quite matter-of-fact*)

Because he will bleed to death without attention?

JULIAN (*To the* CARDINAL)

Help . . . me?

(*In answer, the* CARDINAL *looks back to the* LAWYER, *asking a question with his silence*)

LAWYER (*After a pause*)

No doctor.

BUTLER (*Moving away*)

No doctor.

MISS ALICE

(*To the* LAWYER; *great sadness*)

No?

LAWYER *(Some compassion)*

No.

JULIAN

Father!

CARDINAL *(Anguished)*

Please, Julian.

JULIAN

(Anger through the pain)
In the sight of God? You dare?

LAWYER

Or in the sight of man. He dares. *(Moves to the table, putting the gun away, taking up the briefcase)*

JULIAN *(Again)*

You dare!?

(BUTLER goes to cover something)
(Weak again) Father? *(Pain)* God in heaven!

CARDINAL

(Hand out) Julian . . .

MISS ALICE

Poor Julian!

(Goes to him; they create something of a Pietà)
Rest back; lean on me.

LAWYER

You *will* go on, won't you—red gown and amethyst, until the pelvic cancer comes, or the coronary blacks it out, all of it? The good with it, and the evil? *(Indicates JULIAN)* Even this? In the final mercy?

(The CARDINAL looks straight ahead of him for a moment, hesitates, then walks out, looking neither left nor right)

BUTLER

(Calling after him, half-hearted and intentionally too late)
Any of the cars will do . . . *(Trailing off)* . . . as they're all hired.

JULIAN

Who . . . who left? Who!

MISS ALICE *(Comforting him)*
You're shivering, Julian . . . *so.*

JULIAN *(Almost a laugh)*

Am I?

MISS ALICE (*To* JULIAN)

A blanket?

JULIAN

No. Hold close.

MISS ALICE (*Ibid.*)

I don't want to hurt.

JULIAN

Closer . . . please. Warmth.

MISS ALICE (*Ibid.*)

How like a little boy you are.

JULIAN

I'm lonely.

MISS ALICE

Is being afraid always the same—no matter the circumstances, the age?

JULIAN

It is the attic room, always; the closet. Hold close. . . . and it is very dark; always. And no one will come . . . for the longest time.

MISS ALICE

Yes.

JULIAN

No. No one will come. No one will come . . . for the longest time; if ever.

MISS ALICE (*Agreeing*)

No.

LAWYER

(*To* MISS ALICE, *immediately*)

Are you ready to go?

MISS ALICE

(*Looking up; sad irony*)

Am I ready to go on with it, do you mean? To move to the city now before the train trip south? The private car? The house on the ocean, the . . . same mysteries, the evasions, the perfect plotting? The removed residence, the Rolls twice weekly into the shopping strip . . . all of it?

LAWYER

Yes. All of it.

MISS ALICE

(*Looks to* JULIAN, *considers a moment*)

Are you warm now?

JULIAN

Yes . . . and cold.

MISS ALICE

(Looks up to the LAWYER, *smiles faintly)*
No.

LAWYER

Get up and come along.

MISS ALICE *(To the* LAWYER)
And all the rest of it?

LAWYER

Yes.

MISS ALICE

The years of it . . . to go on? For how long?

LAWYER

Until we are replaced.

MISS ALICE

(With a tiny, tinkling laugh)
Oh God.

LAWYER

Or until everything is desert *(Shrugs)* . . . on the chance that *it* runs out
before *we* do.

BUTLER

(Examining the phrenological head)
I have never even examined phrenology.

LAWYER

But more likely till we are replaced.

JULIAN

(With a sort of quiet wonder)
I am cold at the core . . . where it burns most.

MISS ALICE *(Sad truth)*
Yes. *(Then to the* LAWYER) Yes.

LAWYER *(Almost affectionately)*
Gather yourself.

MISS ALICE *(Restrained pleading)*
But, he is still . . . ill . . .

JULIAN

(To MISS ALICE, *probably, but not at her)*
You wish to go away now?

MISS ALICE *(To the* LAWYER*)*
You see how he takes to me? You see how it *is* natural? Poor Julian.

LAWYER

Let's go.

MISS ALICE *(To* BUTLER*)*
Butler, I have left my wig, it is upstairs . . .

BUTLER *(Rather testy)*
I'm sorry, I'm covering, I'm busy.

LAWYER *(Turning to go)*
Let me; it's such a pretty wig, becomes you so. And there are one or two
other things I'd like to check.

MISS ALICE *(Sad smile)*
The pillowcases? Put your ear against them? To eavesdrop? Or the sheets?
To see if they're still writhing?
   (The LAWYER *almost says something, thinks better of it, exits)*
Poor Julian.

BUTLER

Then we all are to be together.

MISS ALICE *(Small laugh)*
Oh God, you heard him: forever.

BUTLER

I like it where it's warm.

MISS ALICE

I dreaded once, when I was in my teens, that I would grow old, look back,
over the precipice, and discover that I had not lived my life. *(Short abrupt
laugh)* Oh Lord!

JULIAN

(Now a semi-coma, almost sweet)
How long wilt thou forget me, O Lord? Forever?

BUTLER

We live *some*thing.

MISS ALICE

Yes.

JULIAN

How long wilt thou hide thy face from me?

BUTLER *(To* JULIAN*)*

Psalm Thirteen.

MISS ALICE *(To* JULIAN*)*

Yes?

JULIAN

Yes.

BUTLER

How long shall my enemy be exalted over me?

JULIAN

Yes.

MISS ALICE

Not long.

BUTLER *(Looking at a cover)*

Consider and hear me, O Lord, my God.

JULIAN

What does it mean if the pain . . . ebbs?

BUTLER *(Considered; kindly)*

It means the agony is less.

MISS ALICE

Yes.

JULIAN *(Rueful laugh)*

Consciousness, then, is pain. *(Looks up at* MISS ALICE*)* All disappointments, all treacheries. *(Ironic laugh)* Oh, God.

BUTLER

For ages, *I* look at the sheets, listen to the pillowcases, when they're brought down, sidle into the laundry room . . .

MISS ALICE

Don't.

    (JULIAN *makes a sound of great pain)*

Oh! . . .Oh! . . .

JULIAN

    (Commenting on the pain)

Dear . . . God . . . in . . . heaven . . .

MISS ALICE

Calm; be calm now.

BUTLER *(Wistful)*

But you pass through everyone, everything . . . touching just briefly, lightly, passing.

MISS ALICE

My poor Julian. *(To the model)* Receive him? Take him in?

JULIAN *(A little boy, scared)*

Who are you talking to?

MISS ALICE *(Breathing it)*

Alice . . .

JULIAN

Alice? Ah.

BUTLER

Will we be coming back . . . when the weather changes?

MISS ALICE *(Triste)*

Probably.

JULIAN

(Confirming the previous exchange)

Alice?

MISS ALICE

Yes.

JULIAN

Ah.

BUTLER

(Understanding what he has been told)

Ah.

(The LAWYER enters with MISS ALICE's wig)

LAWYER

Bed stripped, mothballs lying on it like hailstones; no sound, movement, nothing.

(Puts the wig on the phrenological head)

Do you want company, Julian? Do you want a friend? *(To MISS ALICE)* Looks nice there. Leave it; we'll get you another. Are you ready to go?

MISS ALICE *(Weary)*

You want me to go now?

LAWYER *(Correcting her)*

Come.

MISS ALICE

Yes. (*Begins to disengage herself*) Butler, come help me; we can't leave Julian just . . .

BUTLER

Yes. (*Moves to help her*)

JULIAN

(*As they take him by the arm*)
Don't do that!

MISS ALICE

Julian, we must move you . . .

JULIAN

Don't.

LAWYER (*Without emotion*)

Leave him where he is.

JULIAN

Leave me . . . be.
(*He slides along the floor, backing up against the model*)
Leave me . . . where I am.

LAWYER

Good pose: leave him there.

BUTLER

(*Getting a chair cushion*)
Cushion.

JULIAN

All . . . hurts.

BUTLER

(*Putting the cushion behind him*)
Easy . . .

JULIAN

ALL HURTS!!

MISS ALICE (*Coming to him*)

Oh, my poor Julian . . .

JULIAN

(*Surprisingly strong, angry*)
LEAVE ME! All of you! Leave me!
(MISS ALICE *considers a moment, moves up out of* JULIAN's *sight-line and stays.*)

LAWYER
(Walks over to JULIAN, *regards him; almost casually)*
Goodbye.

JULIAN
(Softly, but a malediction)
Instrument!

LAWYER
(To MISS ALICE*)*
Are you coming?

MISS ALICE
(Empty and ambiguous.)
Of course.

LAWYER
(Turns on his heel, walks out, saying as he goes)
Butler?
(Exits)

BUTLER
(As LAWYER *goes; abstracted)*
Yes . . . dear.

JULIAN
(Half laughed, pained incredulity)
Good . . . bye!

BUTLER *(Looks about the room)*
All in order, I think.

JULIAN *(Wistful)*
Help me?

BUTLER
My work done.

JULIAN
No?
*(*BUTLER *regards* JULIAN *for a moment, then walks over, bends, kisses* JULIAN *on the forehead, not a quick kiss)*

BUTLER
Goodbye, dear Julian.
(As BUTLER *exits, looks to* MISS ALICE, *who does not gesture. Silence. And then he closes the doors behind him)*

JULIAN

(Alone, for a moment, then, whispered)

Goodbye, dear Julian. *(Pause)* Exit . . . all? *(Softly)* Help me . . . come back, help me. *(Pause)* HELP ME! *(Pause)* No . . . no help. Kiss. A kiss goodbye, from . . . whom? . . . Oh. From, from one . . . an . . . arms: around me; warming. COME BACK AND HELP ME. *(Pause)* If only to stay *with* me, while it . . . *if* . . . while it happens. For . . . you, you would not have left me if it . . . were not . . . would you? No. *(Calling to them)* I HAVE NEVER DREAMED OF IT. NEVER . . . IMAGINED . . . *(To himself again)* what it would be like. *(As if they were near the door)* Ahhhh. Will no one come? *(Looks at the ceiling)* High; high walls . . . summit. *(Eyes on his leg. Cry of pain, then)* Oh . . . GOD! "I come to thee, in agony." *(Cry to the void)* HELP . . . ME! *(Pause)* "How will I know thee, O Lord, when I am in thy sight? How will I know thee?" By my *faith.* Ah, I see. *(Furious, shouting at the roof)* BY FAITH? THE FAITH I HAVE SHOWN THEE? BENT MYSELF? What may we avoid! Not birth! Growing up? Yes. Maturing? Oh, *God!* Growing old, and?. . . yes, growing old; but not the last; merely when. *(Sweet singsong)* But to live again, be born once more, sure in the sight of . . . *(Shouts again)* IS THERE NO ONE? *(Turns his head toward the closed doors, sadly.* MISS ALICE *is visible to us, but not to* JULIAN*)* Unless you are listening there. Unless you have left me, tiptoed off some, stood whispering, smothered giggles, and . . . silently returned, your ears pressed against, or . . . or one eye into the crack so that the air smarts it sifting through. HAVE YOU COME BACK? HAVE YOU NOT LEFT ME? *(Pause)* No. No one. Out in the night . . . nothing. Night? No; what then? IS IT NIGHT . . . OR DAY? *(Great weariness)* Or does it matter? No. How long wilt thou forget me, O Lord? Forever? How long wilt thou hide thy face from me? How long shall my enemy . . . I . . . can . . . barely . . . feel. Which is a sign. A change, at any rate. *(To the rooftops again)* I DO NOT UNDERSTAND, O LORD, MY GOD, WHAT THOU WILT HAVE OF ME! *(More conversational)* I have never dreamed of it, never imagined what it would be like. I have— oh, yes—dwelt *(Laughs at the word)* . . . dwelt . . . on the *fact* of it, the . . . principle, but I have not imagined dying. Death . . . yes. Not being, but not the act of . . . dying? ALICE!? *(Laughs softly)* Oh, Alice, why hast *thou* forsaken me . . . with . . . all the others? *(Laughs again)* Alice? ALICE!? *(Laughs)* "Raise high the roofbeam, for the bridegroom comes." Oh, what a priesthood is this! Oh, what a range of duties, and such parishioners, and such a chapel for my praise. *(Turns some, leans toward the model, where the chapel light shines)* Oh, what a priesthood, see my chapel, how it . . .

(Suddenly the light in the chapel in the model goes out. MISS ALICE *turns, leaves.* JULIAN *starts, makes a sound of surprise and fear)*

Alice? . . God? SOMEONE? Come to Julian as he . . . ebbs.

(We begin to hear it now, faintly at first, slowly growing, so faintly at first it is subliminal: the heartbeat . . . thump thump . . . thump thump . . . And the breathing . . . the intake taking one thump-thump, the exhaling the next. JULIAN neither senses nor hears it yet, however)

Come, comfort him, warm him. He has not been a willful man . . . Oh, willful in his . . . cry to serve, but gentle, would not cause pain, but bear it, *would* bear it . . . has, even. Not much, I suppose. One man's share is not . . . another's burden. *(Notices the wig on the phrenological head; crawls a bit toward it; half kneels in front of it)* Thou art my bride? Thou? For thee have I done my life? Grown to love, entered in, bent . . . accepted? For thee? Is that the . . .awful humor? Art thou the true arms, when the warm flesh I touched . . . rested against, was . . . nothing? And *she* . . . was not real? Is thy stare the true look? Unblinking, outward, through, to some horizon? And her eyes . . . warm, accepting, were they . . . not real? Art thou my bride? *(To the ceiling again)* Ah God! Is that the humor? THE ABSTRACT? . . . REAL? THE REST? . . . FALSE? *(To himself, with terrible irony)* It is what I have wanted, have insisted on. Have nagged . . . for. *(Looking about the room, raging)* IS THIS MY PRIESTHOOD, THEN? THE WORLD? THEN COME SHOW THYSELF! BRIDE? GOD?

(Silence; we hear the heartbeats and the breathing some)

SHOW THYSELF! I DEMAND THEE! *(JULIAN crawls back toward the model; faces it, back to the audience, addresses it)* SHOW THYSELF! FOR THEE I HAVE GAMBLED . . . MY SOUL? I DEMAND THY PRESENCE. ALICE!

(The sounds become louder now, as, in the model, the light fades in the bedroom, begins to move across an upper story. JULIAN's reaction is a muffled cry)

AGHHH! *(On his hands and knees, he backs off a little from the model, still staring at it)* You . . . thou . . . art . . . coming to me? *(Frightened and angry)* . . . *(Sad, defeated)* Art coming to me. *(A shivered prayer, quick)* How long wilt thou forget me, O Lord? Forever? How long wilt thou hide thy face from me? . . . Consider and hear me, O Lord, my God. *(Shouted now)* CONSIDER AND HEAR ME, O LORD, MY GOD. LIGHTEN MY EYES LEST I SLEEP THE SLEEP OF DEATH.

(The lights keep moving; the sounds become louder)

BUT I HAVE TRUSTED IN THY MERCY, O LORD. HOW LONG WILT THOU FORGET ME? *(Softly, whining)* How long wilt thou hide thy face from me? COME, BRIDE! COME, GOD! COME!

(The breathing and heartbeats are much, much louder now. The lights descend a stairway in the model. JULIAN turns, backs against the model, his arms way to the side of him)

Alice? *(Fear and trembling)* Alice? ALICE? MY GOD, WHY HAST
THOU FORSAKEN ME?

*(A great shadow, or darkening, fills the stage; it is the shadow
of a great presence filling the room. The area on* JULIAN *and
around him stays in some light, but, for the rest, it is as if ink
were moving through paper toward a focal point. The sounds
become enormous.* JULIAN *is aware of the presence in the
room, "sees" it, in the sense that his eyes, his head move to all
areas of the room, noticing his engulfment. He almost-whis-
pers loudly)*

The bridegroom waits for thee, my Alice . . . is thine. O Lord, my God, I
have awaited thee, have served thee in thy . . . ALICE? *(His arms are
wide, should resemble a crucifixion. With his hands on the model, he will
raise his body some, backed full up against it)* ALICE? . . . GOD?

(The sounds are deafening. JULIAN *smiles faintly)*

I accept thee, Alice, for thou art come to me. God, Alice . . . I accept thy
will.

(Sounds continue. JULIAN *dies, head bows, body relaxes some,
arms stay wide in the crucifixion. Sounds continue thusly:
thrice after the death . . . thump thump thump thump thump
thump. Absolute silence for two beats. The lights on* JULIAN *fade
slowly to black. Only then, when all is black, does the curtain
slowly fall)*

CURTAIN

Malcolm

FROM THE NOVEL BY
JAMES PURDY

For James Purdy

with ever-growing admiration

FIRST PERFORMANCE

January 11, 1966, New York City,
Shubert Theatre

MALCOLM	*Matthew Cowles*
COX	*Henderson Forsythe*
LAUREEN	*Estelle Parsons*
KERMIT	*John Heffernan*
A YOUNG MAN	*Victor Arnold*
MADAME GIRARD	*Ruth White*
GIRARD GIRARD	*Wyman Pendleton*
A STREETWALKER	*Estelle Parsons*
ELOISA BRACE	*Alice Drummond*
JEROME BRACE	*Donald Hotton*
GUS	*Alan Yorke*
JOCKO	*Robert Viharo*
MELBA	*Jennifer West*
MILES	*Henderson Forsythe*
MADAME ROSITA	*Estelle Parsons*
HELIODORO	*Victor Arnold*
A MAN	*William Callan*
A WASHROOM ATTENDANT	*Henderson Forsythe*
A DOCTOR	*Henderson Forsythe*
VARIOUS PEOPLE	*Vicki Blankenship*
	Joseph Cali
	William Callan
	Robert Viharo

Directed by ALAN SCHNEIDER
Designed by WILLIAM RITMAN
Costumes by WILLA KIM
Lighting by THARON MUSSER
Music by WILLIAM FLANAGAN

ACT ONE

SCENE ONE

(*A golden bench;* MALCOLM *seated on it; no expression save patient waiting.* COX *enters, behind* MALCOLM, *grimaces, stands for a moment, hands on hips, tapping his foot, finally advances*)

COX (*Rather petulantly*)
You seem to be *wedded* to this bench. (MALCOLM *smiles, does not look at* COX, *but, rather, down at the bench*) You!

MALCOLM
(*Looks up; a sweet smile*) Oh, I'm here all the time. (*Tiny pause*) My name is Malcolm.

COX (*A trifle edgy*)
Good morning; my name is Cox. (MALCOLM *smiles, nothing more;* COX *pauses a moment, then*) I suppose, of course, You *are* waiting for somebody; your sister, perhaps.

MALCOLM
(*His attention slipping away*) No. (*Then back*) I'm waiting for nobody at all.

COX
(*Impatient; suspicious*) You have such a waiting *look;* you've been here forever. For months and months.

MALCOLM (*Surprise*)
You've seen me?

COX
Of course I've seen you; this is my . . . I, I walk by here every day.

MALCOLM
Oh. Well, in that case, I suppose I *am* waiting for somebody.

COX

(Helpful; after MALCOLM *says no more)* Yes?

MALCOLM

(Statement of fact) My father has disappeared.

COX

Well, don't tell me you've been waiting for *him* all this time.

MALCOLM

(Thinks for a moment; then) Yes; perhaps I may be waiting for *him. (Then he laughs, openly, agreeably)*

COX *(Snorts)*

Waiting for your father!

MALCOLM

I'm afraid I have nothing better to do.

COX

Ridiculous! I've taken special notice of you, because nobody has ever sat on this bench before. I don't think anybody *should* sit on it, for that matter.

MALCOLM

(Firmly; clearly enunciated) Poppycock.

COX *(Dogmatic)*

I am speaking of the regulations. This bench was set out here in front of the hotel as decoration, to . . . to set things off, and I don't . . .

MALCOLM *(No apology)*

Well, I am a guest in the hotel and I sit where I please.

COX *(Miffed)*

I see! *(Tiny pause)* It's clear you've not heard of me. *(Clears his throat)* I am an astrologer.

MALCOLM

(Innocent delight) People still study the . . . stars . . . for, for . . .?

COX

(Snort of disgust) People!

MALCOLM

(Gentle apology) I'm sorry.

COX

(Regarding MALCOLM *carefully, appraisingly)* Do you have no one, then?

MALCOLM

(As if the question were odd, unfamiliar) No one?

COX

No one.

MALCOLM

(*Clearly dropping the above*) I'd invite you to sit down, sir, but you quite clearly don't think it should be done, and I wouldn't want to ask you if you didn't want to do it.

COX

(*Intentional bored tone*) Your way of refusing to give information?

MALCOLM

Things are, well, a bit too much for me, you see: I'm quite young, I guess. So I sit here all the time . . . I suppose.

COX

Guess!? Suppose!? You *know!*

MALCOLM (*A sweet smile*)

Well, sir; yes; I know.

COX (*Broods*)

Hmmmmmmmm.

MALCOLM (*A fact*)

I suppose, though . . . that if someone would tell me what to do, I would do it.

COX

(*Regards him; chooses his words carefully*) Would that be wise, though? For someone so young?

MALCOLM

(*Finally touching the bench with his hand, to emphasize a point*) If I could leave the bench . . . if I saw some purpose . . . I would risk it.

COX

(*Relieved, energized; takes a notebook and pencil from his pocket*) Good. When were you born, Malcolm? The date of your birth. (MALCOLM *is silent*) Don't tell me you don't know!

MALCOLM

(*Quite simple about it*) I'm afraid you're right: I don't.

COX

Then I don't see how you expect me to help you.

MALCOLM

(*Quietly confused*) Help . . . sir?

COX (*To himself*)

I don't think I've ever met anybody who didn't know when he was born.

MALCOLM

But since he—my father—disappeared, I've had nobody to remind me of dates.

COX

How *old* are you? Do you know *that? Vaguely?*

MALCOLM (*Sweet smile*)

I'm . . . I'm afraid not, sir.

COX

(*Regarding* MALCOLM *closely*) You look really quite young. Well, are you . . . have you . . . do you, uh, have . . . hair?

MALCOLM

Sir?

COX (*Embarrassed*)

Hair. Do you have hair, uh, under your arms, and, uh . . .

MALCOLM

(A *winning smile; laughs*) Oh. Yes. Recently.

COX

Ah, well, then, you are probably . . . Did your father never talk to you about plans? Plans for when you were grown up?

MALCOLM (*Hesitant*)

Grown . . . up?

COX (*Gloomily*)

Grown up.

MALCOLM (A *little sadly*)

No. (*Rather tentative, then growing in pleasure*) My father . . . my father seemed to feel I was always going to stay just the way I was, and that he and I would always be doing just about what we were doing *then*. We were both satisfied. You have no idea, Mr. Cox, sir. (*A faint frown*) We were very happy together, my father and I.

COX

Well, for God's sake, Malcolm, you're not happy now!

MALCOLM (*Quite level*)

No, sir; I'm not.

COX

Well, you've got to do something about it!

MALCOLM

Do?

COX

Yes; *do.*

MALCOLM (*A quiet appeal*)

But, what is there to do?

COX

You must . . . give yourself up to things.

MALCOLM

(*Rises, a little apprehensive*) Give myself up to . . . things?'

COX

Of course, my dear boy. You must begin your education.

MALCOLM

But, my father taught me . . .

COX

Your education to *life,* Malcolm!

MALCOLM

Sir?

COX

Since you are going out into the world—leaving your bench, so to speak—
you must prepare yourself. You have the look of innocence, Malcolm . . .
and that will never do!

MALCOLM

No, sir?

COX

Innocence has the appearance of stupidity, my boy.

MALCOLM

It does, sir?

COX

Yes, the two are easily confused, and people will take the easy road,
Malcolm, and find you stupid. Innocence must go! (*Softer*) And I can help
you; I can give you people, if you think it's people you're looking for . . .
addresses.

MALCOLM (*Confused*)

Addresses, sir?

COX

Addresses. That is, if you want to give yourself to things—to life, as an
older era said.

MALCOLM

Well, I have no choice, have I. But . . . addresses?

COX

(Hands MALCOLM *a calling card; uses his lecturer's voice)* Here is the first. I want you to take this card, and you are to call on the people whose names are written on it, *today,* at five o'clock.

MALCOLM

(After folding his arms, and a long pause) I will *not!* I will do no such thing. *(Then, suddenly he takes the card and studies it, then reacts with consternation. Intense displeasure)* Kermit and Laureen Raphaelson indeed! *(Throws the card on the ground)* I'll have nothing to do with such an absurd introduction. You must be . . . out of your mind.

COX

Pick up that card at once! What would your father think of you!

MALCOLM

Kermit and Laureen Raphaelson indeed!

COX

If you do not obey me . . . I will never speak to you again! *(Scoffs)* Sitting there, day after day, moping over your father, who probably died a long time ago . . .

MALCOLM

Disap*peared,* sir.

COX *(Pushing on)*

Yes, and when help for you arrives in the shape of an address, what do you want to do! Nothing! You prefer to stay on that bench. You prefer that to . . . *beginning.* . . .

MALCOLM

(Reconsiders) Well, I will do as you say in this one case.

COX

You will do as you're told, since you don't know what to do at all.

MALCOLM *(A gentle smile)*

Very well, sir.

COX

And remember the exact hour: five.

MALCOLM

Yes, sir.

COX *(As he leaves)*

Remember, Malcolm . . . you must *begin.*

MALCOLM

(Looking at the card) Yes, sir . . . begin.

COX

You'll rather enjoy Kermit and Laureen, I think . . . they're children—like yourself.

MALCOLM (Disappointed)

Oh? Yes?

COX

Grown-up children. (As he exits) Remember, Malcolm . . . You must begin.

ENTRE-SCENE

(MALCOLM leaves the bench scene, which changes in darkness. He comes forward, broods some, then speaks to his father, rather as if they were standing together)

MALCOLM

Dear father . . . I am to begin. Begin what? I don't know, but . . . something. My education, I believe. Oh, father; I miss you so very much, and I don't understand . . . at all: why you've left me, where you have gone, if you *are*, as they say, dead or if you will ever return. I miss you so. But I am to begin now, it would appear, and I will try to be all you have taught me . . . polite; honest; and . . . what is the rest of it, father? That you have taught me? *(Looks at card)* Do you know . . . do you know Kermit and Laureen Raphaelson, father? By chance, do you know them? Grown-up children, father?

SCENE TWO

(The lights come up on the set of the Raphaelsons' house. LAUREEN is in it. She calls to MALCOLM)

LAUREEN

Malcolm? Hurry up, now. Over here.

MALCOLM

(Moving tentatively into the set) Uh . . . yes. You're . . . uh, Laureen Raphaelson?

LAUREEN

Oh, *am* I. And you! You *are* Malcolm; you *are* from Professor Cox.

MALCOLM

Uh . . . yes, I suppose.

LAUREEN

Kermit is not with us at the moment, as you can see.

MALCOLM

Well, no . . . I . . .

LAUREEN

As a matter of fact, he's in the pantry finishing his supper. He eats in there alone now quite often, just to spite me, I think. I'm afraid Professor Cox may be right . . . that we're headed for the divorce courts. What do you think of that?

MALCOLM

Divorce courts are entirely out of my range of experience. But I'm sorry you're headed for them.

LAUREEN

(Thinking it over) I haven't said divorce is actually imminent, mind you.

MALCOLM

No?

LAUREEN

Though it probably is. My God, you're young, aren't you? (KERMIT *enters;* LAUREEN *sees him*) There he is, Malcolm. It's Kermit! There's Kermit. *(To* KERMIT, *very eager to please)* You have a caller, Dolly.

MALCOLM

(Observing KERMIT, *open-mouthed, as he advances)* Why, who are *you?*

KERMIT

(Rather amused, but slightly imperious) Who am I? You heard her. I am Kermit. *Her* husband. Oh, I can't tell you how glad I am to see somebody nice for a change, and stop looking so surprised, Malcolm, you are Malcolm, right?

MALCOLM

Why . . . uh, yes. . . .

KERMIT

Why don't you just ignore Laureen there, and pay proper attention to *me?* After all, I'm the lonely one.

LAUREEN

Good God alive, it's beginning already. I beg you, Kermit: don't bring on a scene in front of this child.

KERMIT

(Settling into a chair) So . . . you are the boy who is infatuated with his father.

MALCOLM

I? Infatuated?

LAUREEN

Professor Cox has already told us all about you.

MALCOLM

But there's nothing to tell . . . yet.

KERMIT *(Gravely)*

There is always a great deal to tell, Malcolm, as I have learned.

MALCOLM

(To break a stared-at feeling) And you really *are* married.

KERMIT

She proposed.

LAUREEN

I warn you, I will not tolerate your telling secrets about our marriage to a third party again. Ever!

KERMIT

(To MALCOLM; *proudly)* I am the oldest man in the world.

LAUREEN

(Familiar argument) You are not!

KERMIT

I most certainly am!

LAUREEN

You most certainly are not!

KERMIT

(To MALCOLM*)* I am one hundred and ninety-two years old.

LAUREEN

You are no such thing!

KERMIT *(To* LAUREEN*)*

I am one hundred and ninety-two years old.

LAUREEN

You're ninety-seven years old . . . *(Mutters)* for God's sake. *(Louder)* You're not even one hundred.

KERMIT

I'm much too old to argue with you. *(Back to* MALCOLM*)* Why did you decide to come to see us, Malcolm?

LAUREEN *(To herself)*

One hundred and ninety-two years old indeed! *(To* MALCOLM; *something of a challenge)* Yes, why did you come?

MALCOLM

Why did I come to see you? Why, Mr. Cox ordered me to.

LAUREEN

Professor Cox has ruined Kermit here with his ideas. Kermit and I were *so* happy before we met that awful man.

KERMIT

(*Laughs derisively*) Laureen, sweetheart, if you're going to start a sermon, I'll have to ask you to leave the front room and go out and sit in the back parlor with the cats.

LAUREEN

(*Rather steely for all-suffering*) You should tell Malcolm how many cats you have out there so he can have a picture of where you're ordering me to go. (KERMIT *makes a little face;* MALCOLM *stifles giggles*) We have fifteen cats! Malcolm, am I getting across to you?

KERMIT

(*In confidence, to* MALCOLM) Professor Cox has a rather low opinion of Laureen at the moment.

LAUREEN

He has a low opinion of everybody, I would suspect. (*Turns to* MALCOLM) Malcolm, sweetie, do you know what Professor Cox suggested to me, only last week? (MALCOLM *shakes his head*) But you're too young to hear it! Oh, God! So terribly young, and unaware.

KERMIT

Nonsense! No one's too young to hear anything about people! And where's my hot tea, by the way? I asked you for my tea nearly an hour ago.

LAUREEN

(*Hastening to the tea table*) Dolly, didn't I bring you your tea? I won't have it said I've neglected my duties by you, no matter what may happen later on. Malcolm, honey, will you join Kermit in a cup of tea?

MALCOLM

(*Very little boy*) Yes, please.

KERMIT

(*As* LAUREEN *brings the tea*) Just what *did* Professor Cox command you, Laureen? Why don't you regale us with it?

LAUREEN

(*Giving* MALCOLM *his tea, kissing him on the cheek, ignoring* KERMIT'*s last remark*) Here, precious.

MALCOLM

Thank you, Laureen. Yes, what did Mr. Cox command you?

KERMIT

I'll tell you what Mr. Cox commanded her.

LAUREEN

(Put upon) Let me tell it, Kermit; I want the boy to hear it without your embellishments.

KERMIT

Will you allow me to entertain *my* guest in *my* fashion? I am one hundred and ninety-two years old.

LAUREEN

You are not.

KERMIT

(To MALCOLM*)* We are poor people. *(To* LAUREEN*)* Quiet! *(Back to* MAL-COLM*)* And knowing my wife's *propensities,* a long history we need not go into here, Professor Cox merely and sensibly proposed that Laureen go out with certain gentlemen who would pay her for her compliance with their wishes, since she was not entirely unknown for her favors before her sudden proposal of marriage to me. *(To* LAUREEN*)* Silence! *(Back to* MAL-COLM*)* Laureen had promised when she proposed marriage to me and I had agreed to be her husband that my days of struggle and difficulty would be over. *(To* LAUREEN, *as if she were threatening to speak)* YES? *(Back to* MALCOLM*)* The exact opposite, alas, has been true. Since the prolonged weekend of our honeymoon in Pittsburgh, there has not been a day . . .

LAUREEN

(Quite the tragedienne) When one's husband no longer respects one, when he can tell the most intimate secrets of a marriage in front of a third party, there is, indeed, nothing left for one but the streets. Malcolm, baby, do I look like a streetwalker? *(Goes right up to him, towers over him)* Answer me, dear boy, for you're not yet corrupt. *(*MALCOLM *does not answer)* Do I . . . or don't I?

MALCOLM *(Quite confused)*

But aren't you . . . already one, dear Laureen? I . . . I thought your husband said you . . .

KERMIT

(Laughs uproariously) Go back there and talk to the cats; I want to be with Malcolm. Go on! I certainly deserve to see somebody else in the evening besides your own horrible blonde self.

LAUREEN

(Disdainfully, at KERMIT*)* A true pupil of Professor Cox. *(Kisses* MALCOLM *benevolently, retires without looking at* KERMIT *again.)*

KERMIT

(Shouting after her) Back with the other alley cats! *(Laughs pleasantly)*

MALCOLM

Are there really cats back there?

KERMIT

As Laureen said: there are fifteen.

MALCOLM

What an extraordinary number of cats.

KERMIT

Well, I've been collecting them for a while. After all, I'm one hundred and ninety-two years old.

MALCOLM

How . . . how odd that Laureen should be a . . . a . . .

KERMIT

(Quite conversationally) Odd she's a whore? Well, it's the only thing she ever wanted to be, and why she thought marriage would straighten her out, especially marriage with *me,* God only knows.

MALCOLM

I don't seem to recognize women like that when I meet them.

KERMIT

You *do* have beautiful clothes.

MALCOLM

Do I? (Looks down at himself) They're all suits my father picked out years in advance of my being this size. He's picked out suits for me all the way up to the age of eighteen. I think he had a presentiment he'd be called away, and he left me plenty of clothes.

KERMIT

(More polite than anything) Your father was quite extraordinary.

MALCOLM

(A little whine in the voice) That's what I tried to tell Mr. Cox, but he wouldn't believe me. I'm . . . I'm glad you think my father was extraordinary. (Surprisingly near tears) You see, he's all I've got . . . and now I don't have him. (A few brief, genuine sobs)

KERMIT

(After a decent interval) You have *me,* Malcolm; I'll be your friend.

MALCOLM

(Recovering; a sweet smile) Thank . . . thank you, Kermit.

KERMIT

I'll be your friend.

MALCOLM

You . . . you have beautiful clothes, too.

KERMIT *(Modest)*

Oh, well, they're . . . they set me off.

MALCOLM

I've . . . I've never met anybody as old as you are, before.

KERMIT

Well, you haven't met many people, have you, Malcolm?

MALCOLM

No. There's one thing, though, I must get straight. Are . . . are you really as old as you say you are?

KERMIT

(Tossing it off with a little laugh) Well, of course.

MALCOLM

But you can't be!

KERMIT *(Quite petulant)*

Why not?

MALCOLM

Well . . . nobody *could* be!

KERMIT *(Straight curiosity)*

Do you want me to tell you about the Boston Tea Party?

MALCOLM

Uh . . . no. (KERMIT *sticks his tongue out at* MALCOLM) Golly, you look awful when you do that.

KERMIT

(Offhand) I *am* awful sometimes.

MALCOLM

I think I like you, though; you're not usual.

KERMIT

Well, I could say the same thing of you, Malcolm, but I won't. Not that I don't like you; I do—but that you're unusual. You're not bright, I gather, but you have your own charm, an air of . . . innocuous fellowship.

MALCOLM

(Solemnity and awe) Aren't you . . . afraid? I mean . . . well . . . being so old and all . . . aren't you afraid of . . . dying?

KERMIT

(After a mouth-open pause, quite casually calls) Uh, Laureen? Laureen?

MALCOLM

I'm, I'm sorry if I . . .

KERMIT

Laureen?

LAUREEN

(Enters, examining her hand) One of your damn cats bit me. I think it was Peter. Honestly, Kermit, I wish you'd do something about . . .

KERMIT

Laureen, Malcolm just said the oddest thing.

MALCOLM

I'm sorry, Kermit, really I am.

LAUREEN

(Still with her hand, barely interested) Yeah? What did you say, Malcolm?

KERMIT

(As if it were funny) Malcolm asked me if I wasn't afraid of dying.

LAUREEN

(Only the mildest, matter-of-fact criticism, offhand) Oh, you shouldn't say anything like that, Malcolm.

KERMIT

(Just a hint of self-reassurance) When I was your age, Malcolm, the idea of death occurred to me, and I was very frightened.

LAUREEN

I mean, that isn't a nice thing to say at all.

KERMIT

And I lived with it all through my forties and fifties and everything, and by the time I was a hundred or so . . .

LAUREEN

You're ninety-seven. I don't see why we can't get rid of those damn cats.

KERMIT

. . . by the time I was a hundred or so . . . I'd resigned myself to it.

LAUREEN

It just isn't a nice thing to say to anybody, Malcolm.

KERMIT

But on my one hundred and forty-fifth birthday the idea suddenly hit me that there wasn't any death. So when I was a hundred and eighty-five I married Laureen here . . .

LAUREEN

I mean, when you're dealing with a person who's over ninety and all, I . . . I just don't see why you want to scare me like that.

KERMIT
. . . and we have each other, and the cats, and everything. . . .

LAUREEN
I don't think you know how to behave around grownups, boy.

KERMIT
Malcolm doesn't know what life is, Laureen; he just doesn't know, that's all.

MALCOLM
Well, no, I . . . I suppose I don't.

LAUREEN
You come back and see us, Malcolm, some other time. *(Beginning to stroke* KERMIT*)* We wanna be alone for a little now. You'll understand when you're married. We got our own problems, Kermit, being ninety-seven and all. . . .

KERMIT
One hundred and ninety-two.

LAUREEN
But you call us. Call us now, you hear?

MALCOLM
Yes, well . . . thank you both for the evening. Thank you for . . .

KERMIT
(Enjoying being fondled etc.) Come back and see us, Malcolm. Come back and see *me. I'm* the lonely one.

MALCOLM
Yes, I . . . good, goodnight to both of you.

LAUREEN
Goodnight, baby.

KERMIT
I'm your friend, Malcolm, no matter what you think of me. Who knows, I may be your only friend in the world. You can cry here any time.

LAUREEN
Oh, Dolly, you're wonderful, you really are. So wonderful.
    (As this set fades, as MALCOLM *moves away)*

KERMIT *(Cheerfully)*
I'm one hundred and ninety-two years old.

LAUREEN *(Teasing him)*
You are not.

KERMIT
(*A tone creeping in*) I am one hundred and ninety-two years old!!

LAUREEN
Dolly, you are *not* a hundred and ninety-two years old.

ENTRE-SCENE

(MALCOLM *backs away from the Raphaelsons' as it fades to blackness.* MALCOLM *is alone*)

MALCOLM
Love . . . Love is . . . *Marriage* is . . . Married love is the strangest thing of all. (*More or less to his father*) Of everything I have seen, married love is the strangest thing of all. (COX *enters, unseen by* MALCOLM)

COX
What are you doing, Malcolm?

MALCOLM
(*A smile, self-assurance*) Thinking aloud.

COX
Thinking what?

MALCOLM (*A recitation*)
That married love is the strangest thing of all.

COX (*Stern*)
Not true!

MALCOLM (*Quiet smile*)
Ah, well.

COX
I was talking with my wife only last night.

MALCOLM (*Astonishment*)
You mean there is a *Mrs.* Cox?

COX (*Rather sniffy*)
Of course! Everybody is married, Malcolm . . . everybody that counts.

MALCOLM (*Dubiously*)
I don't understand why Laureen won't admit that Kermit is one hundred and ninety-two years old.

COX

(Hedging) Well, she has a certain personal right to deny it, if she wishes to. Besides, maybe he isn't.

MALCOLM

Well, Kermit was very firm about it.

COX

That is so like Kermit!! The day will come . . . the day will come when Laureen will have to admit that Kermit is one hundred and ninety-two years old, or Kermit will have to admit that he isn't.

MALCOLM

You mean they can't both go on believing what they want?

COX

(A flicker of kindness) Well, not if they're the only ones who believe it.

MALCOLM

(Sad glimmer of knowledge) Aaaahhh.

COX

(All business again; takes card from his wallet) Well, here is your second address, Malcolm. Society, great wealth, position, sadness.

MALCOLM *(Rather sadly)*

So soon.

COX

(Brandishing, presenting a card as if on a platter) The Girards. Madame Girard, and her husband. You must hurry, though. The Girards are very wealthy people, and while the very wealthy have no sense of time, their interests do . . . shift, the portals close, the beautifully groomed backs . . . turn . . . no loss . . . but yours.

MALCOLM

(Looking at the card) Mr. and Mrs. Girard . . . "The Mansion."

COX *(Moving off)*

Hurry to them; hurry now.

MALCOLM

(To the retreating COX) Maybe . . . maybe they've met . . . maybe they'll know where my father is!

COX *(Exiting)*

Ah, well . . . if your father exists, or has ever existed . . . perhaps they will. *(Exits)*

SCENE THREE

MALCOLM

(Alone for a moment; the Girard set will light directly. Great bewildered wonder; to himself) If he exists . . . or has existed! *If* he exists! *(To his father, now)* Do you know them, father? . . . Mr. and Mrs. Girard, who live in the mansion? Are very wealthy, have great position, and have . . . beautifully groomed backs—and fronts, I would venture? *(Laughs, joyously)* Is that where you are, father? Will you be waiting for me there?

(A YOUNG MAN *appears)*

YOUNG MAN

Are you Malcolm?

MALCOLM

Oh! Uh, yes, sir, I am.

YOUNG MAN

I thought you were; you look like you should be. Come along now. Madame Girard is demanding a settlement from her husband; you're just in time for the evening performance.

MALCOLM

A settlement? Of what sort?

YOUNG MAN

Money, of course! Divorce. What are settlements for? *(Shrugs)* Peace at the end of wars, settlements, money, what else? Come now.

(They enter the Girard set. MADAME GIRARD *is seated on a throne of sorts.* GIRARD GIRARD *stands near her, another* YOUNG MAN *to the other side of her.* MADAME GIRARD's *make-up is smeared all over her face; she is drinking; is drunk)*

MADAME GIRARD

(As the YOUNG MAN *ushers* MALCOLM *into her presence)* Who admitted this child? *(Takes a drink)*

GIRARD GIRARD

Why, Professor Cox called up, my dear, and asked if this young man could not be received. *(Goes to* MALCOLM, *hand out)* Good evening, Malcolm.

MALCOLM

(After difficulty getting his hands out of his pockets, shakes hands with GIRARD GIRARD*)* Good, good evening, sir.

MADAME GIRARD *(To her husband)*

And who gave you leave, sir, to accept invitations by proxy for me? I have a great mind to take proceedings against you, to in*crease* the settlement, proceedings with reference to the matter we discussed earlier in the evening.

GIRARD GIRARD *(Sotto voce)*

Please try to be more hospitable, Doddy.

MADAME GIRARD

Don't use pet names for me in front of strangers! *(Points to* MALCOLM*)* You! Come here. (MALCOLM *advances;* MADAME GIRARD *looks him over carefully)*

MALCOLM

Is my . . . my tie straight?

MADAME GIRARD

(Wonder and sadness) Heavens! You can't be more than six years old. *(To* GIRARD GIRARD, *peremptorily)* Get him a drink. (GIRARD GIRARD *moves to do so)*

MALCOLM *(To* MADAME GIRARD*)*

Are . . . are all of you friends of Mr. Cox? *(The four* YOUNG MEN *laugh and exchange knowing glances)*

MADAME GIRARD

(Glowering at her husband) Why is it you're not entering into the spirit of the party? Do you want me to begin proceedings against you at once? *(The* YOUNG MEN *giggle)* Well!?

GIRARD GIRARD

(Giving MALCOLM *his drink)* Now, Doddy.

MALCOLM *(To* GIRARD GIRARD*)*

I had no idea it was going to be like this.

MADAME GIRARD

What is *it?*

MALCOLM

(With some distaste) Your party, or . . . gathering, or whatever you call it.

MADAME GIRARD *(Drinking again)*

We are here . . . for the sole purpose of taking proceedings against my husband—boor and lecher—seducer of chambermaids and car hops. . . .

GIRARD GIRARD *(So patiently)*

Now, Doddy . . .

MADAME GIRARD

(*To* MALCOLM, *still*) And I think I can arrange this settlement quite properly without comments from the newly arrived and half-invited.

MALCOLM

(*Rather loud and self-assertive*) Perhaps *Mr.* Girard may want a divorce first!
   (*The* YOUNG MEN *laugh,* GIRARD GIRARD *smiles quietly*)

MADAME GIRARD

Newly arrived and *un*-invited!

MALCOLM

(*Is he a little drunk himself? Still rather loud. Genuine concern*) You must drink a *great* deal, Madame Girard.
   (*Again, guffaws from the* YOUNG MEN)

MADAME GIRARD

(*Crafty, eyes narrowing*) What was it you said, young man?

MALCOLM

I think you are intoxicated, Madame.
   (*Great laughter*)

MADAME GIRARD (*Drunk dignity*)

Do you realize in whose mansion you are?

MALCOLM

Why, Mr. Girard's mansion.

MADAME GIRARD

Clearly you do not.

MALCOLM (*To the others*)

This is only the second place I've visited at Mr. Cox's request, but I can't say it's the more pleasant or comfortable of the two.

MADAME GIRARD

Hear him!? He's not a guest—he's a critic! Not only a critic, but a spy! Throw him out! THROW him OUT!!

GIRARD GIRARD

Doddy; *dear.*

MADAME GIRARD

A filthy spy for that vicious old pederast!

GIRARD GIRARD

Doddy, not in front of a child.

MALCOLM (*Fascinated*)

Old what? Ped . . . what? What did she call him?

GIRARD GIRARD

Doddy, please. *(To* MALCOLM*)* I believe I've heard mention of your father.

MALCOLM

(To GIRARD GIRARD, *with wonder and hope)* You really knew my father!

GIRARD GIRARD

Ah, no; I said, I believe I've heard mention of him.

MADAME GIRARD *(An announcement)*

I . . . do not think your father exists. *(Takes a great gulp)* I have *never* thought he did. (MALCOLM *swallows, stares at her open-mouthed)* And what is more . . . *(Takes another drink)* . . . *nobody* thinks he exists . . . or ever *did* exist.

MALCOLM

That's . . . that's . . . blasphemy . . . or, a thing above it! (MADAME GIRARD *laughs, echoed by the* YOUNG MEN) *And* . . . *(Quite angry now)* . . . this is the first time where I have ever attended a . . . a . . . *meeting* . . . a meeting where the person in charge was *drunk!* (*A strained tiny silence)*

MADAME GIRARD

Oh, my young beauties, see how I'm suffering. *(Stretches out her hands to the* YOUNG MEN, *who take them)* Come and comfort me, beauties.

MALCOLM

(An aside to GIRARD GIRARD*)* What a pretty face she must have under all that melted make-up.

MADAME GIRARD

Oh, dear God, I've been through so much; nobody knows what I've suffered. *(Whimpering)* And now with this spy here from Mr. Cox; he'll go directly back to that old pederast and tell him *everything* about this evening. . . .

MALCOLM

Old *what?* Pederast?

MADAME GIRARD

How I was *not* at the top of my form, and Cox will call his clients and tell *them* I was not at the top of my form, and they in turn will call . . .

GIRARD GIRARD

Would champagne help? *(Solicitously)*

MADAME GIRARD *(Weeping a little)*

Yes; it would help a little; a lot might help a little. (GIRARD GIRARD *motions to one of the* YOUNG MEN, *who fetches champagne)* It's so hard to bear one's burdens sometimes, and we don't *need* Malcolm, do we? *(Refers to the* YOUNG MEN) And haven't I my young beauties around me already. Aren't they enough? Do we need a paid informer? A paid informer in the shape of this brainless, mindless . . . (*Suddenly as if seeing* MALCOLM *for the first time*) . . . this *very* beautiful young boy?

MALCOLM

(*Sort of drunk; flattered, childishly "with it"*) Perhaps we should all drink to Madame Girard.

MADAME GIRARD

My dear, dear young friend. Oh, thank you. Leave Mr. Cox, dearest Malcolm; be mine; be my own Malcolm, not his.

MALCOLM

Let's all drink to Madame Girard!

MADAME GIRARD

(*Approaching him, putting her hands on him, kissing his cheek, etc.*) Do you know, my young, my very young dear friend, the company you've been keeping? Do you know what Mr. Cox *is?*

MALCOLM

(*Raising his glass, in a gleeful toast*) A pederast!

ALL THE OTHERS IN UNISON

WHAT!?

MADAME GIRARD

(*A bemused smile*) What word did I hear? What word, Malcolm? Did you say something?

MALCOLM

(*Draining his glass*) I don't intend to repeat myself. My father never did. Hurrah!

MADAME GIRARD

Champagne! Champagne for everyone; a prince has come among us! Royalty!

GIRARD GIRARD

Champagne! Champagne!

>(*The scene will start fading now . . . swinging off, whatever. Everybody is talking at once. But above it all we hear . . .*)

MADAME GIRARD

Royalty! Real royalty! A prince has come among us! A true prince!

SCENE FOUR

(KERMIT *alone in his set.*)

MALCOLM
(*Enters*) Kermit—Kermit, I've been to the Girards'.

KERMIT
Poor Kermit; poor little man; poor poor little man.

MALCOLM
(*Nodding, embarrassedly*) And . . . and they've accepted me and . . .

KERMIT
I knew you wouldn't fail me . . . as much as one can know anything.
Laureen has left me . . . the bitch has up and taken off.

MALCOLM (*Sympathizing*)
Left *you.*

KERMIT (*Bitterly*)
Oh, what's so surprising about that? (*Grabbing* MALCOLM'S *hand, weeping
freely*) She left me all alone, Malcolm.

MALCOLM
I . . . I . . . (*Shrugs sadly*)

KERMIT
Oh, I'll grant I hadn't really *loved* Laureen in . . . months; she'd lost her
sparkle, and there were times when she almost disgusted me, but I'd got
so *used* to her, her waiting on me, her . . . her being *around.* I'm . . . all
alone now.

MALCOLM
Did she . . . did she run off with somebody?

KERMIT
(*Anger coming back*) How else would she go!? Like a decent human
being? Alone? Of course not! She ran off with a Japanese wrestler!

MALCOLM (*Terribly puzzled*)
But . . . how did she find one?

KERMIT
I don't know!

MALCOLM (*Softly, to solace*)
Was he—the Japanese wrestler—also very old?

KERMIT

He was the . . . usual age for a man.

MALCOLM

It's pretty scary, isn't it, being alone?

KERMIT

We're both alone, you and I. Aren't we lucky Professor Cox brought us together? We're both in an impossible situation.

MALCOLM

Certainly *I* am.

KERMIT

(*Quite put out; after a tiny pause*) Why you more than I?

MALCOLM

Well, you *have* something; your marriage, which means you know *women*. I have . . . nothing; there's nothing I can *do*. All I have is the memory of my father. My father . . .

KERMIT

(*Quivering with rage*) SHIT ON YOUR FATHER!! (*Total silence.* MALCOLM *slowly rises.* KERMIT *slowly comes over to him, tugs at his sleeve*) Malcolm! Forget I ever said that. (MALCOLM *moves away a few feet*) You just listen to me, and forgive me. You must let me apologize, dear, dear Malcolm.

MALCOLM

(*Removed, sort of lost*) How can I ever listen to you *again?* And how can I forgive you? To have said *that* about my father! This is the very last straw of what can happen to me. I'm going to pack up and leave the city today!

KERMIT

You have no right to desert me or, for that matter, desert your father. He . . . he may come back for you. Malcolm, my entire world has gotten out of bed and walked away from me. I'm depending on you so! I have no one else to depend on.

MALCOLM

A likely story coming from a man who insults the dead . . . the *disappeared*.

KERMIT

Forgive me, Malcolm, I only meant irritation. There you were, talking on and on about your father, and I wanted to talk about *my*self, and about the whore of a wife . . . (*Begins sniffing*) . . . who I miss so much. . . .

MALCOLM (*Rather kingly*)

Very well, then, Kermit, you're forgiven for this once.

KERMIT

Laureen, Laureen, Laureen . . .

MALCOLM *(Shyly)*

Kermit? Why did Laureen really leave you?

KERMIT *(Sighs)*

It was so strange. At exactly the same minute I decided to tell her I was only ninety-seven, to make it easier for her, she walked into the room, looking sort of funny, saying she'd decided to live with the fact that I was a hundred and ninety-two. And so we argued about it for a while, me insisting I was only ninety-seven, and she telling me that I was older than hell itself, and then she said she couldn't take it any more, and . . .

MALCOLM

How . . . how old are you? Really?

KERMIT

Hm? Oh . . . well, I don't remember any more. I'm up there, though . . . two . . . two hundred and something.

MALCOLM

I . . . I like you, Kermit. I like you very much.

KERMIT

Yes? Well, come and see me soon, Malcolm. I'm really very lonely now.

ENTRE-SCENE

(MALCOLM, *between sets, alone, stands, shakes his head a little, sadly, suddenly sees, leaning against the proscenium, a* STREET-WALKER *who looks like Laureen, is played by the actress who plays Laureen, false wig, too much make-up, ridiculous dress.* MALCOLM *walks toward her, slowly, mouth open)*

MALCOLM

Why . . . why, *Laureen. (The* STREETWALKER *pretends not to notice him; he speaks now somewhat as if he were punishing a naughty child) Laureen!* You go home at once! Shame on you, leaving Kermit like that.

STREETWALKER

(Bored, tough, not a parody, though) What do *you* want, kid?

MALCOLM

Laureen, it's Malcolm.

STREETWALKER

Laureen!? My name's Ethel.

MALCOLM

Why, it is not! Your name is Laureen Raphaelson, and you're married to Kermit Raphaelson, who is a terribly old man, at least one hundred and ninety-two years old and maybe two hundred and something . . .

STREETWALKER

(Nodding her head as if MALCOLM were insane) My name is Laureen Raphaelson, and I am married to a terribly old man at least one hundred and ninety-two years old and maybe even two hundred and something.

MALCOLM

Yes, and you've left him and you've run off with a Japanese wrestler, and I think you ought to go home right this minute.

STREETWALKER

(Nodding her head even more) My name is Laureen Raphaelson, and I am married to a terribly old man who is at least one hundred and ninety-two years old or maybe even two hundred or something except that I've left him and run off with a Japanese wrestler.

MALCOLM

(Quite stern, oblivious of her incredulity) Yes, and I think you ought to go home right this minute.

STREETWALKER

(Ponders this a little) And where is this Japanese wrestler right now?

MALCOLM

(Flustered for a moment) Why . . . why, wrestling, I'd imagine.

STREETWALKER

Uh huh. I think you better go home yourself, kid.

MALCOLM

No! I think you had. (Whines) Laureen . . . please.

STREETWALKER (Shakes her head)

Amazing. I thought my name was Ethel, and I thought I was not married, save once, a long time ago, for a couple of weeks to a nice kid turned out was a fag and is now shacking up with a cop picked him up one night in a bus depot, very happy I believe, stays home, cleans the gun, cooks . . .

MALCOLM *(Whining)*

Laureeeeeeeeeeeeen!

STREETWALKER

You got a family, kid?

MALCOLM

(Struck by her question) A what? A family?

STREETWALKER

Mommy? Daddy?

MALCOLM

I . . . I *had* a father, but he . . .

STREETWALKER

(Soberly, not unkindly) Died?

MALCOLM *(Nods, solemnly)*

Uh . . . yes, it would seem.

STREETWALKER

Gee, I thought your name was maybe something like Donald or Malcolm, and you lived in a big hotel, except your money was going, and your father wasn't dead, but had only . . . disappeared. Not dead . . . gone away.

MALCOLM

Yes! That's *right*. Disap*peared.*

STREETWALKER

(Walking slowly toward off) You better get home, kid; Mommy and Daddy spank they find you out late, talking to . . . grownups.

MALCOLM

My father isn't dead! He only disap*peared!*

STREETWALKER

Good for you, baby, better go home to Daddy . . . *(Exits)*

MALCOLM

Laur . . . ! *(Pause; softly; alone)* Not dead . . . only gone away. I didn't mean to say that you were dead, father, but you've been . . . disappeared so long, and everybody says . . . I'm sorry, father, but please come back . . . so it won't be true.

> *(Begins to move toward the set of his bedroom in the hotel, which begins to light)*

SCENE FIVE

(Malcolm's hotel bedroom; old, stately furniture. GIRARD GIRARD *is there, his back to the audience.* MALCOLM *enters, not from a door, but right onto the set)*

MALCOLM
(Deep in thought, takes off coat, does not see GIRARD GIRARD *at first, then)*
Why . . . (GIRARD GIRARD *turns around) . . .* why, Girard Girard! What are *you* doing here?

GIRARD GIRARD
My dear Malcolm, my dear boy, I hope you'll forgive me waiting for you in your own bedroom, but I had to see you, and . . .

MALCOLM
(Rather put off) But how did you get in here?

GIRARD GIRARD *(Kindly)*
Getting here was no problem, Malcolm; I own the hotel, and as for *why* I am here . . .

MALCOLM *(Sniffing)*
Well, if you own the hotel, I should think you'd do something about the water pipes: there's rust and it takes ages for the hot water to come.

GIRARD GIRARD
It's an old place, Malcolm, a great one, but old. Besides, when I told you I owned the hotel I didn't mean to suggest that I managed it as well. It is a . . . property, a . . . something that's passing through my portfolio.

MALCOLM *(Quite formal)*
So much for the how, sir; but what of the why? *Why* . . . are you here?

GIRARD GIRARD
If I've disturbed you, I'm deeply sorry, but my coming is dictated by an emergency.

MALCOLM *(Concerned)*
Nothing serious? Madame Girard hasn't taken ill, or died?

GIRARD GIRARD
Madame Girard is at home, sleeping in her private wing of the mansion.

MALCOLM (*Quiet wonder*)
Private wings. Indeed, that *is* an extension of separate rooms, is it not?

GIRARD GIRARD
It is indeed. I've come here to make a very unusual suggestion to you, and I hope you'll hear me out. And I want to make it very clear to you that I've come here on my own volition, despite the fact that Madame Girard herself ordered me to come. Madame Girard has taken such an immediate and violent fancy to you that we wondered—and please don't think us too outrageous—we wondered if you'd care to come with us to our chateau for the summer.

MALCOLM
(*Pacing for a moment*) Why, I'm speechless with surprise at your generosity. It's . . . overwhelming.

GIRARD GIRARD
You have no idea how . . . pleased Madame Girard would be, Malcolm.

MALCOLM
No, sir; of course I haven't.

GIRARD GIRARD
And since you will make both me and my wife very happy if you will come with us to our chateau for the summer, we may expect you?

MALCOLM
. . . No, sir.

GIRARD GIRARD
But, Malcolm!!

MALCOLM
(*Ponders it, then*) You see, I'm terribly afraid of leaving here where I'm always alone, and waiting, and going to where people may demand me at all hours . . .

GIRARD GIRARD
(*A little less patiently than before*) No one will demand anything of you that you don't want to give.

MALCOLM
. . . and then there is the bench.

GIRARD GIRARD
The bench, Malcolm?

MALCOLM
It is where I receive my addresses, sir! Where I have made contact . . . with *people,* sir. And there is Kermit, sir . . .

GIRARD GIRARD

Kermit? Kermit?

MALCOLM

(*Slow and very serious*) My very best friend in the world, I think; one person whom I could never leave.

GIRARD GIRARD

(*Sigh of relief*) Well, then bring him with you—bring your Kermit with you.

MALCOLM

(*Almost thinking aloud*) Perhaps . . . if Kermit were to come . . . perhaps, then, I could accept.

GIRARD GIRARD (*Last lollipop*)

You could have one of the gatehouses, if you liked . . . anything!

MALCOLM (*Very sincere*)

I will try very hard, sir.

GIRARD GIRARD (*So gentle*)

That is all we ask. Come spend the summer with us; be our son.

MALCOLM

Be *like* your son, sir.

GIRARD GIRARD

(*As he prepares to leave the set; wistfully*) Between simile and metaphor lies all the sadness in the world, Malcolm.

MALCOLM

(*As* GIRARD GIRARD *turns, starts to leave*) It does, sir?

GIRARD GIRARD

Do let us know; come with us; be ours.

MALCOLM

(*Nods; not an acquiescence, but a pondering*) Yours.

GIRARD GIRARD (*Leaving*)

Goodnight, Malcolm.

MALCOLM

(GIRARD GIRARD *has left*) Good—goodnight, Mr. Girard . . . sir. (COX *enters from* left—KERMIT *enters from right on his chair on treadmill*) Kermit, we are going to the chateau for the summer. We are going with the Girards.

KERMIT

The Girards . . . the chateau . . .

COX (*To himself*)

Oh, I wouldn't count on that, buddy, if I were you. I wouldn't be so sure about that at all.

MALCOLM

We're on our way, Kermit.

COX

I wouldn't count on anything in this whole damn world.

MALCOLM

We're on our way, Kermit. We're on our way. (*Exits*)

SCENE SIX

(*Kermit's sitting room, but rearranged, this time, so that when* KERMIT *is facing his front door, his back will be to the audience.* COX *standing,* KERMIT *sitting, his knees together, his hands clasped on them*)

COX

I suppose you think you're going to go. (*No answer from* KERMIT) I said: I suppose you think you're going to go. (KERMIT *looks up, but does not speak; his eyes are near tears*) Is there to be a long parade? . . . of all of you? . . . all my students, all whom I've raised from nothing, you, Malcolm, God knows who else? . . . streaming after that pied piper of a Girard woman . . . like rats?

KERMIT

(*A weak whisper*) Mice?

COX

(*Intimidating, loud*) HM? WHAT?

KERMIT

(*Clears his throat; a tiny voice*) Mice. Pied piper: mice. (*A little malice now*) Rats leave a sinking ship.

COX

(*Choosing to ignore it*) All of you, whom I've educated beyond your state, risen up so that you can look at life, if not in the eye, at least at the belt buckle? All of you, running off? No thank you, sir! (KERMIT *says nothing*) Hm? HM?!

KERMIT (*Still cowed*)

I have been asked . . .

COX

SPEAK UP!!

KERMIT

I have been asked.

COX

(Fuming, to himself) It is the fate of sages and saints, I suppose, to serve, teach . . . *give,* if you will, of their substance . . . and be abandoned in the end, left desolate on the crag, like our beloved Francis, while the mice, the *rats,* scurry off . . . playing in the great gardens, nibbling at the pâté, the mousse . . . garnering.

KERMIT

(So timid, apologetic) I have . . . been asked.

COX

(Looks at KERMIT *carefully, changes his tack a little)* Well, yes, of course you have, my fine fellow . . . asked.

KERMIT

Yes!

COX

(Comforting a child) Of course! And you want to go.

KERMIT

(The wonder is too much for him) The . . . Girards . . .

COX

The Girards? Yes?

KERMIT

(Blurting it out) The Girards have invited me to the chateau and it would be wonderful. I'd see nice people . . . and everything might be all right there.

COX

(A vicious confidence) Now look here, I don't mind playing games, but the time comes we gotta get serious, right?

KERMIT

Right.

COX

You're very special, a very special person; you're fragile, Kermit, and your eyes aren't strong; you couldn't stand the . . . grandeur. . . . You'd be blinded by the splendor, Kermit.

KERMIT

(Breathes the word with loss and awe) The . . . splendor.

COX

It'd knock your eyes out, kid; you couldn't take it.

KERMIT

Then I . . . I can't go?

COX

Unh-unh.

KERMIT

I can't go with Malcolm to . . . to the chateau, with Madame Girard and . . .

COX

Unh-unh.

KERMIT

(*Knowing it's all up*) But I'd be so happy there.

COX

You couldn't take the splendor, kid; I'm sorry.

KERMIT

(*As* COX *starts to leave, but not by the front door; off to one side*) I would have been so happy there, with Malcolm, and . . .

> [MALCOLM, GIRARD GIRARD *and* MADAME GIRARD *will come on-stage and move to* KERMIT's *front door*]

COX (Exiting)

Whatever happens, Kermit, don't let them in. Remember, the splendor. (*Exits*)

MALCOLM

(*To the* GIRARDS, *as* KERMIT *huddles within*) . . . and he told me on the phone he washed the walls with ammonia and scented it all with patchouli oil and rosewater, which are your favorites for a dwelling, are they not, Madame Girard?

MADAME GIRARD

They are essential for a habitation. (*Squints*) What a charming little building; you must buy it for me, Girard.

GIRARD GIRARD

All right, Doddy.

MADAME GIRARD

I smell cats!

GIRARD GIRARD (Some wonder)

Do you, Doddy?

MALCOLM (*Eager glee*)

There are fifteen!

KERMIT

(*Huddled in a corner; whispers to himself*) Go away, oh, do go away.

MALCOLM

(*At the front door*) Kermit? Hello?

KERMIT

(*Not heard by the others*) Go away . . . *please*.

MALCOLM (*Knocks*)

Ker-mit. (*No answer; tries the doorknob*) He . . . he doesn't answer.

MADAME GIRARD

Nonsense! (*She tries it, too*) Why doesn't he answer? Is he expecting us?

MALCOLM

Of course! Kermit? Don't play games with me.

GIRARD GIRARD

Perhaps your friend is indisposed.

MADAME GIRARD

When *we* are visiting? Don't be absurd. (MADAME GIRARD *enters imperiously, followed by* MALCOLM *and* GIRARD GIRARD) Do you hear me, my good man? It is I, Madame Girard! I am issuing a command! You are coming with us to the country.

KERMIT

(*Shaking his head, sobbing*) I can't; I . . . cannot.

GIRARD GIRARD

Here, let me try.

MADAME GIRARD

(*Motioning him away*) *You* can't do anything; *I* have the splendor here.

MALCOLM

Kermit! Please! We're going to the chateau! Don't be a coward; come with me; I can't go without you!

KERMIT

(*A trapped animal, very loud*) Go away! I . . . can't bear the splendor!

MALCOLM

(*Whining a little*) Kermit!

MADAME GIRARD

What is it you can't bear?

KERMIT *(Shouting)*

I can't stand the splendor of your presence!

MADAME GIRARD *(Awe and joy)*

The *splendor* of our presence!

MALCOLM *(As above)*

Kermit, please!

KERMIT

(Moans)

MADAME GIRARD

Why, the creature is moaning! *(At which* KERMIT *moans louder)* He is moaning . . . over *us!*

MALCOLM *(Loss)*

Kermit? . . . Please?

KERMIT *(Intensity)*

(Weeping to himself) I . . . I can't. I cannot.

MALCOLM

Kermit! *(The three wait for a little, in silence, the only sound being* KER-MIT's *sobbing as he and his chair slide off)*

MADAME GIRARD *(Finally, softly)*

Well, then, we shall have to go without him. Girard?

GIRARD GIRARD

It would seem so, Doddy. I'm sorry, Malcolm, you shall have to come with us without your friend.

MALCOLM *(Soft, loss)*

Kermit!

MADAME GIRARD

(As they all begin to move away from Kermit's door) Kermit has rejected me.

MALCOLM

It's *me* he has rejected.

MADAME GIRARD *(Patiently)*

He has rejected *all* of us. I must have a drink.

MALCOLM *(Rather severe)*

What of?

MADAME GIRARD

(Sweetly, patiently explaining) Dark rum.

GIRARD GIRARD

Completely out of the question.

MADAME GIRARD

Explain the meaning of that last remark.

GIRARD GIRARD

Your drinking days are over. At any rate, with me around.

MADAME GIRARD

You pronounce my doom with the sang-froid of an ape! You are an ape!

GIRARD GIRARD

I warn you, Madame Girard, I'm at the end of my tether. We must leave for the country at once; my lungs demand the air. Malcolm? You shall have to come with us . . . alone.

MALCOLM

I can't, Mr. Girard, sir; I can't abandon Kermit now.

GIRARD GIRARD *(Sad shrug)*

Alas.

MALCOLM

(Rueful agreement) Yes; alas.

MADAME GIRARD

(Bravura cheerfulness) We have tried and failed. *(Puts her hand out)* Lead me, Girard.

GIRARD GIRARD

Goodbye, Malcolm?

MALCOLM

Goodbye, Mr. Girard, sir; goodbye, Madame Girard.

MADAME GIRARD

(Being led off by GIRARD GIRARD*)* Goodbye, dear child, dear ungrateful child. *(They both exit)*

MALCOLM *(Rather petulant)*

Well, you've made rather a hash of things, I must say, Kermit. A whole summer, two people who loved me, or so they said, a man like Mr. Girard who said he would be like my father—all of it, everything, for *both* of us, and you won't do it! *(Tapping his foot, rather impatient)* Well? What's to become of me now? I hope you've got plans for me. I've given up every-thing for you! *(But* MALCOLM *is alone. Frightened little boy)* What's to become of me?

ENTRE-SCENE

(COX *comes on, sees* MALCOLM *alone*)

COX

(*Feigning surprise*) What? You still here? Lucky boy, aren't you off with the tycoon and his lady, and where is your friend Kermit?

MALCOLM (*Surly*)

You study astrology and things, don't you?

COX

(*Shakes his head*) Tch-tch-tch-tch-tch; up the ladder too quick, down they plunge to the bottom rung, as the saying goes. Arrogant, weren't you, crowing over your triumph and all?

MALCOLM (*A front*)

It's . . . it's just a matter of a day or two, until I get things settled here, and then I'm off.

COX

Good thing, too, I must say, since your room is gone, your bags out in front of the hotel. Checked out, have you?

MALCOLM

Of course! I . . . (*Bursts into tears*) What am I to do? It was all arranged, and then Kermit lost his courage and said he wouldn't go, and . . .

COX

Tears? What would your father, or whoever it is, or was, say? Hm?

MALCOLM

(*Trying to stop crying*) And where has Kermit gone, and what's *wrong* with him?

COX (*Quite casual*)

Kermit, I'm sorry to say, is probably going to have a nearly complete collapse.

MALCOLM

(*Wonder with the stopping tears*) A nearly complete collapse?

COX

Yes, poor little man; the presence of the unattainable often brings one on.

MALCOLM (*Great wonder*)

Poor Kermit.

COX

Yes, but poor Malcolm, too, poor of pocket as well as other resources.

MALCOLM

My bags . . . you say . . . were . . .

COX (*Jolly*)

Out on the curb. Empty, though.

MALCOLM

But my clothes! My shells! My . . .

COX (*Jollier*)

Sold, whisked off, taken in payment, gone.

MALCOLM (*Great awe*)

And what am I to do!?

COX

(*Bringing out another card*) Start lower, I think; ascend again. Oh, you should count yourself lucky I bother with you at all.

MALCOLM

(*Some spunk left*) Should I! Well, let me tell you, everyone in and out of the Girards' speaks slightingly of you.

COX (*Coolly*)

Those in possession of the truth are hardly ever thought well of.

MALCOLM (*Some awe*)

You are in . . . possession of the . . . truth?

COX

(*Calm, with a small smile*) I thought you knew I had it.

MALCOLM

Then, you *are,* as people say, a magician as *well* as an astrologer.

COX (*Tossing it off*)

I merely try to help—sometimes I fail, as in your case, child. You are very difficult to educate. (*Handing* MALCOLM *a card*) Here. Take it.

MALCOLM

(*Some enthusiasm*) *Another* address, sir?

COX

Not so much enthusiasm, Malcolm. What did your father— such as he was or was not—teach you?

MALCOLM (*Ingenuous*)

To be polite, sir, and honest.

COX (*A little sour*)
Your father spoke in contradictions, then.

MALCOLM
Sir?

COX
These people . . . be cautious.

MALCOLM (*Genuine alarm*)
But why are you sending me to them, Mr. Cox, sir!?

COX (*A great shrug*)
What is left for you, Malcolm? Maybe you're on the way down, for good;
maybe not. 'S'up to you. Besides, it's the only card I happen to have with
me. (*Starts to go*) Goodnight, kiddie.

MALCOLM
(*Looks above, sees it has gone dark*) Why . . . it *is* night.

COX
Yes, gets dark pretty quick around here, don't it?

MALCOLM (*Still amazed*)
Yes; very. (*Sees that* COX *is leaving*) Mr. Cox!

COX
Hm?

MALCOLM (*Real anger*)
I don't understand your world, Mr. Cox, sir! Not one bit!

COX
You will, sonny, you will. (*Walks offstage, leaving* MALCOLM *alone*)

SCENE SEVEN

(*Eloisa Brace's studio begins to light.* ELOISA *is in it, in the growing light. There is distant jazz music going on*)

MALCOLM
(*Half calling after* COX, *half talking to himself*) Not a bit of your . . . world,
Mr. Cox, sir, not one little bit. Caution? How do I do that?

ELOISA
(*Having listened to* MALCOLM) O.K., kid; all right, O.K. All right?

MALCOLM

(*Startled to see her*) Oh! My goodness.

ELOISA

You the new kid, hunh? Malcolm? Is it you? (MALCOLM *nods*)
Practicing caution?

MALCOLM

Is that what I'm doing? Are you . . .?

ELOISA

O.K., then, either come in or go out. You can't just stand there, O.K., you
know? I'm giving a concert.

MALCOLM (*Enthusiasm*)

Are you!

ELOISA

I'm Eloisa Brace, O.K.?

MALCOLM

How do you do? Mr. Cox . . .

ELOISA (*Irritable*)

Yeah, yeah, O.K.

MALCOLM

(*Entering the set*) You're awfully cross tonight, aren't you?

ELOISA

Look, buddy, if you had a bunch of musicians lying around the house . . .

MALCOLM

I'm sorry!

ELOISA

Yeah? O.K. Hey! I'm gonna paint your portrait. (MALCOLM *only smiles a
little*) I said: I'm gonna do a picture of you. Paint. O.K.?

MALCOLM

Are . . . are you a painter?

ELOISA

(*A little suspicious*) I don't know where we're gonna put you while you're
living here, every bed in the damn place is full of musicians and all, but
you look pretty small, we'll find part of a bed for you. O.K.? My God, I
hate kids how old are you!

MALCOLM

Well, I think I must be fifteen by . . .

ELOISA

O.K.! There's that face of yours, I'm gonna paint. *(Rather mysterious)* It's like a commission: I mean, I think I can sell it right away I got it done. O.K.?

MALCOLM

O-O.K.

JEROME

(Entering) Is that the new boy? *(Sees* MALCOLM*)* Ooh, yes, it does look to be.

ELOISA

Will you please take over from here, O.K.? You know I can't stand kids, and I got all these musicians waiting.

JEROME

(Rather sweet, urging her out) O.K., baby.

ELOISA

(To MALCOLM, *as she exits)* I gonna paint the hell out of you, kid. O.K.?

MALCOLM

(As she goes) Y-yes . . . certainly.

JEROME

(Taking MALCOLM *by the arm, walking him further into the set)* My wife is a bit nervous when we have these concerts.

MALCOLM *(Astonished)*

Eloisa Brace is *your* wife?

JEROME *(Nods)*

Oh, yes. *(Leads* MALCOLM *further)* But do come clear into the room, why don't you—where I can see you.

MALCOLM *(Uncertainly)*

Sure.

JEROME

(Looking at MALCOLM *carefully)* Yup, you're just as Mr. Cox described you. Yup. *(Nods several times)* Would you like some wine, Malcolm?

MALCOLM

(As a glass is being poured for him) I usually don't drink.

JEROME

(Hands MALCOLM *a glass, takes one himself)* Do have some.

MALCOLM

You're so . . . very polite.

JEROME

(Returning the compliment) You're much nicer than I even thought you would be for a boy of your class. My name, by the way, is Jerome. *(They shake hands. Hope and enthusiasm in his voice now)* I don't suppose you've heard of me. I'm an ex-con, a burglar. You're not drinking up. *(Pours* MALCOLM *more wine)*

MALCOLM

(Rather drunk, vague) But you see . . . I don't drink. Jerome, what *is* an ex-con?

JEROME

A man who's been in prison. An ex-convict.

MALCOLM

Ah; I see!

JEROME

I wrote a book about it.

MALCOLM

How *difficult* that must have been!

JEROME

(Going to get a copy) Would you like to read my book?

MALCOLM

Well, I . . . I don't know; I've . . . I've never read a complete book—all the way through.

JEROME *(Leering some)*

You'll read this one. *(Hands it to* MALCOLM*)* It's called *They Could Have Me Back*.

MALCOLM

(Looking the book over) What a nice title. Is that you naked on the cover? *(*JEROME *smiles, touches* MALCOLM *lightly on the ear)* I . . . I don't read very much.

JEROME

(Touches MALCOLM *gently on the ear again)* Do you dig that music, kid?

MALCOLM

(Touching his ear where JEROME *had touched it)* What did you do that for?

JEROME

(Pouring MALCOLM *more wine)* Look, Malcolm, I know you make a point of being dumb, but you're not *that* dumb. *(*JEROME *sits at* MALCOLM's *feet, his arm around his leg, his head against his knee)* I *do* want you to read my book; I want you to, well, because, because I guess you don't seem to have

any pre-judgments about anything. Your eyes are completely open. (MAL-COLM *jumps a little as* JEROME *starts stroking his thigh*) Look, Malcolm, I'm not a queer or anything, so don't jump like that.

MALCOLM *(Drunk, vague)*

I see.

JEROME

Will you be a good friend, then?

MALCOLM *(From far away)*

Of course, Jerome.

JEROME

Thank you, Malcolm. It's going to be a wonderful friendship. *(Strokes some more)* But I think you better give up Girard Girard and Mr. Cox and all those people, because they don't believe in what you and I believe in. . . .

MALCOLM *(Very dizzy)*

But what do we believe in, Jerome?

JEROME

What do we believe in, Malc? What a lovely question, and you said we; I'll appreciate that for one hell of a long time. One hell of a long time from now I'll think of that question of yours, Malc: What do *we* believe in? You carry me right back to something. . . .

MALCOLM

(The jazz music is louder, MALCOLM's *head spins)* But you see, I don't know what I believe in, or any . . .

JEROME

Don't spoil it, Malc! Don't say another word!

MALCOLM

(A tiny voice; he is about to pass out) Jerome . . .

JEROME

Don't say a word, now. Shhhh . . . *(At this moment the glass falls out of* MALCOLM's *hand, and he topples from the chair, head first, across* JEROME's *lap)* Jesus Christ! Malc? *(Shakes* MALCOLM, *but he has passed out)* MALC?

(Lights fade on the tableau)

SCENE EIGHT

(Eloisa Brace's studio again. ELOISA *and* COX *swing on, with portrait, etc.)*

ELOISA

Well, whatta ya think of the portrait, hunh?

COX

It's . . . it's . . . very interesting.

ELOISA

(Put out) Oh? Really?

COX

I mean . . . it's beautiful.

ELOISA

I thought that's what you meant.

COX

It's lovely, my dear.

ELOISA

It has a certain . . . *him* about it, don't you think?

COX

Well, that depends on what you mean, Eloisa. It doesn't look exactly like *him*—or he doesn't look exactly like *it.* . . . Maybe it's a picture of what he used to be . . . or what he's becoming.

ELOISA

(Her leg is being pulled) Ooohhh . . . you astrologers, you're something.

COX

(Down to business) I happened—just in passing, you understand—to mention the portrait of Malcolm to Madame Girard.

ELOISA

(Going along with it) Just in passing.

COX

Yes, and she seemed—well, how shall I put it?—she seemed beside her-self.

ELOISA

(Feigned lack of interest) Oh? Yes?

COX

Ah. How we dissemble.

ELOISA

I can't imagine what you're talking about.

COX

Madame Girard finds herself in the curious dilemma of, on the one hand, feeling that Malcolm is the most ungrateful child who ever lived, and, on the other hand, retaining for the boy—or, to put it most accurately, for the fact of him—a possessiveness that borders on mania.

ELOISA

(*More openly interested*) Oh, really?

COX

Yes; and when I mentioned to her that you were painting his portrait, her eyes flashed with the singular fire that's the exclusive property of the obsessed.

ELOISA (*Tiny pause*)

Meaning?

COX

Meaning simply that Madame Girard will stop at nothing to have Malcolm's portrait. That I think you've got a big sale coming.

ELOISA (*Knowingly*)

Yeah? And?

COX

And that I hope you'll not forget my commission.

ELOISA (*Airily*)

Oh, Professor Cox, you'll have your ten percent.

COX (*Clears his throat*)

Uh, twenty.

ELOISA (*Steely*)

Fifteen.

COX

Agreed.

MADAME GIRARD'S VOICE (*offstage*)

Eloisa Brace? Eloisa Brace?

COX

Aha! You see? I think I'll go out this way, if you don't mind.

MADAME GIRARD'S VOICE

Eloisa Brace?

COX

And leave you two ladies to your business.

ELOISA

(Fact, but no judgment) You're a terrible man, Professor Cox.

COX *(Exiting)*

Yes? Well, do keep in the back of your mind that the role of a post-Christian martyr is not an easy one.

ELOISA *(As* COX *exits)*

A post-Christian martyr!

MADAME GIRARD *(Entering)*

Eloisa Brace? It is I!

ELOISA

(Feigned surprise) Why, Madame Girard!

MADAME GIRARD

I'm lonely, my dear.

ELOISA

Well, sure you're lonely, but . . .

MADAME GIRARD

You have a young man named Malcolm here, and don't pretend you've not.

ELOISA

Why, yes! I'm painting his portrait.

MADAME GIRARD

Oh? Then I must buy it at once! I've not been so taken with a person in years.

ELOISA

(Drinking, or pouring brandy) But, lady, I haven't finished it yet, and . . .

MADAME GIRARD

What are you doing?

ELOISA

I'm sipping brandy.

MADAME GIRARD

At nine-thirty in the morning?

ELOISA

You upset me so, Madame Girard, as you well know, and sometimes a finger of brandy helps me get through.

MADAME GIRARD

I know nothing of your anxieties. All I know is Malcolm is here and you are painting his portrait. *I* discovered *him,* and *I* claim *it.*

ELOISA

Madame Girard! Listen to reason!

MADAME GIRARD

I am claiming my own is all. If that is decent brandy, I might just have a taste.

ELOISA

Oh, please! You know we buy only a cheap domestic.

MADAME GIRARD

(*Sniffs with displeasure*) Well, naturally, what can one expect?

ELOISA

Why don't you just toot along, Madame Girard? Your wealth and position don't entitle you to come into a private house and . . .

MADAME GIRARD (*Snorts*)

A public house, from what I've heard! The things you've done to that sweet, though ungrateful child.

ELOISA

Like what!

MADAME GIRARD

(*Momentarily stopped*) Well, you have *done* something to him, haven't you?

ELOISA

Well, it's a little crowded around here—what with musicians coming and going at all hours—and there aren't enough *beds,* so Malcolm gets shifted around sometimes, in the middle of the night—you know, from bed to bed and all, and sometimes we gotta put *three* people in one bed. . . .

MADAME GIRARD

Three! People!

ELOISA

(*Puzzling it through*) Yeah; Malcolm said it was like traveling in Czechoslovakia during a war. Though how Malcolm could know that, I can't imagine.

MADAME GIRARD

I'm glad for his own sake that Malcolm's father, or whatever he was, died or whatever he did.

ELOISA

There you go: your middle-class prejudices coming out. Everybody's gotta begin sometime. (*Exits*)

MADAME GIRARD

Eloisa! Eloisa Brace!

(MALCOLM *enters, sees* MADAME GIRARD)

MALCOLM

Madame Girard!

MADAME GIRARD

Are you all right, dear child? Loss? What have they done to you?

MALCOLM

Not . . . not much.

MADAME GIRARD

Have you kept your innocence! Oh, Malcolm, have they *used* you?

MALCOLM

Well, it *is* a little crowded when it comes to bedtime, and I suppose I've . . .

MADAME GIRARD (*Envelops him*)

Oh, my dear child!

GIRARD GIRARD (*Entering*)

Monstre! Take your hands off Malcolm at once!

MALCOLM

Mr. Girard!

MADAME GIRARD

Is that you, Girard Girard?

GIRARD GIRARD

It is I, Madame Girard.

MALCOLM

How . . . how wonderful.

MADAME GIRARD (*Still sweet*)

Why aren't you in the midst of one of your adulteries, Girard Girard?

GIRARD GIRARD

I have been in Idaho, Madame Girard, making six million dollars.

MADAME GIRARD

You said you would be in Iowa, making four.

GIRARD GIRARD

You misheard me, then, when I told you where I was going and to what end.

MADAME GIRARD

All I can believe is what the detectives say is so.

GIRARD GIRARD

And all I can believe, Madame Girard, is what my wits tell me is so.

MADAME GIRARD *(So sweet)*

Then I have the better of it, Girard Girard.

GIRARD GIRARD

This once, my dear, I think it is I.

MADAME GIRARD

(After a tiny pause) Ooooooooohhhh?

MALCOLM

(To GIRARD GIRARD*)* I'm so glad to see you!

GIRARD GIRARD

(Not too unpleasantly) Be quiet, Malcolm.

MADAME GIRARD

Why are you here, Girard Girard?

GIRARD GIRARD

I have come for something of great value.

MADAME GIRARD

Yes? As have I! And you shall not have it, sir!

GIRARD GIRARD

I am in the habit of finding my desires satisfied, Madame Girard.

MADAME GIRARD

Oooohhhh, are you ever!

GIRARD GIRARD

But since I find you here, let me speak of a related matter. Do you remember, Madame Girard, that night, so long ago, when we sat in the dark woods, near the lagoon, by the Javanese temples . . .?

MADAME GIRARD

When I gave you your victory, Girard Girard? The night I surrendered myself to your blandishments and agreed to become your wife?

GIRARD GIRARD

That very night.

MADAME GIRARD

I recall it. I gave up . . . everything, my life, in return for but one thing, which now I cherish: my name—Madame Girard.

GIRARD GIRARD

It is that which I propose to take from you now.

MADAME GIRARD (*After a pause*)

I do not think . . I hear you well.

GIRARD GIRARD

I have decided, my dear, upon reflection, to give you the separation which you have demanded without cease since the melancholy day of our marriage.

MADAME GIRARD

Certainly, sir, you will let me determine the relationship between what I wish and what I say I wish.

GIRARD GIRARD (*Doom-ridden*)

No longer! I am divorcing you, Madame Girard.

MADAME GIRARD (*Haughty*)

You will do no such thing, sir.

MALCOLM

Please.

GIRARD GIRARD

Listen carefully to what I say: I am divorcing you, Madame Girard; I am marrying Laureen Raphaelson.

MALCOLM

Laureen Raphaelson!

MADAME GIRARD

That slattern.

GIRARD GIRARD

I am taking your name from you, the name I gave you many years ago.

MADAME GIRARD

You have taken many things from me, Girard Girard: my youth, my job, my self-respect, but there is one thing you may never take from me—my name.

GIRARD GIRARD

You may have the mansion and the chateau, and wealth enough to satisfy your every whim. I will take but two things: myself and your name.

MADAME GIRARD

Never, sir!

GIRARD GIRARD

You are history, Madame Girard; you no longer exist.

MADAME GIRARD *(After reflection)*

I will die, Girard Girard; I shall take my life.

GIRARD GIRARD

I think not, madame.

MADAME GIRARD *(Very genteel)*

But what will become of me? *(Loud)* YOU PIG!

GIRARD GIRARD

(A little weary, a little sad) You will move from the mansion to the chateau, and from the chateau back. You will surround yourself with your young beauties, and hide your liquor where you will. You will . . . go on, my dear.

MADAME GIRARD

Girard Girard!! The name!! The name is mine!!

GIRARD GIRARD

No longer, my dear. You are history. And now I think I shall obtain what I came here for.

MADAME GIRARD

Never, sir!! You may not have everything!!

GIRARD GIRARD

Is that a rule, madame? *(Calls, begins moving off)* Eloisa and Jerome Brace? Are you there? It is I, Girard Girard.

MADAME GIRARD

(Moving off in the opposite direction, taking Malcolm's portrait with her) Eloisa! Eloisa!

GIRARD GIRARD

It is I, Girard Girard. *(Exits)*

MADAME GIRARD

Eloisa? Eloisa Brace? *(Exits, leaving* MALCOLM *alone onstage)*

MALCOLM

Girard Girard, sir! Madame Gi . . . everything . . . everything I touch is . . . each place I go, the . . . the, THE WHOLE WORLD IS FLYING APART!! The . . . the whole world is . . . Have . . . have I done this? Is . . . is this because of me? I've . . . I've been polite, and honest, and . . . I've *tried.* I don't understand the world. No, I don't understand it at all. I feel that thing, father . . . Loss. Loss . . . father?

SCENE NINE

(Still Eloisa Brace's studio, immediately following. ELOISA *precedes* JEROME *onstage)*

ELOISA *(Shrugs)*

O.K. *(Calls)* Uh, Malcolm, baby!

JEROME

How's the old Malc!?

MALCOLM

(Patient, but confused) I'm *fine*, Jerome.

JEROME

(False heartiness) Well, good, kid!

ELOISA

(Hating to start) Uh . . . Malcolm . . .

JEROME

(Coming to her aid) Malc, we think it's time you were moving on, boy.

MALCOLM

Moving? On?

JEROME

(False heartiness) Sure, you don't wanna spend your life in a place like this, buncha jazz musicians, concerts going on, lotta drinking and all, you wanna . . . you wanna go be with your own type, Malc.

MALCOLM

But . . . don't you like me here? *(Looks from one to the other)* I mean, where would I go?

JEROME

Oh, that's all set, kid. . . .

ELOISA

Malcolm, Jerome and I have come into quite a bit of money . . . and we're gonna close up shop for a couple 'a months, an' . . . take a little trip. You know? O.K.?

JEROME

(As MALCOLM *is silent)* Fact is, Malc, Madame Girard got what she came for . . .

ELOISA

. . . your portrait, sweetheart . . .

MALCOLM *(Confused)*
She . . . she really wanted the picture?

JEROME
Well, she must of, kid; I mean, that lady right next to you there is happy possessor of the check for the sale of one portrait of someone looks very much like you.

ELOISA
(Patting her bodice) Ten thousand dollars, Malcolm. I am, next to Madame Girard, probably the happiest woman on God's green earth.

MALCOLM *(Amazed)*
Ten . . . thousand . . . dollars?

ELOISA *(Blushing)*
Yup!

MALCOLM
(Doubt on his face, and confusion) For . . . that *painting?*

ELOISA *(Ire rising)*
Well, some people think my brushwork is worth a great deal more than others, it would appear.

MALCOLM *(Lying nicely)*
I didn't mean *that,* Eloisa; it's a . . . it was a lovely painting.

JEROME
Ten thousand bucks lovely, Malc.

MALCOLM
(Thinks a moment, then) Wow.

ELOISA
And Jerome's come into a little money, too, himself.

JEROME *(Blushing)*
Aw, you don't have to mention that, baby. . . .

MALCOLM
Do . . . do you paint, too, Jerome?

JEROME
(Explaining away something a little shady) Well, no kid, not that, I . . . well, you see, Malc . . .

ELOISA
You see, Malcolm, with Madame Girard getting the painting and all, Girard Girard wondered if he couldn't have you. And we told him, naturally, that you were happy here, with us, and our friends, and all, and that

we didn't see any reason why *he* should have you when we were all so happy *together.* I mean with Madame Girard coming along and practically stealing your portrait right from under our collective nose—for a song!—and now all we have left *is* you . . .

JEROME

. . . and why would he want to take *that* away from us, too . . .

ELOISA

. . . exactly.

MALCOLM

(After a short pause; rather unhappy) Did you *sell* me to him, Jerome? Did you sell me to Mr. Girard?

JEROME *(Whining)*

Aw, now, Malc . . .

ELOISA

(Rather put out) I wouldn't put it *that* way, Malcolm. . . .

MALCOLM

How much did you *get* for me, Jerome? *(Jerome fidgets, doesn't answer)* How much did I fetch?

ELOISA

(To fill an awkward silence) I'm afraid you didn't do quite as well as your picture, sweetheart. . . .

MALCOLM

(Sad, but steely) How much did you sell me for, Jerome?

JEROME

Thirty-five hundred dollars.

MALCOLM

(Sad, nodding) I see.

JEROME

You'll be happy with Mr. Girard, Malc.

ELOISA

Oh, you *will*, sweetie!

MALCOLM *(Tiny voice)*

Where am I to go? *(Clears his throat)* I say, where am I to go?

JEROME

He's waiting for you . . .

ELOISA *(Enthusiastically)*

. . . at the entrance to the botanical gardens.

JEROME *(Soft)*

Right now!

ELOISA

Unh-hunh.

MALCOLM

(Confused, lost) Well . . . well, I think I'll say goodbye, then.

JEROME

Not goodbye, Malc; au revoir!

ELOISA

You come see us when we get back . . . if we go.

MALCOLM

(As things fly apart, as the BRACES *vanish)* Yes, well . . . Goodbye, Jerome the burglar, goodbye, Eloisa Brace. Goodbye. Goodbye. *(Alone)* Sold? Sold to Mr. Girard? Like a . . . a white slave or something? Well, why not? I mean, I suppose it's as natural as anything in the world. But really! You'd think I could stick . . . somewhere! Sold? SOLD? The . . . THE WHOLE WORLD IS FLYING APART! And . . . what's to become of me? WHAT'S TO BECOME OF ME NOW!!??

ACT TWO

SCENE ONE

(The entrance to the botanical gardens. Daylight. MALCOLM *asleep.* GUS *enters: tall, brawny, got up in motorcycle uniform; regards* MALCOLM *briefly, kicks him gently)*

GUS

Hey, buddy; hey; hey, you, there.

MALCOLM

(Waking up, sort of beside himself) Hm? Hm? Girard Girard, is that . . . ? Oh; excuse me; I'm sorry.

GUS

(Not unfriendly; just all business) You a contemporary?

MALCOLM

(Looking around for GIRARD GIRARD*)* Have you seen . . . you haven't seen Mr. Girard Girard nearby, have you?

GUS

Don't kid around, buddy.

MALCOLM *(Very sincere)*

Oh, I'm not kidding around. I assure you, I'm quite serious. He was supposed to be here last night, and he and I . . .

GUS

Unh-hunh. I said: you a contemporary?

MALCOLM *(Ponders it)*

A contemporary of *what*?

GUS

(Not understanding) What?

MALCOLM

Of *what*?

GUS

(A little edge to his tone) I don't know what you talkin' about, mister.

MALCOLM

(Rubbing his eyes) Well, I'm afraid I don't know what you're talking about, either.

GUS *(Shrugs)*

Don't matter. If you one of the contemporaries, we go right on over to Melba's. If you ain't, it don't matter too awful much anyhow, on account of you are the *type*.

MALCOLM *(Rather abstracted)*

You don't seem to understand. I came here yesterday afternoon, at the—I suppose I should say invitation—of Mr. Girard Girard—I'm sure you've heard of him—the magnate?

GUS

(Shaking his head) Unh-unh.

MALCOLM

Well; I would have thought everybody had.

GUS

Let's go.

MALCOLM *(Rather panicky)*

Go! I can't go anywhere, I've been too far already. You don't know what's happened to me, sir!

GUS

(Firm, but not ugly) Stow it, buddy! Now, come on.

MALCOLM

No! I won't! *I can't!*

GUS

You really waiting for anybody?

MALCOLM *(Small, lost)*

I . . . thought I was.

GUS

Unh-hunh. Figgered. Come on, boy.

MALCOLM *(Being dragged)*

Who is . . . who is . . . Melba?

GUS

Melba? You don't know who Melba is?

MALCOLM

I've heard of who Melba was, but this can't possibly be the same lady.

GUS

Where you been living, boy?

MALCOLM

Oh, lots of places.

GUS

An' you never heard of Melba. Well, buddy, you got a pleasure comin'. Melba is a *singer.* And she ain't just any singer, she is . . . man, she got solid gold records stacked up like they was dishes.

MALCOLM *(Quite pleased)*

Really?

GUS

You ain't never heard her records? . . . *Hot in the Rocker?*

MALCOLM

N . . . nooo.

GUS

Or, *When You Said Goodbye, Dark Daddy?*

MALCOLM *(Uncertain)*

I . . . don't think so; no.

GUS

Boy! You ain't been anywhere. *(Sings)*
　　"When you said goodbye, dark daddy,
　　Did you know I'd not yet said hello?"

MALCOLM

(Somewhat dubious) That's . . . very catchy.

GUS

She sold eight million of that one.

MALCOLM

(Fascinated by the high figure, nothing else) Eight million! Really!

GUS

Melba gonna like you. Boy, I *hope* she like you. She say to me, Gus, you go out and find me a contemporary. *(Small threat)* You better be a contemporary.

MALCOLM

(Noticing where they're coming to) Well, I'm bound to be, aren't I, of . . . something.

GUS

(Shaking his head) You better be, that's all I gotta say.

SCENE TWO

(We have come to the backstage area of the club wherein MELBA
is performing; we hear screaming from "onstage," and we hear
MELBA *singing, vaguely; what we hear mostly is applause and
screaming)*

MALCOLM

Where *are* we?

GUS

You hear that? You hear them people?

MALCOLM

(Rather put off) Yes, what . . . what *is* all this?

GUS *(Proud)*

That's Melba. Listen to 'em yellin. Boy! She gets 'em. *(Shouting)* GO TO
IT, MELBA, BABY!

MALCOLM

But, where are we?

GUS

Why'n't you sit yourself down wait a bit. GO TO IT, BABY. GIVE IT
TO 'EM!

MALCOLM *(Whining some)*

I shouldn't be here; Mr. Girard won't know where to find me, and . . .
or anything.

GUS

Melba be offstage soon, you just sit wait on her. (WAITER *enters)* Hey,
Jocko, give us a couple of drinks, now, I brought me a contemporary.

JOCKO

Usual, Gus?

GUS

Natcherly. What you wanna drink, boy?

MALCOLM

(To JOCKO, *sensing he looks familiar)* How do you do? *(To* GUS) I . . . I don't
know; I don't drink very . . .

GUS

Two of the usual, Jocko-boy; two big ones. (JOCKO *nods, begins to exit)* She
knockin'em out, hey?

JOCKO

Right out flat. Two big ones. *(Exits)*
(The song ends, great screaming, shouting. MELBA *backs onstage)*

MELBA

All right! All right! Jesus! God, they love me! Give me a drink. JOCKO!

JOCKO

Here you go, Melba: a big one, the usual.

MELBA

Oh, Jocko baby, you like chimes. *(To them all)* Listen to those bastards out
there. Doesn't that warm the old cockles? Wow!

JOCKO

They love you, Melba.

MELBA *(About "them")*

Nudnicks.

MALCOLM *(To* JOCKO)

Th-thank you.

MELBA *(Shouting)*

ALL RIGHT! I'LL BE OUT! SHUT THE . . . *(Mutters)* Bums. *(Notices*
MALCOLM) What you got here, Gus?

JOCKO *(Exiting)*

Something mighty young, Melba.

GUS

Hey, Melba? You asked me to go find you a contemporary. How's this? He
contemporary enough?

MELBA *(Circles* MALCOLM)

Hmmmm. What's your name, baby?

MALCOLM

M-Malcolm . . . Melba.

GUS *(Proud)*

He a contemporary or not?

MELBA *(Still appraising)*

Unh-hunh. Yup, that's what it is.

GUS *(Proud)*

I knew I could do it.

MELBA

(Sitting next to Malcolm, putting her arm on him) I'm Melba, honey . . .
sweet little Malcolm.

MALCOLM *(Blushing)*

Aw, gee . . .

MELBA

(Stroking his cheek) You like me a little bit, Malcolm, baby?

MALCOLM

(About to say something else, does not, kisses MELBA's *hand)* I've . . . I've had such a . . . long . . . short . . . life.

MELBA

(Raises her glass) To Malcolm, and his long short life. *(Leaning to him)* I could marry you, baby. (MALCOLM *kisses her hand again)*

GUS

You can't get married again, Melba; think of . . .

MELBA *(Threatening)*

That will do, Gus. *(To* MALCOLM, *now)* Gus was my first husband, old number one, as we sometimes call him.

GUS

I'm not ashamed of it, Melba.

MELBA

I'm so glad he found you, baby. *(Kisses* MALCOLM *on the mouth)* Do you think you could find happiness with me? Hunh?

MALCOLM

(Hesitates briefly, then in tearful, tired relief) Oh, yes I do, Melba; I really do.

MELBA *(To* GUS)

Isn't it wonderful? Us young people are so . . . are you sulking again? *(No answer; addresses* MALCOLM *again) Would* you marry me, Malcolm?

GUS *(Some anguish)*

It's too sudden. Wait till Thursday, or somethin'.

MELBA *(To* MALCOLM)

Do you really care for me? I mean, honest-really?

MALCOLM *(Slowly, seriously)*

I . . . I do, Melba. I've lost so much. *(Kisses her on the throat, impulsively)* I DO, MELBA: I DO!

MELBA

I have never been so quickly surprised, or so quickly happy. *(To* GUS; *rather ugly)* You begrudge me this happiness, don't you! You begrudge me this tiny, tiny bit of happiness in my life of pettiness and struggle. . . .

GUS

Melba, honey, happiness is the last thing I begrudge you, but I don't want
you to rush into matrimony this here time; think of all the other times you
done got stung. Think of the courts, Melba, honey.

MELBA *(To* MALCOLM*)*

He begrudges me. *(Snuggles)* God, we'll be happy—for a long, long time.

MALCOLM

(A gurgling sound, resembling a coo) Rrrooooooooo. *(Sits up, startled)*

MELBA

Isn't he beautiful, Gus? You notice the dimples when he smiles. *(Snuggles
again)* Aw, *sweet*heart!

MALCOLM

Rrrrooooooo. But *you're* beautiful, Melba. You're the beautiful one.

MELBA

And you really feel you want to marry me, dearest?

GUS *(A cry of pain)*

MELBA, SWEET JESUS!!

MELBA *(To* MALCOLM*)*

He's carrying a torch, sweetheart; don't pay any attention to him.

MALCOLM

(Stammering) You're . . . my girl . . . Melba.

MELBA

(Sighing happily) I've simply got it is all; it's come like lightning, and . . .
well, I've been got.

GUS

I may be carryin' a torch, Melba, honey, but SWEET JESUS, HE AIN'T
OLD ENOUGH!

MELBA

(Stopping MALCOLM's *ears)* Don't listen to him; jealousy and rage, that's all
it is. Six weeks of marriage teaches you an awful lot about a man. But *our*
marriage, Malcolm, will last on, and on . . . precious.

MALCOLM

(About to swoon with joy) Oh, Melba!

MELBA

(Rising, more businesslike) Good boy. Now, I gotta go out and sing some
more, sing for our wedding supper, babyface.

MALCOLM

But . . . but, Melba!

MELBA

No buts, baby. Momma gotta work.

MALCOLM

Aw, Melba . . .

MELBA *(Hand on hip)*

Well, of course, I *could* quit my career, honey, and you could go out run telegrams or something.

MALCOLM *(Little boy)*

I . . . I understand, Melba.

MELBA *(Effusive again)*

Aw, give me a kiss, sweetheart. *(Engulfs* MALCOLM *again, kisses him lots)*

MALCOLM

Rrrrrrrooooooo.

MELBA

You hear those bastards out there? They're my public, angel-face, those no-goods. You my private. See ya Thursday, hunh?

MALCOLM *(Very serious)*

Till . . . till Thursday . . . Melba.

MELBA

Bye, sweetpants. *(As the crowd sounds increase)* I'M COMING! YA BUMS! *(To* MALCOLM, *kissing him one last time)* Gus'll take real good care of you, baby. *(To* GUS) Gus, you take real good care of, uh, Malcolm here, ya hear? *(Waving at* MALCOLM, *blowing him a kiss. Sotto voce to* GUS, *taking money from her bodice, giving it to* GUS) Mature him up a little, you know? You know what I mean? Mature him up a little.

*(*MELBA *exits, the crowd sounds swell.)*

ENTRE-SCENE

(GUS *and* MALCOLM *walking, the last scene having faded*)

GUS

(*Shaking his head*) I don't know; I just don't know.

MALCOLM (*Lost little boy*)

Gus? . . . What have I done?

GUS

(*Talking more or less to himself*) Mature him up a little bit, she says. Mature him up! How the hell I gonna do that, hunh?

MALCOLM

Gus? What have I done?

GUS

Hm?

MALCOLM

What have I done?

GUS

What have you done!? You have got yourself engaged to Melba baby, that what you done.

MALCOLM

I don't under*stand*.

GUS (*Remembering*)

She sure is a knockout, hunh?

MALCOLM

I mean, I've never *felt* like that before, and everything happened so quickly, and . . .

GUS

Bang! it hits! Unh? The old kazamm; pow!

MALCOLM (*Wonder*)

But I just met her, and . . .

GUS

Well, you get a chance to get to know her some.

MALCOLM

It's . . . it's being so close to her like that . . . when she . . . hugs and every-thing.

GUS *(Pained)*

Don't talk about it, boy.

MALCOLM *(Blushing)*

And . . . and when she kisses and all . . .

GUS *(Anguish)*

Just *don't!* Don't *stir* me.

MALCOLM

. . . and everything happens, and . . .

GUS

(Returning slowly to businesslike stature) An' . . . an' now we gotta mature you up some. *(Shows* MALCOLM *the money)* See this? This is money to mature you up, boy. Now, look, Malco-boy, I gotta ask you a plain question.

MALCOLM

(Nodding happily) Yes.

GUS

To put it delicate-like, boy, have you ever been completely and solidly joined to a woman? Have you ever been joined to a woman the way nature meant? Yes or no.

MALCOLM

(After a puzzled pause) Well, it's always been so very dark— where I was— and people were—shifting so . . .

GUS

I can see you ain't, and that's what Melba meant—what she sent us out for, to mature you up.

SCENE THREE

(Set comes on. Sign saying PRIVATE AND TURKISH BATHS. CABINETS AND OVERNIGHT COTTAGES. $2.00*)*

GUS

You see that place over there? That's where I'm gonna take you: Rosita's. Madame Rosita they used to call her. You heard of her?

MALCOLM

(Shakes his head) No.

GUS

You ain't heard of anything! Well, that's what I'm here for. *(Mumbles)* That what sweet Melba told me t'do—get you ready. . . .

MALCOLM
(A little confused) You're . . . you're very kind, Gus.

GUS
(Gives MALCOLM *a funny look; calls)* Hey, Miles, Miles? *(A seedy man comes out, green visor; played by the actor who plays* COX*)* Miles? How you doin', boy?

MILES
Gus, is that really you? Well, I'll be damned. *(Looks at* MALCOLM, *who is staring at him, open-mouthed)* Where'd you get him—the one with his mouth hangin' open?

MALCOLM *(Rather hurt)*
But, Mr. Cox!

MILES
(It is not COX, *of course)* Name is Miles, boy. Gus, how long's it been?

GUS
(Bringing out the money) Need some work done, Miles; quick and special.

MALCOLM *(Very hurt)*
Mr. Cox!

MILES *(Very straight)*
That ain't my name, boy. Work, Gus?

GUS *(Yawning)*
Yeah, house special for the boy.

MILES
(Looks at MALCOLM *dubiously)* I was just wonderin' if you'd noticed this kid here is sorta young.

GUS
(Waves the money under MILES' *nose)* Oh, I don't know.

MILES
Yeah, well, looks is deceiving.

GUS
He gonna marry Melba.

MILES
Hunh! Who ain't!

MALCOLM *(Offended)*
Please!

GUS *(To* MALCOLM*)*
Now, upstairs is where you're gonna go, kiddie. When you through, you come down here an' wake me up. Which is my room, Miles?

MILES

(Counting the money) You pick one out; nobody here tonight at all.

GUS

O.K., I take me old number twenty-two. *(To MALCOLM)* You got that, boy? Twenty-two.

MALCOLM

(Shivering a little) R-right.
> *(Enters a woman of indeterminate age, a parody of a whore; to be played by the actress who plays LAUREEN)*

ROSITA

Gus! Baby! It's been years! *(Goes to embrace him)*

GUS

It's the boy this time, uh, sweetheart. I just gonna get me a shower and a snooze; I ain't had no sleep in a week, if you know what I mean.

ROSITA

Let me get this all down. You are sending *him* . . . upstairs for *you*.

GUS

Break him in, for Christ's sake, will ya?

MALCOLM (A *little scared*)

I could swear I know you, madame.

GUS

(To MALCOLM; weary) You do like I told you now, back in the street. I want you to go through it all just like I told you nature meant.

ROSITA

(Gives GUS a quiet raspberry; says to MALCOLM) O.K., you come on with me, honey. *(Begins dragging MALCOLM off)*

GUS

(To MALCOLM as he is exited) An' don't you come back down without you had it, you hear?

MALCOLM (*Being exited*)

Had . . . had what!

ROSITA

Come on.

MILES

(Shakes his head; laughs) Jesus!

GUS (*Chuckling*)

Poor baby boy.

MILES

Gonna shack up with Melba, hunh?

GUS

Weddin' bells and all. *(Moving off, slowly, wearily)* Oh, I tell you, Miles, I am so weary, so sad. . . . I think I'll lie down, not wake up again. Wouldn't matter . . . 'cept for the kid, there.

MILES *(As they exit)*

How old *is* he?

GUS

Malco? I don't know: fourteen, fifteen, maybe. Don't matter: Melba'll age him up a little.

(MILES *and* GUS *have exited*)

SCENE FOUR

(MALCOLM *and* ROSITA *come on,* MALCOLM *carrying the locket*)

ROSITA

Well, goodbye and God bless, kiddie. You're the real stuff.

MALCOLM

Gee, thanks, Rosita.

ROSITA

You've made an old woman very happy. *(She exits as soon as possible)*

MALCOLM

(Left alone, joyous) Melba? Melba? (MELBA *appears, way down right, say, with open arms*)

MELBA

Here I am, baby. Come to Momma!

MALCOLM

(Going to her, puppylike enthusiasm) I . . . I did it, Melba, all the way through . . . three times! Wow! It looks like I'll be a bridegroom after all.

MELBA *(Pleased)*

Yeah?

MALCOLM

Yes, and Madame Rosita paid me a compliment; she said I was the real stuff, and she gave me tea . . . in between . . . and when we were all done she gave me this locket, which has a real, little tiny American flag all rolled up inside.

MELBA

Yeah; that's great. Let's go to Chicago, baby!

MALCOLM

But . . . but why?

MELBA

You ever been married in Chicago?

MALCOLM

Well . . . no!

MELBA

Well, neither have I, baby! Let's go! *(They race off together)*

ENTRE-SCENE

(Another no-set promenade. MADAME GIRARD *comes on, followed by* KERMIT; *they stroll)*

MADAME GIRARD

(Not looking at KERMIT *as they walk;* KERMIT *keeps eyeing her, with a set mouth and mistrustful eyes)* I understand—though one is never sure of one's information in a world of gossips—that they were married in Chicago. Would you like a peppermint? No? That they were married in Chicago, by some defrocked justice of the peace—a scandal, if you care for my opinion—stop eyeing me—that they flew to the Caribbean for a honeymoon which was interrupted by their having to move from hotel to hotel, country to country, that they have returned here, where that loathsome brat of a chanteuse has resumed her career of caterwauling, and that Malcolm—that poor, dear child—walk with me, can you?— is virtually a prisoner in some den she keeps. *(Sobs)* I have written *letters!* I have *tele*phoned! My calls have been answered by a manservant who sounds Cuban at the least, and my letters! Stop staring at me! My letters have been returned to me, unopened, with semi-literate notes, scrawled by that girl Svengali, informing me that Malcolm—oh, dear God, child, come back to me!—is busy at being married, is too occupied and happy to be, as she puts it, dragged under by his past! If you will not walk like a proper companion, we shall both stand still. *(They stand still)* Too occupied! Too happy! Dear Lord, can people be that? *(*KERMIT *stands in front of her, rather like a bulldog about to spring)* Are you going to bite me? You?—you who ruined everything? You who cringed when we came to take you with us? You, but for whom we should all be together now, Malcolm with us? Malcolm's picture! His picture stares at me, and tells me, "It is not I, dear Madame Girard, not

I. Not I, dear Madame Girard, not I." I can't look at it any more! It is *not* my Malcolm. Help me! Help me, please! Get me my Malcolm back! (KERMIT *starts walking off*) Wait! Help me! Dearest Kermit! Wait! (*She exits after him*)

SCENE FIVE

(*As* MADAME GIRARD *exits, we hear* MALCOLM *and* MELBA *giggling, she shrieking a little, too. Lights come up on* MALCOLM *in bed, naked to the waist, or wearing pajamas, depending on the build of the actor playing the part.* MELBA *in a negligee, on the bed beside him.* MELBA *is tickling him*)

MALCOLM

(*Very ticklish, speaks between giggles*) Melba . . . honey . . . please . . . Melba . . .

MELBA

How's my kitchy-koo? Kitchy-kitchy-kitchy? Hmmmm?

MALCOLM (*A cry-giggle*)

MMMM EEEEELLLLLBBBBB AAAAA

MELBA

Kitchy-kitchy-kitchy? Aw, sweetheart. (*Kisses him all over*) Aw, baby. Come to Melba.

MALCOLM

(*Giggles subsiding some*) Aw, honest, Melba, I love you; I do.

MELBA

(*Seriously, sensuously; hand on his crotch*) Oh, I do love you, too, sweet pants. Yes, I do. . . . You have *got* it, baby; you have got what Melba wants.

MALCOLM

We . . . do an awful lot of being married, don't we, Melba?

MELBA (*Eyes closed*)

Oooooh, you are good at marriage, sweetheart, yes, you are. Gimme that mouth of yours, tonguey-boy. Ummmmmmmm. (*Kisses him fervently*) Oh baby let's do marriage right this second sweetheart lover baby dollface, c'mon, C'MON!

MALCOLM

(*Seeing that* HELIODORO, *the Cuban valet, has entered with a tray of coffee*) Uh, Melba . . .

MELBA

C'mon, sweetpants, let's get some action goin'. . . .

MALCOLM

Uh . . . good—good morning, Heliodoro.

MELBA

Hunh? *(Sees* HELIODORO*)* What the hell do you want?

HELIODORO

(Who is played by one of the YOUNG MEN*)* Coffee; coffee time.

MELBA

Nuts! It's take the frigging coffee and get the hell out of the bedroom time; that's what time it is.

MALCOLM

I'd . . . *(timidly)* . . . I'd like some coffee, Melba, and . . . and maybe some breakfast? Breakfast, too?

MELBA *(Mock tough)*

Married six weeks, an' he's cold as a stone. Look at 'im. *(Cuddles)* Baby want breakfast?

MALCOLM

Just . . . just a little.

MELBA

*(Gets *up off the bed, stretches, shows off a little for* HELIODORO)* O.K. Momma got to go to work anyway. But you stay right there, sweetheart; you just lie there an' read a funny-book, or somethin', so Momma know where you are when she want you. O.K.?

MALCOLM *(So smitten)*

I'll . . . be right here where you want me, Melba.

MELBA

Right on top, baby! That's where I want you. Hey, don't forget, hotrocks, we're goin' out clubbin' tonight after I get done work.

MALCOLM

(Small protest in this) We go . . . to a nightclub *every* night, Melba. At least one.

MELBA *(To a child)*

Well, I'm proud of my baby. *(To* HELIODORO*)* Fix him a Bloody Mary or somethin', will you?

HELIODORO

Maybe he shouldn't drink so . . .

MELBA *(Murderous)*

Fix him a goddam Bloody Mary! *(Blows* MALCOLM *a kiss)* See you, sweet-heart. *(Exits)*

HELIODORO

You want coffee?

MALCOLM

Yes, please, and . . . I don't need a Bloody Mary, O.K.? Some . . . eggs and toast and bacon, and . . .

HELIODORO

You gettin' thin.

MALCOLM

(Sweet and innocent) Melba says marriage is a thinning business.

HELIODORO *(Shrugs)*

I suppose she oughta know.

MALCOLM

Have you been married, Heliodoro?

HELIODORO *(Laughs)*

Me? No, I'm too young.

MALCOLM

How old *are* you?

HELIODORO

Twenty-two.

MALCOLM *(Sad)*

Yes, that's very young. *(Brightly)* I'm . . . fifteen, I think.

HELIODORO

(Changing the subject) That . . . that lady called again today.

MALCOLM *(Some gloom)*

I don't know why Melba won't let me see Madame Girard or . . . or any-body . . . any of my friends. I . . . well, I love Melba like all get-out, and everything . . . but . . I get lonely . . . just being here like this.

HELIODORO

(A little embarrassed) You . . . you want to start your Bloody Marys?

MALCOLM

(Weary; head back on pillow) I suppose so; I suppose I'd better if Melba thinks I should.

HELIODORO

I'll bring you a Bloody Mary.

MALCOLM *(Weary)*

I suppose you should: I've got a long, hard day ahead of me.

(FADE)

ENTRE-SCENE

*(*ELOISA *and* JEROME *come on, huffily, pursued by* GIRARD GIRARD.
No set needed; this can *be in the nature of a promenade)*

ELOISA

I have never been so insulted; never, in my long and scrabby life—the life
of an artist, always hurt, always wanting—have I been so insulted. Jerome?
Don't talk to the man.

GIRARD GIRARD

But my dear Mrs. Brace . . .

ELOISA

Never.

GIRARD GIRARD

(Both of the others are huffily silent. Reasoning) I have come to you,
beseeching, a humble man, casting about in the dark . . .

ELOISA

You have not! You came in here, you came upon us, near-*flagrante*, howling your insults. . . .

GIRARD GIRARD

I DID NO SUCH THING!

ELOISA

(Snappish; for confirmation) Jerome?

JEROME

Never, in all my years behind bars . . .

GIRARD GIRARD *(Anguish)*

Where is Malcolm? Please!

ELOISA

Hah! Accusing us again, are you?

GIRARD GIRARD

(Patient) I have accused you of nothing, my good woman. I merely
explained that I had a business matter of some urgency to settle and when
I arrived at the botanical gardens, some hours later than I had intended
to . . .

ELOISA

He'd gone!

GIRARD GIRARD

Yes!

ELOISA

And that *we* had stolen him!

GIRARD GIRARD

No!

JEROME   *(Sneering)*

We heard you.

GIRARD GIRARD

I suggested no such thing!

ELOISA

We may be poor . . .

JEROME

. . . and I may have a record a yard long, but . . .

GIRARD GIRARD

WHERE IS MALCOLM!?

ELOISA

(Sniffs. After a tiny pause) I'm sure we don't know.

JEROME

(Oily) It's out of our hands, buddy; we delivered the merchandise, free and clear, good condition; we don't take no responsibility for . . .

GIRARD GIRARD

Please! I must have him!

ELOISA   *(Grand)*

It would seem to me that if you're careless enough to . . . abandon the child under some bushes somewhere while you go about your filthy money-making . . .

JEROME

. . . that it's hardly our affair.

ELOISA

We did not steal him.

GIRARD GIRARD *(Sad, defeated)*

I . . . I merely wondered.

ELOISA

Well, we . . . we have problems enough of our own, without running any sort of . . .

GIRARD GIRARD

If . . . if he returns to you . . .

ELOISA

There you go again.

JEROME

Prison was nothing! The unimaginable indignities of the cell block were .
. . were frolic next to . . . to your vile and tawdry suggestion, sir.

GIRARD GIRARD

Jerome, I merely . . .

ELOISA

Never! Tell me this, Girard Girard: do you think your wealth entitles you?
Do you?

JEROME

The older prisoners, after lights out, making straight for the cells where the
younger inmates cower, their rough blankets pulled over their heads . . .

GIRARD GIRARD

My dear friends . . .

ELOISA

La vie de Boheme, Girard Girard, may indeed seem loose and unprinci-
pled to some, but . . .

JEROME

. . . or the entrapments in the shower room, two or three, coming at you . . .
lathered bodies, all glistening, slow smiles . .

ELOISA *(An aside)*

Control yourself, Jerome.

SCENE SIX

(To one side of the stage, a nightclub table, with MALCOLM *and*
MELBA *at it, both noticeably drunk. Lots of noise in the background, music, chattering)*

MELBA

You like rum sours, baby?

MALCOLM

I would seem to, Melba-honey. This is number . . . what?

MELBA

Who cares? Drink up.

MALCOLM

(Notices MELBA *open a vial)* Melba, what *is* that stuff you're always putting in our drinks and all?

MELBA

(Pouring some in their drinks) Magic, sweetheart, magic; makes you feel all athletic when we get home, right?

MALCOLM *(Giggles sillily)*

Right, baby.

MELBA

And, of course, I *didn't* marry you for your mind.

MALCOLM

(Drunken pondering) I . . . noticed that.

MELBA

You're gettin' awful thin, big boy. I *like* you thin, you understand, but I suppose I'd like you fat, too.

MALCOLM *(Puppydog)*

I . . . I like you, too, Melba-pussy.

MELBA

(Abrupt, faintly histrionic) Don't call me that; number three called me that; it's sacred.

MALCOLM

What is?

MELBA

(Embarrassed at the sacredness; almost whispers it) Melba-pussy.

MALCOLM *(Laughs)*

Well, what shall I call you? Melba-puppy? *(Laughs greatly, happily)* Melba-puppy?

MELBA

You're annoying, kiddie, you really are.

MALCOLM

(Having noticed a man walk across the stage to a dark area)
That's HE . . . THAT'S MY FATHER! *(Rises)*

MELBA

Sit down, baby.

MALCOLM

(Moving to go after the MAN*)* THAT'S MY FATHER.

MELBA *(Sharp)*

Come back here, Malcolm!

MALCOLM

(Unrestrainable, moving to the other side of the stage) THAT'S MY
FATHER!

SCENE SEVEN

(The area on MELBA *blacks out, and the lights come up on the*
MAN, *in a washroom, facing the audience, washing his hands at a*
basin)

MALCOLM

(Stretching his arms out to the MAN, *weaving a little)* Father! Where did
you *go* all this time? *(The* MAN *either touches his hair or his mustache, does*
not reply or take notice of MALCOLM) Don't you *recognize* me? I'd . . . I'd
recognize *you* anywhere. *(Still no response from the* MAN) Father! *(Goes*
up to him, puts his arm on his shoulder) Please, father . . .

MAN

(Looks straight at MALCOLM, *no recognition; cold)* Would you allow me
to pass?

MALCOLM

You're . . . you're pretending not to recognize me! Is it . . . is it because I
married Melba, or because I left the bench, or because I . . .

MAN

(Making an effort to get by) Allow me to pass!

MALCOLM

(Starting to grapple with the MAN; *the struggle gets hotter)* Please, father!
It's me! It's Malcolm!

MAN

Help! Help!

MALCOLM *(Grappling)*

Please, father! I've missed you so, and I've been so lonely, and . . .

MAN

(Struggling) Let go of me!

MALCOLM

(In tears now) Father! Father!

(The MAN *seizes* MALCOLM *and throws him hard;* MALCOLM *hits either the washbasin or the floor, heavily. An* ATTENDANT *enters, played by the actor who plays* COX)

MAN

(Pointing to the crumpled MALCOLM) Have that child arrested. He attacked me!

MALCOLM

(Weeping, from the floor) Father, I am Malcolm!

MAN

Indeed! *(Turns on his heel, walks into blackness)*

ATTENDANT

Well, now, what's going on? (MALCOLM *babbles a few thank yous as the* ATTENDANT *helps him to a sitting position)*

MALCOLM

Melba? Have you seen my wife, sir?

ATTENDANT *(Incredulous)*

You? Are married?

MALCOLM

(Cheerful through the pain) Yes, sir! Would you like to meet my wife?

ATTENDANT

(Examining MALCOLM'S *head)* You're bleeding, boy.

MALCOLM

I . . . I am?

ATTENDANT

That's quite a cut.

MALCOLM

My father refused to recognize me.

ATTENDANT

Who?

MALCOLM

My . . . my father.

ATTENDANT

That couldn't have been your father, sonny.

MALCOLM

N-no?

ATTENDANT

That old pot's been coming here for years. He's nobody's father.

MALCOLM

I . . . I thought it was my father.

ATTENDANT

Better get you home, kid. You don't look so hot.

MALCOLM

Maybe . . . maybe my father . . . never existed.

ATTENDANT

Who knows, son? Better get you to a doctor before you bleed to death, or something.

MALCOLM

Maybe he never existed at all!

SCENE EIGHT

(MADAME GIRARD *and* HELIODORO *walk on. They are moving toward the solarium*)

MADAME GIRARD

(*All camp is gone from here to the end of the play*) I apologize to you, young man, if I have bothered you with my calls, my constant ringing.

HELIODORO

That's O.K.

MADAME GIRARD

My search for the one decent thing in this entire world.

HELIODORO

It's O.K.

MADAME GIRARD

Where is my Malcolm? And where is that girl?

HELIODORO

She—an' you mean, I think, great Melba-baby—is with the doctor.

MADAME GIRARD

Why was I not told until now?

HELIODORO

You wanna come in the solarium?

MADAME GIRARD

Of course I want to come into the solarium. My God, what a bright solarium! Where *is* she? Where is that filthy girl?

HELIODORO

(*Embarrassed*) You better watch who you talkin' about, buddy.

(MELBA *enters*)

MADAME GIRARD

Is that her?

HELIODORO

She call you filthy, baby.

MELBA

(*Indifferent*) Yeah? Go fix us a drink. (*As* HELIODORO *hangs back*) Well, go on, kiddo.

HELIODORO

I don't wanna leave you here with her, baby.

MELBA

Aw, go be a sweetheart and go get us a drink, hunh?

MADAME GIRARD

Keep your hands off the servants. You are a married woman, if you care to remember.

HELIODORO

See? (*Exits*)

MELBA

(*Braying*) Yeah? Well, look here, Madame Hotsy-Totsy, or whatever your name used to be . . .

MADAME GIRARD

IS!

MELBA

I been married a few times, you know? And I know how to act.

MADAME GIRARD

Have pity on us human beings, please!

MELBA

What do you want, a job or something? You looking for work?

MADAME GIRARD

I am looking for Malcolm!

MELBA

Yeah? Well, I got him, lady; move on.

MADAME GIRARD

I can have you arrested, you know that?

MELBA

Get the hell out of here, will . . .

MADAME GIRARD

THE CHILD IS FIFTEEN YEARS OLD!!!!

MELBA

GET OUT!!

MADAME GIRARD

I warn you, youngish woman, if there is so much as one hair of his precious head that I find damaged, you'll rue the day you ever took it on
yourself to . . .

MELBA

(Really beside herself) GET OUT!!!!

MADAME GIRARD

(While the DOCTOR *is entering)* THERE ARE THINGS IN THIS LIFE
WHICH MAY NOT BE PERMITTED!! *(Sees him)* Are you the doctor?

DOCTOR

I am.

MADAME GIRARD

How is my Malcolm!?

DOCTOR

Are you family?

MADAME GIRARD

I am more than family.

DOCTOR

(Picking his words carefully) He . . . is beyond human care. (MADAME
GIRARD *stifles a cry.)*

MELBA

(Dryly, after a moment) What do you mean, buddy?

DOCTOR

(Looking at neither of them) The child is dying.

MADAME GIRARD

DYING!!

MELBA

(Pause) Don't be stupid.

DOCTOR

There is nothing that can be done: give him rest, a bed to himself, quiet.
He is very near death.

MADAME GIRARD

You are a *quack!*

DOCTOR

I may have seen better days, lady, but I know dying when I look at it.

MELBA

(Clears her throat) Uh, what is my Malcolm-baby dying of?

MADAME GIRARD

(Hoping to make it true) This man doesn't know what he's talking about. People like Malcolm do not die: there isn't room for it.

MELBA *(Rather harsh)*

What's he dying of, hunh?

DOCTOR *(Reticent)*

The . . . young man . . . is dying of a combination of acute alcoholism and, uh, sexual hyperaesthesia, to put it simply.

MADAME GIRARD *(A command)*

NO!

MELBA

(To the doctor; wincing a little) I, uh, didn't get you, baby.

MADAME GIRARD

(Turning full, loss and sickened wrath on MELBA*)* You . . . you . . . WAN-TON! Malcolm? MALCOLM? *(Runs off into the blackness)*

DOCTOR

(Repeating it, mumbling some) Acute alcoholism and sexual hyperaesthesia: the combination of the two . . . well, one would be enough, but . . .

MELBA

(Trying to avoid it, quite nervous) Look, uh, what is this . . . this sexual stuff, hunh? I mean, he's only been with me, and . . .

DOCTOR

Sexual hyperaesthesia?

MELBA

Uh, yeah; that.

DOCTOR

Sexual hperaesthesia is, or can be more easily described as, a violent protracted excess of sexual intercourse. (MELBA *just stares at him)* I can give you a prescription . . . for the child . . . useless, of course. . . . *(Sees the answer is "no," shrugs, exits)*

HELIODORO

(Who is entering as the DOCTOR *exits)* You O.K., baby? (MELBA *is just standing there, swaying a little)* Hey . . . Melba . . . you O.K.?

MELBA

(Preoccupied, a little sad, but calm) Hunh? *(Puts her hand out for his)* Hey, give me a hand, will ya, sweetie? This just ain't a good day. Old Malcolm's gonna die. He's gonna leave us.

HELIODORO *(Quiet surprise)*

Yeah? *(They exit)*

SCENE NINE

(Malcolm's bedroom. MALCOLM *propped up on pillows, pale, half-conscious. The room in near-darkness.* MADAME GIRARD *enters, hesitantly, comes to the bed)*

MADAME GIRARD

Malcolm? Malcolm? Can I help?

MALCOLM *(Little boy)*

Is it . . . true? Am I going to die?

MADAME GIRARD

(Not looking at him; softly) Well . . . who is to say?

MALCOLM *(Home truth)*

You.

MADAME GIRARD

I . . . suspect it may be so.

MALCOLM

(Sits up in bed, says, with great force) BUT I'M NOT EVEN TWENTY! IT'S . . . NOT BEEN TWENTY YEARS!

MADAME GIRARD

(Easing him back to the pillows) Malcolm . . . please.

MALCOLM

(Lying back, a little delirious) I've . . . lost so much, I've . . . lost so very much. (MADAME GIRARD *gets up, moves a little away, doesn't look at* MALCOLM) And . . . everyone has . . . swept by . . . Kermit and, and Mr. Girard . . . (MADAME GIRARD *stiffens a little*) . . . and even Mr. Cox *(She thinks to speak; does not)* . . . and . . . my father . . . my FATHER! . . . What . . . *(softly)* what have I not lost?

MADAME GIRARD

(Waits, expecting more, nodding. Waits, suddenly realizes, turns) No . . . *(shakes her head)* . . . no . . . PRINCE! *(Goes to the bed, touches him, takes her hand away)* Say . . . say . . . more. . . . There's more. *(Begins to cry)*

There's . . . much, much more. More, oh, Malcolm . . . oh, child. My Malcolm. What have you not lost? . . . And I . . . And all . . . What have *we* not lost? What, indeed. Did none of us ever care? *(The others start coming on, will group near, around, behind the bed)* You, my poor husband, with that woman you choose to call your wife? Or you? Or you? Or even you. Malcolm is dead.

KERMIT

Malcolm? Dead?

LAUREEN

Dead?

ELOISA

Just like that?

JEROME *(Quiet awe)*

Wow.

MADAME GIRARD

No, not just like that.

COX

I suppose he didn't have the stuff, that's all. God knows, I tried.

MADAME GIRARD

Oh, yes, we tried . . . we all tried.

MELBA

I'm . . . I'm cold.

MADAME GIRARD

And you, my husband? Silent?

GIRARD GIRARD *(Considerable pain)*

Let it go, my dear. He . . . he passed through so quickly; none of us could grasp hold.

LAUREEN

We tried.

ELOISA

Sure; we tried.

JEROME

Sure.

LAUREEN

He was a sweet kid.

KERMIT

I tried . . . as much as I could.